EU Internet Law

ELGAR EUROPEAN LAW

Founding Editor: John Usher, *formerly Professor of European Law and Head, School of Law, University of Exeter, UK*

European integration is the driving force behind constant evolution and change in the laws of the member states and the institutions of the European Union. This important series will offer short, state-of-the-art overviews of many specific areas of EU law, from competition law to consumer law and from environmental law to labour law. Whilst most books will take a thematic, vertical approach, others will offer a more horizontal approach and consider the overarching themes of EU law.

Distilled from rigorous substantive analysis, and written by some of the best names in the field, as well as the new generation of scholars, these books are designed both to guide the reader through the changing legislation itself, and to provide a firm theoretical foundation for advanced study. They will be an invaluable source of reference for scholars and postgraduate students in the fields of EU law and European integration, as well as lawyers from the respective individual fields and policymakers within the EU.

Titles in the series include:

EU Intellectual Property Law and Policy
Catherine Seville

EU Private International Law
Second Edition
Peter Stone

EU Labour Law
A.C.L. Davies

EU Public Procurement Law
Second Edition
Christopher H. Bovis

EU Internet Law
Andrej Savin

EU Consumer Law and Policy
Second Edition
Stephen Weatherill

EU Private International Law
Third Edition
Peter Stone

EU Intellectual Property Law and Policy
Second Edition
Catherine Seville

EU Environmental Law
Geert Van Calster and Leonie Reins

EU Internet Law
Second Edition
Andrej Savin

EU Internet Law

Second Edition

Andrej Savin

Associate Professor, Copenhagen Business School, Denmark

ELGAR EUROPEAN LAW

 Edward Elgar
PUBLISHING

Cheltenham, UK • Northampton, MA, USA

Published by
Edward Elgar Publishing Limited
The Lypiatts
15 Lansdown Road
Cheltenham
Glos GL50 2JA
UK

Edward Elgar Publishing, Inc.
William Pratt House
9 Dewey Court
Northampton
Massachusetts 01060
USA

Paperback edition 2018

A catalogue record for this book
is available from the British Library

Library of Congress Control Number: 2016953945

This book is available electronically in the **Elgar**online
Law subject collection
DOI 10.4337/9781784717971

ISBN 978 1 78471 795 7 (cased)
ISBN 978 1 78471 797 1 (eBook)
ISBN 978 1 78471 796 4 (paperback)

Typeset by Columns Design XML Ltd, Reading
Printed and bound by CPI Group (UK) Ltd, Croydon CR0 4YY

To Henriette

Contents

Preface

This book analyses Internet regulation in the European Union (EU). Frank Easterbrook, pointing out the danger of collecting different strands of study into a unified one, famously called Internet law 'the Law of the Horse'.[1] His warning is still valid today. Assuming that Internet law is a unified field, we run the danger of forgetting that its regulation arises out of more general, older legal disciplines. Nevertheless, the Internet has been part of our reality for two decades. Today it penetrates our lives to an unprecedented extent and we can no longer be happy attempting to view it through the prism of other disciplines. Although it may have earlier been true to say that intellectual property or contract law was sufficient to explain the Internet, this is no longer true. There are two reasons for this. First, as a result of the digital revolution, rather than applying the inherited concepts to the digital world, the traditional phenomena such as property, privacy and identity need to be reconceptualised in a broader non-digital frame. Second, the ubiquitous new phenomena, such as user-generated content or social networks, bring new rules, a new language and a new social context that do not easily lend themselves to traditional legal classification.

In this book we understand the Internet to mean a World Wide Web of interconnected computers that use the same language (protocol) to communicate. As such, we do not distinguish between the Internet provided through the regular broadband pipe and through other means (LAN networks, new generation 4G or 5G mobile networks, etc.) This approach inevitably means that a range of phenomena typically relevant in information technology (but which do not involve publicly accessible connected networks) are out of the scope of this book. In other words, this book is not about information technology systems in general but only those which operate on the publicly accessible World Wide Web.

Three other remarks about this book's scope are in order.

---

[1]   Easterbrook, F.H, "Cyberspace and the Law of the Horse" 1996 University of Chicago Legal Forum 207.

First, a number of works have already been written on the subject of electronic commerce, both in the EU and abroad. Although it is tempting to view the Internet purely as an electronic commerce phenomenon, this would be both wrong and misleading. Although most activities on the World Wide Web have commercial aspects, only some of them take place in the purchase–sale form. A regular visit to a free news website, for instance, is commercial only in that the site generates revenue from advertising, but does not take place in the form of a purchase of a subscription and is outside the scope of a simple electronic sales contract. In other words, Internet regulation is wider than the regulation of sales transactions that take place on the Internet.

Second, excellent works exist on EU intellectual property, EU copyright, EU telecommunications, EU privacy or EU consumer protection. The work that we offer is meant neither to replace nor to compete with them. Instead, we attempt to provide an overview of how these disciplines fit together in situations concerning Internet regulation. As such, the work is not meant as a simple catalogue of disparate legal disciplines but as an attempt to understand their interaction. The chapters that follow represent a collection of what are typically encountered as legal problems in Member States' courts, although the order in which they are presented does not reflect their relative importance.

Third, the Internet has two components. The first is the infrastructure on which the content is transmitted. The second is the content itself. The former is subject to a separate and relatively complex legal discipline called telecommunications (or electronic communications) law. The second is the subject of various legal disciplines that are covered in this book. The decision not to talk about telecommunications regulation is a result of two factors. The first are space constraints. The second is the existence of a conceptual difference between the regulatory environment that applies to the wires as opposed to that which applies to the content. In addition to that, media law, which regulates broadcasting (traditionally understood as distribution of audio or video content through the audio magnetic spectrum) is also largely outside the scope of this book.[2] Although television or radio share many features with the Internet, they are, as a rule, non-interactive and distributed from the centre to the periphery.

This book is not an attempt to analyse the Internet as a Single Market phenomenon. Although the European Commission often uses Article 114 of the Treaty on the Functioning of the European Union (TFEU) as a

---

[2] Except where media laws apply to on-demand radio and television.

legal basis when regulating the Internet, the main reason for harmonization is arguably not the fear that disparity between Member States'
laws would slow the economic development but rather that a lack of a
coherent vision would have a negative impact on such development in the
EU. The EU law-maker, in other words, acts not so much as a
harmonizer as it acts as a policy-maker.

The EU's efforts in Internet regulation may at first appear confusing.
Instruments are numerous, policies difficult to distinguish, court decisions conflicting, official statements contradictory, proposals incoherent.
But these problems can only partially be attributed to systemic or
bureaucratic failures. Arguably, there are two reasons for this apparent
failure. The first concerns the radical rethinking of the user/consumer's
role. Few media have contributed to turning the world into McLuhan's
'global village'[3] as much as the Internet has. The reason why it surpassed
newspapers, radio, television and other communication media is simple:
it allows participation. It turns passive consumers into active players and
contributors. The implications of such a new global village for the
economy and society at large are as yet unknown. But some elements of
the picture are already beginning to emerge. We know that participation
increases the number of players (and therefore interests) on the board
exponentially. This is the second reason for the apparent failure. We are
aware that holders of vested rights are fighting innovation that they
perceive is endangering their interests. We know that governments,
corporations and other individuals all have their own interests in violating
privacy. We are aware of the crucial role of consumers. These disparate
interests are not easy to balance and this is evident in EU laws.

The Internet gives us the opportunity to rethink the world we live in. It
is a thought experiment in developing legal rules for new social contexts.
But the Internet also creates these new social contexts. The motivation
for this book on EU Internet law comes from the desire to systematize
many instruments that either apply to Internet regulation or have been
specifically drafted for that purpose. Today, the United States stands at
the forefront of Internet development. Most of what other jurisdictions do
can be interpreted as a response or reaction to a trend that comes from
the US. The European Union has answered most of these challenges.
Sometimes, these answers are distinct, even original or unique. That is
the case with at least the introduction of the country of origin principle in
the Electronic Commerce Directive. On the other hand, occasionally, the

---

[3] M. McLuhan, *The Gutenberg Galaxy: The Making of Typographic Man*
(University of Toronto Press, 1962), p. 21.

solutions are questioned by businesses and the wider public alike. In any case, European regulation of the Internet is a reality.

* * *

This book is a result of a long-lasting interest in Internet regulation. Thanks are due to many individuals and institutions with which the author was fortunate to interact over many years. The author wishes to specially thank the staff and colleagues at the Law Faculty, University of Cambridge, Emmanuel College and Kings College, Cambridge, where he lectured and was a fellow from 2001–07. I am grateful to my colleagues at the Law Department, Copenhagen Business School, where I have worked since 2007. Finally, I am greatly in debt to my family and in particular to my wife, Henriette, whose patience and support has been material to this work's completion.

* * *

NOTE ON THE SECOND EDITION

This second edition presents a thoroughly updated and revised text. This has become necessary for three reasons. The first is that a comprehensive review is currently being undertaken in the telecommunications, data protection and copyright fields with laws in the first two already passed. The second is that a multitude of cases originating with the Court of Justice of the European Union, in particular in the area of copyright, consumer protection and private international law, have clarified some important obscurities in the law. The third is that small-scale changes have taken place in most of the other areas covered such as, for example, electronic commerce, content regulation, digital identity or cybercrime. Where necessary, draft Directives have been presented in full or in part. Even though it is likely that these will be changed in the adopted versions, it is necessary to present the readers with the law-makers' intentions. Two fundamental proposals have been made in September 2016: a new telecommunications framework and a new proposal on copyright in the Digital Single Market. Since both will be subject to intensive debate and successive amendments, they are only presented very briefly at the end of Chapters 1 and 6, respectively.

As with the previous edition, it has been necessary to exclude a number of areas that would otherwise have been relevant. The Council of Europe's efforts and the cases of the European Court of Human Rights have only been included sporadically and when necessary. Competition law, which has in recent years become very important in both the carrier (telecommunications) and the content (e-commerce, media) layers, have also been left out due to space constraints.

The law is up to date as of 1 October 2016.

Table of cases of the Court of Justice of the European Union

Note: Electronic Reports of Cases (ECLI) numbers are given for all cases filed in 2010 or after.

Table of secondary legislation

1. Internet regulation in the European Union

1 CHALLENGES OF CYBERSPACE

The modern world has been subject to information and communication technology (ICT) penetration at an unprecedented level. The main aspect of this phenomenon has been the ability to distribute information and knowledge widely and at great speed. This is a phenomenon that predates our decade and even the last century. But the Internet, as its latest manifestation, is fundamentally different from a television transmission or a newspaper, neither in its purpose nor in its ability to reach audiences instantaneously but in its capacity to involve them as active participants. This active participation and its networking potential are unique to the Internet and a direct result of its architecture, which promises low costs, decentralization and anonymity. To maintain this liberating potential, prudent regulation is needed. At the beginning of the Internet's history, however, it was believed that cyberspace could not be regulated at all and ought to be left to its own means. We now know this not to be true, but we still do not know how to regulate it.

The Internet attracts and empowers people but at the same time makes itself a target of control and a battleground of interests. On one hand, with its vast potential for information distribution, the Internet is often viewed by the general public only or primarily in light of its liberating potential. Regulation is here perceived as something restrictive that endangers and limits the acquired liberties. On the other, a different trend is emerging: the Internet is gaining a reputation as dangerous, morally dubious and difficult to control. Consumers are attracted to the potential that the Internet opens up for them but are afraid of the lack of protection. Businesses are eager to benefit from electronic commerce (e-commerce) but wary of having to become accustomed to different legal systems or of becoming liable in different jurisdictions. Content producers see new business opportunities but are loath to abandon habits formed in the old world. In this duality of character lies the power, the danger and the difficulty of governing the Internet.

1

The fact that the modern Internet is influenced by a multiplicity of actors, ranging from governments, corporations, regional organizations, non-governmental entities and individual users means that it is today more meaningful to talk about 'governance' as a process rather than 'regulation' as a single government-directed activity.[1] Nevertheless, the primary actors in the Internet regulation of today are still nation-states.[2] Both the United States and the European Union have decisively shaped the Internet as we know it today. As a result of its economic strength and of its strong starting position, the United States has been the dominant force behind the Internet's expansion, although the European Union followed in its steps. The Internet's emergence as a global medium of communication made a quick impression on the European Union. In little more than a decade, it adopted laws on issues as wide in range as intellectual property, electronic commerce, data protection and privacy, consumer protection and criminal law. Initiatives were tabled as quickly as various technological developments allowed and policies were drafted with an atypical enthusiasm.[3] To an outside observer, this flurry of activity and abundance of documents in the EU makes clear the perceived importance of the Internet but at the same time disguises the fact that Internet regulation remains difficult and ambiguous.

Towards the end of the last century, the number of Internet users started to increase dramatically.[4] Two ideas motivated the EU's intervention in this area. First, the European Union acknowledged that the Internet promises further economic development, which cannot be tapped into without intervention in the areas where it directly bears on the Internal Market. The EU began to view electronic commerce as a vital tool in keeping the Single Market competitive. On the other hand, the EU also realized that the development and spreading of the Internet had a direct influence on the protection of individuals as consumers and as private persons since the global impact of the Internet was felt in everyday activities, including the actions of private individuals. The

---

[1]   See I. Brown (ed.), *Research Handbook on Governance of the Internet* (Edward Elgar Publishing, Cheltenham and Northampton, MA, 2013).

[2]   See D. Drezner, 'The Global Governance of the Internet: Bringing the State Back In' (2004) 119 *Political Science Quarterly* 477.

[3]   Dickie has aptly called this state of affairs a mixture of 'soft- and hard-law, and of established, pending and proposed law', J. Dickie, *Internet and Electronic Commerce Law in the EU* (Hart, Oxford/Portland, OR, 1999), p. 103.

[4]   For statistics on Internet usage in the EU, see Eurostat and European Commission, *Science, Technology and Innovation in Europe* (Publications Office of the European Union, Luxembourg, 2013).

intervention, therefore, could not concentrate on furthering only the Single Market aims but had to include individual freedoms. As a result of this tension, two focal points of EU intervention in the field of Internet law began to crystallize: one centred around the Single Market and the other around consumers.[5] The first reflected the ideal of a unified European market for goods, services, people and capital and the belief that this aim cannot be achieved without a single market for electronic commerce. The second reflected the EU's determination to protect the individual. Both aims were asserted strongly, beginning from treaty provisions, through Directives and judgments. The presence of both aims in EU instruments gave, as will be argued elsewhere in this book, conflicting results.

As a result of fast-paced legislative activity in many loosely connected areas, the Community body of laws relating to the Internet, at present, is not joined in a common overarching structure, guided by Single Market-informed policies. Instead, it is an aggregate of loosely connected secondary laws reliant on the European Commission ('the Commission')'s interpretation as the cases slowly trickle through the Court of Justice of the European Union (CJEU). The instruments normally referred to as 'Framework Directives' act as frameworks only for the specific areas they cover (such as electronic commerce or telecommunications). The policy instruments (such as Action Plans or Green and White Papers) have indirect influence on the multitude of Directives in fields other than their own. Many projects were begun in the 1990s, at a time when the Internet was in its infancy and its potential impact poorly understood. Other projects were drafted in fulfilment of the European Union's international obligations, partially under the influence of commercial forces and lobbies. Others yet were a result of the work of the Council of Europe, the EU lacking the required competence.

At the same time, policies and legislation on the other side of the Atlantic appeared more transparent, individual interests were easier to trace and public debate seemed louder. The drafting of such laws as the hotly disputed 1998 Digital Millennium Copyright Act (DMCA)[6] in the United States was followed by a public and academic debate, the formation of interest groups and clashes in Congress. In the United States, the battles also raged over speech regulation on the Internet in light of the First Amendment, as well as over privacy and the role of

---

  [5] Cf. J. Dickie, *Consumers and Producers in EU E-Commerce Law* (Hart, Oxford/Portland, OR, 2005), especially Chapters 1 and 7.
  [6] H.R. 2281.

intermediaries. In Europe, some of these issues remained altogether unnoticed while many others were observed dispassionately. Where even stricter regimes than those found in the United States came into place beginning in the 2000s, none of the public excitement seen in the US was evident and general interests seemed to be lost in complicated law-making procedures that demonstrated the less democratic traits of EU law-making only too well. It was only after 2011, with the net neutrality debate and the Snowden revelations, that public interest in telecommunications and data protection regimes respectively began to stir.

In the meantime, the Internet as it was in the 1990s and early 2000s had gradually transformed. What influenced the Internet of the twenty-first century more than any other development was the presence and expansion of collaborative efforts.[7] The exclusive and limited network of the early 1990s had turned into a global decentralized phenomenon. From a linear model characterized by exclusive content being placed by individual corporations, the Web has moved towards a collaborative, interoperable, user-centred platform sometimes referred to as Web 2.0 and, further, to a platform enabling large degrees of personalization.

At the same time, the telecommunications (carrier) and audio-visual and e-commerce worlds (content) began to converge. Services which had hitherto been the privilege of traditional providers (such as telephony, text messages or television) increasingly started to be provided through disruptive business models which use the Internet as their universal pipeline. The Internet itself gradually started to be more accessible through mobile platforms such as smartphones and SIM-enabled tablets and laptops.

But it is not only the content distribution model that has changed. The Web itself has evolved from a passive medium into a platform, from a released and finished package into a constantly changing, dynamic 'permanent beta'.[8] The concepts of open access and open source are some examples of not only how the Internet can transform the social milieu from which it arose but also of how traditional patterns of regulation can be transformed. At the same time, much of daily life had

---

[7] R. Ghosh (ed.), *Code: Collaborative Ownership and the Digital Economy* (MIT Press, Cambridge, MA, 2005); Y. Benkler, *The Wealth of Networks: How Social Production Transforms Markets and Freedom* (Yale University Press, London/New Haven, CT, 2006).

[8] On Web 2.0, see T. O'Reilly, 'What is Web 2.0? Design Patterns and Business Models for the Next Generation of Software', available at www.oreillynet.com/pub/a/oreilly/tim/news/2005/09/30/what-is-web-20.html.

migrated to the Internet to the extent that the Internet became representative of our culture. We, the users, at the same time, have transformed our identities. The Internet, whose regulation is also in the hands of the European Union, is built on an architecture different from any other medium before it.

2 INTERNET ARCHITECTURE

The uniqueness of Internet architecture rests on three groups of features: its layered structure, its end-to-end nature and its neutrality. This architecture led some authors to declare that it also determines its governance method.[9] Technology here determines regulatory policy, which then influences that very technology.

The idea of the *layered structure* describes the Internet's heterogeneous nature and the complexities of its hardware, software and substance: the Internet is not homogenous but rather composed of different layers.[10] In order to regulate the Internet properly one has to embrace and understand its layered structure. Or, in other words, 'regulation should be directed at or match the layer where the problematic conduct arises'.[11]

The *end-to-end architecture* refers to the Internet's decentralized nature and its lack of dependency on a central distribution system. This architecture depends on packet switching, decentralized standard-setting, cryptography and anonymity.[12]

Packet switching is a technology that is inherently difficult to control by traditional mechanisms applied to telecommunications. The computers are independently managed but connected in a network and adhere to a common standard enabling them to communicate (the TCP/IP protocol). The most important feature of the protocol is that it enables the data to be broken into packets, which are then transmitted through the network of intermediaries and reassembled in the target computer. The data can use any route available on the way but the route chosen does not have an

---

[9] The clearest exposition of this term is Lessig's 'code is law' thesis. See L. Lessig, *Code 2.0* (Basic Books, New York, 2006).

[10] L.B. Solum and M. Chung, *The Layers Principle: Internet Architecture and the Law*, U San Diego Public Law Research Paper No. 55, available at http://ssrn.com/abstract=416263.

[11] *Ibid.* 104.

[12] M. Froomkin, 'The Internet as a Source of Regulatory Arbitrage' in B. Kahin and C. Nesson (eds.), *Borders in Cyberspace* (MIT Press, Cambridge, MA. 1996), pp. 129–63.

impact on the quality of the ultimate information received. This feature of the Internet is a result of the desire of the original client (the US Defense Department) to make the network resistant to failures of individual communication lines.

Directly in connection with this is the decentralized standard-setting. Although the original network arose under the auspices of the US government, the actual standard-setting is performed by non-governmental bodies. The first among these is the Internet Engineering Task Force (IETF). Another significant body is the World Wide Web Consortium (W3C). The very influential organization in charge of the domain names is the Internet Corporation for Assigned Names and Numbers (ICANN).[13]

Connected with these features are anonymity and cryptography. A varying degree of anonymity is available and even guaranteed to users on the Internet. Following from this last feature is what Froomkin[14] calls regulatory arbitrage: the ability of Internet users to evade unfavourable regulatory regimes by choosing to subject their transaction to more liberal ones. The first consequence of this is that proper censorship is difficult. A website can be registered under any one of a multitude of domain names (every country has one, plus there are a number of universal ones such as .biz, .org, .eu, or others). The content itself can be offered for hosting to any one of the thousands of hosting services across the globe. Cryptography can be used on any content crossing the borders. The second consequence is that it is often easier to speak freely on the Internet than it is on traditional media. The countries that do control the Internet with varying degrees of success[15] face rising costs and difficulties as the customer base and the number of services grow.

Alongside its architecture, which opens up its liberating potential, the Internet is also influenced by the regulatory regime to which it is subject. That regime has been described by Oxman[16] as having succeeded due to

---

[13] On the role that the United States plays here, see T. Wu, E. Dyson, M. Froomkin and D. Gross, 'On the Future of Internet Governance', American Society of International Law, Proceedings of the Annual Meeting, vol. 101, available at http://ssrn.com/abstract=992805.

[14] Froomkin, 'The Internet as a Source of Regulatory Arbitrage', note 12 above, p. 142.

[15] Such as China, Saudi Arabia or Iran. On this see J. Goldsmith and T. Wu, *Who Controls the Internet: Illusions of a Borderless World* (OUP, Oxford, 2006).

[16] J. Oxman, *The FCC and the Unregulation of the Internet*, OPP Working Paper No. 31 in B. Fitzgerald, *Cyberlaw I and II* (Ashgate, Dartmouth, 2006), vol. I, p. 77, at pp. 78 and 99–101.

three factors. First, no legacy solutions were imposed on new technologies. The Federal Communications Commission (FCC) has treated information technology (IT) services as unregulated from the moment they appeared. They were transmitted through telephone infrastructure, and yet they were not regulated as telephone services. Secondly, as Internet services began replacing legacy services, the former were not forced into regulatory models of the latter but, rather, remained unregulated. As services such as Voice over Internet Protocol (VOIP) and wireless access spread, this should have the effect of removing the regulatory burdens from legacy services. Finally, competition was strictly monitored and preserved, and the responses to violations were targeted and minimal – they addressed specific problems rather than the whole industry.

The final of the three defining features of the Internet is its *neutrality*.[17] In simplest terms it is a concept that describes how the Internet relates to the content posted on it or, in other words, the relationship of the Internet towards applications or services that run on it. More precisely, it refers to the belief that governments should step in to actively prevent the Internet service providers (ISPs) from discriminating between types of data on the network. Presently, the Internet provides the same standards of service (upstream and downstream download speeds, bandwidth, quality of signal) irrespective of the application or content used and distributed. The question has distinctly political undertones (see section 6 below).

Importantly, network neutrality is a result of Internet architecture. This architecture, as was indicated above, rests on the end-to-end principle: the core of the network is simply a protocol that describes *how* the neutral machines placed at the end of the network communicate. *What* exactly is placed on the network is not a result of a decision made at the core but, on the contrary, on the periphery, where ultimate users reside[18] and changing this balance may damage the Internet.

As a consequence of the described architecture, the Internet is open – not susceptible to authorizations either at the production or at the user end. At the same time, these features make it a subject and target of

---

[17] See D. Nunizato, *Virtual Freedom: Net Neutrality and Free Speech in the Internet Age* (Stanford University Press, Stanford, CA, 2009). See also T.W. Hazlett, *The Fallacy of Net Neutrality* (Encounter Books, New York, 2011).

[18] For more on the consequences of this design and the potential dangers, see J. Zittrain, 'The Generative Internet' (2005–2006) 119 *Harvard Law Review* 1975.

numerous interests: international, national, corporate and individual.[19] In summary, understanding the Internet's architecture is a prerequisite for good governance of the Internet. Although this point does not have a particularly European flavour it is perhaps worth recalling the complexities of the EU law-making process and emphasizing that good flexible solutions, although much needed, are also the most difficult to achieve.

3   MAKING LAWS FOR THE INTERNET: INTERNET GOVERNANCE

Many ideas about governing the Internet have crystallized since its emergence.[20] Some are idealistic.[21] Others repeat the metaphor of cyberspace as a separate place.[22] A preliminary question, popular at the onset of the debate about Internet regulation, asked whether the Internet can be governed at all. The wave of popular enthusiasm that followed the discovery of the medium's potential dictated a certain kind of optimism that was empowering but ill-suited to the Internet of today. The best representative of that mood is the famous 'A Declaration of the Independence of Cyberspace' written by John Parry Barlow.[23] In memorable words, Barlow said:

> We have no elected government, nor are we likely to have one, so I address you with no greater authority than that with which liberty itself always speaks. I declare the global social space we are building to be naturally

---

[19]   Specifically, on the unobserved security concerns of such an Internet, see J. Zittrain, *The Future of the Internet and How to Stop it* (Allen Lane, London, 2008).

[20]   For a detailed overview of issues concerning governance and policies in the IT sector in the EU, see G. Christou and S. Simpson, *The New Electronic Marketplace: European Governance Strategies in a Globalising Economy* (Edward Elgar Publishing, Cheltenham and Northampton, MA, 2007). See also L. Bygrave and J. Bing, *Internet Governance: Infrastructure and Institutions* (OUP, Oxford, 2009). In this book we understand 'governance' to mean the problem of ruling the Internet in general and not just the issue of domain name regulation.

[21]   J.P. Barlow, 'A Declaration of Independence of Cyberspace' in B. Fitzgerald (ed.), *Cyberlaw I and II* (Ashgate, Dartmouth, 2006), vol. I, p. 129.

[22]   On the problems associated with this and the dangers arising from it for the judiciary, see D. Hunter, 'Cyberspace as Place' (2003) 91 *California Law Review* 439 and M. Lemely, 'Place and Cyberspace' (2003) 91 *California Law Review* 521.

[23]   Barlow, 'A Declaration of Independence of Cyberspace', note 21 above.

independent of the tyrannies you seek to impose on us. You have no moral right to rule us nor do you possess any methods of enforcement we have true reason to fear.

We now know that the 'global social space we are building' is not naturally independent of tyrannies[24] and that governments do have methods of enforcement that both corporations and individuals have reasons to fear.

Other ideas, however, have crystallized into policy and decidedly shaped the Internet. Among these, few are as indicative of the formative phase of the Internet or as important for the course that it took as ex-President William Clinton's 'A Framework for Global Electronic Commerce'.[25] The principles which it contains, informed by the liberal 1990s, have pushed the Internet from a purely regulatory environment into governance, from hard to soft law and from public to private regulation. The Clinton framework notes that the expansion of the Internet has been driven primarily by investment from private corporations. In order to maintain the acquired freedom, the regulatory 'nudge' is supplied in the form of a simple idea that the Internet must not be regulated but ought to be market-driven, and that markets and not governments are the most efficient regulators. To ensure future development, businesses and consumers should maintain their central role with as little government intervention as possible. On the contrary, governments should encourage self-regulation and create such environments that would enable free and unhindered development of the Internet. Following from that, governments should avoid undue restrictions and, where their involvement is needed, 'its aim should be to support and enforce a predictable, minimalist, consistent and simple legal environment for commerce'. Governments should also recognize the unique qualities of the Internet and not attempt to fit the Internet to the legacy regime developed for telecommunication services. Finally, e-commerce should be facilitated on a global basis. The ideas developed here were followed and copied in the European Union's Initiative in Electronic Commerce

---

[24]   For an empirical study of the Chinese government's measures to control the early Internet, see J. Zitrain, *Internet Filtering in China*, Harvard Law School Public Law Research Paper No. 62 (IEEE Computing, March/April 2003), p. 70.

[25]   W. Clinton, 'A Framework for Global Electronic Commerce' in B. Fitzgerald (ed.), *Cyberlaw I and II* (Ashgate, Dartmouth, 2006), vol. I, p. 133.

from 1997 and permanently informed most of the core EU Internet regulatory efforts.[26]

Internet governance does not have a precise definition. The Working Group of Internet Governance defines Internet governance in the following manner:[27]

> Internet governance is the development and application by Governments, the private sector and civil society, in their respective roles, of shared principles, norms, rules, decision-making procedures, and programmes that shape the evolution and use of the Internet.

As is apparent, one important feature distinguishes 'governance' from pure regulation: governance applies to international organizations, citizens and businesses in addition to governments as is understood in a traditional sense. Governance, in other words, is an attempt to address a global phenomenon by global action. The importance of the above definition lies in the recognition of the fact that the Internet is not ruled or shaped purely by *laws* or *regulation* but that it spreads to all 'principles, norms, rules, decision-making procedures, and programmes' that shape the Internet. The Internet, in other words, requires something more than pure traditional regulation.

In recent years, the concept of 'new governance' has been extensively discussed in the European Union.[28] Although the term does not have a firm definition, many of its features are known. It suggests alternative legal paradigms for regulating issues ranging from environment to education and others. It was said[29] that the mere usage of the term governance suggests that the approach in the EU is already changing from 'command-and-control' towards a 'regulatory' one. Some of the features that can be used to describe it include 'diversity', 'revisability' and provisional character. Others are participation of the affected, transparency, openness, evaluation and review. A central authority would have

---

[26] European Commission, *A European Initiative in Electronic Commerce, Communication to the European Parliament, the Council, the Economic and Social Committee and the Committee of the Regions*, COM(97)157 (15 April 1997).

[27] Working Group on Internet Governance (July 2005), available at www.wgig.org/docs/WGIGREPORT.pdf.

[28] For an overview of the issues involved, see G. de Búrca and J. Scott (eds.), *Law and New Governance in the EU and the US* (Hart Publishing, Oxford/Portland, OR, 2006).

[29] *Ibid.* 2.

the task of coordinating the new governance and facilitating 'the emergence of new infrastructure'.

Another term which has an autonomous EU meaning is multi-stakeholder governance.[30] This simply means that different stakeholders, including non-government and commercial entities, are all involved in Internet governance. Since its inception in 2009, the approach has already found its way into several initiatives. An example of this is the European Multi Stakeholder Platform (MSP) on ICT standardization set up at the end of 2011. The MSP typically holds four meetings a year and helps with ICT standardization.

We suggest, and will demonstrate in different parts of this book, that the dominant EU paradigm is, therefore, that the Internet ought to be *governed* rather than purely *regulated*. But how is the right balance chosen between intervention of national governments, involvement of independent bodies and of corporations and the power of the medium, which has, it seems, a significant potential to regulate itself?[31] Which governance model preserves the autonomy of the Internet, its liberalizing potential and its networking power while enabling the state to regulate? Looking purely in terms of traditional regulation, there are four (exclusive or concurrent) potentially applicable governance models.[32] They can briefly be described as follows.

The first model presupposes the extension of territorial sovereignty. This model assumes that the present legal paradigm based on state territorial sovereignty is adequate for Internet regulation, and its proponents say that the state can simply adapt its current laws to apply to the Internet. The latter is not a separate entity that exists outside national borders, but, on the contrary, is largely subject to national jurisdictions which states can and should take advantage of. A large proportion of activity on the Web does rely on this model, ranging from protection and enforcement of intellectual property rights to data protection, taxation or

---

[30] See Commission Communication, *Internet Policy and Governance: Europe's Role in Shaping the Future of Internet Governance*, COM(2014)072 final (12 December 2014). See also Commission Communication, *Cybersecurity Strategy of the European Union*, JOIN(2013)1 final (7 February 2013) and Commission Communication, *Internet Governance: The Next Steps*, COM(2009)277 final (18 June 2009).

[31] On the issue of regulating cyberspace through technology, see J. Reidenberg, 'Lex Informatica: The Formulation of Information Policy Rules Through Technology' (1998) 76 *Texas Law Review* 553. See also L. Lessig, 'The Law of the Horse: What Cyberlaw Might Teach' (1999) 113 *Harvard Law Review* 501.

[32] See D.R. Johnson and D.G. Post, 'Law and Borders: The Rise of Law in Cyberspace' (1996) 48 *Stanford Law Review* 1367.

consumer protection. In fact, it would be difficult to claim that this model is anything but dominant today. This does not automatically mean that the Internet is illiberal and subject to government restrictions, or liable to adapt to the standard of the most restrictive state. The application of this model simply means that the Internet can be contained. In as much as this localization is present, that is, to the extent that the users and the networks are found in individual geographic locations, the rules that apply to them will also be local. This prevents neither the globalizing nor the liberalizing effect of the Internet which both derive from its architecture. In fact, one can go as far as to say that Internet architecture encourages regulatory competition and forces governments to be liberal rather than restrictive regulators. This competition has been especially evident in the case of electronic commerce, where businesses tend to place themselves in jurisdictions legally and financially more favourable to them.

At the same time, it would be wrong to say that complete reliance on national regulation is a desirable model. First, the relationship between regulation and innovation is still largely unknown. An overly restrictive regulatory climate *may* create a less competitive, less innovative digital economy. Second, a significant number of areas (such as regulation of spam, child pornography, domain names or data transfer between states) require either cooperation between states, or corporate involvement, or both.

The second model relies on international agreements and international regulatory efforts. The Internet, its proponents argue, should be left to international agreements, concluded between sovereign Member States. The record of such achievements is, at least at the present time, poor although existent.[33] A practical example of this approach is found in the EU–United States Agreement on transfers of passenger data.[34] The EU regime forbids private data transfer outside the European Union unless specific, very strict conditions have been met. This transfer agreement introduces a special regime for data transfer across the Atlantic as a way of overcoming these limitations. The US security regulations require that

---

[33] For the Cybercrime Treaty, see Chapter 10.

[34] Agreement between the United States of America and the European Union on the use and transfer of passenger name records to the United States Department of Homeland Security [2012] OJ L215/5, 11 August 2012. A previous Council Decision 2004/496/EC of 17 May 2004, on the conclusion of an Agreement was annulled by the European Court of Justice. See C-317/04 and C-318/04 *European Parliament v Council of the European Union and Commission of the European Communities* [2006] ECR I-4721, 30 May 2006.

all passenger airline data is transferred, and the two parties managed to negotiate a deal setting the conditions on which such data can be provided to the United States.

The third model of regulation relies on new international organizations. This model presupposes the creation of new international organizations formed specifically to deal with the Internet and entrusted with its regulation. Examples of organizations which have operated with success include the Internet Corporation for Assigned Names and Numbers (ICANN), the World Wide Web Consortium (W3C) or the Internet Society (ISOC).

The nature of these organizations varies. The first, ICANN, is a non-profit organization created in 1998 to supervise the performance of a number of Internet-related tasks of which the most notable is the assignment of Internet names and addresses. The second, the World Wide Web Consortium, is a standards organization for the World Wide Web. It is a consortium of member organizations, of which there are presently over 400, which it coordinates in their job of setting Internet standards. The third, the Internet Society, is an international organization for the promotion of Internet use.

Some of the organizations are unique and historical. Such is the position of ICANN, whose importance cannot be replicated. Others, such as W3C, are, although successful, entrusted with standard-setting rather than regulation. Others, yet, play a limited role. Arguably, this model has not had a significant success rate in any of the Internet governance areas today.

The final model emphasizes Internet architecture and its regulatory potential.[35] This idea has in the past been influential and important but also poorly understood.[36] In simple terms, the architecture or 'code' of the Internet produces regulatory effects. The Internet is governed not only by traditional regulatory methods in the form of legal norms but also and primarily by the architecture it is based on. Any impact on the regulatory regime also brings changes to the architecture itself, making it more or less restrictive. The present Internet is liberal only because it is built on architecture not easily subject to centralized control. But, although this

---

[35] Although Lessig is usually credited with the metaphor, it originated with Mitchell, see W. Mitchell, *City of Bits: Space, Place, and the Infobahn* (MIT Press, Cambridge, MA, 1995), p. 111. For another early version of the metaphor, see J. Reidenberg, 'Lex Informatica: The Formulation of Information Policy Rules Through Technology' (1998) 76 *Texas Law Review* 553.

[36] See T. Wu, 'When Code Isn't Law' (2003) 89 *Virginia Law Review* 103, who looks at the problem from the perspective of the interest group behaviour.

may evoke the vision of the invisible hand leading the Internet, one of Lessig's most important ideas is that cyberspace should *not* be left to the invisible hand:

> [W]e have every reason to believe that cyberspace, left to itself, will not fulfil the promise of freedom. Left to itself, cyberspace will become a perfect tool of control ... The invisible hand, through commerce, is constructing an architecture that perfects control.[37]

Or, in another place:

> We can build, or architect, or code cyberspace to protect values that we believe are fundamental. Or we can build, or architect, or code cyberspace to allow those values to disappear.[38]

However, the issues are of considerable complexity.[39] The idea that code can have a regulatory effect seems foreign to an ordinary legal mind and its implications are hotly debated.[40]

Closely related to the link between code and law is the idea that the Internet is not suited to direct legal control and needs a more flexible approach in the form of self-regulation.[41] In this context, self-regulation is the delegation of regulatory powers from state to non-state entities comprising of industry representatives. As such, self-regulation is not synonymous with deregulation, which is the reduction of excessive governmental control, or with non-regulation, which is complete absence

---

[37] L. Lessig, *Code and Other Laws of Cyberspace* (Basic Books, New York, 1999), pp. 5–6.

[38] L. Lessig, *Code V 2.0* (Basic Books, New York, 2006), p. 6.

[39] For a general debate about code as code and some issues that highlight the difficulties of the relationship between Information Technology and regulation, see E. Dommerin and L. Asscher, *Coding Regulation: Essays on the Normative Role of Information Technology* (T.M.C. Asser Press, The Hague, 2006). See also T. Wu, 'When Code Isn't Law', n. 36 above, on instances where code acts against regulation. On the problem with the idea that code must be subject to political action, see G. Post, 'What Larry Doesn't Get: Code, Law and Liberty in Cyberspace' (2000) 52 *Stanford Law Review* 1439.

[40] See E. Dommerin, 'Regulating Technology: Code is Not Law' in E. Dommerin and L. Asscher, *Coding Regulation: Essays on the Normative Role of Information Technology* (T.M.C. Asser Press, The Hague, 2006), p. 1.

[41] See M. Price and S. Verhulst, *Self-Regulation and the Internet* (Kluwer, The Hague, 2005), p. 19.

of regulation. Likewise, self-regulation is not synonymous with govern-ance, which is a general term for a move from regulation to less government-oriented approaches.

In Europe, self-regulation started to gain prominence in the Internet area in the late 1990s. Today, self-regulatory authorities and codes of conduct are widespread. In a study of Internet self-regulation in the EU, the Oxford Internet Institute found that self-regulation had worked best where there was a firm legal basis, where codes of practice were well known and where clarity and transparency were not at issue.[42] The EU itself supports self-regulation, which is mentioned in various EU policy documents,[43] but also endorses co-regulation, which is a combination of state and non-state regulation. In the 2005 EU-commissioned study on co-regulation,[44] this model was seen as a viable option as long as transparency and openness were maintained.

Article 16 of the 2000 Electronic Commerce Directive, entitled 'Codes of Conduct' specifically supports self regulation. It provides that Member States and the Commission shall encourage:

(a) the drawing up of codes of conduct at Community level, by trade, professional and consumer associations or organisations, designed to contribute to the proper implementation of Articles 5 to 15;
(b) the voluntary transmission of draft codes of conduct at national or Community level to the Commission;
(c) the accessibility of these codes of conduct in the Community languages by electronic means;
(d) the communication to the Member States and the Commission, by trade, professional and consumer associations or organisations, of their assess-ment of the application of their codes of conduct and their impact upon practices, habits or customs relating to electronic commerce;
(e) the drawing up of codes of conduct regarding the protection of minors and human dignity.

In addition, Member States and the Commission shall encourage 'the involvement of associations or organisations representing consumers' in the drafting and implementation of codes of conduct affecting their interests and drawn up in accordance with paragraph (a). 'Where

---

[42] Oxford Internet Institute, *Internet Self-Regulation: An Overview*, EU No. 27180-IAPCODE.
[43] See references in section 5 below.
[44] Hans-Bredow-Institut, *Final Report Study on Co-Regulation Measures in the Media Sector, Study for European Commission*, available at http://ec. europa.eu/avpolicy/docs/library/studies/coregul/final_rep_en.pdf.

appropriate, to take account of their specific needs, associations representing the visually impaired and disabled should be consulted.'

The European Union, as will be seen further in this book, relies on all
four models of regulation. But the coexistence of the models does not
ensure a 'free' Internet nor does it make the EU a liberal regulator. The
perceived and desired freedom of the Internet is a function of many
factors. In the European Union, first among them is the Single Market.
As the *raison d'être* of the Community, this aim features prominently in
all Community legislative measures. However, tensions are present
between the Single Market, on the one hand, and other treaty values,
such as the protection of private life, fundamental rights or consumer
protection, on the other.

Furthermore, the Internet originated in the United States[45] and much of
the development and control as well as legal problems, are inextricably
tied to it. Solutions to problems in cyberspace inevitably often also need
to be American solutions. A large number of questions, if not all of them,
have a trans-Atlantic dimension. In this book, we will also look at these
problems from the United States' perspective. In fact, one of the biggest
challenges placed before EU regulators today is facing the United States'
regulatory power and providing an alternative to it.[46]

The Internet developed in the United States and its current 'look and
feel' is a result of that development.[47] Its main features were a result of
both the architecture and the deregulatory approach mandated by the
Federal Communications Commission.[48] The architecture, set up in the
early 1960s and 1970s, and careful regulation in the 1980s led to
the booming of the medium in the 1990s and its ubiquity in the
twenty-first century. The European Union can never match this historically given fact. Neither does it have to. Its regulatory choices are
determined by its own history and environment.

---

[45]   On the Internet's origins, see B. Leiner, V. Cerf *et al.*, 'A Brief History of
the Internet' in B. Fitzgerald (ed.), *Cyberlaw I and II* (Ashgate, Dartmouth,
2006), vol. I, p. 3.
[46]   For more detail on this issue, see B. May, J.C. Chen and and K.W. Wen,
'The Differences of Regulatory Models and Internet Regulation in the European
Union and the United States' (2004) 13 *Information and Communication
Technology Law* 259.
[47]   For a concise history, see Leiner, Cerf *et al.*, 'A Brief History of the
Internet', note 45 above, p. 3.
[48]   See J. Oxman, *The FCC and the Unregulation of the Internet*, OPP
Working Paper, No. 31 in B. Fitzgerald (ed.), *Cyberlaw I and II* (Ashgate,
Dartmouth, 2006), vol. I, p. 77.

3.1 Domain Name Regulation as an Aspect of Governance

The control of domain name assignment was from the very beginning conducted on behalf of the US government by other organizations, notably the Internet Assigned Numbers Authority (IANA).[49] This organization was established under a contract with the US Department of Defence and put in charge of overseeing global Internet Protocol (IP) address allocation, Domain Name System (DNS) root zone management, and other Internet Protocol assignments. In reality, it was a small group of people, directly supervised by Jon Postel of the Information Society Institute of the University of South California. On 24 December 1998, IANA entered into a transition agreement with the Internet Corporation for Assigned Names and Numbers (ICANN) and transferred its functions to it, effective on 1 January 1999. The United States has, directly or indirectly, been in charge of assignment of names and addresses since the inception of the Internet and is very reluctant to hand over that control to an international body.[50]

At a World Summit on the Information Society held in Tunisia in 2005, a broader international participation was requested. The EU along with some other members proposed a new way of regulating the Internet that relied on cooperation between governments and the private sector.[51] These proposals were defeated at the conference. On 30 June 2005, the United States issued Principles on the Internet's Domain Name and Addressing System.[52] The principles provided:

(a)   The United States will continue with its special role to guarantee the security and stability of the Internet.
(b)   The United States recognizes the legitimate interests of governments over the national domain name space.

---

[49]   For an overview of domain name regulation in the world see T. Bettinger and A. Waddell, *Domain Name Law and Practice* (Oxford, Oxford University Press, 2015).

[50]   W. Kleinwachter, 'WSIS and Internet Governance: The Struggle over the Core Resources of the Internet' (2006) 11 *Communications Law* 3.

[51]   'Proposal for addition to Chair's paper Sub-Com A Internet Governance on Paragraph 5, Follow-up and Possible Arrangements'', WSIS-II/PC-3/DT/21-E of the WSIS Summit, 30 September 2005. For comments, see Kleinwachter, 'WSIS and Internet Governance', n. 50 above.

[52]   National Telecommuncations and Information Administration, Principles on the Internet's Domain Name and Addressing System, 30 June 2005, available at www.ntia.doc.gov/legacy/reportsarchives.html.

(c) For the United States, ICANN is the main body for the technical management of the Internet core resources.
(d) The United States supports a continuing dialogue on Internet governance.

The most important of these is item (c), ICANN is the appropriate technical manager of the Internet DNS. This shows primarily that the United States is unwilling to relinquish the control of the DNS management to an international body.

The EU proposals, radically different from the American, relied on the public–private cooperation model:

(a) [the model] should not replace existing mechanisms or institutions, but should build on the existing structures of Internet Governance, with a special emphasis on the complementarity between all the actors involved in this process, including governments, the private sector, civil society and international organisations each of them in its field of competence;
(b) this new public-private co-operation model should contribute to the sustainable stability and robustness of the Internet by addressing appropriately public policy issues related to key elements of Internet Governance;
(c) the role of governments in the new co-operation model should be mainly focused on principle issues of public policy, excluding any involvement in the day-to-day operations;
(d) the importance of respecting the architectural principles of the Internet, including the interoperability, openness and the end-to-end principle.

The notable feature of this model is the public–private cooperation. The private sector would lead the daily operations but governments would be in charge of overseeing them. Importantly, however, this was seen as a movement away from ICANN control and towards an intergovernmental, possibly United Nations-led, effort. The US government, backed by the media,[53] vigorously opposed the idea, seeing it as vague and ineffective in practice. The final agreement was a compromise that included wider participation of governments of world nations. This equality of governments, however, is limited to control of their own top-level domains.

---

[53] The papers engaged in a vigorous campaign. The US government, however, exercised pressure on the EU to withdraw the proposal. See letter from Condoleezza Rice and Carlos Gutierrez to Jack Straw, 7 November 2005, available at www.theregister.co.uk/2005/12/02/rice_eu_letter/. For more on EU–US policy differences, see also D. Drissel, 'Internet Governance in a Multipolar World: Challenging American Hegemony' (2006) 19 *Cambridge Review of International Affairs* 105.

In 2016, an agreement had been reached to end direct US oversight of the domain name system. The model that replaces it is a multi-stakeholder governance model. This means that from late 2016, ICANN, which remains in existence, answers to multiple parties rather than only to the US government. The model, which had been agreed on in 2014,[54] is a result of voluntary agreement between ICANN and the US Department of Defence (DOD).

Today, it does not seem that the ability to control Internet domains really represents the feared power. In our time, the threat to the Internet comes mostly from other sides.[55] Nevertheless, it is a fact that the European Union plays but a marginal role in this sphere of Internet governance.

4 EU COMPETENCE TO REGULATE

When transferring parts of their sovereignty to the Union, Member States placed safeguards in the Treaty on European Union (TEU) ensuring that EU legislation has a proper legal basis, is proportionate to the objective to be achieved and does not violate the principle of subsidiarity.[56] The authority to legislate in the sphere of information technology, intellectual property, telecommunications or, specifically, the Internet derives from several legal bases and is subject to different procedures. Among these are free movement of services provisions, Articles 49 and 56 TFEU. The Single Market legal basis, contained in Article 114 TFEU, is the most widely used legal basis in the EU, both in general and for various laws affecting the Internet.

The use of the Single Market legal basis has been subject to judicial scrutiny since its introduction in the Single European Act in 1986. In order to speed up the completion of the Single Market, it enabled laws to be adopted more easily with only a qualified majority instead of the more common uniformity. It quickly became popular and was used even when the original purpose was not fulfilled. The culmination came in 1998 with the *Tobacco Advertising*[57] judgment in which the (then) European Court of Justice ruled that Article 114 TFEU could not be used as a

---

[54]   Details of the agreement are available at https://www.ntia.doc.gov/other-publication/2016/q-and-iana-stewardship-transition-0.

[55]   See Zittrain, 'The Generative Internet', note 18 above.

[56]   Article 5 TEU.

[57]   C-376/98 *Federal Republic of Germany v European Parliament and Council of the European Union* [2000] ECR I-08419.

general legal basis in the absence of other bases. On the contrary, that basis is available only when there is a genuine Single Market aim. After the *Tobacco Advertising* judgment, in other words, it is much more difficult to rely on the Single Market basis.

In spite of relative clarity of Article 114 TFEU, doubts remain as to whether the breadth and the scope of intervention which it enables in Internet regulation can be squared with the principles of subsidiarity and proportionality. It is doubtful whether subsidiarity, which is the idea that law-making powers should be located at the lowest level of government, close to the citizens, is duly taken into consideration in some of the Directives. Subsidiarity rests upon a dual test: not only are Member States not in a position to achieve the objective but the Community itself, by reasons of scale or effect, is better suited to the task.

The claim that serious disruptions in the Internal Market result from lack of harmonization in these areas is tenuous. A typical instance is found in Recital 6 of the Preamble to the Data Retention Directive:[58]

> The legal and technical differences between national provisions concerning the retention of data for the purpose of prevention, investigation, detection and prosecution of criminal offences present obstacles to the internal market for electronic communications, since service providers are faced with different requirements regarding the types of traffic and location data to be retained and the conditions and periods of retention.

No 'obstacles to the internal market for electronic communications' had been presented by industry representatives in the months leading to the adoption of the Directive. On the contrary, it is possible to argue that the new requirements present an additional burden for corporations. The principal objective, moreover, is not to contribute to the Internal Market but to help combat serious crime. Examples of these kinds of problems can be found in almost every EU Directive affecting Internet law.

On the surface, the EU seems to respect the principle of proportionality as it opts for Directives more often than Regulations and for framework instruments when possible.[59] On the other hand, on a more substantial level, it can be argued that some Community Directives, at least, lack proportionality.

The TFEU provisions serve not only as a legal basis for most of the EU's Internet laws but also as a general backdrop for Internet activity in

---

[58]   More on the Directive can be found in Chapter 8.

[59]   See Protocol on the Application of the Principles of Subsidiarity and Proportionality, [2004] OJ C310/207, 16 December 2004.

the Community. In that sense, it is to be expected that the Community Single Market law will be applicable in this area. That law, as developed in the CJEU's cases, states that both discriminatory and non-discriminatory obstacles to trade in goods and services are illegal unless specifically justified in the Treaty or by reference to the Court's own exceptions.

Very few cases concerning the Single Market coming from the CJEU specifically focus on the Internet and those that do, do not necessarily establish far-reaching principles. Nevertheless, the cases serve to support the point that measures restricting the sale of goods or provision of services on the Internet are illegal, unless otherwise justified in the Treaty or by reference to the Court's case law.

An example of the Court's approach to a purely Single Market case is found in *DocMorris*.[60] In that case the issue was whether a Dutch company which legally provided pharmaceutical services via a dispensary in The Netherlands, by mail order and on the Internet, can also provide them on the Internet in Germany, where such sales are restricted to authorized pharmacies. The Court, after careful consideration of all the conditions of sale and the classification of drugs, decided that a national measure restricting such sales is a measure having equivalent effect, normally justifiable under Article 36 TFEU but not so if the prohibition is absolute. In *Gambelli*,[61] it was held that the Italian prohibition on online gambling was in violation of the provisions on free movement of services. Both cases illustrate nothing more than the Court's willingness to apply its developed Single Market doctrines to the Internet. The CJEU cases, although numerous, do not normally revolve around constitutional protections of the four freedoms but concentrate instead on these freedoms' implementation in the specific Directives.

5 EUROPEAN POLICY ON INFORMATION TECHNOLOGY

5.1 History

The history of the EU's interest in Internet law is relatively brief. Although relevant intellectual property (IP) and data protection laws

---

[60] C-322/01 *Deutscher Apothekerverband eV v 0800 DocMorris NV* [2003] ECR 14887.

[61] C-243/01 *Criminal Proceedings against Piergiorgio Gambelli and others* [2003] ECR I-13031.

predate the earliest Internet laws, specific e-commerce initiatives can be dated to the mid-1990s.[62] On the other hand, someone attempting to find a single EU-endorsed policy document on Internet law or even just electronic commerce from that period would be looking in vain. Doubts remain even over the question whether the European Union actually has a coherent Internet policy rather than a set of mini-policies. This is true in spite of an abundance of official agendas. Nevertheless, several documents provide an indication of the drive behind the EU Directives to be analysed further in the book.

Historically, the first document of interest to Internet law and the one to colour the EU's subsequent approach to the Internet is the European Initiative in Electronic Commerce from 1997.[63] The purpose of the document was to encourage the growth of e-commerce but its specific interest lies in the Commission's desire to create a 'coherent regulatory framework'. This was to be built on existing 'Single Market legislation which already creates the right conditions for online businesses'.[64] Four guiding principles were developed for the framework. The first related to technology: the EU must 'promote technology and infrastructure' necessary to ensure competitiveness. The second related to regulation: the EU must enable a coherent regulatory framework based on the Single Market. The third related to promotion: the EU was to make consumers and industries aware of the opportunities that electronic commerce enables. The last was related to the international dimension: the EU was to ensure effective international participation.

At the same time, four principles were to provide an 'adaptable and appropriate' framework for legislation:

- no regulation for regulation's sake;
- all regulation based on Single Market freedoms;
- all regulation to take account of business realities;
- all interests to be reached effectively and objectively.

---

[62] Y. Poullet, 'Towards Confidence: Views from Brussels: A European Internet Law? Some Thoughts on the Specific Nature of the European Regulatory Approach to Cyberspace' in G. Chatillon, *Internet International Law* (Bruylant, Brussels, 2005), p. 123. For a more detailed overview, see Chapter 5 in Christou and Simpson, *The New Electronic Marketplace*, note 20 above.

[63] European Commission, *A European Initiative in Electronic Commerce, Communication to the European Parliament, the Council, the Economic and Social Committee and the Committee of the Regions*, COM(97)157 (Brussels, 15 April 1997).

[64] *Ibid.* III(38).

Several observations must be made about the Initiative. The first is that the Community is signalling its preference for a flexible approach, which includes self-regulation. This largely follows in the steps of the Clinton administration's 'A Framework for Global Electronic Commerce',[65] which is itself a model of liberal, non-state initiated regulation. The second is that the balance between producers' and consumers' interests is taken into account.[66]

A new policy on Information Technology was initiated under the Council of Europe at the Strasbourg Summit in 1997 and developed in 1999.[67] Stressing the significant potential of digital technologies, particularly for such issues as freedom of expression, transparency, pluralism, and so on, the document is also interesting for highlighting the darker side of information technology such as cybercrime and threats to privacy. The Declaration talks about access as particularly important for any potential success of information technology. Further to this, important conventions have been drafted under the auspices of the Council of Europe, such as the Data Processing Convention.[68]

The third historically significant step was taken with the Lisbon Declaration and the e-Europe initiative.[69] The initiative was to make Europe the most dynamic 'knowledge-based economy in the world' by 2010. Among the declared goals that were to help achieve this were those that related to Internet access (then judged to be slow, uncertain and expensive) and the development of electronic commerce. Internet penetration, it was thought, had to be wider and electronic commerce needed to meet with better acceptance. Both problems were directly related to the need to liberalize the telecommunications sector in the Member States, a difficult step taken only reluctantly, but also due to the lack of a proper legislative framework. In light of this, work was initiated on a number of Directives, including the E-Commerce Directive. In addition

---

[65] See note 25 above.

[66] Although, in reality, there are reasons to believe that it is tilted in favour of producers. See, e.g., Dickie, *Consumers and Producers in EU E-Commerce Law,* note 3 above and Christou and Simpson, *The New Electronic Marketplace*, note 20 above, p. 99.

[67] Declaration on a European Policy for New Information Technologies, adopted by the Committee of Ministers, Dec(1999)NTI, 7 May 1999.

[68] Convention for the Protection of Individuals with regard to Automatic Processing of Personal Data, Strasbourg, 28 January 1981.

[69] Communication from the European Commission, *E-Europe: An Information Society for All*, COM(1999)687 (8 December 1999), repeated in the conclusion of the Stockholm European Council on 23 March 2001.

to this, self-regulation was promoted as was the creation of a separate .eu
domain name.

The practical blueprints for Internet regulation in most of the 2000s
were two action plans: eEurope 2002[70] and its continuation eEurope
2005.[71] The 2002 Action Plan had Internet penetration as its main task. It
contributed significantly to the 2002 revision of telecommunications
regulation. The 2005 Action Plan had connectivity as its main focus in
addition to services such as e-health, e-government, e-learning and
e-business. The 2005 plan was reviewed in 2009.[72]

'i2010: A European Information Society for Growth and Employment'[73] is an information society initiative launched in June 2005 as a
new strategic framework defining rather broad policy guidelines for the
information society and the media. It has three aims: to create a 'Single
European Information Space'; to strengthen investment in innovation and
information technology; and to improve public services and quality of
life through better use of ICT. In essence, this document is just a
continuation of the previous initiative.

5.2   Current Framework

Two documents play a particularly important role in outlining current
policy goals for Internet regulation: the 2010 Agenda and the 2015
Strategy. While the former replaces all the previously mentioned policy
instruments, the latter updates it to the demands of new technologies.

A Digital Agenda for Europe[74] is a 2010 initiative within the Europe
2020 strategy.[75] The Digital Agenda is an action plan which aims to help

---

[70]   Commission Communication, *eEurope 2002: Impact and Priorities: A
Communication to the Spring European Council in Stockholm, 23–24 March
2001*, COM(2001)140 final (13 March 2001).
[71]   Communication from the Commission to the Council, the European
Parliament, the Economic and Social Committee and the Committee of the
Regions, *The eEurope 2005 Action Plan: An Information Society for Everyone*,
COM(2002)263 final (28 May 2002).
[72]   Communication from the Commission, *Final Evaluation of the eEurope
2005 Action Plan*, COM/2009/0432 final (21 August 2009).
[73]   Commission Staff Working Paper, Communication from the Commission,
SEC(2005)717/2 (1 June 2005).
[74]   Communication from the Commission, *A Digital Agenda for Europe*,
COM(2010)245 (Brussels, 19 May 2010).
[75]   Communication from the Commission, *Europe 2020: A Strategy for
Smart, Sustainable and Inclusive Growth*, COM(2010)2020 final (3 March
2010).

deliver a digital Single Market.[76] It is, to date, possibly the most comprehensive policy document in the sphere of Internet regulation. It contains seven key 'pillars', which are: Digital Single Market, interoperability and standards; ICT standard-setting and interoperability; trust and security; access to fast Internet; improved ICT research and innovation; enhanced digital literacy and digital skills; and ICT-enabled societal benefits.[77] The Agenda is also a list of 101 actions which need to be undertaken to achieve these goals. Among these are legislative actions, such as amending the Electronic Signatures and the Electronic Commerce Directives (Actions 8 and 9).

Each of the seven pillars is a framework in itself, outlining the presently persisting problems but also giving a general direction in which the area ought to advance. These are then developed in further policy documents. Copyright, audio-video services or consumer protection, for example, feature within one or more Agenda pillars but are subject to their own policies, legislative revisions, etc. In that sense, it is possible to talk not only about EU Internet policy but also, for example, about EU digital copyright policy, EU cybercrime policy, etc.

The second document is the 2015 Digital Single Market Strategy for Europe.[78] This document should be treated both as an update to the 2010 Digital Agenda and as a completely new policy framework. This is because, while keeping the 2010 aims intact, the 2015 Strategy introduces new political goals.

The 2015 Strategy starts from the viewpoint that the Digital Single Market has not yet been achieved and that specific actions can be taken within the coming years to make it more realistic. These are: better online access to consumers and businesses; level playing field for networks and services; and maximizing the growth potential of the digital economy. Each of the three policy sections has a specific timeframe and each has specific sub-goals, which are a result of extensive input which the Commission had received from both businesses and consumers.

Within 'better access' policy area, the Commission suggests harmonized cross-border e-commerce rules for 'digital content' and 'key mandatory EU contractual rights' for online sales. This essentially means

---

[76] See also study: P. Van Eecke and M. Truyens, *Legal Analysis of a Single Market for the Information Society*, SMART 2007/0037 (30 May 2011).

[77] On these aims in detail, see G. Spindler, 'EU Internet Policy' in A. Savin and J. Trzaskowski, *Research Handbook on EU Internet Law* (Edward Elgar Publishing, Cheltenham and Northampton, MA, 2013), p. 3.

[78] Communication from the Commission, *A Digital Single Market Strategy for Europe*, COM(2015)192 final (6 May 2015).

partial harmonization of contract law. It also calls for better cross-border parcel delivery, removal of unjustified geo-blocking, a more modern EU copyright framework and reducing VAT-related burdens.

Within the 'level playing field' policy goal, the Commission calls for telecommunications rules 'fit for purpose' and proposes an overhaul of telecommunications rules including improving spectrum policy and tackling regulatory fragmentation. Importantly, it also calls for incentivising investment in high-speed broadband and the creation of a 'level playing field'. The latter essentially means same or similar conditions for traditional telecommunications services and for over-the-top providers (OTTs). OTTs, such as Skype, Netflix and others, are not subject to the regulatory burden the traditional telecommunications providers are normally subject to. They are able to provide cheaper and popular alternatives to services which have customarily been a revenue source for traditional telecoms (such as messaging, or streaming). Putting the 'level playing field' as a policy goal is a sign of increased anxiety and lobbying from traditional operators who fear that they are subject to unfair competition while being required to invest in next-generation networks. Within the same policy goal, the Commission also proposes an overhaul of the audio-video regulatory framework and a reassessment of the role of platforms (including intermediaries).

The introduction to the Strategy emphasizes that the three strategic EU Internet policy goals are the removal of roaming charges; the removal of unjustified geo-blocking; and the creation of the level playing field. Prioritizing these three goals over others does not seem to be the most rational choice. First, it is not clear why roaming ought to be prioritized over improving fixed and mobile telecommunications networks where the EU is beginning to fall behind rivals. While roaming charges may be frustrating, they are not seriously hampering the development of the digital single market and present a source of extra revenue for the beleaguered telecoms providers. Geo-blocking in content industry, while inconvenient, is mostly a result of the existence of 28 copyright regimes in the Member States. It is not clear how it could be removed without the copyright framework and licensing rules being fully harmonized at the same time. Finally, the level playing field is often emphasized as a desire by the traditional telecommunications providers but it involves extending telecommunications regulatory framework to OTT providers, a risky enterprise at the best of times and potentially a disastrous one.

The prioritization of the three mentioned goals shows confusion in EU policy-making. This is because it demonstrates the lack of clear goals in the telecommunications policy (see section 6 below), hesitance about deeper copyright reform (see Chapter 6) and a focus on secondary problems while ignoring the deeper underlying structural challenges on both the content and the carrier levels.

5.3 Institutional Ecology

The EU Internet policy, both in its formation and implementation aspects, is a result of cooperation between several institutions, where the role of each is well defined. The final documents are a result of this institutional structure, which also means that they are a product of compromises and intense lobbying.

The Commission has the sole right of legislative initiative.[79] The 2015 Commission, headed by Jean-Claude Juncker, assigned the role of coordination of digital policy-making to a Vice-President for the Digital Single Market. This change is meant to improve efficiency and solve the problem of coordination between different parts of the Commission. The Vice-President's role is to coordinate all the work on Digital Single Market issues otherwise performed by different Directorates General (DGs). This could reduce some of the problems associated with different DGs normally being involved in creation of Internet legislation.

In the current Commission, other than the Vice-President, two officers play a crucial role in Internet policy creation. The first is the Commissioner for Digital Economy and Society who coordinates DG Connect (Communications, Network, Content and Technology). This DG is the one directly charged with policy-making in the ICT area. The second is the Competition Commissioner, who is in charge of DG Competition. In addition to this, DG Informatics, DG Internal Market and Services, DG Trade and DG Justice and Consumers all play significant roles. Drafting of Directives is normally a product of collaboration between different DGs, which sometimes causes agendas and goals to clash.

The Commission's proposals are normally adopted in the ordinary legislative procedure[80] which requires cooperation between the Council and the European Parliament. A text cannot be adopted unless there is agreement between these two bodies. This is usually the point where intense lobbying alters the Commission's drafts. Transparent lobbying begins in the Parliament in Brussels as various stakeholders push MEPs for the protection of their interests. It then continues in each of the Member States' capitals when the text moves to the Council. At this point transparency decreases significantly as the sitting Minister in the Council

---

[79] Article 17(2) TEU.
[80] Article 289(1) TFEU.

changes for each proposal and as pressure dissipates between 28 different state bureaucracies. In recent years, this mechanism was most dramatically at work when the controversial measures in the telecommunications and privacy packages were being negotiated. In both cases, the original draft was altered many times on its way from the Commission to the Parliament, to the Council and back to the Parliament in a procedure that took several years. In both cases, intense negotiations between the Council and the Parliament were needed to reach a compromise and in both cases the public attention had diminished significantly by the time that compromise was reached.

Harmonization of Internet law is normally not full harmonization, which would completely replace Member States' laws, but only a partial one. This means that only the essential rules (the minimum) are harmonized whereas the rest is subject to mutual recognition of each other's laws. While this mechanism produces the desired flexibility and preserves Member States' sovereignty, it increases uncertainty and brings with it the need for interpretation. This is coming from the CJEU, which has the competence to interpret the Treaties and secondary legislation and rule on the validity and interpretation of secondary legislation.[81] The Court's work has played an invaluable role in most of the areas discussed in this book. In copyright, civil jurisdiction or privacy, for example, the legal picture would be completely different, had it not been for the Court's interventions. In Internet law, the Court had mostly been an activist court.

Finally, even outside of the European Union framework, a number of initiatives have concentrated on the regulation of the Internet. The most notable of these come from the Council of Europe, which has contributed vigorously to information and communications technology regulation by drafting a number of policies, issuing policy statements and working on important conventions.[82] Importantly, the aims of the Council are markedly different from that of the European Union. Unlike the latter, whose primary concern is trade between Member States, the former deals with human rights, democracy and the rule of law. The interpretation of the Council's documents in the European Court of Human Rights (ECtHR) had sometimes led to clashes with EU law.[83]

---

[81]   Article 19 TEU.

[82]   For an overview of their efforts, see K. Oakley, *Highway to Democracy: The Council of Europe and the Information Society* (Council of Europe Publishing, Strasbourg, 2003).

[83]   See discussion of the ECtHR *Delfi v Estonia* case in Chapter 5.

The picture that emerges from this multitude of policies and instruments is complex and occasionally confusing. Not only is it often not clear which authority stands behind different policies but it is also evident that policy goals may occasionally be confusing and contradictory. Nevertheless, what can be extracted from these instruments is a desire to keep Europe competitive and the idea that a link between technology and development is a key for achieving that aim.

6 EU TELECOMMUNICATIONS LAW AND THE INTERNET

While the subject of this book is mainly the top and the middle layers of the Internet, that is, the providers' network and the actual content, the EU also regulates the bottom layer – the physical layer used to convey the signals. The term telecommunications regulation today refers to legislation pertaining to the physical layer: linear broadcasting through cable and satellite (such as radio and television), regular telecommunications (fixed and mobile telephony) and provision of Internet access through broadband, wireless and other means.

The telecommunications regulatory framework does not regulate content. This is emphasized in the Framework Directive which separates the 'regulation of transmission' from the 'regulation of content'.[84] In other words, the regulatory framework says nothing about electronic contracts, about the IP status of the material provided, about the privacy of users or the providers, the appropriateness of the content or the possible criminal sanctions. These issues are covered in various other EU and national instruments on electronic commerce, copyright and others and, in the case of audio-visual services, in a separate EU Directive.[85]

The importance of telecommunications regulation for the Internet lies primarily in the phenomenon known as 'convergence'. Convergence means the coming together of different technologies – telecommunications, IT

---

[84] Directive 2002/21/EC of 7 March 2002 on a common regulatory framework for electronic communications networks and services [2002] OJ L108/33, 24 April 2002. See Recital 10, which specifically excludes most information society services because they do not consist of 'the conveyance of signals on electronic communications networks'. Web-based content is specifically excluded from the framework.

[85] Directive 2010/13/EU 'Audiovisual Media Services Directive' [2010] OJ L95/1, 15 April 2010.

and media – in a single device.[86] Today's devices, mobile phones, tablets, laptops and other SIM-enabled devices, are capable of serving the same content as traditional 'wired' media (such as telecoms companies or cable TV providers). The problem arises from the lack of convergence in the *regulatory* sector; while services and technologies may be converging in the *physical* world, the law-makers still operate with the three largely independent frameworks. These are the telecommunications framework described here, the audio-visual framework (see Chapter 4) and the e-commerce framework (see Chapter 2). This presents two Internet-specific problems: first, traditional telecommunications and cable providers are burdened by potentially onerous legislation which does not affect providers which are only subject to the e-commerce framework (e.g. OTTs such as Netflix). Second, it may not be clear to a new entrant to the market which legislative framework(s) it may be subject to.

6.1   Current Framework

The EU regulates the telecommunications sector extensively.[87] Telecommunications services have for years been subject to national monopolies and were limited to radio, television and voice telephony. With the technological advances in the 1980s and 1990s, it became necessary to liberalize them and maximize the advantages of the Single Market while increasing competition. This resulted in a number of liberalizing Directives in the areas of telecommunications terminals, services and infrastructure.[88] The main goal of these Directives was to remove the existing national monopolies and to prevent the creation of the new ones. Full liberalization of telecommunications networks and services had been achieved in 1998.[89]

As indicated in section 4 above, the EU only has legislative competence in those fields where the treaties specifically give it such competence. The basis for telecommunications regulation is found in several Articles. First, there is the general Single Market basis (Article 114 TFEU). Further to this, there is Article 106 TFEU which provides for the abolition of special or exclusive rights granted to undertakings. The

---

[86]   Green Paper, *Preparing for a Fully Converged Audiovisual World: Growth, Creation and Value* COM(2013)231 final (24 April 2013).

[87]   In detail see P. Nihoul and P. Rodford, *EU Electronic Communications Law* (OUP, Oxford, 2011).

[88]   *Ibid*. 4.

[89]   See in detail J. Scherer (ed.), *Telecommunication Laws in Europe*, 6th edn (Bloomsbury, West Sussex, 2013), pp. 4–8.

first paragraph of Article 106 prohibits Member States from discriminating on the basis of nationality as well as violating EU competition rules. The second paragraph covers services of general economic interest and subjects them to the Treaty's rules, including those on competition, provided that these do not 'obstruct the performance ... of the particular tasks assigned to them'. The last paragraph of Article 106 gives the Commission the appropriate law-making powers necessary to ensure the application of the Article. Finally, Articles 170–172 TFEU add explicit telecommunications policy goals for trans-European telecommunications networks.

The European Union has a dual regulatory approach in the telecommunications field. On one side, Article 106 TFEU authorizes the EU to liberalize the telecommunications sector. On the other, Article 114 TFEU authorizes it to harmonize the Single Market conditions. This division is not just a simple legacy of the initial set-up under which telecommunications became an interest in the EU. More than that, it hides true tensions between Member States who wish to preserve their competence in this field, on one side, and the EU on the other, which believes that only full harmonization can overcome fragmentation and truly open up the competitive potential of EU markets.

The regulatory framework on telecommunications in the European Union is complex, consisting of over 20 different Regulations, Directives and Decisions. As a result of developments in the broadcasting, telecommunications and information technologies, the EU adopted a new regulatory framework in 2002.[90] The new regime was meant to simplify and consolidate the current laws, deal with convergence issues and introduce more flexibility. The new framework was designed to cover both the Single Market and competition issues and to improve the development of new infrastructures and technologies. Additionally, the framework addresses specifically the convergence between fixed and mobile telecommunications as well as convergence between broadcasting, telecommunications and information technologies. The new framework, which is a consolidation of the previous Directives in the telecommunications sector, puts telecommunications services under a single regulatory framework without creating a central regulatory authority.

The three key instruments of the new regime are the Framework, Authorisation and Access Directives. The general framework of the new

---

[90] The framework was revised in 2009. The amending Directives are the First Amending Directive [2009] OJ L337/11, 18 December 2009, and the Second Amending Directive [2009] OJ L337/37, 18 December 2009.

regime is provided in the Framework Directive.[91] The Directive defines the applicability scope of the new regime, defines its terms and explains the fundamental policy goals. The Framework Directive also introduces national regulatory authorities (NRAs), which are supposed to be independent. The market entry is regulated in the Authorisation Directive[92] which simplifies access conditions for electronic networks and services. Wholesale access is covered in the Access Directive.[93] In order to prevent distortion of competition in services of general interest (referred to in Article 106(2)), the Universal Services Directive ensures the availability of a minimum standard of high-quality services to end-users while establishing their rights and imposing obligations on companies.[94]

The 2009 reform[95] introduced some important changes to the 2002 Framework, without altering its substance. The network of NRAs was kept in place but the previous European Regulators Group for Electronic Communications Networks and Services (ERG) was replaced by the Body of European Regulators for Electronic Communication (BEREC). BEREC, which is a Member State-controlled body, mainly has an advisory function. The 2009 package also sought to improve broadband penetration, increase some consumer rights, introduce an 'Internet freedom provision' securing citizens' access rights, and secure net neutrality.

The 2009 package was subject to further reform that concluded with the 2015 'Connected Continent' reform.[96] In spite of the somewhat ambitious title, the 2015 package is also a limited reform. Faced with the same policy choices as in 2002 and 2009, the 2015 regulation again decided against introducing a single telecommunications regulator. In essence, the Connected Continent Regulation only introduces two novelties. The first is the removal of mobile roaming charges. The second is the introduction of certain measures pertaining to end-users' Internet access (see section 6.2 below). As such, it is not offering a solution to the most pressing issues in the telecommunications world (competition from OTTs, mergers, investment in infrastructure).

---

[91]   [2002] OJ L108/33, 24 April 2002, amended in 2009.
[92]   [2002] OJ L108/21, 24 April 2002, amended in 2009.
[93]   [2002] OJ L108/7, 24 April 2002, amended in 2009.
[94]   [2002] OJ L108/51, 24 April 2002, amended in 2009.
[95]   European Commission, *Regulatory Framework for Electronic Communications in the European Union, Situation in December 2009* (Publications Office of the European Union, 2010).
[96]   Final text of Regulation 2015/2120 (EU) of the European Parliament and of the Council of 25 November 2015 [2015] OJ L310/1, 26 November 2015.

With the new updated framework, the general operation of the bottom Internet layer and access to it has been submitted to a uniform but still exceedingly complex and Member State-controlled regime at European level. This complexity, as well as the lack of a central EU telecommunications authority, has a negative impact on the effectiveness of EU telecommunications services in the Single Market and their competitiveness. With the fears that the EU is not investing enough in next-generation networks, the telecommunications framework is on schedule for revision in 2016. That revision will have to focus more on the convergence between IT, telecommunications and media technologies.

In September 2016, the Commission proposed the most comprehensive telecommunications reform since 2002. The reform consists in one framework directive, an action plan for 5G[97] and several other communications. The main document – Proposal for a European Electronic Communications Code[98] – is a recast of the four 2009 directives. The new Directive is meant to simplify the current rules (deregulation) while incentivising investment and solving systemic problems in the telecommunications sector: fierce competition between the incumbents and the disruptive OTTs, large discrepancies in Internet (both broadband and mobile) availability, penetration and use between the poorer and more developed parts of the EU and convergence between content and carrier. The Proposal redefines the term 'electronic communication services' partially subjecting OTT services to regulation and partially removing regulation from traditional services. Considering the importance of telecommunications and the political difficulties usually associated with this field, it is to be expected that the original Proposal would be subject to further amendments.

6.2 Net Neutrality

Net neutrality is a principle of Internet regulation requiring that Internet service providers (ISPs) do not favour application or content based on their source.[99] In other words, the principle is both stating that the present Internet does not discriminate on the basis of content and that legislation ought to be introduced to maintain this. The principle is meant to operate on the last mile only, that is, only between the ISPs and the end-users. It does not control the peering arrangements which are happening on the

---

97 5G for Europe, An Action Plan, Brussels, 14.9.2016 COM(2016) 588 final.
98 Proposal, Brussels, 14.9.2016 COM(2016) 590 final.
99 T. Wu, 'Network Neutrality, Broadband Discrimination' (2003) 2 *Journal of Telecommunications and High Technology Law* 141.

Internet backbone. Legislation protecting net neutrality normally consists in rules prohibiting providers from introducing differential treatment of some over other kinds of traffic.

Net neutrality is a highly politicized but extremely poorly understood issue.[100] The difficulties arise from the fact that although technical arrangements on the Internet have a very significant impact on political rights and citizens' freedoms they remain poorly understood by those making policy decisions.[101] In the past five years, the United States went from limited net neutrality to no net neutrality to pretty comprehensive neutrality.[102] The European Union, on the other hand, went from very strong net neutrality amendments to the Connected Continent package (resulting from the opposite trends in the United States) to limited net neutrality in the final version.[103]

With the 2009 telecommunications framework,[104] the EU has taken basic measures to ensure net neutrality and some of its provisions are of significance. Article 3(a) of the Second Amending Directive, the 'Internet freedom provision', provides that measures taken by Member States regarding end-users' access to electronic communications networks shall respect the fundamental rights and freedoms of natural persons, as guaranteed by the 1950 European Convention for the Protection of Human Rights and Fundamental Freedoms (ECHR) and general principles of Community law. Any restrictions may only be imposed if they are 'appropriate, proportionate and necessary within a democratic society' and must in any case be subject to proper judicial safeguards.

There are two ways in which this can be read.[105] The first is the right to access the Internet, which may mean that Internet access in itself is a fundamental right, although this remains untested in most national courts. The second relates to prosecution of national non-commercial copyright infringements which, although allowed, may not disproportionately and unnecessarily restrict the users' access.

---

[100] On the politics and law of net neutrality see L. Belli and P. De Filippi, *Net Neutrality Compendium* (Springer, London/New York, 2016).

[101] On this issue in general see L. DeNardis, *The Global War for Internet Governance* (Yale University Press, London/New Haven, CT, 2014).

[102] The latest iteration is FCC Rules passed on 26 January 2015. Federal Communications Commission doc. FCC 15-24, available at http://transition.fcc.gov/Daily_Releases/Daily_Business/2015/db0312/FCC-15-24A1.pdf.

[103] Regulation 2015/2120 (EU) [2015] OJ L310/1, 26 November 2015.

[104] Second Amending Directive: Directive 2009/140/EC of the European Parliament and of the Council of 25 November 2009 [2009] OJ L337/37, 18 December 2009.

[105] See Scherer, *Telecommunication Laws in Europe*, note 89 above, p. 28.

Several other provisions are of significance. First, under the 2009 telecommunications framework,[106] 'national regulatory authorities' are required to promote 'the ability of end-users to access and distribute information or run applications and services of their choice'. Secondly, Article 22(3) of the Universal Service Directive[107] further allows the creation of safeguarding powers for national regulatory authorities to prevent the degradation of services and the hindering or slowing down of traffic over public networks. This provision simply means that national regulatory authorities, after consulting the Commission, can set a minimum quality of service requirements if a problem arises. Finally, articles 20(1)(b) and 21(3)(c) and (d) of the Universal Services Directive further strengthen transparency requirements related to the treatment of consumers. These provisions are designed to enable consumers to better understand the Internet.

The 2015 Connected Continent Regulation[108] introduces only limited net neutrality. Article 3(1) and (3) guarantee the right of access for end-users. Article 3(3) provides that:

> Providers of internet access services shall treat all traffic equally, when providing internet access services, without discrimination, restriction or interference, and irrespective of the sender and receiver, the content accessed or distributed, the applications or services used or provided, or the terminal equipment used.

At the same time, the same article allows the implementation of 'reasonable traffic management measures'. The ISPs are obliged not to:

> block, slow down, alter, restrict, interfere with, degrade or discriminate between specific content, applications or services, or specific categories thereof, except as necessary, and only for as long as necessary.

The ISPs are allowed to restrict in order to comply with EU or national laws or to preserve the integrity or security of network or services or to prevent congestion.

Possibly even more importantly, article 3(4) allows the so-called specialized services which are 'services other than internet access services which are optimised for specific content, applications or services'. These can be, for example, various TV, music and gaming subscriptions,

---

[106]   Framework Directive, art. 8(4)(g).
[107]   Directive 2002/22/EC [2002] OJ L108/51, 24 April 2002.
[108]   Regulation 2015/2120 (EU) of the European Parliament and of the Council of 25 November 2015 [2015] OJ L310/1, 26 November 2015.

Internet to businesses or public organizations, special data storage, etc. The service providers have lobbied for these to be allowed, claiming that providing extra services in no way influences the regular operation of the Internet and that their enabling does not mean that certain popular applications (such as, for example, YouTube) would instantly be treated as 'special' and thus charged extra. The 2015 framework also provides for transparency measures (article 4) and supervision mechanisms (article 5) as well as penalties for violation (article 6).

On 6 June 2016, BEREC published its draft Guidelines on the Implementation of European Net Neutrality Rules.[109] The Guidelines are drafted in accordance with article 5(3) of the 2015 reform package, which demands that they be published but does not specify their scope. The Guidelines to article 3 point out that operators are allowed to offer free access to applications (such as a streaming music service) as long as this is not subject to preferential traffic. On the other hand, when assessing the so-called 'zero-rating', a practice where the operator applies zero price towards certain applications or groups of applications (usually the ones they own or promote for other reasons), the BEREC Guidelines point out that any blocking or slowing down of all applications except those zero-rated once the data cap is reached would be illegal. Other aspects of zero-rating need to be assessed by national authorities, which need to have the aims of the Regulation in mind. In relation to specialized services, the Guidelines point out that these can only be offered if regular services are in no way affected and not as a higher-price alternative to otherwise degraded basic services.

It is this author's position that net neutrality at present is largely a solution in search of a problem. This is for several reasons. First, the European telecommunications market is significantly more competitive than the American one where the danger of a monopolist provider of services discriminating is significantly higher. Secondly, the evidence of actual discrimination on the last mile is either non-existent or limited to isolated examples of blocking and throttling by vertically-integrated ISPs. Thirdly, net neutrality legislation, which is by definition on the last mile only, does not effectively deal with problems that arise on the backbone and these problems are better dealt with by competition and contract law anyway. Finally, there are commercial and organizational reasons why service providers ought to be allowed to provide separately charged specialized services while at the same level providing the 'best effort'

---

[109] BEREC Guidelines on the Implementation by National Regulators of European Net Neutrality Rules, BoR(16)94 (June 2016).

guarantee for the general Internet. It is submitted here that present EU rules provide an adequate guarantee for this.

7 CONCLUSION

The debate about Internet law is often subject to simplification as issues are politically coloured or portrayed in black and white. In fact, Internet regulation remains an elusive concept. While the early battles over Internet regulation have largely subsided, the debate about who regulates and when and the share of work between the actors has not. The latest interest in governance, self-regulation and home country control has demonstrated the Internet's adaptability in the face of increasingly complex demands put on it but it has also demonstrated its vulnerability. The Internet is remarkably susceptible to traditional methods of regulation, to traditional models of political pressure and traditional policy-making, none of which should be underestimated. Poor choices lead to an economy that is less dynamic and less competitive but also to a society that is less free.

The European Union has played a crucial part in Internet regulation in Member States. Large parts of electronic commerce, privacy, copyright protection and other areas are extensively covered by EU instruments. Globally, the European Union has a potential to hold a unique position. Its quasi-federal status, so often a source of problems, is also a starting place for regulatory competition and a drive for introducing decentralized solutions. Its desire to introduce new governance models is an asset in a battle to find the right solution, as is its bias in favour of a public over the private model of regulation. Its economic strength makes it a plausible alternative to the pervasive power of the United States. The choice of governance models is therefore crucial for the development of a new electronic economy in the EU as it is for the preservation of the individual freedoms of its citizens.

One of the theses of this book is that the fluid status of the Internet, its little-explored consequences and its unknown impact warrant as liberal a regulatory approach as possible and a balance between governmental intervention and self-regulation, careful participation in governance efforts and recognition of the exceptional features of the Internet's architecture. As will be demonstrated in the chapters to follow, this is a task that is not always easy to fulfil.

2. Electronic commerce

1 REGULATING ELECTRONIC COMMERCE IN EUROPE

Electronic commerce has a deceptively simple definition: it is the act of buying or selling goods or services by means of electronic resources. The straightforwardness of this explanation hides the complexity facing the regulator and the great economic importance of the phenomenon. Since the public rise of the Internet in the mid-1990s and through its wide penetration at the turn of the century, the law-makers across the globe have repeatedly tried to address a host of questions relating to the conclusion of electronic contracts and its consequences. When can contracts be formed on the Internet? Is a simple exchange of emails sufficient? When does clicking on the words 'I Agree' on the seller's webpage bind the parties? This anxiety is a result of the Internet's often real but sometimes only perceived borderlessness. In a transaction concluded on the Internet the parties are 'not present'. But this does not differ from contracts concluded over other modes of communication. Sending an offer and receiving acceptance happens in much the same way over email or by clicking the 'I Agree' button on the webpage of the supplier as it does by phone, regular mail or fax transmission. From this perspective, it is not surprising that special rules on electronic contracts were rare both in national and EU law.

On the other hand, the Internet brings real problems, some of which do not appear with other media. If a dispute arises, what courts will have jurisdiction? Will consumers be able to avail themselves of their local protective regime? How can an online payment be processed? The European Union as a developed industrial economy has been exposed to these dilemmas for over 20 years. Here, like elsewhere, the key problems have been the adequacy and the adaptive power of traditional rules and the extent of the potential intervention. Part of the European answer to these dilemmas comes in the form of the E-Commerce Directive[1] which became a backbone for European regulation in this area.

The Internet's potential lies in the employment opportunities it provides and the growth it brings through investment in innovation and increased competition.[2] The Community legal order, with its liberal regime for the movement of factors of production, represents a particularly positive climate for the development of electronic commerce. The current volume of electronic commerce amounts to over 57 per cent of manufacturing shipments,[3] and with a growth rate of 15 per cent per annum its future potential is considerable. After a boom in the late 1990s and a bust in 2000, the trade has recovered in the early years of the century and medium- as well as long-term predictions seem to be optimistic. The services sector, which in the developed countries forms the larger part of gross national product, is already heavily dependent on the information society and will be more so in the future. In 2015, the Internet penetration in Europe for households stands at about 80 per cent[4] and for businesses at almost 100 per cent. Most companies have a website and an increasing number use the Internet as a business tool. At the moment, e-commerce represents over 40 per cent of retail sales in Europe since this number increased from €10 billion in 2000 to €70 billion in 2003 to predicted €233 billion in 2018 and after. Advertising can be singled out as another growing sector in recent years with businesses spending more on online advertisement placements than those in traditional media.

Few laws in the European digital context are as far-reaching in practice as the E-Commerce Directive.[5] Not only is the Directive designed to

---

[1] Directive 2000/31/EC on certain legal aspects of information society services, in particular electronic commerce, in the Internal Market [2000] OJ L178/1. The proposal was adopted in 1998, amended by the European Parliament in 1999 and finally adopted in 2000. The Parliament's most important amendment was to allow ISP liability for breaches of intellectual property rights under certain circumstances.

[2] These are also emphasized in Recital 3 of the Directive.

[3] As of 2013, US Census Bureau E-Stats, 28 May 2015, available at www.census.gov/econ/estats/e13-estats.pdf.

[4] Eurostat, *Information Society Statistics: Households and Individuals* (June 2015), available at http://ec.europa.eu/eurostat/statistics-explained/index.php/Main_Page.

[5] On the historical development of the Directive, see G. Pearce and N. Platten, 'Promoting the Information Society: The EU Directive on Electronic Commerce' (2000) 6 *European Law Journal* 363.

provide an overall framework for electronic commerce,[6] a difficult achievement in any context, but its ambition is also to provide the basis for competing with the United States in encouraging the use of the Internet in commerce. Although the recitals of the Directive contain the familiar EU Single Market invocation, it is also clear that the Directive aims to do more than just reinforce free movement of goods and services.

It can be said with some confidence that the E-Commerce Directive is one of the more successful initiatives in electronic commerce in modern times. The Commission reported positively on the Directive in 2003 and confirmed that there was no need for a revision.[7] The two studies on the Directive commissioned since, the Study on the Economic Impact of the Electronic Commerce Directive[8] and the Study on the Liability of Internet Intermediaries[9] have also had positive results. For Europe, the Directive was the beginning of a crucial phase of wider regulation of the Internet, but for the outside world, in the form of the 'country of origin rule', it proved an intriguing approach to the difficult issue of legislative jurisdiction.

Nevertheless, the 2015 Digital Single Market Strategy[10] emphasizes that, in spite of the successes, large areas are still in need of intervention. The Strategy emphasizes that three issues are of particular need of further intervention. The first is the existence of affordable high-quality cross-border parcel delivery where postal rates charged for cross-border services are often many times higher than domestic rates. The second is better access to digital content including the prevention of unjustified geo-blocking. The third is the reduction of VAT-related obstacles in cross-border sales. For each of these issues the Commission has submitted legislative proposals in 2016.

In this chapter, we will talk about the pursued aims of the E-commerce Directive, look at its main provisions and analyse its modus operandi. We

---

[6]   On three regulatory layers applying to the Internet see Chapter 1, section 6.

[7]   Report from the Commission to the European Parliament, the Council and the European Economic and Social Committee, *First Report on the Application of Directive 2000/31/EC of the European Parliament and of the Council of 8 June 2000 on Certain Legal Aspects of Information Society Services, in particular Electronic Commerce, in the Internal Market (Directive on Electronic Commerce)*, COM(2003)0702 final, 21 November 2003.

[8]   European Commission, DG Internal Market and Services Unit E, *Final Report* (7 September 2007).

[9]   T.V. Ulys *et al.*, *Study on the Liability of Internet Intermediaries*, Markt/2006/09/E (12 November 2007).

[10]   Communication from the Commission, *A Digital Single Market Strategy for Europe*, COM(2015)192 final (6 May 2015).

so look at its provisions concerning the conclusion of electronic
ts and the country of origin rule. Jurisdiction issues arising out of
f the provisions of the Directive will be addressed in Chapter 3,
issues in Chapter 5 and consumer issues in Chapter 7. But, since
ective itself is not harmonizing contract law as such, in the final
the chapter we will provide an overview of various EU proposed
ization measures in the field of electronic commerce regulation.

COMMERCE DIRECTIVE: THE FRAMEWORK

rly Community project on electronic commerce was the action
p.... *Europe's Way Forward to the Information Society*.[11] More tangibly,
in 1997 the Commission published the *European Initiative in Electronic
Commerce*.[12] Its four guiding principles were to: (a) promote the technology and infrastructure; (b) capitalize on the Single Market by ensuring
a coherent regulatory framework for e-commerce; (c) foster a favourable
business environment; and (d) reach a common European position. It was
to prove the right document for boosting both the interest in electronic
commerce among Member States and the awareness of businesses and
consumers alike. But the Initiative had an important source of inspiration
in the form of the US Clinton administration document *A Framework for
Global Electronic Commerce*[13] which emphasized the belief that the
Internet should be market-driven and not regulated. Five principles of the
Clinton document were to inform Internet governance: (1) the private
sector should lead; (2) governments should avoid undue restrictions on
electronic commerce; (3) where governments do need to intervene, it
should be to support a simple and minimalist legal environment; (4)
governments should recognize the unique qualities of the Internet; and
(5) electronic commerce should be facilitated globally. The Framework,

[11] Communication to the Council, the European Parliament, the Economic
and Social Committee and Committee of the Regions, COM(94)347 final (19
July 1994). This was preceded by the 1993 Commission *White Paper on Growth,
Competitiveness and Employment: The Challenges and Ways Forward into the
21st Century*, COM(93)700 final (5 December 1993), which discussed new
technologies and their importance for Europe's economy.
[12] Communication to the Council, the European Parliament, the Economic
and Social Committee and Committee of the Regions, COM(97)157, 15 April
1997.
[13] W. Clinton, 'A Framework for Global Electronic Commerce' in B.
Fitzgerald (ed.), *Cyberlaw I and II* (Ashgate, Dartmouth, 2006), vol. I, p. 133.

which inspired other regulators including European, remains one of the strongest statements of a 'hands-free' approach.

The 1997 EU Initiative had been created independently from the Clinton framework but under its influence, a fact which can be deduced from each document's content. Among areas for future action, the Initiative identified the 'access to infrastructure' and the 'creation of a legal framework'. Both frameworks identified the 'new economy' as an area of utmost importance. The Europe Union observed that initiatives had to be implemented by 2000 if Europe was to benefit from the development of the Internet.[14] The plan, the true beginning of e-commerce regulation in Europe, was a starting point for a number of legal initiatives discussed in this and other chapters of the book. It drew inspiration both from the American efforts and from the UNCITRAL Model Law on Electronic Commerce,[15] recasting some of the fundamental principles in the Single Market context.

Some policy values and guiding principles which remain today were also first introduced in the EU Initiative. Their principal aim was to control the new regulatory framework.[16] According to the general EU principle of subsidiarity, Community harmonization should only take place where other integration mechanisms prove insufficient. Accordingly, 'no regulation for regulation's sake' is the first guiding principle. Mutual recognition and home country control should take priority over full regulation. Secondly, the new rules should be compatible with the Internal Market and not conflict with it. Thirdly, the new regulation should follow the realities of the business cycle. Finally, public interests should be taken into consideration, including consumer protection.

The preparatory work on the Directive, in the form of first proposals and comments received on them, both from competent Community institutions and from the general public, reveals that the Community had specific goals in mind. Primarily, and in accordance with Article 18 of the Treaty on the Functioning of the European Union (TFEU), the aim was to prevent discrimination between Member States of 'information society service (ISSs) providers'.[17] Further to that, the aim was to remove other 'non-discriminatory obstacles'. These were addressed throughout

---

[14]   In reality the implementation dragged on well into the 2000s.
[15]   UNCITRAL Model Law on Electronic Commerce with Guide to Enactment 1996, United Nations Publications, No. E.99.V.4.
[16]   G. Pearce and Platten, 'Promoting the Information Society', note 5 above, pp. 366–7.
[17]   To distinguish them from conceptually narrower Internet service providers (ISPs), information service providers are here referred to as ISSs.

the Directive. To achieve this, the Community expected the Directive to be not only part of a wider scheme of instruments on e-commerce but also to rely on the *acquis communautaire*.

Possibly the most important feature of the E-Commerce Directive is its ambition to be the 'Framework Directive'. Directive 2000/31 is meant to be part of a larger number of initiatives covering trading that takes place on the Internet. More narrowly defined, this area encompasses measures on the protection of consumers (see Chapter 7), on electronic signatures (see Chapter 9), on e-commerce (this Chapter) and on copyright and related rights (see Chapter 6). More widely defined, it includes a number of other initiatives concerning money, financial services, taxation and others, also discussed within the mentioned chapters.

The Directive and its counterparts reflect the 'life cycle of electronic commerce activities'.[18] It starts with the establishment of information society service providers, moving on to commercial communication and contracts concluded by electronic means, to end with the liability of intermediary service providers. In spite of this, it is evident that this is not an all-encompassing law on electronic commerce. Indeed, such laws rarely exist at national levels and are of modest success at international levels.[19] The Directive covers what were believed to be the most contentious areas only. Furthermore, the Community, limited by principles of subsidiarity and proportionality as expressly recognized in Recital 10, sought to address only the obstacles to electronic commerce between Member States rather than to harmonize the law of contracts on the Internet.

The Internal Market was set as the framework for the Directive.[20] Article 114 TFEU on the Internal Market is used as a legal basis, together with Articles 52 TFEU on establishment and 62 TFEU on services, clearly placing it in a Single Market context and suggesting its main purpose. The purpose of the Directive and other instruments from the framework is to enable the free movement of information society services. This fits within the general concept of the four freedoms, as

---

[18]   A. Lodder, 'Directive 2000/31 on Certain Legal Aspects of Information Society Services, in particular Electronic Commerce, in the Internal Market' in A. Lodder and H. Kaspersen (eds.), *eDirectives: Guide to European Union Law on E-Commerce* (Kluwer Law International, The Hague/London/New York, 2002), p. 69.

[19]   On the UN Convention on the Use of Electronic Communications in International Contracts, see C. Connolly and P. Ravindra, 'First UN Convention on E-Commerce Finalized' (2006) 22 *Computer Law and Security Report* 31.

[20]   See Recitals 4, 5, 6 or 59.

they are set out in the TFEU and developed by the Court of Justice of the European Union (CJEU).

It is worth remarking that the main idea behind the four freedoms[21] is the prohibition of any restrictions on movement of goods, services, people and capital between Member States. Initially, this was taken to mean discrimination based on nationality.[22] Very importantly, however, in the practice of the Court,[23] the freedoms have been interpreted as including non-discriminatory barriers to movement, those that place an equal burden in law (thus avoiding the difference based on nationality) but a different burden in fact (making it in practice more costly and less competitive for the provider from another Member State). In reality, however, since the Internet is subject to a number of harmonization Directives discussed in this book, national courts very rarely decide cases directly on the basis of the four freedoms.

A total replacement of national law on contract formation, on the Internet or otherwise, was never contemplated and the framework regime is intended to supplement it only. In EU terms, this can be understood as a 'minimum harmonization' measure, providing only the harmonized basis that must be respected throughout the Community and requiring Member States to recognize that entities and activities are subject to regulation in the country of origin. This is among the more original but also controversial features as demonstrated by the 2004 Services Directive.[24] It is worth adding that some EU measures are full harmonization measures, pre-empting further national legislation even where this increases the protection standards.[25]

The Internal Market was not the only perspective that the legislator had in mind, however. Although the Directive only operates within the EU, relations with third states were clearly in the mind of the regulators, as they thought not only that Europe should have a strong negotiating position (Recital 59) but also that Europe and major non-European areas need to consult each other (Recital 60). There have not been any major

---

[21]   See Arts 34–62 TFEU.

[22]   Also set out as a general Treaty principle in Art. 18 TFEU.

[23]   See C-120/78 *Rewe-Zentral AG v Bundesmonopolverwaltung fhr Brannt-wein* [1979] ECR 649 for goods; C-55/94 *Gebhard* [1995] ECR I-4165 for establishment; and C-76/90 *Saeger* [1991] ECR I-4221 for services.

[24]   See original proposal: European Commission, Proposal for a Directive of the European Parliament and of the Council on services in the internal market, COM(2004)0002 final, 25 February 2004.

[25]   Most notably the Unfair Commercial Practices (UCP) Directive [2005] OJ L149/22, 11 June 2005.

attempts at international harmonization of electronic commerce law other than the mentioned UNCITRAL Model law.

3 E-COMMERCE DIRECTIVE: AIMS AND SCOPE

The Directive applies both to business-to-business (B2B) and business-to-consumer (B2C) transactions. Consumer protection, a specifically business-to-consumer area, is not the focus of the Directive but is recognized by reference in several recitals and in the idea that consumers benefit from electronic commerce by being exposed to greater choices and lower prices. This double nature of the Directive can be explained by the desire to create a universal instrument which can be supplemented by special consumer protection rules, as needed.

The objectives of the Directive are set out in article 1, the first paragraph of which refers to the Internal Market. The purpose of the Directive is free movement of information society services between Member States. The Preamble proclaimed that hindrance to trade and lack of harmony in Member States in the mentioned areas were primary motivating factors for harmonization. Article 1(2) states that the tool which will be used is the approximation of laws and summarizes the main activity areas in the Directive. These are:

- the establishment of service providers;
- commercial communications;
- electronic contracts;
- intermediary liability;
- out-of-court dispute settlement.

There were several reasons for focusing the activity on the afore-mentioned areas of harmonization. Primarily, the problem of the form of an electronic contract was being addressed differently in Member States. Secondly, the problem of the point of creation was increasingly gaining in importance.[26] Thirdly, the issue of whether Internet service providers were liable for the content they transmitted was unresolved and was threatening to slow the Internet's development down. The Directive was therefore meant as a set of solutions to a cluster of connected problems.

---

[26] A. Murray, 'Entering into Contract Electronically: The Real WWW' in L. Edwards and C. Waelde (eds.), *Law and the Internet: A Framework for Electronic Commerce* (Hart Publishing, Oxford, 2000).

Despite ambitious declarations, the authors were aware of the difficulties involved in attempting to harmonize contract law. Their dilemmas are apparent in the revision history and in the limitations introduced in Article 1.[27] Article 1(3) provides that the Directive does not prejudice any protection of public health or of consumers 'in so far as this does not restrict the freedom to provide information society services'. Furthermore, the Directive does not establish additional rules on private international law and does not deal with the jurisdiction of the courts.[28] Article 1(5) excludes the application of the Directive to taxation, data protection, telecommunications, cartel law, notaries, advocates or gambling. Finally, article 1(6) excludes measures taken in protection of linguistic or cultural diversity or pluralism.

Each of the limitations to the Directives can be understood in its own context although not all seem entirely justified and a number are not drafted ideally. Article 1(3) would suggest that freedom to provide services prevails over public health or consumer protection, as the latter are only protected in so far as they do not restrict the freedom to provide services. Since the priority is clearly set in favour of both public health and consumer protection in other provisions, not least in the Single Market Treaty provisions, this must be interpreted as a mistake. Article 1(4) concerning private international law, although seemingly written in a neutral way, created a lot of controversy over its relationship with the principle of the country of origin. Article 1(5) refers to measures where proper EU harmonization has not happened (for example, the professions) or where resistance from Member States might be too difficult to overcome.

Article 2 defines crucial terms of the Directive. Somewhat curiously, it does not define information services themselves. For that, reference must be made to Recitals 17 and 18 of the Directive. This, in turn, copies a definition given in the Technical Standards Directive.[29] Recital 17 thus says that information society services are:

---

[27]   For the history of some of the provisions of the Directive, see A. Murray, 'Articles 9–11, ECD: Contracting Electronically in the Shadow of the E-Commerce Directive' in L. Edwards (ed.), *The New Legal Framework for E-Commerce in Europe* (Hart Publishing, Oxford, 2005), p. 67.

[28]   Art. 1(4). For a detailed discussion of this question, see Chapter 3.

[29]   Directive 98/34 of 22 June 1998 laying down a procedure for the provision of information in the field of technical standards and regulations and of rules on Information Society services [1998] OJ L204, 21 July 1998.

provided for remuneration, at a distance, by means of electronic equipment for the processing ... and storage of data, and at the individual request of a recipient of a service.

This definition is meant to encompass a large number of transactions and the E-Commerce Directive is wider in scope than its title might suggest. This is not surprising. First, as mentioned, it was designed as a framework instrument, part of a broader set. More importantly, it covers the wider business of receiving information society services rather than the narrower act of an online sale, as can be seen in the definition provisions. This makes it applicable in situations not involving trade. Importantly, Recital 18 sets out to explain the nature of the information society services beyond the above definition. In doing so, it emphasizes that they are not restricted to online contracting but include those services where information is provided. Another important requirement is the individual demand. Where this is lacking, the Directive does not cover the services. Therefore, television and radio broadcasting fall without, since they are subject to the Audiovisual Media Services (AVMS) Directive (2010/13/EU), whereas email or on-demand video are within.

The basic elements of the definition are fourfold. First, the service must be provided for remuneration although the cost need not necessarily be borne by the final recipient. A number of extremely important information services, such as web mail or search engines, rely on advertising for their income. In the *Pappasavas* case, the CJEU expressly ruled that 'the concept of "information society services" ... covers the provision of online information services for which the service provider is remunerated, not by the recipient, but by income generated by advertisements posted on a website'.[30] Secondly, the service must be provided at a distance. This should be taken to mean that there must have existed electronic communication between the parties at the time when the contract was concluded. Thirdly, the service must be made by electronic means. Other distance-selling methods are not covered. Finally, the service must be provided at the individual request of a recipient. The last point was introduced to distinguish information society services from television and other broadcasting services under the AVMS Directive. The question remains open, at this point, as to how streaming services (such as Netflix or iTunes), television provided through mobile devices (smart phones, tablets, etc.) and television provided through personal computers ought to be classified. They contain elements both of

---

[30] C-291/13 *Sotiris Papasavvas v O Fileleftheros Dimosia Etairia Ltd, Takis Kounnafi, Giorgos Sertis*, ECLI:EU:C:2014:2209, 11 September 2014.

on-demand and traditional services, in that the service is provided or requested for, usually through some form of web access, but also that they fall under broadcasting and can mostly also be accessed on traditional media. Until the Court provides further clarification, it should be assumed that such services fall both under the E-Commerce and the AVMS regimes.

Article 2(c) defines the place of establishment of a service provider. This will be the place where the provider has a 'fixed establishment for an indefinite period'. The presence of technical equipment does not, in itself, constitute establishment. The last is an important point, as servers and other equipment are often located in places away from the provider's establishment.

The purpose behind the definition, as behind the introduction of the country of origin rule, seems to be to establish clear rules in the climate where several connecting factors may be relevant. In that sense, neither the place where the corporation is doing business, nor the place where the equipment is located matter.

The Electronic Commerce Directive is addressed to the Member States and therefore is meant to apply to information society service providers established in the European Union. If a third-country provider has an establishment in the EU, they would be subject to the rights and obligations of the Directive. If a third-country provider operates by directly offering services to consumers, they may be covered by other EU laws, such as privacy or consumer protection rules, but will not be directly under the Electronic Commerce Directive.

In recent years, a question regarding the nature of information society services arose in the context of transport provision. Uber is a multi-national taxi dispatch company that relies on the Internet to market and sell its services. In many European countries, national taxi service providers staged protests claiming that Uber was operating an otherwise regulated activity (passenger transport) without complying with national laws. In 2015, a Spanish judge referred the question to the CJEU, asking whether Uber provided a 'transport service' or 'an electronic intermediary service or an information society service' in Europe.[31] Uber's argument was that they provided an information society service under the EU freedom of establishment and that, as such, they required no authorization. The question is important because an increasing number of disruptive services rely on electronic commerce to make themselves

---

[31]   C-434/15 *Asociación Profesional Élite Taxi v Uber Systems Spain, SL* (not yet decided).

more competitive, thus circumventing traditional regulatory frameworks. In such a situation, the outer limits of states' ability to regulate such services need to be established both for purposes of maintaining public interests and for decreasing the danger of stifling innovation through overregulation.

4 E-COMMERCE DIRECTIVE: OPERATION

The E-Commerce Directive achieves four major goals. First, it eases the establishment and operation of information service providers throughout the EU. Secondly, it demands that the seller provides particular kinds of information in electronic contracts. Thirdly, it introduces measures that facilitate the conclusion of electronic contracts. Finally, it limits the liability of information society service providers. The first and the third of the features are analysed in this chapter while the second and fourth are looked at in Chapters 7 and 5, respectively.

4.1 Establishment of the Information Service Provider

The Directive's first task is to enable easy establishment of information service providers. Recital 19 sheds light on the term 'establishment' in the Internal Market context. The recital provides that the 'place at which a service provider is established should be determined in conformity with the case-law of the Court of Justice' on establishment. The concept of establishment, as developed in that case law[32] is identified by virtue of the presence of a fixed establishment pursuing activity for an indefinite period. Since establishment is a more permanent presence, and therefore subject to the more stringent control of the 'host state', providers will often seek to avail themselves of more favourable terms of the freedom to provide services. This has resulted in a Communication from the Commission helping to distinguish between the two.[33]

For information society services which operate through websites, the place of establishment is not the place where the technology supporting the website is located, nor the place where the site is accessible, but

---

[32] See C-55/94 *Reinhard Gebhard v Consiglio dell'Ordine degli Avvocati e Procuratori di Milano* [1995] ECR 4165.

[33] For difficulties in distinguishing services from establishment in the banking and insurance sectors, see the Commission's Interpretative Communications on the Second Banking Directive, SEC(97)1193 final (Brussels, 20 June 1997) and the Third Insurance Directive [2000] OJ C43/5, 16 February 2000.

rather the place where the provider pursues its economic activity. Where the provider has several places of establishment or where it is difficult or impossible to determine one, it will be the place where the provider has a centre of activities relating to the particular service.[34] The definitions, although helpful, are not precise and it is possible to imagine an operator pursuing economic activity in several centres.

Articles 4 and 5 deal with the establishment of information society service providers. The guiding principle behind these articles seems to be the ease of access to the information required. They demand that recipients of services be able to quickly and easily understand the kind of service they receive and its source.

Article 4 introduces the principle of exclusion of prior authorization. The taking up and pursuit of ISS activities does not depend on any prior requirement. Specifically excluded from this are authorization schemes not specifically targeted at ISS providers and telecommunications services.

Article 5 establishes the obligation of the ISS provider to provide information about itself. This includes its name, address, contact details, authorization details, and so on. The aim of this is simply to give the other party as much real world information about the trader as possible. A special requirement in article 5(2) relates to prices, which are often a source of confusion. The first draft provided that 'prices of Information Society services are indicated accurately and unequivocally'. In the second draft, it was added that these prices must also include all additional costs. The final text states that prices should be indicated 'clearly and unambiguously' and that they must specify whether they are inclusive of VAT and delivery, where applicable.

4.2   Commercial Communications

Section 2 of the second chapter (articles 6 to 8) of the Directive deals with commercial communications directed at recipients. Advertising, marketing, unsolicited emails and similar phenomena have grown in importance as electronic commerce developed. At the same time, the development of electronic advertising has exceeded expectations. The Directive provides minimum requirements regarding the provider of services and the commercial activity it engages in. The information requirement is not specifically targeting consumers but also applies to business-to-business (B2B) transactions. Same or similar information

---

[34]   See Recital 19.

requirements are repeated in a number of other EU Directives covering this field, leading to the serious questioning of the cost they impose on the provider and their effectiveness.[35]

Article 6 establishes information obligations which are additional to other requirements imposed on the ISS provider elsewhere. The commercial communication must, according to this article, be identifiable as such, as must be the entity on whose behalf this is provided. The regulation of promotional offers, discounts and similar incentives is left to Member States but must be identifiable as must be any conditions necessary to qualify for them, where permitted. Finally, competitions and games are also left for regulation by Member States but the same conditions apply to them as to promotional offers. In the area of financial services, the Commission issued a Communication concerning the application to them of article 3(4) to 6,[36] which was a result of a concern expressed by financial service providers about the areas which did not yet converge.

Article 7 deals with unsolicited commercial communication, or spam, as this is more commonly referred to today.[37] At this stage we will only say that the provision, as adopted in the Directive, was always inadequate to cope with the sheer volume of such communication. The provision leaves the legality of spam to Member States but obliges them to introduce provisions which would oblige the sender of a communication to identify it as such as soon as received. Further to that, article 7(2) obliges the Member States to take measures to make sure that service providers respect opt-out registers containing the names of those not wishing to receive such communication. Since unsolicited commercial communication was subject to further legislation, article 7 is of little practical importance today.

In light of the recent developments in this area, it is submitted that the area of commercial communication as set out in this part of the Directive is out of date. The Community left it to Member States to actually make unsolicited commercial communication illegal and limited itself to imposing information requirements (which have already been covered in

---

[35] Specifically, on the multiplication of information requirements in different directives see A. Lodder, 'Information Requirements Overload? Assessing Disclosure Duties under the E-Commerce Directive, Services Directive and Consumer Directive' in A. Savin and J. Trzaskowski, *Research Handbook on EU Internet Law* (Edward Elgar Publishing, Cheltenham and Northampton, MA, 2014).

[36] COM(2003)259 final (14 May 2003).

[37] Spam will be dealt with in more detail in Chapter 8.

the Distance Selling Directive (97/7/EC). More importantly, unsolicited communication is undesirable by virtue of its cost rather than the annoyance factor to the end-user/recipient. The Directive does little to address this or the problem of unsolicited communication coming from third states[38] and arguably does not have the potential to cover more sophisticated forms of electronic advertising available today.

Article 8 covers regulated professions. Services provided by a member of a regulated profession (such as solicitors, notaries, etc.) are allowed, subject to compliance with the general rules but also any professional rules (such as those concerning conduct, secrecy and such). Professional associations are encouraged to provide codes of conduct at Community level. The Electronic Commerce Directive does not prejudice other Community instruments regulating professional conduct.

4.3   Concluding Contracts on the Internet

The E-Commerce Directive is not a model law for electronic commerce.[39] It does not replace national civil law rules and does not give the answer to such questions as existence of offer or acceptance, the place of performance or consequences of breach. Such rules come from national laws and remain unchanged (although not unrecognized) by EU rules.

In the previous chapter we have examined some of the issues concerning regulatory competence in Internet law and identified some of the powers that the EU relies on to regulate in that area. The European Union, we have concluded, has the legislative competence to act. But, this is not necessarily the case in civil law where the EU has only limited powers to regulate and is generally not in a better position than Member States to do so.[40] These powers have always been used with restraint and, despite occasional doubts, are usually accepted by Member States.[41]

Article 9 of the E-Commerce Directive imposes a requirement that Member States make it possible for contracts to be concluded by

---

[38]   Such communication largely remains out of the scope of EU law.

[39]   Such a document has been created in 1996 under the auspices of UNCITRAL as the UNCITRAL Model Law on Electronic Commerce with Guide to Enactment, General Assembly Resolution 51/162 (United Nations, 1996). See also United Nations Convention on the Use of Electronic Communications in International Contracts, UN Publ. A/Res/60/21, 5 December 2005.

[40]   For attempts to create mandatory and optional European sales laws, see section 6 below.

[41]   For an overview of the EU regulatory efforts in private law, see C. Twigg-Flesner (ed.), *European Union Private Law* (CUP, Cambridge, 2010).

electronic means. This reflects a desire for electronic contracts to be concluded in a manner as close as possible to regular contracts. Member States are under an obligation to ensure that legal requirements applicable to the contractual process do not create obstacles for the use of electronic contracts nor result 'in such contracts being deprived of legal effectiveness and validity on account of their having been made by electronic means'.

The E-Commerce Directive does not cover the typical life-cycle of a contract, which includes negotiations, formation, performance and possible remedies and dispute resolution. Section 3 of the Directive, entitled 'Contracts concluded by electronic means' contains some important elements, but does not suggest a full harmonization of the area. It is interesting to note that the original draft for the Directive was somewhat more ambitious in including more detailed provisions on the formation of the contract. These can still be found hidden in the preparatory works. Even when other e-commerce-related Directives are included, no comprehensive system of electronic contracts emerges: the instruments such as the E-Money Directive[42] complement the picture but do not create a system of Internet contract law.

The answer to why this is the case can be found in the 1997 Initiative,[43] which clearly shows that the extent of the Commission's intentions were limited. Looking through the lens of concern for how the existence of multiple regulatory systems might affect electronic commerce, the following is said:

A number of Member States' rules governing the formation and the performance of contracts are not appropriate for an electronic commerce environment and are generating uncertainties relating to the validity and enforceability of electronic contracts (for example the requirements for written documents, for hand written signatures, or the rules of evidence that do not take into account electronic documents). The Commission will take concrete steps to address the problem of how to *eliminate barriers for the legal recognition of electronic contracts* within the Single Market. Furthermore, as regards *consumer protection* in the field of electronic commerce, this point shall be dealt with in the Communication on the Consumer Dimension of the Information Society. (emphasis added)

---

[42] See Chapter 9, section 3.
[43] COM(97)157, 15 April 1997.

On an international plane the Directive is also not unique. An important inspiration, the UNCITRAL Model Law,[44] was published in 1996. It sought to improve legal certainty and predictability for e-commerce transactions. The UN Convention on E-Commerce followed in 2005.[45] The basic principles of the Convention are functional equivalence (paper documents equal electronic ones) and technology neutrality (the law does not discriminate between forms of technology).[46] The Convention maintains party autonomy, also present in other UNCITRAL documents.[47] Most of the solutions in the Directive correspond to those in the Model Law and this relationship is expressly referred to in the Commission's 2003 Report.[48]

The Community's legal effort regarding electronic contracts, however, should not be underestimated. The intervention is extensive, with wide and varying issues covered, ranging from payment and consumer protection to various aspects of jurisdiction. Even where the instruments are general in scope, such as the European Regulation on recognition and enforcement of foreign judgments ('Brussels I Regulation (Recast)'),[49] some thought has been given to the issue of electronic commerce and the effects it might have. The E-Commerce Directive itself covers a range of issues. In the area of pre-offer information, for instance, the Directive requires the ISPs to make certain information available,[50] regulates the establishment of providers[51] and regulates certain aspects of the placing of the order.[52] Although various aspects concerning offer and acceptance are covered in the following sections, it is sufficient to point out here the

---

[44]   Both the United States and the European Union have adopted the Model Law. In the United States, this has been done in the Uniform Electronic Transactions Act (UETA), approved by the National Conference of Commissioners on Uniform State Laws (NCCUSL) on 23 July 1999, which has now been adopted in most of the federal units. In the EU, the adopting document is the Electronic Commerce Directive.

[45]   See note 39 above.

[46]   See in particular articles 8 and 9.

[47]   Article 3.

[48]   See Commission Report, note 7 above, point 97.

[49]   See Chapter 3.

[50]   Article 10.

[51]   Articles 4 and 5.

[52]   Article 11.

fact that the national law of a Member State will apply to general issues concerning electronic contract formation. These laws will not be analysed here.[53]

Section 3 of the Directive covers contracts concluded by electronic means. As was said above, this section does not harmonize contract law or replace national provisions in this area. This is clear from Section 3 as it is from the Preamble to the Directive. The legislative history of Section 3, however, reveals some earlier, more ambitious attempts.

While the UNCITRAL Model Law is only concerned with recognition of electronic commerce acts, the Electronic Commerce Directive, in articles 10 and 11 (discussed below), makes an attempt at harmonizing contract formation rules in electronic contracts.[54]

Article 9 mirrors article 6 of the Model Law. Article 9(1) obliges Member States to ensure electronic contracts are allowed. It stipulates that legal requirements must be such that they do not deprive the contracts of 'effectiveness and validity' purely on account of them having been made by electronic means. Article 9(2), however, creates a list of contracts that Member States may exclude from the scope of the general rules. First in this list are contracts that create or transfer rights in real estate. Second are the ones requiring the involvement of courts or other public authorities. Further to that are added contracts of suretyship and those governed by family law. Member States are under an obligation to notify the Commission of those contracts which they intend to exclude from paragraph 1. Most of the exclusions are understandable, although the drafting of at least one is somewhat ambiguous. Whereas real estate contracts (under paragraph (a)) and family law contracts (under (d)) were always treated as separate, paragraph (b) originally spoke of the contracts that need to be registered in order to be valid. It is not entirely clear what had been gained by changing this requirement to contracts requiring the 'involvement of courts', as there are very few contracts that require this rather than registration.

Article 10 of the Directive addresses issues of transparency. The minimum information to be provided by the ISS providers prior to the conclusion of the transaction includes: technical steps to follow the conclusion of the contract (article 10(1)(a)); whether the contracts will be filed and accessible by ISPs (article 10(1)(b)); technical means for identifying and correcting input (article 10(1)(c)); and languages offered

---

[53] For an example of the relationship between national law and EU law in electronic contracts, see Part III, 'Denmark', *Cyberlaw*, in *International Encyclopaedia of Laws* (Kluwer Law International, The Hague, 2007).

[54] See Murray, 'Entering into Contract Electronically', note 26 above, p. 70.

for the conclusion (article 10(1)(d)). Further to this, any codes of conduct (article 10(2)) must be made available as well as contractual terms and conditions (article 10(3)). The previous conditions do not apply to contracts concluded exclusively by email. There is evidence that some of the requirements introduced in this article are of limited use, either because national laws already provide sufficient incentives to provide the requested information or because such information is not needed.

Article 11 ensures that the ISPs acknowledge the receipt of the order without delay, by electronic means. The order and acknowledgement of receipt are considered to be received when the parties to whom they are addressed can access them. The drafts of article 11 were more ambitious. The first two drafts were entitled 'Moment at which the contract is concluded'[55] whereas the actual title of article 11 is 'Placing of the order'.

Why has the final version been watered down? Contract laws in Member States are different. In some countries, the contract is concluded after the offer has been accepted. In others, the process has three stages. In the United Kingdom, the invitation to treat is followed by the offer, which in turn is followed by the acceptance. The first draft article brought confusion by introducing the fourth step of the confirmation of the acknowledgement of receipt. It provided that:

> the contract is concluded when the recipient of the service (i) has received from the service provider, electronically, an acknowledgement of receipt of recipient's acceptance, and (ii) has confirmed receipt of the acknowledgement of receipt.
>
> Acknowledgement of receipt is deemed to be received and confirmation is deemed to have been given when the parties to whom they are addressed are able to access them.

Draft article 11(1) seeks to regulate the moment when the contract is concluded. This, it will be observed from the above, is at the moment when the confirmation of the acknowledgement of the receipt is received by the recipient of the service. This step is unnecessary and it is not clear what the draft wanted to achieve. The fourth step is counterproductive, making the process more cumbersome. This is reflected in the second draft, where article 11 provides that the contract is concluded when the recipient of the service received the acknowledgement of the receipt from

---

[55]   Proposal for a European Parliament and Council Directive on certain legal aspects of electronic commerce in the Internal Market, COM(1998)586, 18 November 1998.

the provider. This solution was better, closer to systems in many states and more practical for consumers and traders alike.

The existing solution in the E-Commerce Directive is modest. Article 11 demands that the service provider has to acknowledge the receipt of the recipient's order without undue delay and by electronic means. The order and the acknowledgement of receipt are deemed to be received when the parties to whom they are addressed are able to access them. Finally, the service provider must make available to the recipient of the service appropriate, effective and accessible technical means allowing him to identify and correct input errors, prior to the placing of the order. Business (non-consumer) parties are allowed to contract out of these provisions and regulate the relationship differently.

5 COUNTRY OF ORIGIN PRINCIPLE

The country of origin principle is a potentially wide-reaching idea that Internet services should be entitled to free movement if they are lawful according to the law of the state from where they originate. A simple definition is that the country of origin rule is a rule of international law allocating competence between Member States.[56] More precisely, it is a rule that gives the competence to the state where the service (in this case, information society) originates. This is a term from the arsenal of legislative competence and determines which state, among several that possess the competence, shall exercise it.

To those proponents of the country of origin as a wider solution to problems of regulation on the Internet, this idea must seem attractive. The countless problems caused by borderlessness of the Internet disappear by a simple stroke, giving the competence to a single state. But, even if the idea has the potential to resolve these difficulties, it is limited to EU Member States and even then it is unclear what scope it might have.

Article 3 of the E-Commerce Directive says that, where the ISS provider is established on the territory of a Member State, *that state* shall ensure that its own national laws apply to the provider. This is the basic operation of the country of origin rule, giving the legislative competence to the 'home state'. Article 3(2) then adds that Member States will not,

---

[56] See J. Hörnle, 'The UK Perspective on the Country of Origin Rule in the E-Commerce Directive: A Rule of Administrative Law Applicable to Private Law Disputes?' (2004) 12 *International Journal of Law and Information Technology* 333.

for reasons falling within the *coordinated field*,[57] restrict the freedom to provide information society services. This article applies to host states, sending them a signal that they, in principle, are not allowed to regulate information society services where these originate outside that Member State.

The list of derogations from article 3 is given in the Annex to the Directive. This is largely because they are covered in other measures from the European Union arsenal or because interests of the host state warrant the application of its law. The mentioned areas, copyright and neighbouring rights, electronic money, choice of law, consumer contracts, real estate contracts and spam, have all been covered in other EU instruments.[58]

In further derogation from the principle of country of origin, and in consistency with other EU Directives and the general approach to the Internal Market, Member States will be able to derogate from article 3(2). Host states will therefore be able to impose their own regulation for reasons of public policy, public health, public security or protection of consumers. The measures thus imposed must be: (a) necessary for one of the mentioned reasons; (b) taken against an ISS provider that endangers the objectives mentioned or presents a serious and grave risk to them; and (c) be proportionate. To ensure that the spirit of the country of origin rule is preserved, article 3(4) also provides that the host state shall request that the home state takes the measures in question and waits for their outcome. Only if the home state has not taken them or if they prove to be inadequate will the host state act. Furthermore, the host state will notify the Commission and the home state of the measures that it intends to take. These precautions will only be derogated from in cases of urgency.[59] The Commission is given the power of monitoring the derogations taken under article 3(4) and it has the power to ask the host state to refrain from taking them or put an end to them.[60] It is not clear what sanction might be available to the Commission in case of non-compliance.

---

[57] Coordinated field is defined in art. 2 as 'requirements laid down in Member States' legal systems applicable to information society service providers or information society services, regardless of whether they are of a general nature or specifically designed for them'.

[58] Covered in Chapters 6, 9, 3 and 7, respectively.

[59] Article 3(5).

[60] Article 3(6).

It is apparent from these provisions that the legislator has proposed a system of communication between Member States. The latter are supposed to notify each other of contentious areas and resolve possible disputes in an amicable way. The restrictive use of article 3(4), furthermore, fits very well with the general idea of the protection of certainty, which seems to be the highlight of the E-Commerce Directive. The evidence suggests that derogations have, so far, been used very restrictively.[61] This, in turn, might indicate both that the area of regulation does not seem to be problematic and that Member States are tolerant and willing to recognize rules of the home state.

The country of origin principle is an idea sometimes ascribed extraordinary regulatory potential. Some authors claim that 'country of origin regulation ... is the only regulatory model so far attempted which ... is capable of resolving the conflicts between the multifarious and overlapping claims by national jurisdictions to regulate particular Internet activities'.[62] In the view of the author, the key is in the word 'capable'. If by capable we mean that the concept, if agreed on universally and enforced properly, can resolve the legislative jurisdiction disputes and conflicts where two or more states both purport to regulate the same subject matter, this is, in theory, possible. The concept, taken on its own, has that potential. On the other hand, it is unrealistic to expect that aim ever to be truly achieved. It is fair to say that, in its present incarnation in the E-Commerce Directive, the country of origin principle achieved some limited, if welcome, success. In a 2011 judgment,[63] the CJEU rejected the principle's conflict-of-laws operation and further clarified its true scope:

> Article 3 ... must be interpreted as not requiring transposition in the form of a specific conflict-of-laws rule. Nevertheless, in relation to the coordinated field, Member States must ensure that, subject to the derogations authorised in accordance with the conditions set out in Article 3(4) of Directive 2000/31, *the provider of an electronic commerce service is not made subject to stricter*

---

[61] *Report from the Commission on Directive 2000/31/EC*, COM(2003)702 final (Brussels, 21 November 2003) suggests (see para. 4.1) that there have only been five notifications under art. 3, of which only two used the emergency procedure of para. 5.

[62] C. Reed, *Internet Law: Text and Materials* (CUP, Cambridge, 2004), p. 250.

[63] Joined Cases C-509/09 and C-161/10 *eDate Advertising GmbH v X; Olivier Martinez, Robert Martinez v MGN Ltd*, ECLI:EU:C:2011:685, 25 October 2011.

> *requirements than those provided for by the substantive law applicable in the*
> *Member State in which that service provider is established.* (emphasis added)

In other words, the judgment emphasizes that the rule has a public law and not conflict-of-laws character. The present situation (minimum harmonization accompanied by mutual recognition and mandatory requirements) grants the host state some space for maintaining its potentially restrictive laws in place. Article 3 was necessary as a broadly drafted warning not to subject e-commerce services to stricter domestic laws.

In addition to the mentioned difficulties, which arise out of the context in which the country of origin rule developed, there are others. The country of origin rule can be described as a rule of legislative juris-diction, in other words a rule of competence, not a rule of adjudicative jurisdiction. It determines which state's laws apply to information society services but does not determine which courts have jurisdiction. Arguably, a large number of Internet issues concern adjudicative rather than legislative jurisdiction. Similarly, country of origin is not a choice of law principle, as is clear from the *eDate* case, which aims to limit its operation to public law cases.

In *deVisser*, the CJEU ruled that article 3 'does not apply to a situation where the place of establishment of the information society services provider is unknown, since application of that provision is subject to identification of the Member State in whose territory the service provider in question is actually established'.[64]

6 HARMONIZATION OF SALES LAW

Although no full harmonization of the law of obligations had ever been undertaken at EU level,[65] serious academic work in this area has been going on for several decades. The purpose of this work was to find a common set of rules – a frame of reference – on the law of obligations common to all EU Member States. The work of the so-called Lando Commission[66] in the 1990s has been taken over in the Draft Common

---

[64] C-292/10 *G v Cornelius de Visser*, ECLI:EU:C:2012:142, 15 March 2012.
[65] Except for a small part of consumer sales discussed in section 6.1 below.
[66] O. Lando (ed.), *The Principles of European Contract Law, Parts I and II* (Kluwer, The Hague, 1999).

Frame of Reference (DCFR),⁶⁷ which itself was promoted by the Commission's 2003 Action Plan on contract law.⁶⁸ The DCFR informed the idea of an optional instrument which would partially solve the difficulties arising out of disparate contract regimes. This resulted in the 2011 EU proposal for an optional Common European Sales Law, the idea which was only abandoned in 2015 in favour of mandatory Directives on online sale of goods and supply of digital content. These proposals, the adoption of which remains as yet uncertain, are discussed in the following sections.

6.1 Consumer Rights Directive

In spite of the lack of harmonization of the law of obligations in the EU, partial harmonization of some aspects of contract law as applied to consumers has been attempted in the Consumer Rights Directive.⁶⁹ That Directive contains harmonized rules on delivery and passing of the risk applicable only to business-to-consumer (B2C) contracts. These rules are generic in nature, i.e. they apply to all sales of consumer goods, digital or otherwise.

Article 19 provides that the trader must deliver the goods by transferring the physical possession or control to the consumer without delay but not later than 30 days from contract conclusion. This means that the trader has the right to deliver at any point within 30 days unless something else has been agreed. It seems that an indication of the availability and possible shipping dates on a website should not be taken as a promise of a specific delivery date in terms of article 19 but only as an indication. The words 'guaranteed delivery' or similar, on the other hand, should be taken to represent a specific promise.

Where the trader fails to deliver, the consumer may be given an appropriate additional period. No details are given on what a specific period might be but this ought not to be longer than the original period. The right to terminate the contract arises in cases where no delivery has

---

⁶⁷   Ch. Von Bar, *Principles, Definitions and Model Rules of European Private Law: Draft Common Frame of Reference (DCFR) Outline Edition* (Sellier, Munich, 2009).

⁶⁸   European Commission, *Action Plan on a More Coherent European Contract Law* (15 March 2003) [2003] OJ C63/01.

⁶⁹   Directive 2011/83/EC of 25 October 2011 of the European Parliament and of the Council on consumer rights [2011] OJ L304/64, 22 November 2011. See Chapter 7 for more detail.

been undertaken after the expiry of the additional period. On the other hand, no additional period is necessary where the timely delivery is essential or where the seller refused to deliver.

The passing of the risk is covered in article 20 which provides that the risk of loss or damage passes to the consumer when he or a third party had acquired the physical possession of the goods. This means that the seller bears the burden of potential damage to the goods or their loss in transit.

Article 22 prevents the seller from requiring extra payments resulting from any pre-selected default options (e.g. extra insurance, extra guarantees, payment protection plans, etc.) which the consumer would have to click on to opt out from. This means that such extra services are only allowed if the consumers actively select them.

6.2   Common European Sales Law

A Common European Sales Law[70] (CESL) was proposed as a way of partially addressing differences between contract laws of Member States. In order to avoid the uncertainties of foreign laws in unfamiliar states, the parties would have an option to resort to one EU-wide sales law. Traders' fear of contract law barriers is quoted in the proposal as the main reason for the initiative.[71] By opting for the sales law, the traders gain the opportunity to rely on a common set of contract rules. Unusually for an EU source, the CESL was meant to apply both to B2C and business-to-small and medium-sized enterprise (B2SME) relations.

Article 3 of the proposed Regulation emphasizes the law's optional nature. The law is activated only if the parties specifically opt in. In that case, the law governs the sale of goods, the supply of digital content and the provision of services. The law is used for cross-border contracts between traders, which are defined as contracts between parties who have habitual residences in different countries where at least one is a Member State.[72] If, on the other hand, the contract is between a trader and a consumer, it will be considered cross-border if either the address the

---

[70]   Proposal for a Regulation of the European Parliament and of the Council on a Common European Sales Law, COM(2011)635 (11 October 2011). See H.W. Micklitz and N. Reich, *The Commission Proposal for a "Regulation on a Common European Sales Law (CESL)": Too Broad or Not Broad Enough?*, EUI LAW Working Paper No. 2012/04 (1 February 2012).

[71]   Recital 3.

[72]   See art. 4(2).

consumer indicated, the delivery address or the billing address are located in a country other than the trader's habitual residence and if at least one of these is a Member State.

The CESL can be used for sales contracts including contracts for the supply of digital content.[73] This may, but need not be, on a tangible medium. In light of the fact that digital content is often supplied in combination with goods or in exchange for information (such as shopping habits), the proposed law applies irrespective of whether the content is supplied in exchange for a price. The law also applies to service contracts. The law may only be used if the supplier is a trader.[74] The trader, on the other hand, can be either a legal or a natural person acting for the purposes of that person's business (article 2(e) of the Regulation). If both parties are traders, one needs to be a small or medium-sized enterprise (SME), a term which has an autonomous definition in the Regulation.

Digital content is defined in article 2 of the Regulation as:

data which are produced and supplied in digital form, whether or not according to the buyer's specifications, including video, audio, picture or written digital content, digital games, software and digital content which makes it possible to personalise existing hardware or software;

but excluding financial services and advice, online banking, legal advice, electronic healthcare, electronic communications (i.e. telecoms), gambling and:

the creation of new digital content and the amendment of existing digital content by consumers or any other interaction with the creations of other users.

The last exclusion seems to be targeting private content and user-generated content (UGC). If so, the definition chosen is peculiar, as is the exclusion. User-generated content may and does have a commercial dimension and can be traded.

The law contains a number of provisions of interest to electronic commerce. Section 1 contains a list of pre-contractual requirements to be given by a trader. Article 13 contains a special list of information for distance contracts. These conditions are largely similar to general information requirements arising from the E-Commerce Directive and special requirements arising from consumer or financial Directives. Of particular

---

[73] Proposal, art. 5(b).
[74] Proposal, art. 7.

interest is the obligation to give information on any technological protection (such as digital rights management) or interoperability.[75]

Section 3 covers contracts concluded by electronic means. Article 24 stipulates that such contracts are not concluded by electronic means in cases where emails only have been used, presumably because emails have been equated with ordinary mail communication. The trader is obliged to give the other party technical means for correcting errors. The trader is obliged to provide information on a number of technical and other issues. Contractual terms, in particular, need to be accessible. In contracts requiring payment, the trader is under a special obligation (article 25) to inform the consumer of the general information from article 13, including price information under article 14 and the duration of the contract. In particular, the consumer must be informed of the contract's duration. The trader must, under article 25(3), indicate any delivery restrictions and methods of payment.

The rest of the law contains much of what is expected in such documents, with rights and obligations of the parties, withdrawal, unfair terms, remedies, damages, risk passing and other provisions. Of interest to Internet users is article 100 which contains criteria for conformity of, among other things, digital goods. These must be fit for any particular purpose and in particular the purpose which they ordinarily have. Article 100(h) provides that, when determining what qualities digital goods must possess, regard is to be had to whether or not the content is supplied free of charge or not. This would seem to establish a presumption that goods supplied free of charge may be of lower quality than those provided for remuneration. This is typically the case, for instance, when audio and video content is streamed at different qualities to paying and non-paying customers.

Article 101 contains a peculiar provision according to which the incorrect installation of 'goods or digital content' must be regarded as non-conformity either when the seller installs it or when the consumer who is so authorized does but the incorrect installation is due to poor instructions. There is no guidance as to what constitutes poor instructions.

Under article 103, digital content is not to be considered as non-conforming simply because an updated version has become available in the meantime. Furthermore, article 105 obliges the trader to keep the digital content conforming even in cases where the content must be subsequently updated. For content not supplied in exchange for payment,

---

[75]   CESL, art. 13(1)(h)–(i).

the buyer can resort to one remedy only: damages for property resulting from non-conformity.[76]

Although the CESL was abandoned in 2015 after several years of intense criticism, some of the ideas it contained have made their way into two proposals on sales of distance and online goods tabled in late 2015. Also important is the fact that the CESL is the first European contract law document with specifically designed rules applying only to the digital world.

6.3 Distance Sale of Goods

The Directive[77] on certain aspects of online and other distance sales was proposed as part of a replacement solution when the Commission abandoned the CESL in 2015. The Directive, instead of being optional like its predecessor, is a targeted full harmonization. The Directive is meant to remove 'contract law-related barriers hindering cross-border trade'. While certain aspects of sale of goods and associated guarantees had been harmonized in 1999,[78] a number of differences in Member States' laws remain. It is these that the current proposal seeks to overcome, specifically talking about 'a full harmonisation of the conformity criteria for the goods, of the hierarchy of the remedies, available to consumers and of the periods for the reversal of burden of proof and the legal guarantees'. In addition to the 1999 Directive, the proposal would amend the Consumer Rights Directive (see Chapter 7) and the E-Commerce Directive, while keeping the Unfair Contract Terms Directive (see Chapter 7) intact.

Article 1 defines the scope of the Directive. It applies to distance sale of goods between sellers and consumers. It specifically excludes provision of services (article 1(2)), as they are the subject of a separate proposal, but includes mixed contracts in the part which covers goods only. The Directive does not apply to cases involving durable media (such as CDs, Blu-ray discs, etc.) which are used exclusively as carriers. Article 1(4) provides that national contract laws will remain intact in parts not otherwise covered by the Directive.

---

[76] CESL, arts. 106 and 107.

[77] Proposal for a Directive on certain aspects concerning contracts for the online and other distance sales of goods, COM(2015)635 final (9 December 2015).

[78] Directive 1999/44/EC of the European Parliament and of the Council of 25 May 1999 on certain aspects of the sale of consumer goods and associated guarantees [1999] OJ L171, 7 July 1999.

Article 2 provides definitions in the usual manner consistent with other EU Directives (see Chapter 7). Article 3 emphasizes the fact that the Directive is a full harmonization.

Articles 4 to 7 deal with conformity of goods. The goods conform when the conditions from all articles have been fulfilled. Article 4 provides that goods conform when and if they are of a 'quantity, quality and description required by the contract', when they are fit for a 'particular purpose' which the consumer made known to the seller or 'indicated in any pre-contractual statement which forms an integral part of the contract'. Article 5 provides that the goods need to be fit for ordinary purposes, be delivered with all the necessary accessories and instructions and possess qualities and performance capabilities normal for goods of that type. Statements made earlier by the seller or the producer concerning quality need to be taken into account. Installation faults are, as per article 6, regarded as lack of conformity either when the seller was responsible for installation or when the instructions were faulty. Article 7 obliges the seller to provide the goods free of any third party's rights including intellectual property rights. Article 8 regulates the relevant time for establishing conformity. The consumer is given an absolute deadline of two years in article 8(4), which is repeated in article 14.

Article 9 provides the relevant remedies for the lack of conformity. The initial position is that the consumer can choose repair or replacement, within a reasonable time, according to the rules set out in articles 10 (replacement) and 11 (choice between repair or replacement). The consumer is also entitled to a reduction of the price (according to article 12) or termination of the contract (according to article 13). This is only possible where repair or replacement is impossible or unlawful; where the seller had not completed them upon request; where they would be significantly inconvenient for the consumer; or where the seller had made it clear that the goods would not be brought into conformity. The consumer is entitled to payment withdrawal until goods had been brought into conformity but is not entitled to remedies to the extent that they contributed themselves to non-conformity.

The rules on termination of the contract (article 13) allow partial termination which applies only to those goods which are not in conformity. Termination, which is subject to the consumer's notice to the seller and the mentioned conditions from article 9, triggers the seller's obligation to reimburse the price to the consumer within a maximum of 14 days and the consumer's obligation to return the goods.

Commercial guarantees are obligations undertaken by the seller or the producer to repair or replace the goods in addition to their usual obligations. Article 15 sets out transparency requirements for these. It says that guarantees laid down in pre-contractual information, in advertising or in the guarantee statement shall be binding. Article 15(2) introduces some requirements for the guarantees, including that the agreement needs to be made on a durable medium and be drafted in plain and intelligible language and needs to include information on duration, transferability and scope. The seller needs to emphasize that the guarantee does not affect the rights which arise from the Directive.

Article 17 splits enforcement among various national bodies, including public bodies, consumer organizations and professional organizations. The purpose of this provision is to give persons or organizations which have a legitimate interest in protecting consumer rights the ability to initiate proceedings, before a court or before a relevant administrative body competent to hear complaints.

Some of the provisions of the Directive are mandatory. Article 18 emphasizes that contractual derogations from the provisions of the Directive which are detrimental to the consumer will not be binding. An exception is found in article 4(3) which allows the seller to limit the operation of the conformity requirements in cases where the consumer was expressly told of this before contract conclusion.

The purpose of the Directive is a limited harmonization of the online law of sales. There are three reasons to believe that the proposal may indeed bring some harmony to disparate national laws. First, the Commission has had extensive experience from the input it received (a significant part of which was negative) from the Common European Sales Law proposal. Secondly, the new proposal is narrower in scope, more focused and it is not optional. Thirdly, the proposed Directive works in harmony with the private international law rules on jurisdiction and the applicable law.[79] All this may mean both that potential adoption would be more likely and that the effect on consumer sales would be positive.

6.4 Supply of Digital Content

The proposed Directive[80] is the second of the two intended to replace the Common European Sales Law. The Commission clarifies that the proposal is meant to complement the rules in the Consumer Rights Directive

---

[79] See Chapter 3.
[80] Proposal for a Directive on certain aspects concerning contracts for the supply of digital content, COM(2015) 634 final (9 December 2015).

which already contain some harmonizing measures on contractual information requirements and the right of withdrawal.[81] The purpose is to introduce specific EU rules to protect consumers against digital content which is not in conformity with the contract and to harmonize remedies for non-conformity (article 1). In addition to conformity, the proposal deals with the rules on modification and termination of long-term contracts. In line with the proposed Directive on sale of goods, the proposed Directive on supply of digital content is a full harmonization measure (article 4) with mandatory effect (article 19). This means not only that Member States would not be entitled to regulate this area (not even to introduce more protective measures) but also that any contractually agreed provisions which conflict with the protection given in the Directive would have to be eliminated.

Digital content is defined in article 2 as either: (a) data produced or supplied in digital form (including video or audio, software or games); (b) a service allowing creation, processing or storage of consumer-supplied data (such as, for example, file or photo repositories); or (c) a service allowing sharing or interaction with data provided by other users (such as, for example, social networks). The definition takes into consideration both the commercially provided content services and the user-generated ones.

The Directive applies in all cases where digital content is supplied in exchange for a paid price but also where the consumer 'actively provides counter-performance other than money in the form of personal data or any other data'.[82] It would appear that the word 'actively' means that only websites that openly demand that consumers submit their data in exchange for content are covered. This leaves open a number of situations where websites appear to provide free content (or may even have both a commercial and a free edition) but collect data through 'cookies' or other means.

The Directive also applies to contracts for the supply of digital products made to customer specifications (article 3(2)) and to contracts involving durable media (article 3(3)). The former would typically involve web design, web marketing and software design. The latter may involve any combination of digital product production and delivery where durable medium is only used as a carrier.

The Directive does not apply (article 3(5)) to services with a predominant element of human intervention with the digital format used as a

---

[81]   See section above and Chapter 7.
[82]   Article 3.

carrier only, to electronic communication services as defined in the Telecommunications Framework Directive (2002/21/EC), to healthcare services, gambling services or to financial services.

The Directive does not affect parts of national contract law on formation, validity or consequences of termination that are not already covered in the Directive. Article 4 clarifies that this is a full harmon-ization measure, preventing conflicting national legislation with a differ-ent level of consumer protection.

Article 5 provides simply that content can be supplied directly to the consumer or to a third party operating a physical or a virtual facility. The supplier is obliged to provide the content immediately unless agreed otherwise.

Conformity is regulated in article 6. The content must be of the quality, quantity, duration, version or functionality as required by contract. In addition, it must possess other agreed features such as interoperability, accessibility or security. If the consumer had made a particular purpose known to the supplier, and if the supplier had accepted such purpose then the content must fit such a purpose. Instructions ought to be provided with the contract and the updates performed according to the agreement.

If the contract does not provide any specifications or details, then it must be fit for ordinary purposes (article 6(2)). In determining whether such content complies, regard will be had to whether it had been provided for free or against payment, whether any international technical standards exist and whether the supplier had made any public statement about the content's quality and features. Therefore, for example, where an audio and video streaming service makes no promise of a particular streaming quality (bit rate, resolution, etc.), the customer can expect an average quality unless specific declarations have been made.

Incorrectly integrated content will be regarded as lack of conformity (article 7) only if the supplier had been responsible for such integration or the supplier gave incorrect instructions to the consumer. Digital content must be free of any third party claims at the time of supply (article 8).

Article 9 covers the important issue of the burden of proof in cases of non-conformity. While the burden of proof is normally on the supplier, it will shift to the consumer in cases where the supplier had informed the consumer of the problems in the consumer's digital environment before the conclusion of the contract. The consumer is supposed to cooperate with the supplier on the environmental suitability but the means for that ought to be least intrusive. In a typical situation involving the supply of digital content (e.g. video streaming) this should be taken to mean that the clearly published system requirements would probably satisfy the condition. In more complex cases (involving, for example, demanding video games) it should be expected that the supplier's obligation to ensure that the consumer's environment is actually compliant would be more stringent.

The suppliers' liability extends to failure to supply, lack of conformity at the time of supply or for the duration of supply if the contract extends over a period of time (article 10). Each of these is covered in a separate article. Article 11 allows the consumer to terminate the contract where the supplier failed to supply the digital content. Article 12 provides remedies for lack of conformity while article 13 regulates termination of contract.

The consumer has, according to article 12, the right to have non-conforming digital content brought into conformity unless this is impossible, unlawful or is unreasonably costly. The content needs to be made conforming within a reasonable period of time. The consumer is entitled to either the reduction of the price or termination according to rules set out in article 12(3) to (5). This will be the case where the remedy is impossible or has been denied, has not been completed or would significantly inconvenience the consumer.

Termination, according to article 12(5), is only allowed 'if the lack of conformity impairs functionality, interoperability' or other 'main performance features'. Reduction in price must be proportionate to the decrease in value suffered. Where the consumer has the right to terminate, this right is exercised, according to article 13, by giving a notice to the supplier. The consequence is the supplier's obligation to reimburse the consumer no later than 14 days after the receipt of notice.

Since the supply of digital content is different in nature from the supply of digital goods in that copies can easily be produced, special provisions exist that deal with the consequences of termination. Article 13(2)(b) obliges the supplier who received data or other non-pecuniary counter-performance to refrain from keeping the data, while article 13(2)(d) obliges the consumer to refrain from using the digital content or giving it away to third parties. Consumers are, by virtue of article 13(2)(c), entitled to retrieve any content generated through the use of the service. A consumer who had not received a physical copy is obliged to delete the content or render it unintelligible. Where the content had been supplied on durable medium, the consumer is obliged to return it within 14 days and to delete any copies made. In addition to that, the supplier has the right to prevent consumer's access to content by, for example, disabling the account. Article 13(4) exonerates the consumer from having to make payments for use made prior to termination but allows the supplier who charges on a termly basis (e.g. once a month) to charge for the periods used prior to termination.

Article 14 regulates the right to damages. The supplier is liable for 'economic damage to the digital environment' caused by lack of conformity or a failure to supply. In spite of this, no further harmonization is offered as the Member States are directed to regulate the exercise of this right in their own national laws.

The supplier is allowed, according to article 15, to modify the 'functionality, interoperability and other main performance features' of the content only if the contract so allows, the consumer is duly notified and the consumer is given the right to terminate the contract without charge and within 30 days of being notified.

Long-term contracts, defined in article 16 as those whose renewal periods exceed 12 months, can also be terminated after the first 12 months had expired. Other rules are the same or similar to short-term contracts.

7 CONCLUSION

Electronic commerce is playing an ever-increasing role in the European Union. The regulatory climate is stable with the relatively uncontroversial E-Commerce Directive and with more recent proposals for harmonization of sales law.

The success and importance of the E-Commerce Directive can be summarized in three points. First, it creates a framework for other Directives in the field and forms a basis for an evolving flexible system. Secondly, it uses the principle of the country of origin creatively, opening up a possibly new avenue of regulation. Finally, it encourages alternative dispute resolution mechanisms.

As a legislative model, the E-Commerce Directive, in spite of containing a number of good solutions, has its limitations. It is a law designed to operate within the EU environment. As such, it reaps all the benefits that the organization offers, but is also subject to its weaknesses. Ultimately, the success of the E-Commerce Directive depends on the success of the approach it has chosen to take. In the United States, self-regulation has been the model for regulating the Internet since its inception.[83] The law-maker has occasionally intervened, sometimes strongly, but the bulk

---

[83] See N. Cox, 'The Regulation of Cyberspace and the Loss of National Sovereignty' (2002) 11 *Information and Communication Technology Law* 241, 249.

of regulation was left to businesses. Contrary to this, the European Union advocates a combined approach, following direct regulation in a number of areas but relying on the principle of subsidiarity, which involves less direct intervention, through minimum harmonization and mutual recognition. Additionally, the core of the regulatory interest in EU Internet law revolves around balancing the rights of producers with those of consumers, where the former lobby for liberalization and the latter for greater protection. The E-Commerce Directive addresses the interests of both with the emphasis on businesses.[84] The Directive is an Internal Market instrument, a fact that limits its scope from the outset. Furthermore, as a Framework Directive, it chose a flexible structure that has the potential to adapt itself to further changes.

In light of these circumstances, it is important to see the E-Commerce Directive in a proper perspective, as a successful Internal Market instrument, and to give it credit for what it has achieved. Ultimately, the main objective of the Directive, for Europe 'to become the most competitive and dynamic knowledge-based economy in the world capable of sustainable economic growth with more and better jobs and greater social cohesion',[85] may depend less on the choice and design of the Directive and more on other factors.

---

[84]   Consumers are also addressed in other Directives (see Chapter 7).
[85]   Presidency Conclusions, Lisbon European Council, 23 and 24 March 2000.

3. International jurisdiction and applicable law

1 THE INTERNET AND MODERN CONFLICT OF LAWS

One of the most important and most difficult questions surrounding the Internet concerns resolving civil disputes in regular courts. Although the claim that the Internet ought to be subject to regular civil courts and regular civil procedure seems natural today, it has not always been so. In its early days, it was thought that the Internet, inherently present or accessible 'everywhere', makes the traditional premises upon which private international law rests unworkable.[1] Courts ought to exercise care, these arguments ran, when they assume jurisdiction over webpages not connected in any way with their own forum. The Internet is borderless and should not be subject to the same rules as regular transactions.[2] It would be impossible or improper to impose local jurisdiction and local laws on a global phenomenon with little or no local presence.[3] The courts should let the Internet develop as freely as possible and should approach the issue with an eye for the medium's particular qualities.

Today, few if any of these claims have support. The courts do assert jurisdiction locally over absent defendants who post globally and apply

---

[1]   For an overview of US scholarship in the area see J. Reidenberg *et al.*, Internet Jurisdiction: A Survey of Legal Scholarship Published in English and United States Case Law Fordham Law Legal Studies Research Paper No. 2309526 (30 June 2013), available at SSRN, http://ssrn.com/abstract=2309526. For an overview of EU law see A. Saraf and A. Kazi, 'Analysing the Application of Brussels I in Regulating E-Commerce Jurisdiction in the European Union: Success, Deficiencies and Proposed Changes' (2013) 29 *Computer Law and Security Review* 127.

[2]   D. Goldsmith, 'The Internet and the Abiding Significance of Territorial Sovereignty' (1998) 5 *Indiana Journal of Global Legal Studies* 475; D. Post 'Against "Against Cyberanarchy"' (2002) 17 *Berkeley Technology Law Journal* 1365.

[3]   See D. Johnson and D. Post, 'Law and Borders: The Rise of Law in Cyberspace' (1996) 48 *Stanford Law Review* 1367.

national laws to trans-border cases. Since the majority of situations in a cyberspace setting do not differ much from their non-electronic counterparts, there are today no separate private international law rules for cyberspace, although newer instruments (such as the Brussels I Regulation (Recast) and the Rome II Regulation, discussed below) do recognize some situations specific to electronic communications.

In spite of the willingness to take Internet disputes, both the courts and the litigants keep struggling to understand how to localize disputes that arise from a medium which in its very nature seems to be delocalized. From the viewpoint of the claimant, the successful outcome of a dispute in international civil litigation depends on whether a particular set of facts can be connected to a state more favourable to their interests. Once the location has been established, the courts can proceed to resolve the dispute by applying the proper law. With the Internet, the certainty which traditional conflicts rules provide disappears and is replaced by a recurrent fear that one's actions will be subject to jurisdictions of remote courts and to laws of unknown lands.

Legal uncertainties surrounding the Internet begin with determining the courts' jurisdiction. Events in cyberspace, which appear to happen simultaneously in several jurisdictions, are difficult to localize and connect to a particular court. In civil law traditions, *general jurisdiction,* which is the court's authority to hear all cases irrespective of the nature of the claim, is based on the defendant's nationality, domicile or habitual residence, depending on the context. But while it may be possible to sue the defendant in, for example, the place where it is domiciled, this may not be a very suitable forum for a plaintiff located in another land. *Special jurisdiction* is exercised only if there is a connection between a claim and the jurisdiction in question. The fact that goods are ordered by a consumer from a particular country or that a personal reputation had been harmed in that country may or may not amount to such a connection. Uncertainties also abound in cases involving intellectual property (IP) or personality rights violations perpetrated on the Net. In such cases, the question usually takes the form of: how strong does a web presence in a foreign country need to be to translate into solid special jurisdiction?

Choice-of-law questions are conceptually equally difficult. What law applies to the Internet will be decided by rules which typically refer to party autonomy or, in its absence, assign the matter to laws of the state with which the dispute is, in one manner or another, most closely connected. But in such situations, a number of difficulties arise. What law will apply to claims where the claimant accessed the material posted globally in the state where they are resident? Will consumers who bought online be able to avail themselves of a more favourable regime of their place of habitual residence in case they want to sue or are sued? What law will apply to situations involving violations of IP rights?

Finally, judgments obtained in one state may have to be recognized in others, in recognition and enforcement procedures that may be controversial and are subject to local public policy standards. In a typical example, a judgment delivered in an EU state awarding damages for a defamatory publication on a webpage may not be recognizable in the United States, where free speech enjoys stronger constitutional protection.

This chapter will look at dispute resolution in the European Union, beginning with an overview of the rules concerning jurisdiction in civil and commercial disputes and enforcement of judgments. Applicable law will be looked at next, including the implications of the country of origin rule. The next section looks at alternative and online dispute resolution. The chapter will conclude with some observations on the approach taken in the United States. Consumer protection rules in private international law are analysed in section 5 of Chapter 7.

2 JURISDICTION IN DISPUTES CONCERNING THE INTERNET

The European Union conflicts system consists of rules on jurisdiction in civil and commercial matters,[4] rules on law applicable to contract[5] and tort[6] and various secondary instruments.[7] In addition to this, the primary Community law (Treaties) and secondary Community law (Directives, Regulations, and court judgments) also have an impact on private international law. This section explores the EU rules on civil jurisdiction and their impact on the Internet.

---

[4] Regulation (EU) 1215/2012 of 12 December 2012 on jurisdiction and the recognition and enforcement of judgments in civil and commercial matters [2012] OJ L351/1, 20 December 2012. For a detailed overview of the field, see P. Stone, *EU Private International Law* (3rd edn, Edward Elgar Publishing, Cheltenham and Northampton, MA, 2014). See A. Dickinson and E. Lein (eds.), *The Brussels I Regulation Recast* (OUP, Oxford, 2015).

[5] Rome I Regulation on the law applicable to contractual obligations (formerly Rome Convention) [2008] OJ L177/6, 4 July 2008. See F. Ferrari and S. Leible (eds.), *The Rome I Regulation* (Sellier, Munich, 2009).

[6] Rome II Regulation on the law applicable to non-contractual obligations [2007] OJ L199/40, 31 July 2007. See A. Dickinson, *The Rome II Regulation* (OUP, Oxford, 2010).

[7] Stone, *EU Private International Law*, note 4 above.

2.1 General Jurisdiction

Jurisdiction rules for civil and commercial cases in the European Union are located in the European Regulation on Recognition and Enforcement of Foreign Judgments ('Brussels I Regulation (Recast)'). The original instrument for jurisdiction and recognition and enforcement of judgments was the 1968 Brussels Convention,[8] which in 2001, with slight changes, became a Regulation.[9] This Regulation, in turn, was partially reformed in 2012 and it is this version that represents current law for all proceedings instituted on or after 10 January 2015.

Article 4, the general jurisdiction rule, provides that jurisdiction exists in the courts where the defendant is domiciled.[10] Article 4 further clarifies that defendants not domiciled in the EU will not be subject to rules in the Regulation but to traditional pre-Brussels I rules. The claimant's domicile is irrelevant, as is the parties' nationality, thus enabling EU defendants to enjoy the Regulation's benefits even against non-EU claimants.

Article 6(1) has the effect of excluding the operation of the Regulation for defendants domiciled outside the EU even where they are EU citizens. This also means that US-domiciled information society service providers would be subject to residual national (non-Brussels) rules of jurisdiction in all cases where they are not domiciled in the EU. This, in turn, does not mean that EU courts would automatically be inaccessible to them but only that jurisdiction rules on the basis of which such courts might take jurisdiction are national non-Brussels rules (residual rules). This is of considerable significance in situations involving claimants who would like to sue American Internet companies in the EU.

Article 6(1) is further modified for employees and consumers, both categories enjoying special protection. Thus, a consumer may bring proceedings against a non-domiciled defendant pursuant to article 18(1). According to that article, a consumer can bring proceedings either in the defendant's domicile or the place of the consumer's domicile. A consumer wishing to sue an Internet provider domiciled in the United States but targeting EU consumers would, therefore, be able to do so in the place of his or her own domicile.[11] This is a deliberate change from the

---

[8] [1972] OJ L299, 31 December 1972.

[9] [2001] OJ L12/1, 16 January 2001.

[10] Article 62 regulates domicile of individuals while art. 63 deals with that of corporations.

[11] It is worth noting, however, that a jurisdiction agreement in such a consumer contract may modify the situation. See section 2.4 below.

original Regulation which did not allow consumers to sue non-domiciled defendants according to Brussels I rules at all.

Domicile of private individuals is determined for each Member State by reference to that state's law (article 62). Thus, whether the defendant is domiciled in, for example, France, will be determined according to French law. If the defendant has domicile in several states, he can be sued in each of those, at the plaintiff's discretion. The *DeVisser* case discussed the situation where the defendant's domicile is unknown.[12] The case involved an action for damages arising out of violation of personality rights by posting images online. Since it was impossible to determine where in the EU the defendant had domicile, but it was likely that he was an EU citizen, and the court seised did not hold conclusive evidence that he was domiciled outside the EU, uniform jurisdiction rules of the Brussels I Regulation (Recast) were applicable.

Article 63 gives an EU-wide definition of corporate domicile. The latter exists where a company has a statutory seat, or central administration, or a principal place of business in a Member State. The criteria are independent, which means that if only one of them exists in a Member State, the defendant can be sued there, irrespective of the fact that others may also exist in different Member States. This also means that, where several of the criteria exist at once (e.g. a corporation has a statutory seat in England but a principal place of business in the Netherlands) each of the criteria are capable of triggering jurisdiction.

If the defendant is *not* domiciled in the Member States, the courts will determine jurisdiction using traditional rules, which include exorbitant bases enumerated in Annex I to the Regulation. States vary as to the exact circumstances in which courts can assume jurisdiction over non-present defendants but this is generally possible in common law systems. English courts, for example, assert jurisdiction in defamation cases where no English nationals suffered harm, as long as the claimant can establish a reputation in England. Thus, in *Berezovsky v Forbes*,[13] an American magazine was sued in England for defamation. Although the Russian claimants were not truly present in England, they alleged that their reputation in England was harmed. The House of Lords refused to decline jurisdiction on the basis of *forum non conveniens*. Somewhat worrying is the possibility that such judgments can be recognized and enforced in other Member States, as the recognizing court is never in the position to question the adjudicating court's jurisdiction (article 45(3)).

---

[12] C-292/10 *G v Cornelius de Visser* (2012) ECLI:EU:C:2012:142.
[13] [2000] 1 WLR 104 (HL).

The public policy rule, which can normally be used to monitor foreign judgments (article 45(1)), is interpreted restrictively and should not be expected to prevent any but most abusive forms of this rule's operation.

2.2 Special Jurisdiction: Cybercontracts

Special jurisdiction rules exist concurrently, in those situations where the defendant is already domiciled as per article 4 but an additional point of contact exists, giving the claimant the choice of suing in a court different than the court of the defendant's domicile. In contractual obligations this will be the place of performance of the obligation in question.[14] In tort cases it will be in the courts for the place where the harmful event occurred or may occur.[15] Jurisdiction also exists in the place where a branch, agency or other establishment is located but only for disputes arising out of their operation.[16] Once the claimant opts for one of the article 7 bases, courts do not have discretion to decline jurisdiction, a feature inserted for purposes of maintaining certainty and simplicity.

Article 7(1)(a) gives jurisdiction to courts of the place of performance of the obligation. Article 7(1)(b) allows for the possibility that the parties agreed on the place of performance, in which case this agreement will also determine the court's jurisdiction. In the absence of this agreement, a rebuttable assumption is made in respect of both goods and services. For goods, the place of performance is assumed to be the place of delivery of the goods. In a contract concluded on the Internet, this is the place to which goods ordered online are physically shipped, subject to any exceptions available to consumers. The article clarifies that, for the sale of goods, this will be the place where the goods either were or ought to have been delivered under the contract.

In the case of provision of services, article 7(1)(b) also gives jurisdiction to the courts for the place of performance of the obligation. For services, this is the place where, under the contract, the services either were provided or should have been provided. Where services are provided in several states, the court which has jurisdiction to hear all the claims is the court in whose jurisdiction the place of the *main* provision of services was situated.[17]

---

[14] Article 7(1)(a).
[15] Article 7(2).
[16] Article 7(5).
[17] C-19/09 *Wood Floor Solutions Andreas Domberger GmbH v Silva Trade SA* [2010] ECR I-02121.

In *GIE Groupe Concorde*,[18] the Court of Justice of the European Union (CJEU) discussed whether the expression 'place of performance' had an independent meaning or should be determined according to the applicable law of the court seised. It was said there that determining the place of performance does indeed depend on the applicable law, the determination of which essentially consists of three steps. First, the contractual obligation in question needs to be classified. Secondly, the law applicable to it needs to be applied by reference to the Rome I Regulation. Thirdly, that law will determine the place of performance.

It is not clear if computer programs can be regarded as services for the purposes of article 7(1). In the early days of the Internet, software was customarily provided on a tangible carrier such as a tape or a disk. Whereas this is still true to some extent, the dominant model today is for an IP right/licence to be transferred (on a one-off or subscription basis) with the product being directly downloaded. This may or may not be accompanied by a carrier disk. In a corporate environment, the two are normally distinct. A typical situation involving a sale of boxed software would fall under article 7(1)(b), first indent (sale of goods). However, in *Falco and Rebitsch*, the CJEU said that a contract under which the owner of an intellectual property right grants its contractual partner the right to use that right in return for remuneration is not a contract for the provision of services within the meaning of article 7(1)(b), second indent.[19] Such contracts fall within the default position of article 7(1)(a) and will be decided in the courts of the place of performance.

Some doubts may also exist in regard to the provision of audio-visual content over the Internet. Since there is neither a community-wide definition of services, nor can the definition from various EU Directives be automatically applied, whether something is a service and therefore falls under article 7(1)(b), second indent, would still be a matter for national courts. As the CJEU in *Falco v Rebitsch* said, 'a contract under which the owner of an intellectual property right grants its contractual partner the right to use that right in return for remuneration' lacks an important feature of a services contract: 'that the party who provides the service carries out a particular activity in return for remuneration'. This simply means that contracts concerning the supply of audio-visual material will not be defaulted to the place of performance but will be scrutinized for a dominant element as per article 7(1)(a).

---

[18] C-440/97 *Gie Groupe Concorde and others v. Master of the Vessel Suhadiwarno Panjan and others* [1999] ECR 6308.

[19] C-533/07 *Falco Privatstiftung and Thomas Rabitsch v Gisela Weller-Lindhorst* [2009] ECR I-03327.

2.3 Special Jurisdiction: Cybertorts

Special jurisdiction under article 7(2) gives the claimant an option to sue in the courts for the place where the harmful event occurred or may occur.[20] In tort cases, in *Bier BV v Mines de Potasse D'Alsace SA*,[21] the place where the harmful event occurred was said to be both the place where the event giving rise to the damage occurred and the place where the damage itself occurred. This case, which had a straightforward application in non-digital cases, had to be reinterpreted in a series of cases involving the digital world. Most cases involving torts on the Internet that the CJEU had dealt with can be divided in two categories. The first are defamation cases, torts arising out of harming one's reputation on the Web. The second are cases involving violation of intellectual property on the Internet. The latter usually involve copyright violations or trademark infringements. To this should be added other digital torts for which there are no clear guidelines from the Court, such as fraud, breaches of IT systems, privacy violations, etc.

In *defamation* cases, the (then) European Court of Justice's ruling in *Shevill v Presse Alliance SA*[22] gave the claimant a wide choice of courts in which to sue for libel in a newspaper article distributed in several Member States. The issue for the Court was the appropriate forum for a libel by a newspaper article circulated in several Member States. The Court, reinterpreting the *Bier* case for newspaper publication, ruled that the claimant may start proceedings in the place of the publisher's establishment as a place giving rise to the damage, but also in any of the places where the publication is distributed (as a place where the damage occurs). The claimant may recover the whole amount in the former case, and in the latter only the amount suffered for loss of reputation in the place concerned. This gives the plaintiff the flexibility of suing in a more familiar forum for a localized tort while still protecting the defendant for torts that would encompass the whole EU. Whereas such jurisdiction cannot be described as exorbitant, its application to Internet cases depends on the interpretation of the word 'publication' for web content available in national and European contexts. The Regulation does not overtly require the courts to engage in the measuring of the contacts

---

[20] Article 5(3). See T.C. Hartley, '"Libel Tourism" and Conflict of Laws' (2010) 59 *ICLQ* 25.
[21] C-21/76 *Bier BV v Mines de Potasse D'Alsace SA* [1978] ECR 1735.
[22] C-68/93 *Shevill v Presse Alliance SA* [1995] ECR I-415.

between the defendant and the Member States in question, but such measuring was nevertheless necessary, as will be seen from the following cases.

The *eDate Advertising* case resolves some of the difficulties.[23] The case involved a website operator established in Austria and a German plaintiff whose personal rights were allegedly violated in a publication on that website. The Court ruled that:

> Article [7(2)] must be interpreted as meaning that, in the event of an alleged infringement of personality rights by means of content placed online on an internet website, the person who considers that his rights have been infringed has the option of bringing an action for liability, in respect of all the damage caused, either before the courts of the Member State in which the publisher of that content is established or before the courts of the Member State in which the centre of his interests is based. That person may also, instead of an action for liability in respect of all the damage caused, bring his action before the courts of each Member State in the territory of which content placed online is or has been accessible. Those courts have jurisdiction only in respect of the damage caused in the territory of the Member State of the court seised.

The approach of this case is largely consistent with what was seen in *Shevill*. In both instances, there is the possibility to recover both the whole amount and individual amounts. The notable difference lies in the addition of the option to sue for the whole amount at the place where the person whose personality rights had been infringed has its 'centre of interests'. This place, the Court confirmed, normally coincides with the place where that person has its habitual residence. The suggested 'centre of gravity' is the spot where the reputation both has a strong interest in being defended and a spot where the information expressed has an interest in being communicated. It would make more sense to be able to sue in that state than, for example, in the state where the plaintiff is domiciled but does not live. Primary centre of interests need not coincide with habitual residence and a link may be formed with another state either through the exercise of a professional activity or through other means.

The practical consequences of the *eDate* solution are significant as the case objectively expands the number of jurisdictions where the publisher could be sued. If the Internet publisher, a corporation or an individual, is domiciled in the European Union, it can be sued in the state where it is established. But, in addition to that, it can be summoned to any

---

[23] C-509/09 *eDate Advertising GmbH v X and Olivier Martinez*; *Robert Martinez v MGN Ltd*, ECLI:EU:C:2011:685, 25 October 2011.

jurisdiction where the defendant has its centre of interests. Finally, it can also be sued where the harmful content had been accessed, at least in respect of the damage sustained in that state. This, in practice, can mean any combination of 28 Member States. If the defamation involves several subjects, it can reasonably be expected that some would sue in the place of establishment whereas others would sue in their own 'centre of interests' states.

The second group of article 7(2) cybertorts involve *violations of intellectual property rights*.[24] Determining jurisdiction in these cases is among the conceptually more difficult tasks. This is primarily because localizing the violation committed by electronic means is more complicated than localizing other violations since the act usually takes place in several states simultaneously. Whereas disputes involving the *registration and validity* of IP rights are always subject to the exclusive jurisdiction of article 24(4), the Regulation is silent about other cases involving intellectual property rights. Article 7(2) has the potential to provide jurisdiction to the court of the place where the infringement of an IP right took place.[25] This application of article 7(2) can be used in respect of the restitution of profits and preventive actions.[26]

The *Pinckney* case[27] was an action commenced in the French courts by a French national against an Austrian company for copyright violation. Mr Pinckney authored some songs which had been illegally pressed on to a CD by KDG Mediatech and made available online. Pinckney was suing Mediatech for violation of copyright. The question posed to the CJEU was: does the person alleging an infringement have the option of bringing action either in each state where the content is accessible or does the content need to be *directed* to a specific territory. The referring court also asked if 'some other clear connection factor' ought to be present for websites that engage in copyright infringement.

---

[24] See A. Nuyts, 'Suing at the Place of Infringement: The Application of Article 5(3) of Regulation 44/2001 to IP Matters and Internet Disputes' in A. Nuyts (ed.), *International Litigation in Intellectual Property and Information Technology* (Kluwer, The Hague, 2008), p. 105.

[25] Which is otherwise available in the Trade Mark Regulation (Council Regulation (EC) 207/2009 of 26 February 2009 [2009] OJ L78/1) and the Design Regulation (Council Regulation (EC) 6/2002 of 12 December 2001 [2002] OJ 3/1).

[26] This in spite of the *GAT* case, C-4/03 *Gesellschaft für Antriebstechnik mbH & Co. KG v Lamellen und Kupplungsbau Beteiligungs KG* [2006] ECR I-6509.

[27] C-170/12 *Peter Pinckney v KDG Mediatech AG*, ECLI:EU:C:2013:635, 3 October 2013.

The Advocate General convincingly argued that mere accessibility of content does not amount to jurisdiction. In his words 'such a point of connection would encourage forum shopping, contrary to the case-law of the Court'. The Advocate General also excluded Mr Pinckney's idea that the place of the centre of interests introduced in *eDate Advertising* case should, by analogy, be applied here. Centre of interests is more suitable for violations of personality rights where a distortion of the normal operation of article 4 is justified by virtue of the fact that the dispute is more closely connected with the place where the plaintiff has his centre of interests. The Advocate General's solution was to allow the person claiming infringement to bring proceedings in the place of establishment of the infringer – to recover for all damage suffered – or in the place where the infringing website aimed its activity for the damage suffered only in that territory.

In the final judgment, the Court changed the formulation of the question referred, narrowing it down from what was a question about targeting to what is essentially a very narrow and specific question about distribution of media which are in a material form but which are sold electronically. The Court then answered such a narrowly reformulated question in the affirmative, saying that the courts in a Member State have jurisdiction against a 'company established in another Member State and which has, in the latter State, reproduced that work ... also accessible with the jurisdiction of the court seised'. Such jurisdiction only covers the damages in the state in question.

Looking into the criterion of directing, the Court made an analogy with article 18, which covers consumer contracts. That article has been interpreted in Joined Cases *Peter Pammer and Hotel Alpenhoff*[28] in light of website *targeting* and a non-exclusive list of criteria had been developed which would help interpret situations where a website directs its activities to consumers in other Member States. The *Pinckney* Court specifically stated that article 7(2) does not require directing. The Court also rejected criteria of substantive law.

The solution the Court offered differs significantly from the Advocate General's idea, which was wider in scope and easier to apply. It is doubtful that the *Pinckney* Court contributed anything to the understanding of the operation of article 7(2) in online copyright infringement

---

[28] C-585/08 and C-144/09 *Pammer and Hotel Alpenhoff* [2010] ECR I-12527. See Chapter 7.

cases.[29] The essential question – what connecting factors ought to be considered when infringing websites are accessible in multiple Member States – remains unanswered.

Hi Hotel[30] was a case involving multiple violators of copyright located in different Member States. A photographer was contracted to take pictures of a hotel interior but the pictures were, contrary to the agreement, passed by a French-based HiHotel on to a publishing company in Germany where they were used in a book on interior decoration. The photographer brought action in Germany alleging that the harmful event occurred there, although the hotel that had violated his rights had its establishment in France. The Court held that:

> where there are several supposed perpetrators of damage allegedly caused to rights of copyright protected in the Member State of the court seised, [article 7(2)] does not allow jurisdiction to be established, on the basis of the causal event of the damage, of a court within whose jurisdiction the supposed perpetrator who is being sued did not act.

This means that German courts cannot have jurisdiction by virtue of article 7(2) if the violation in Germany is only a causal event of a damage that actually took place elsewhere. However, the Court said that article 7(2): 'does allow the jurisdiction of that court to be established on the basis of the place where the alleged damage occurs, provided that the damage may occur within the jurisdiction of the court seised'. If the latter, the court can only decide on the damage in that state. It seems that the CJEU's intention here is to avoid lawsuits in states where the non-domiciled co-infringer had neither acted nor where real damage has taken place, but to allow them in states where there is real damage even where the infringer had not necessarily acted in them.

In *Pez Hejduk*,[31] Ms Hejduk, a professional architecture photographer, took photos of an Austrian architect's work. These photos were made available for downloading by EnergieAgentur, a German company based in Düsseldorf, without the author's consent. Ms Hedjuk, relying on article 7(2), sought to recover damages in an Austrian court, claiming that

---

[29] See S. Brachotte and A. Nuyts, 'Jurisdiction over Cyber Torts under the Brussels I Regulation' in A. Savin and J. Trzaskowski (eds.), *Research Handbook on EU Internet Law* (Edward Elgar Publishing, Cheltenham and Northampton, MA, 2014), pp. 243–51.

[30] C-387/12 *Hi Hotel HCF SARL v Uwe Spoering*, ECLI:EU:C:2014:215, 3 April 2014.

[31] C-441/13 *Pez Hejduk v EnergieAgentur.NRW GmbH*, ECLI:EU:C:2015:28, 22 January 2015.

courts in Austria had jurisdiction based on the fact that the harmful event had taken place in Austria where photographs could be downloaded. EnergieAgentur claimed that Austria had not specifically been targeted. The question referred was, in cases where rights were infringed by a website (EnergieAgentur) whose top-level domain is not that of the country where the proprietor of the right is domiciled (Austria), does jurisdiction exists only in places where the alleged infringer is established or also in courts where the content is directed?

The Advocate General's Opinion emphasized that automatic application of *Pinckney* would not be practicable as *Pinckney* had been interpreted as a territorial case, even though the medium used had been the Internet. In the present case, the damage was delocalized precisely by virtue of Internet distribution. Here 'it is not possible to apply the criterion of the place where the damage occurred' as 'an applicant in a case like the present one will not be able to produce verifiable material which precisely delimits only the damage sustained in the Member State where proceedings have been brought'. The Advocate General suggested, therefore, that the only just solution would be to limit the operation of article 7(2) to states where the event giving rise to the damage had occurred, completely eliminating the harmful effect which could not be determined accurately.

The Court did not follow the Advocate General, emphasizing that the causal event giving rise to the damage did not matter in the case. That place, the Court said, can only be the place where EnergieAgentur had its place of business because that is where the technical act of posting the photographs took place. On the other hand, the Court reiterated its *Pinckney* position that the likelihood of damage in a state is subject to the condition that the rights are protected. Noting that the allegedly infringing website's domain is .de (for Germany), the Court re-emphasized the irrelevance of directing towards Austria. Instead, it said that 'the occurrence of damage and/or the likelihood of its occurrence arise from the accessibility in the Member State of the referring court, via the website of EnergieAgentur, of the photographs to which the rights relied on by Ms Hejduk pertain'. In other words, whatever the targeting intentions of EnergieAgentur, the fact that the rights were protected in Austria and that the infringing act caused damage in Austria, activated the operation of article 7(2).

Electronic *trademark infringements* were discussed in the *Winter-steiger*[32] case which was a reference concerning the use by search engines of AdWords allegedly breaching the plaintiff's trademark. Win-tersteiger was a producer of ski equipment based in Austria, whereas Products 4U Sondermaschinenbau GmbH was also a ski producer based in Germany who produced accessories for Wintersteiger machines. The plaintiff did not authorize these accessories but they were nevertheless advertised as Wintersteiger accessories. In 2008, Products 4U reserved Google.de AdWords 'Wintersteiger' and a search on Wintersteiger regu-larly produced not only results involving the original ski equipment maker but also Products 4U in the advertisement section. Wintersteiger commenced proceedings against Products 4U in Austrian courts, alleging trademark infringement and claiming that Google.de was regularly accessed in Austria. Products 4U claimed that Austrian courts lacked jurisdiction and that the AdWord was exclusively for German use. No targeting of the Austrian market was taking place, it was claimed, since no AdWord had been booked for the Austrian site, Google.at.

The problem arose from difficulties in establishing the place where the harmful event giving rise to the damage occurred if the place where the site can be accessed is different from the state where the site is registered. In this case, there was no doubt that the lawsuit ought to be brought at the place of infringement and the problem lay only in determining where the place of infringement was located. In relation to the place of the event giving rise to the damage, the Court said that the advertisement creation was the key factor and not the display of the advertisement itself. The Court held that 'it is the advertiser choosing a keyword identical to the trade mark, and not the provider of the referencing service, who uses it in the course of trade' which creates the event giving rise to the damage. The place of the location of the server could not, due to its uncertainty and lack of predictability, be taken to be a determining factor. The place of the establishment of the advertiser, by contrast, was determinable and easy to ascertain.

In relation to the place where the damage occurred, the Court made a distinction between personality rights infringements cases, such as *eDate Advertising*, and intellectual property rights infringements cases, such as the one at present, as the latter should not be subject to the criteria developed in the former. The Court emphasized the territoriality of trademark and the importance of the place where the trademark was

---

[32] C-523/10 *Wintersteiger AG v Products 4U Sondermaschinenbau GmbH*, ECLI:EU:C:2012:220, 19 April 2012.

registered. The courts of the state where the trademark was registered were best able to assess whether an infringement had occurred or not and should, therefore, have jurisdiction. The final solution was, therefore, that an action for trademark infringement on the Internet could be brought either in the place where the advertiser was established or the place where the trademark was registered.

Football Dataco[33] was a case involving online use of *databases. Football Dataco* was a UK company operating a database relating to football matches. They claimed a *sui generis* right in a 'Football Live' database, which was a compilation of data about matches in progress. Sportradar GmbH was a German company providing sports statistics online through a website called 'Sport Live Data'. Sportradar was alleged to have copied the data from 'Football Live' and made it available to its customers in the United Kingdom. Football Dataco and others brought proceedings against Sportradar in the United Kingdom, alleging violations of its *sui generis* right.

The CJEU held that (paragraph 36):

> the mere fact that the website containing the data in question is accessible in a particular national territory is not a sufficient basis for concluding that the operator of the website is performing an act of re-utilisation.

Instead, the Court looked for evidence of targeting. The Court said that the damage was located in the state where the members of the public re-utilizing the database were being targeted. The Court rejected the server approach as being too uncertain since it was difficult to localize the server and an infringement might involve multiple servers. The Court instead made the link with the intended market which was, in this case, specifically targeted.

Article 7(5) gives jurisdiction to courts of the place where a *branch, agency or other establishment* is situated, provided that the contract arises out of the operations concerning that establishment. As with other headings of article 5, the effect is simply to add another forum to the one provided in article 4. This will only be in cases where the dispute arises out of dealings with the branch. As such, this provision is not going to be of particular significance in Internet cases, except in situations where a large corporation, for instance, an e-commerce website, operates through national branches.

---

[33] C-173/11 *Football Dataco Ltd and others*, ECLI:EU:C:2012:642, 18 October 2012.

2.4   Jurisdiction Agreements

Electronic commerce contracts as well as other types of contracts on the Internet normally contain choice-of-forum clauses or clauses involving alternative dispute resolution. Jurisdiction clauses are subject to Brussels I Regulation (Recast), article 25, which allows jurisdiction agreements between parties regardless of their domicile in a Member State. This means that two non-EU corporate entities or persons can agree on an EU court's jurisdiction. It also means that a company based in the United States can agree to resolve all disputes with its customers who may or may not be domiciled in the EU, in the courts of one of the Member States. If the same company agrees to resolve disputes in the United States, however, the situation changes dramatically, as this eventuality is not covered in article 25.[34] Such agreements would be subject to each Member State's rules, but with limitations imposed in articles 18 and 19 (consumer contracts), which only allow jurisdiction agreements entered into after the dispute had arisen in all cases involving EU consumers.

Jurisdiction agreements need to be in writing or evidenced in writing or 'in a form which accords with practices which the parties have established between themselves'. Article 25(2) provides that this can also be in 'any communication by electronic means which provides a durable record of the agreement'. An electronically stored copy of a contract will, therefore, be adequate.

The jurisdiction so conferred is exclusive unless agreed otherwise. If the parties agree on non-exclusive jurisdiction, the effect will be to add another forum to those in Articles 4 and 7. The plaintiff will then be able to exercise discretion as to what court to sue in. The effect of an exclusive clause is to confer sole jurisdiction on the chosen court. Such a court has no discretion to decline jurisdiction if the formal conditions have been met.

If proceedings are started in courts other than the ones chosen in the exclusive jurisdiction clause (in error or deliberately as part of a strategy of slowing things down), such courts must of their own motion declare that they have no jurisdiction. Article 31(2) provides that:

> where a court of a Member State on which an agreement as referred to in Article 25 confers exclusive jurisdiction is seised, any court of another Member State shall stay the proceedings until such time as the court seised on the basis of the agreement declares that it has no jurisdiction under the agreement.

---

[34]   Article 25 refers to 'courts of a Member State'.

If, for example, vexatious proceedings are commenced in another juris-diction in violation of the jurisdiction agreement, that is, if a court other than the one designated in the exclusive jurisdiction clause is first seised, such court has no possibility of continuing unless the court designated in the exclusive jurisdiction establishes that it has no jurisdiction. This solution is an improvement over the previous version of the Regulation whose interpretation in court[35] had been widely criticized.[36]

A valid jurisdiction agreement cannot annul the effects of consumer protection law (article 25(4) is explicit on this) but remains valid if it does not contradict them, that is, if it works in the consumer's favour. Article 19 allows departures from the protective regime applicable to consumers in cases where agreements have been entered into after the dispute had arisen or where such agreements provide forums additional to the ones listed in Section 4 of the Regulation or in cases where both the provider and the consumer are domiciled or habitually resident in the same Member State and the agreement confers jurisdiction on that state. The life of an exclusive jurisdiction clause inserted into a standard consumer contract depends, therefore, on whether it satisfies these conditions. In principle, such a clause might have the effect of a non-exclusive jurisdiction clause in all situations involving a Member State or may be completely invalid if it involves a third state.

There is some doubt as to whether an exclusive clause conferring jurisdiction on courts of *third* states (for example, the United States) would be valid. It is possible to conclude, looking at articles 6 and 19 that it might not be. Article 6 provides that non-domiciled defendants are subject to national (non-Brussels rules) *except for*, among others, article 18. In other words, the main consumer protection rules apply whether the potential targeted trader is domiciled in the EU or not. Article 19, on the other hand, is not mentioned in that context, suggesting that it applies only to jurisdiction agreements where parties are in Member States. On the other hand, article 19 does not expressly mention Member States, leading one to believe that it might apply universally. Article 25(4) simply states that violations of, among others, article 19 shall have no legal force but article 25 only applies for prorogation of jurisdiction of Member States. It is possible to conclude that, although jurisdiction agreements of this kind are governed by national law and not Brussels I

---

[35] See C-116/02 *Erich Gasser GmbH v MISAT Srl* [2003] ECR I-14693.

[36] See e.g., R. Fentiman, '*Erich Gasser GmbH v MISAT Srl*' (2005) 42 *Common Market Law Review* 241.

(Recast) they would, nevertheless, be subject to Article 19 limitations.[37] An alternative conclusion would be, as it had been under the original Brussels I Regulation, that this is a matter for national law.

A jurisdiction clause may in the eyes of a court of a *third* country validly confer jurisdiction but the resulting judgment, if any, might be declined recognition and enforcement. This is not by force of article 45(1)(e)(i), which specifically prohibits recognition and enforcement of a judgment which conflicts with, among others, rules on consumer protection where the consumer was the defendant but which only applies to recognition of judgments of Member States. Potential refusal of recognition will most likely come from national application of public policy rules.

Jurisdiction clauses are on the Internet usually part of a 'click-wrap' agreement, which are agreements presented to consumers purchasing goods or services or electronic content online. In such cases, the consumer has the option either to accept or to reject the whole agreement, without having a say as to whether individual clauses may or may not form its part. In *Jaouad El Majdoub*,[38] a car dealer from Germany purchased a vehicle from a dealer with the registered office in Germany but a parent company in Belgium. Since the vehicle had not been delivered, the buyer plaintiff commenced proceedings in Germany. The seller contended that Belgian courts should hear the case since the buyer accepted the general terms and conditions on the website by going through the necessary steps. The CJEU held that:

> the method of accepting the general terms and conditions of a contract for sale by 'click-wrapping', such as that at issue in the main proceedings, concluded by electronic means, which contains an agreement conferring jurisdiction, constitutes a communication by electronic means which provides a durable record of the agreement, within the meaning of that provision, where that method makes it possible to print and save the text of those terms and conditions before the conclusion of the contract.

It should be noted, however, that the main question here was not whether the agreement is unfair or not as such but only whether the 'click-wrapping' constitutes a durable record. In this instance, the fact that the buyer had access to terms and could print them out constituted such record but this should not be taken as an all-out endorsement of all such

---

[37] See A. Dickinson and E. Lein (eds.), *The Brussels I Regulation Recast* (OUP, Oxford, 2015), p. 235.

[38] C-322/14 *Jaouad El Majdoub v CarsOnTheWeb.Deutschland GmbH*, ECLI:EU:C:2015:334, 21 May 2015.

clauses. The Unfair Terms Directive[39] refers to 'excluding or hindering the consumer's right to take legal action or exercise any other legal remedy' as one of the grounds on which contract can be declared to be unfair. However, since articles 18 and 19 already provide significant protection against jurisdiction agreements, which may harm consumer's interests, the Directive's scope would here be limited to cases where a clause allowed under article 19 may be unfair on grounds other than the location of the forum.

3 ENFORCEMENT OF FOREIGN JUDGMENTS

Chapter III of the Brussels I Regulation deals with recognition and enforcement of judgments. The general rule is that the regime will apply to *all* EU judgments, irrespective of the rules of jurisdiction under which they were given. Therefore, a judgment given in a Member State and based on non-Brussels jurisdiction rules would still be recognized under the Brussels regime.

The most important feature of the regime is the simplified procedure for recognition and enforcement. A judgment from another Member State will be recognized without any special procedure (article 36), without opening the case on the merits and without questioning the deciding court's jurisdiction. The latter is the case even where the judgment was made on one of the exorbitant bases of jurisdiction normally prohibited under the Regulation.

Article 45 only allows a limited number of defences to recognition that the CJEU has interpreted narrowly. The only general basis that is non-procedural in nature concerns judgments manifestly contrary to the recognizing state's public policy (article 45(1)). This ground has had very limited and specific use in national courts, which is the interpretation encouraged by the Court. Nothing in the Brussels I Regulation regime indicates that judgments relating to Internet disputes in general or electronic commerce in particular would be accorded special treatment.

From the European perspective, a judgment from a non-EU Member State will be recognized according to each Member State's traditional rules. If a foreign judgment was obtained on the basis of exorbitant jurisdiction of a non-EU court, there exists a possibility that such judgment will be recognized and enforced although the ultimate result will depend on national rules.

---

[39]   Unfair Terms in Consumer Contracts Directive [1993] OJ L95/29, 21 April 1993.

The principles that govern recognition and enforcement in the United States prevent recognition of judgments that endanger free speech. 'As the First Amendment prevents a state from adopting England's defamation law or France's hate speech law, an American court's enforcement of a foreign judgment based on the English or French law likewise would violate the First Amendment.'[40] Courts in the United States will not enforce a foreign defamation judgment.[41] The leading case in this area is *Matusevich v Telnikoff*,[42] where the District Court for Columbia refused to enforce a British libel judgment. It was said that recognition would violate both the First and Fourteenth Amendments, the basis of the court's finding being that the libellous speech would have been legal under the First Amendment. The *Matusevich* principle was further applied in the *Yahoo US* case,[43] where Yahoo United States argued that a French injunction is not enforceable in the United States. The court confirmed, in principle, the *Matusevich* rule for Internet cases. Foreign libel laws thus cannot be applied in US courts whenever this jeopardizes the protection given by the First Amendment.

No similar rule or practice exists in the European Union, which stands on politically different grounds regarding free speech. Whereas the First Amendment protection is broad in scope and strong in enforcement, the EU Member States typically prohibit certain forms of hate speech and would not refuse recognition and enforcement for all but the strongest reasons of procedural or public policy nature. Neither would they refuse recognition on the account of protection of free speech under the traditional non-Brussels I regime. Under the Brussels I Regulation (Recast) rules, with their narrow grounds for objection, this is even less likely.

The Brussels I regime creates certainty and opts for speed. Interested in easing the free flow of judgments between Member States and not designed to police the quality and political values embedded in foreign judgments, it lacks the tools necessary to 'correct' the foreign courts' output. Although this creates an efficient system of recognition, it

---

[40]   M. Rosen, 'Exporting the Constitution' (2004) 53 *Emory Law Journal* 171.
[41]   The basis for that is found in several provisions, including *Restatement Third of the Foreign Relations Law of the United States* (American Law Institute, 1987), para. 482.
[42]   877 F. Supp. 1 (D.D.C. 1995), US District Court for the District of Columbia.
[43]   *Yahoo! Inc. v La Ligue Contre le Racisme et l'Antisemitisme* 169 F. Supp. 2d 1181 (N.D. Cal. 2001).

possibly makes redundant a valuable tool that could have been used in borderline Internet cases.

4 APPLICABLE LAW

Once jurisdiction of the relevant court is determined, the law applicable to the legal relationship needs to be found. The EU has harmonized rules for determining the law applicable to both contracts and torts. In a large number of modern contracts, the law applicable will be agreed on by the parties and this is accepted in legislation but if the parties had not agreed, both the Rome I and the Rome II Regulations contain default rules.

4.1 Rome I Regulation on the Law Applicable to Contracts

The European Union regime for determining the law applicable to contracts is found in the Rome Regulation on the law applicable to contractual obligations ('Rome I Regulation'),[44] previously the Rome Convention.[45] The Regulation applies to contractual obligations in civil and commercial matters (article 1). Article 2 provides that any law that the Regulation specifies is applied whether or not it is the law of a Member State. This means that the law specified in the Regulation is applied even if it is the law of a non-member. Unlike Brussels I Regulation (Recast), which requires that the defendant is domiciled in the EU (and points to non-Brussels rules if this is not the case), Rome I Regulation replaces traditional choice-of-law rules and applies to all cases within its scope, irrespective of the parties' nationality, domicile, etc.

The general rule in the Regulation is freedom of choice coupled with default rules applicable in the absence of choice and mandatory rules applicable in special situations, including consumer protection. In a large number of situations, it is precisely the rules on consumer protection that will be relevant for transactions on the Internet.

Article 3 allows the parties to choose the law applicable to their transaction. The choice must be 'expressly or clearly demonstrated by the terms of the contract or the circumstances of the case'. The parties may subject different parts of the contract to different laws and can at any

---

[44] Regulation (EC) 593/2008 of the European Parliament and of the Council of 17 June 2008 on the law applicable to contractual obligations ('Rome I Regulation') [2008] OJ L177/6, 4 July 2008.

[45] [1980] OJ L266, 9 October 1980.

time agree on different applicable law. The existence and validity of their choice will be determined in accordance with articles 10, 11 and 13 of the Regulation. Since article 2 states that the law means any law, whether it is the law of a Member State or not, the choice of law of a third state is also valid. The parties' choice will, however, be limited by mandatory rules which protect particularly vulnerable categories such as consumers and employees.[46] Consumer contracts with companies based in the United States typically contain choice of law clauses pointing to the law of one of the US states but the operation of article 6 makes such choice invalid in respect of mandatory consumer protection rules.

Article 4 helps the courts determine the applicable law in the absence of choice. This is done through the concept of the closest connection. The first paragraph introduces assumptions concerning individual types of contract and the corresponding applicable law. For a contract for the sale of goods, this will be the law of the country where the seller has his habitual residence. For the contract for the provision of services, it will be the law of the country where the service provider has his habitual residence. Where the contract is not covered by any of the headings of article 4(1), or where the elements of the contract would be covered by more than one of them, the law of the country where the party required to effect the characteristic performance has his habitual residence will govern the contract (article 4(2)). The laws designated by the first two paragraphs may nevertheless be overridden in cases where it is clear from all the circumstances of the case that the contract is manifestly more closely connected with a country other than that indicated in paragraphs 1 or 2 (article 4(3)). If it is, however, altogether impossible to determine the applicable law, article 4(5) provides that the contract will be governed by the law of the country with which it is most closely connected.

Article 6 contains special rules applicable to consumer contracts. All or many business-to-consumer (B2C) transactions on the Internet will be subject to this regime. A consumer is defined in article 6 as a person who concludes contracts for purposes that lie outside their profession. The default provision is that such contracts are governed by the law of the place where the consumer has habitual residence provided that the professional either pursues their activities in the country where the consumer is habitually resident or 'by any means, directs such activities to that country or to several countries including that country'. The

---

[46]   See Chapter 7.

directing of activities must, by analogy, be understood in light of the *Hotel Alpenhoff* judgment:[47]

> The following matters, the list of which is not exhaustive, are capable of constituting evidence from which it may be concluded that the trader's activity is directed to the Member State of the consumer's domicile, namely the international nature of the activity, mention of itineraries from other Member States for going to the place where the trader is established, use of a language or a currency other than the language or currency generally used in the Member State in which the trader is established with the possibility of making and confirming the reservation in that other language, mention of telephone numbers with an international code, outlay of expenditure on an internet referencing service in order to facilitate access to the trader's site or that of its intermediary by consumers domiciled in other Member States, use of a top-level domain name other than that of the Member State in which the trader is established, and mention of an international clientele composed of customers domiciled in various Member States. It is for the national courts to ascertain whether such evidence exists.

The parties are, as per article 6(2), allowed to choose the applicable law. No choice that the parties make may have the effect of depriving the consumer of the protection of mandatory rules of the law that would have applied in the absence of choice.

Article 6(4)(a) excludes the consumer regime in cases of contracts for the supply of services where these services are to be supplied to the consumer in a country other than that of his habitual residence. This provision targets situations where the consumer cannot reasonably claim protection of the country where they habitually reside since services were marketed in the consumer's state but performed entirely out of it.[48] The solution is not entirely in harmony with article 18 of Brussels I Regulation nor particularly consistent with the overall aim of EU consumer protection rules.

The Rome I Regulation contains a number of mandatory rules, which are rules whose application cannot be derogated from by the parties' choice and which protect fundamental interests. The Regulation operates with two distinct categories of mandatory rules. The first, broader category refers to rules that cannot be derogated from by contract. This applies to consumer, employee or similar protection rules all of which

---

[47] Joint Cases C-585/08 *Peter Pammer v Reederie Karl Schlüter Gmbh & Co. KG* and C-144/09 *Hotel Alpenhof GESmbh v Oliver Heller* [2010] ECR I-12527. See also Chapter 7, section 5.1.

[48] Package holidays are expressly excluded from this regime as they are subject to special regulation.

exist both in European and in national laws. It also introduces a new, narrower category of mandatory rules which article 9 defines as those 'the respect for which is regarded as crucial by a country for safeguarding its public interests, such as its political, social or economic organisation' and which, under Recital 37, need to be construed more restrictively than ordinary mandatory rules. The definition corresponds to some extent to the concept of mandatory rules articles 3 and 7 of the Rome Convention but is also an attempt to address some of the criticism directed at the Rome Convention's treatment of mandatory rules.

Article 3(3) and (4) operate with the broader understanding of mandatory rules. Article 3(3) provides that parties' evasive choice of law in situations where the contract has no significant foreign element cannot avoid the application of internal overriding rules of the forum. In other words, this article allows the parties to choose foreign law in a totally domestic situation, but not to override mandatory rules. Article 3(4) provides that choice of law of a third, non-Member State, cannot have as the effect the avoidance of Community mandatory rules. This has the same effect as article 3(3) but on an EU level. An example of such rules would be, for instance, EU rules on contracts concluded at a distance. A choice of US law, therefore, may be valid but will not achieve the avoidance of Community consumer law or employment laws.

Article 9(2) provides that nothing in the Regulation can restrict the overriding mandatory provisions of the forum. The law chosen by the parties, or arrived at by virtue of article 4, will be applied to the extent that it does not contradict such mandatory rules. Article 9(3), on the other hand, allows effect to be given to overriding mandatory provisions of the law of the country 'where the obligations arising out of the contract have to be or have been performed, in so far as those overriding mandatory provisions render the performance of the contract unlawful'. This provision addresses the illegality of the contract at the place of its performance only. As per article 21, public policy rules of the forum may also apply.

4.2 Rome II Regulation on the Law Applicable to Tort

Finding the law applicable to torts committed on the Internet is a difficult and potentially sensitive issue. Many solutions have been proposed in literature and those applied in practice in courts of different states remain controversial. The difficulty lies in the fact that content published on the Internet crosses national borders while potential defendants usually do not. In a case of defamation, for example, where both a defamatory statement and the defendant publisher are located in the same Member State, the law applicable will usually be the law of that state. But what happens when the defamatory statement was posted on the Internet? Traditional choice-of-law mechanisms for finding the law applicable may point to a state with which the tort has the closest connection. But, what law should be applicable in cases where the contents are accessed and read in several states? The European Union regulates the law applicable to torts in the Rome Regulation on the law applicable to tort ('Rome II Regulation').[49]

The general regime in article 4 is that the law applicable is that of the country in which the damage occurs, irrespective of the country in which the event giving rise to the damage occurs and irrespective of the country in which indirect consequences occur. Where both persons have habitual residence in the same country, the law of that country applies. On the other hand, where it is clear that the tort is manifestly more closely connected with a third country, the law of that country will apply. All of this leaves a certain degree of uncertainty as to which country's laws apply since the answer would only be clear in single-state torts. Where a tort is committed in several states, it would be necessary to find out which country the damage had occurred in, or which country the tort might be 'manifestly' more connected to, if any.

The general regime outlined above applies to some but not all Internet torts. Internet torts most often relate either to privacy/defamation, to unfair competition or to intellectual property violations. Various fraudulent actions and unlawful interferences with computer systems ('hacking') also remain a possible target for the Rome II rules but this has not been tested in court. Privacy is explicitly excluded from the scope of the Regulation. Unfair competition is subject to a special regime. Intellectual property (IP) is also to some extent but where it is not, the location of the damage and, hence, the applicable law remains uncertain.

Marketing and advertising through the Internet is subject to an unfair competition conflicts regime in article 6. The law applicable to a non-contractual obligation arising out of an act of unfair competition is the law of the country 'where competitive relations or the collective interests of consumers are, or are likely to be, affected'. Where, on the other hand, the interests affect one competitor only, the regular regime in article 4 will apply. This article covers defamation as an act of unfair competition in spite of the exclusion of article 1.

---

[49] Regulation (EC) 864/2007 of the European Parliament and of the Council of 11 July 2007 on the law applicable to non-contractual obligations ('Rome II Regulation') [2007] OJ L199/40, 31 July 2007.

4.2.1 Privacy and rights relating to personality

The history of the Regulation is of some interest concerning the law applicable to defamation torts. In 2002, the European Commission published a preliminary draft Proposal for a Council Regulation on the law applicable to non-contractual obligations[50] and amended it in 2006.[51] The Proposal contained several controversial solutions. In relation to the violation of 'private or personal rights or from defamation', article 7 provided the law applicable to be the 'law of the country where the victim is habitually resident at the time of the tort or delict'. The proposal spurred a debate, with the media lobby expressing concern. This solution, it was argued, would unduly restrict the publishers' freedom and make them liable in the state with potentially markedly lower standards of speech protection.

A later draft, in recognition of the criticism, pointed to the law of the place where 'direct injury' was sustained. This was to be the place where the publication was commercially distributed. Additionally, article 6 of the Proposal provided that law applicable 'arising out of a violation of privacy or rights relating to the personality shall be the law of the forum' where application of the host state's laws would be 'contrary to the fundamental principles of the forum as regards freedom of expression and information'. In addition, the original proposal had the intention of giving precedence to the rules of the country of origin. Article 23(2) seems to have been drafted specifically with this purpose in mind.[52] It said that:

> This regulation shall not prejudice the application of Community instruments which, in relation to particular matters and in areas coordinated by such instruments, subject the supply of services or goods to the laws of the Member State where the service-provider is established and, in the area coordinated, allow restrictions on freedom to provide services or goods originating in another Member State only in limited circumstances.

---

[50] Proposal for a Regulation of the European Parliament and the Council on the law applicable to non-contractual obligations ('Rome II'), COM/2003/0427 (22 July 2003).

[51] Amended Proposal for a European Parliament and Council Regulation on the law applicable to non-contractual obligations ('Rome II'), COM(2006)83 final (21 February 2006).

[52] See M. Hellner, 'The Country of Origin Principle in the E-Commerce Directive: A Conflict with Conflict of Laws?' (2004) 12 *European Review of Private Law* 193.

The provision, as proposed, was insufficiently clear. For either it repeated what the first paragraph already said about Community mandatory rules or public policy, or, in the alternative, it invoked a norm which already had a basis in the EU Treaties and therefore did not need a specific embodiment. For these reasons, the Commission had the provision redrafted, completely removing the second paragraph, and changed the context of the provision: from one dealing with country of origin rule to one dealing with other international conventions.

Other interventions came from the European Parliament, which expressed concern that it was not clear what the most significant element of the damage was in cases concerning media. Thus, Recital 25a stated that 'the country in which the most significant element or elements of the damage occur or are likely to occur should be deemed to be the country to which the publication or broadcasting service is principally directed or, if this is not apparent, the country in which editorial control is exercised'.

In spite of the original desire to include defamation and violation of privacy, article 1(2)(g) of the Regulation excludes non-contractual obligations arising out of violations of privacy and rights relating to personality, including defamation. It is worth noting that the exclusion does not relate to other torts committed by the media, such as disclosure of confidential data or data theft.[53] The former is of increasing relevance, especially in relation to user-generated websites, including social networks, while the latter have an even wider scope.

In 2011, the European Parliament proposed adding violations of privacy and personality rights to the Rome II Regulation.[54] The Proposal is based on the developments following the *Shevill* case, namely in *eDate Advertising*, as well as in other cases and the comparative study commissioned on the subject.[55] In particular, the Proposal mentions the phenomenon of 'libel tourism'.[56] The Parliament proposed adding a new article to the Rome II Regulation:

---

[53] See I. Bach, 'Comment on Article 1' in P. Huber (ed.), *Rome II Regulation: Pocket Commentary* (Sellier, Munich, 2011), p. 54.

[54] European Parliament, Resolution of 10 May 2012 with recommendations to the Commission on the amendment of Regulation (EC) 864/2007 on the law applicable to non-contractual obligations (Rome II) 2009/2170(INI) (2 December 2011).

[55] *Comparative Study on the Situation in the 27 Member States as Regards the Law Applicable to Non-Contractual Obligations Arising Out of Violations of Privacy and Rights Relating to Personality, Final Report*, JLS/2007/C4/028 (February 2009).

[56] Hartley, '"Libel Tourism" and Conflict of Laws', note 20 above.

(1) Without prejudice to Article 4(2) and (3), the law applicable to a non-contractual obligation arising out of violations of privacy and rights relating to personality, including defamation, shall be the law of the country in which the rights of the person seeking compensation for damage are, or are likely to be, directly and substantially affected. However, the law applicable shall be the law of the country in which the person claimed to be liable is habitually resident if he or she could not reasonably have foreseen substantial consequences of his or her act occurring in the country designated by the first sentence.

(2) When the rights of the person seeking compensation for damage are, or are likely to be, affected in more than one country, and that person sues in the court of the domicile of the defendant, the claimant may instead choose to base his or her claim on the law of the court seised.

(3) The law applicable to the right of reply or equivalent measures shall be the law of the country in which the broadcaster or publisher has its habitual residence.

(4) The law applicable under this Article may be derogated from by an agreement pursuant to Article 14.

The Proposal's main position is that the law applicable should be the law of the state where the injured party's interests are. This reverts to the law of the plaintiff's habitual residence where the plaintiff did not and could not have foreseen the consequences. This provision brings the needed flexibility but opens up the term 'foreseen' to interpretation. Other solutions follow *eDate Advertising*'s logic in opting for the law of the defendant's domicile. The law of the broadcaster's habitual residence, proposed in the paragraph (3) right-of-reply situation, would have to be interpreted for situations involving Internet publishers.

4.2.2 Violations of intellectual property rights

According to article 8(1), the law applicable to non-contractual obligations arising out of infringements of intellectual property rights is the law of the country for which the protection is sought (*lex protectionis*). This is a logical solution that arises out of the territorial character of IP rights. It means that whether a right exists at all and what remedies might be available for its infringement would be determined according to the law of the country where the protection is claimed.[57]

If the tort arises out of an infringement of a unitary Community intellectual property right,[58] as per article 8(2), the law applicable is the

---

[57] See art. 15.
[58] Trademarks, designs, plant varieties and geographical indications.

law of the country in which the infringing act was committed for any issue not already covered by the said Community instrument. The draft Proposal had the general regime (article 4) apply to IP torts but the present special regime was introduced as a reaction to the criticism received. Choice of law is allowed under the conditions described in article 15 but is expressly excluded in cases involving violations of IP rights.

Since intellectual property rights are territorial, a violation on the Internet by, for example, publishing a copyright-protected material without permission or by violating a trademark, may lead to litigation in several states based on jurisdiction rules (described in Chapter 2, section 2.3). Litigation needs to be commenced in each of the states in which the protection is sought, with the law of each of them respectively being applicable. In terms of jurisdiction, the courts of the place where the infringer is domiciled will have jurisdiction as per article 4 of the Brussels I Regulation (Recast) whereas the courts in each of the states where the infringement took place will have jurisdiction under article 7(2) of that Regulation.

4.3 Country of Origin Principle

In Chapter 2, we have discussed the scope and importance of the country of origin principle. The claim examined here is that home country control has the potential to interfere with the operation of the choice-of-law rules. In spite of the disproportionate amount of interest and legal writing that the principle has generated with conflicts lawyers, much remains ambiguous. Although some scholars believe the impact to be significant,[59] the settled opinion is now that the principle exercises a limited influence on conflict-of-laws process, ranging from weak, where national judges are obliged to take account of the EU four freedoms without the obligation to do anything in particular to enforce it, to stronger, where EU law corrects an incompatible national law.

---

[59] See J. Basedow, 'Der kollisionsrechtliche gehalt der Produktfreiheiten im europäischen Binnenmarkt: favor offerentis' ['The Conflict-of-Laws Content of the Four Freedoms in the European Single Market: favor offerentis'] (1995) 59 *RabelsZ* 1; L. Radicati di Brozolo, 'L'influence sur les conflits de lois des principes de droit communautaire en matière de liberté de circulation' ['The Impact of Community Free Movement Principles on Conflict of Laws'] (1993) 82 *RCDIP* 401.

The home country control approach has been used in, among others, the Electronic Commerce Directive,[60] which extends the validity of the 'passport' obtained in one state to other Member States. The Directive concerns nearly all information society services (ISS), with exemptions[61] enumerated in article 1(5). It uses the so-called coordinated field[62] to indicate to the Member States the areas in which they are obliged to take action. The purpose is to avoid fragmentation of the market, as only one Member State is in charge of the supervision. Recital 22 of the E-Commerce Directive reinforces the importance of subjecting information and communications technology (ICT) services to the supervision of the country of origin. The recital specifically states that 'information society services should in principle be subject to the law of the Member State in which the service provider is established'. Article 3, on the Internal Market, states:

1. Each Member State shall ensure that the information society services provided by a service provider established on its territory comply with the national provisions applicable in the Member State in question which fall within the coordinated field.
2. Member States may not, for reasons falling within the coordinated field, restrict the freedom to provide information society services from another Member State.

This provision is to be read in conjunction with article 1(4):

This Directive does not establish additional rules on private international law nor does it deal with the jurisdiction of Courts.

The main function of the Directive is to ensure that information society services, within the coordinated field, are supervised at the *source* of the activity. Service providers are thus subject to prescriptive jurisdiction and laws of the Member State in which they are established. Host states are not allowed to regulate information services, except those that fall outside the Directive's scope and those that, although within its scope, can be justified in the interests of public policy, public health, public security and/or protection of consumers, provided that they are proportionate to the aim that they wish to achieve.

---

[60]   For more detail, see Chapter 2.
[61]   Relating to taxation, data protection, notaries, gambling and representation in court.
[62]   Articles 2(h) and 3, determining the scope of provisions needing harmonization.

While article 3(3) excludes the area outside the coordinated field from the scope of home country control, article 1(4) of the Directive specifically excludes its application to issues concerning choice of law and jurisdiction. The express exclusion of article 1(4) is coupled with Recital 23 that emphasizes that the Directive 'neither aims to establish additional rules on private international law relating to conflicts of law nor does it deal with the jurisdiction of Courts'. The Recital mentions only the negative impact of home country control, saying that private international law must not 'restrict the freedom to provide information society services as established in this Directive'.

Article 2, which contains the definition of the coordinated field, says nothing about whether it applies to private law.[63] Certain national implementations limit the scope of the E-Commerce Directive to public law, therefore excluding the private sphere and solving the problem of the potential conflict with e-commerce law.[64]

Looking at articles 1(4) and 3 of the E-Commerce Directive, as well as at article 23 of the original Proposal, it seems that the EU legislator could have had any of the three possibilities in mind.[65] According to the first, the country of origin rule acts as a choice-of-law rule.[66] There can be two interpretations of the first possibility. According to one, article 3 means *the law of the state of origin is the applicable law*.[67] According to the other, the private international law rules of the country of origin should *determine* the applicable law.[68] Support for this argument in EU law itself is not strong. According to the second possibility, the country of origin rule can be treated as a mandatory rule. In EU law, however, the use of

---

[63]   On the other hand, the originally proposed draft does include a wide interpretation and art. 3 excludes specific areas of private law, implying that others are included.

[64]   Thus, art. 2(8) of Danish Lov No. 227 of 22 April 2002 om tjenester i informationssamfundet, herunder visse aspekter af elektronisk handel – e-handelsloven [Law on information society services including various aspects of electronic commerce and e-commerce law]. Also Swedish Lag am elektronisk handel och andra informationssamhällets tjänster m.m. [Law on electronic commerce and other information society services] Prop. 2001/02:150.

[65]   See Hellner, 'The Country of Origin Principle', note 52 above, p. 109.

[66]   The main proponents of this have been Basedow and Radicati di Brozzolo. See note 59.

[67]   See C. Waelde, 'Article 3 ECD: Internal Market Clause' in L. Edwards (ed.), *The New Legal Framework for E-Commerce in Europe* (Hart, Oxford/Portland, OR, 2005), pp. 3, 8.

[68]   Waelde, 'Article 3 ECD', note 67 above, p. 8.

mandatory rules is almost always preceded by specific language[69] and the intention to use the home country principle as a mandatory rule would have been indicated. According to the third possibility, the country of origin rule limits the application of the designated law, in a manner similar to the *ordre public* provision, after choice of law had been allowed to operate.

It is possible to interpret the four freedoms as having no effect on conflict of laws. Primarily, the country of origin principle is not a connecting factor and was not designed to demand the application of the law of the country of origin, or to request the jurisdiction of particular civil courts. And, if the result of the conflict-of-laws process is incompatible with EU law, this is incidental and not connected to the main issues in private international law. There is support for this view in the fact that secondary instruments, such as the E-Commerce Directive, expressly rule out potential effects that they might have on conflict of laws.

The *eDate Advertising* case resolves most of the difficulties of the home country control principle. The referring court asked if article 3(1) and (2) of the E-Commerce Directive must be interpreted as having a conflict-of-laws character in the sense that they also require the exclusive application of the law applicable in the country of origin, to the exclusion of national conflict-of-laws rules or only as a corrective at a substantive law level, by means of which the substantive law outcome is altered and adjusted to the requirements of the country of origin.

The CJEU's decision in the *eDate Advertising* case was that:

> Article 3 of Directive 2000/31/EC of the European Parliament and of the Council of 8 June 2000 on certain legal aspects of information society services, in particular electronic commerce, in the Internal Market ('Directive on electronic commerce'), must be interpreted as *not requiring transposition in the form of a specific conflict-of-laws rule*. Nevertheless, in relation to the coordinated field, Member States must ensure that, subject to the derogations authorised in accordance with the conditions set out in Article 3(4) of Directive 2000/31, the provider of an electronic commerce service is not made subject to stricter requirements than those provided for by the substantive law applicable in the Member State in which that service provider is established. (emphasis added)

This passage must be interpreted to mean that the choice-of-law process needs to be allowed to operate without interference. In paragraph 61, the

---

[69]   Although there may be confusion there as well. See C-381/98 *Ingmar GB Ltd v Eaton Leonard Technologies Inc.* [2000] ECR I-9305.

Court emphasizes that article 3(1) does impose on a Member State an obligation to ensure that ISS services on their territory comply with the national provisions of that state. The Court proceeds to say that this is not, in nature, a conflicts rule. To the question concerning the clash of such laws with laws of other states in which ISSs operate, the Court, in paragraph 67, stated:

> In relation to the mechanism provided for by Article 3 of the Directive, it must be held that the fact of making electronic commerce services subject to the legal system of the Member State in which their providers are established pursuant to Article 3(1) does not allow the free movement of services to be fully guaranteed if the service providers must ultimately comply, in the host Member State, with stricter requirements than those applicable to them in the Member State in which they are established.

A provider, therefore, cannot be subject to stricter requirements than those in the home state. The solution is phrased differently from that found in Advocate General Cruz Villalón's Opinion. On this point the Advocate General insisted that article 3(1) imposed neither a choice-of-law rule nor a 'corrective at a substantive law level'. The article, in his view:

> gives concrete legislative expression, in terms of harmonisation, to the freedom to provide services as applied to electronic commerce, while also empowering the Member States, within the margin of discretion granted to them by the directive and by Article 56 TFEU, to lay down measures for the protection of rights which warrant special safeguards, by way of a derogation from the freedom to provide services.

It is difficult to escape the conclusion that the chosen solution treats article 3(1) as a specific form of an EU mandatory rule which operates as a corrective to substantive law. This is reinforced in paragraph 64 where the Court insists that 'it must be possible to apply mandatory provisions of a directive that are necessary to achieve the objectives of the internal market notwithstanding a choice of different law'. In light of such a solution, which clearly contradicts article 1(4), it is to be expected that the Commission will, in due course, suggest a change to one of the presently contradictory articles.

5   THE INTERNET AND ALTERNATIVE DISPUTE RESOLUTION

Alternative dispute resolution (ADR) is a term that refers to a number of techniques and processes for conflict resolution that do not involve formal litigation. While various forms exist, negotiation, mediation and arbitration are the most widely practised ones. Disputes that arise in relation to the use of the Internet (either in business-to-business (B2B) or B2C contexts) and which can be resolved by reference to an ADR mechanism are conceptually somewhat different from online dispute resolution (ODR),[70] which involves communication, mediation or resolution online. Several EU instruments deal with alternative dispute resolution.

Out-of-court dispute settlement is covered in article 17 of the E-Commerce Directive. The primary obligation is not to hamper the use of out-of-court schemes that are available under national law in any dispute involving an information society services provider and the recipient of services. The addressees of this obligation are the governments and the obligation specifically includes electronic means of dispute resolution. In addition, Member States have the duty to encourage the bodies responsible for out-of-court settlement to operate in a way which provides adequate procedural guarantees for the parties concerned. This specifically includes consumer disputes. Finally, Member States must encourage the same out-of-court dispute settlement bodies to inform the Commission of the significant decisions they take regarding information society services and to transmit any other information on the practices, usages or customs relating to electronic commerce.

Since a large number of consumer contracts are concluded by reference to the seller's standard terms and since these terms often refer to mandatory arbitration, the question imposes itself whether such arbitration is binding on the consumer. In terms of consumer protection, mandatory EU rules apply. Directive 93/13 on unfair terms in consumer contracts[71] prohibits clauses that are:

> excluding or hindering the consumer's right to take legal action or exercise any other legal remedy, particularly by requiring the consumer to take

---

[70]   For an overview of ODR, see S. Kierkegaard, 'Online Alternative Dispute Resolution' in R. Nielssen, S.S.Jacobsen and J. Trzaskowski (eds.), *EU Electronic Commerce Law* (Djøf, Copenhagen, 2004), p. 177.

[71]   Unfair Terms in Consumer Contracts Directive [1993] OJ L95/29, 21 April 1993.

disputes exclusively to arbitration not covered by legal provisions, unduly restricting the evidence available to him or imposing on him a burden of proof which, according to the applicable law, should lie with another party to the contract.

The situation is somewhat complicated by the presence of the new EU 2011 ADR Directive (see below). That Directive allows Member States to opt for consumer arbitration but, if they do, forces them to abide by certain standards set out in articles 10 and 11. Moreover, the Directive is only applicable if the consumer initiates proceedings but not if the trader does. In latter cases, general EU rules on unfair terms apply which only partially harmonize the rules, allowing for different views in different Member States. Thus, consumer arbitration remains prohibited in states such as France and limited in Germany, Spain and some other EU countries.[72]

The question was addressed in several of the CJEU's judgments. In *Katalin*,[73] a consumer had concluded a mortgage loan contract that contained a mandatory arbitration clause. The consumer contended that the mandatory arbitration clause was unfair as per Unfair Terms Directive, article 3(2). The Court ruled that it was for the national court to determine if such a clause was unfair.[74] The Court did, however, give two important guidelines. First, it must be verified whether 'the clause at issue has the object or effect of excluding or hindering the consumer's right to take legal action or exercise any other legal remedy'. Second, the fact that the consumer had been told, before the conclusion of the contract, about the differences between arbitration proceedings and ordinary legal proceedings cannot, in and of itself, 'rule out the unfairness of that clause'. This is in addition to an earlier case where the Court held that national courts must of their own motion determine if such clauses are unfair even if the consumer in question is not raising it as an issue.[75]

---

[72] See N. Reich, 'Party Autonomy and Consumer Arbitration in Contract: A "Trojan Horse" in the Access to Justice in the EU ADR-Directive 2013/11?' (2015) 4 *Penn State Journal of Law and International Affairs* 290.

[73] C-342/13 *Katalin Sebestyén v Zsolt Csaba Kővári and others*, ECLI: EU:C:2014:1857, 3 April 2014.

[74] This is in line with C-237/02 *Freiburger Kommunalbauten* [2004] ECR I-03403 where the CJEU confirmed that unfairness of the contract in terms of art. 3(1) is an issue for the national court.

[75] C-168/05 *Mostaza Claro* [2006] ECR I-10421.

Alternative and online dispute resolution have been the target of consistent efforts since 2008. The 2008 Mediation Directive[76] encourages the use of mediation as a means of settling disputes. The Directive applies to cross-border civil and commercial matters, with certain exclusions. Its main task is to compel Member States to authorize courts to suggest mediation, without making it mandatory. As such, the Directive does not contain detailed rules on mediation but provides guidelines concerning ensuring quality of mediation (article 4); appropriateness of a court's call to mediation (article 5); enforceability (Article 6); confidentiality (Article 7); and effect of mediation (Article 8).

The 2013 Directive on ADR in consumer disputes[77] is meant to improve redress for consumers in the context of the internal market. The addressees of the Directive are Member States and their main obligation is to facilitate consumers' access to ADR and improve the benefits they can obtain from such a system. As such, the Directive aims to improve access to ADR facilities and procedures (article 5); ensure expertise, independence and impartiality (article 6); and improve transparency (article 7); effectiveness (article 8); and fairness (article 9). The Directive specifically covers consumer standard terms which contain ADR clauses in article 10(1):

> Member States shall ensure that an agreement between a consumer and a trader to submit complaints to an ADR entity is not binding on the consumer if it was concluded before the dispute has materialised and if it has the effect of depriving the consumer of his right to bring an action before the courts for the settlement of the dispute.

Article 10(2) adds that particular solutions are only binding on parties if they had been informed of their binding nature in advance and 'specifically accepted this'. Furthermore, article 11 covers mandatory consumer protection rules in cases where a solution had been imposed on a consumer. In cases where both the trader and the consumer are habitually resident in one state, that state's consumer protection rules cannot be derogated from. Where they are not in the same state and the law applicable is determined by virtue of article 6 of the Rome I Regulation,

---

[76]   Directive 2008/52/EC of the European Parliament and of the Council of 21 May 2008 on certain aspects of mediation in civil and commercial matters [2008] OJ L136/3, 24 May 2008.

[77]   Directive 2013/11/EU of the European Parliament and of the Council of 21 May 2013 on alternative dispute resolution for consumer disputes and amending Regulation (EC) 2006/2004 and Directive 2009/22/EC (Directive on consumer ADR) [2013] OJ L165/63, 18 June 2013.

the protection afforded by that article cannot be derogated from. The Directive contains further provisions on information to the consumers and cooperation between ADR entities (Chapter III) and on the role of competent authorities (Chapter IV).

Drafted at the same time and meant to complement the former is the 2013 Regulation on consumer online dispute resolution,[78] which aims to create an online dispute resolution system for consumers. Unlike the ADR Directive, which only aims at facilitating alternative dispute resolution otherwise provided at national level, the ODR Regulation aims at creating an EU ODR platform. The Regulation applies to 'contractual obligations stemming from online sales or service contracts between a consumer resident in the Union and a trader established in the Union' provided that the ADR entity in question is listed in accordance with article 20 of the ADR Directive. The Regulation covers disputes that are initiated by the consumer but leaves the question of disputes which the trader initiates for the legislation of the state where the *consumer* is habitually resident. The Commission is in charge of establishing and maintaining the ODR platform (articles 6, 7). The Regulation further covers the submission (article 8), the processing and transmission of the complaint (article 9), and the resolution of the dispute (article 10). Articles 12 and 13 cover data protection while article 13 ensures that the consumer is adequately informed at all times. The platform was launched on 15 February 2016.

6 APPROACH IN THE UNITED STATES AND THE EU

Two general features distinguish the European rules-based system from the US discretion-based system.[79] First, the European system is more rigid than the American. National courts acting under Brussels I Regulation (Recast) *are obliged* to take jurisdiction and have no discretion to act otherwise. This means less flexibility but more certainty. Second, the European Regulation is not activated unless the defendant is domiciled in the Member State. If the defendant *is* domiciled in a Member State,

---

[78]   Regulation (EU) 524/2013 of the European Parliament and of the Council of 21 May 2013 on online dispute resolution for consumer disputes and amending Regulation (EC) 2006/2004 and Directive 2009/22/EC (Regulation on consumer ODR) [2013] OJ L165/1, 18 June 2013.

[79]   In detail see P. Borchers, 'Tort and Contract Jurisdiction via the Internet: The "Minimum Contacts" Test and the Brussels Regulation Compared' (2003) 50 *Netherlands International Law Review* 401.

traditional rules of jurisdiction do not operate at all and the use of the Regulation is mandatory.

US rules on jurisdiction *in personam* are complex, but can be described in outline as follows: a court is allowed to exercise jurisdiction *in personam* on the basis of presence, domicile, consent or activities having effect in the forum, the latter existing where the defendant's contacts with a jurisdiction were 'continuous or systematic'.[80] Formally, *general* international civil jurisdiction exists in the United States if the service of process can be effected and exists irrespective of the nature of the claim. If the defendant's activities in a state gave rise to the claim, such jurisdiction is *special* jurisdiction. If there is no general jurisdiction, specific jurisdiction may exist where the action relates to a single activity or relationship between the defendant and the forum, if it falls within the 'minimum contacts' framework and the jurisdiction is exercised reasonably. Sporadic or casual activity does not justify assertion of jurisdiction. For a non-resident defendant, jurisdiction is based on a continuous activity or presence. If the defendant is not resident in the jurisdiction, to comply with due process principles in terms of exercising jurisdiction over non-resident defendants, the defendant must have substantial or continuous and systematic contacts with the forum state.

In Internet disputes, US courts have experimented with various approaches. In *Inset Systems Inc. v Instruction Set*,[81] a Connecticut District Court said that purposefully directing web advertising activities towards Connecticut on a continuous basis satisfies the minimum contacts test. This meant that a simple creation of a webpage amounted to 'purposeful availment' and that the Web was equated to ordinary advertising.[82] An alternative approach was developed in *Bensusan*.[83] In that case, a New York District Court looked at specific circumstances of the case and introduced a difference between active and passive websites. The former actively target persons in the forum, by virtue of advertising, promotion or otherwise, the latter do not.

---

[80] *International Shoe Co. v Washington* 326 US 310, 316 (1945), US Supreme Court. See also *World-Wide Volkswagen Corp. v Woodson* 444 US 286, 291–2 (1980), US Supreme Court.

[81] 937 F. Supp. 161 (D. Conn. 1996).

[82] See M. Geist, 'The Shift Toward "Targeting" for Internet Jurisdiction' in A. Thierer and C. Crewds (eds.), *Who Rules the Net?* (Cato Institute, Washington, DC, 2003), p. 95.

[83] *Bensusan Restaurant Corp. v King* 126 F.3d 25, 29 (2d Cir. 1997).

An important publishing case, *Calder v Jones*,[84] involved a libellous article published in one but accessed in another state. Here the US Supreme Court held that a state could assert personal jurisdiction over the author and editor of a national magazine, which published an allegedly libellous article about a resident of that state, where the magazine had wide circulation in that state. The activities here (newspaper publishing) were intentionally directed at a California resident and could constitute jurisdiction.

A new Internet-specific approach to jurisdiction was adopted in 1997 in *Zippo Manufacturing Co. v. Zippo Dot Com Inc.* (the 'Zippo Test').[85] The court there distinguished the cases where the defendant does business over the Internet from situations where information is simply posted on the website. The former are active, the latter passive, but there are a number of situations in between where some form of interaction takes place. In the latter case, the court should examine the exercise of the existing level of interactivity:

> This sliding scale is consistent with well developed personal jurisdiction principles. At one end of the spectrum are situations where a defendant clearly does business over the Internet. If the defendant enters into contracts with residents of a foreign jurisdiction that involve the knowing and repeated transmission of computer files over the Internet, personal jurisdiction is proper. At the opposite end are situations where a defendant has simply posted information on an Internet Web site which is accessible to users in foreign jurisdictions. A passive Web site that does little more than make information available to those who are interested in it is not grounds for the exercise [of] personal jurisdiction. The middle ground is occupied by inter-active Web sites where a user can exchange information with the host computer. In these cases, the exercise of jurisdiction is determined by examining the level of interactivity and commercial nature of the exchange of information that occurs on the Web site.

For a while, the *Zippo* Test was dominant. But, in the first years of this century, US courts shifted towards a more sophisticated approach originally developed in *Calder v Jones*.[86] The question asked was: may a State court exercise jurisdiction over a non-resident newspaper, editor and its reporters in a libel action filed by a forum resident when the newspaper has a substantial circulation in the forum State and the newspaper, its

---

[84]   465 US 783 (1984).
[85]   952 F. Supp. 1119, 1126 (W.D. Pa. 1997), United States District Court for the Western District of Pennsylvania.
[86]   465 US 783 (1984).

editors and reporters aimed the article at the complaining forum resident
knowing it was likely to cause harm against the forum resident? This
approach, called the 'Effects Test', is based on a simple idea that
personal jurisdiction exists where the defendant's tort is aimed towards
the forum. At the same time, the defendant must have had knowledge that
harm will result from its actions. A strong confirmation of the targeting
doctrine happened in May 2003 when the Supreme Court rejected an
application for leave to appeal against a decision of the US Court of
Appeal in *Young v New Haven Advocate*.[87] The court held that defamation proceedings relating to material published online in Connecticut
cannot be commenced in Virginia. The court held that courts in Virginia
have no jurisdiction where the newspapers in question did not 'manifest
an intent to aim their websites or the posted articles at a Virginian
audience'.

Courts in the United States, unlike European and common law courts,
will not recognize and enforce foreign defamation judgments.[88] The
Internet as a 'brave new world of free speech'[89] requires that information
and ideas published be protected robustly and the First Amendment has
so far successfully provided that protection. While freedom of speech is a
basic human right, which enjoys considerable protection in many jurisdictions, no other state provides such extensive protection as the United
States.

Finally, criteria for choice of law rules (i.e. choice of choice-of-law
rules) are different in the United States and in Europe. Whereas the
United States relies on issue-selective approaches,[90] Europe uses a
rule-selection method. The result is more flexibility and less certainty in
the former and the opposite in the latter. In the United States, there has
never been much consensus on appropriate laws for multistate defamation[91] and it now seems that traditional rules, based on the plaintiff's

---

[87]   315 F. 3d 256 (4th Cir. 2002), United States Court of Appeals, Fourth
Circuit. See also *Revell v Lidov*, No. 01-10521 (5th Cir. Dec., 2002), United
States Court of Appeals, Fifth Circuit.
[88]   *Yahoo! v LICRA*, 169 F. Supp. 2d 1181 (N.D. Cal. 2001), United States
District Court, Northern District of California.
[89]   *Blumenthal v Drudge*, 992 F. Supp. 44 (D.D.C. 1998), United States
District Court, District of Columbia.
[90]   Such as those listed in *Restatement Second of Conflict of Laws*, para. 6.
[91]   See J. Pielemeier, 'Choice of Law for Multistate Defamation' (2003) 35
Arizona State Law Journal 55, 42.

domicile and contacts, may be out of date. It has been suggested[92] that specific rules for the Internet should be developed, but this suggestion remains doubtful.[93]

---

[92] Johnson and Post, 'Law and Borders', note 3 above, p. 1378.
[93] For other views, see L. Lessig, *Free Culture* (Penguin, London, 2004), pp. 277–87.

4. Speech and content regulation

The Internet was born with a promise of bringing a world without national boundaries, where content is distributed not from the centre but supplied and consumed at a low cost from the periphery. Such an Internet was supposed to be free of national control as it was assumed that content placed on it either cannot or will not be regulated.[1] Although this view proved to be an illusion, the exact extent to which the Internet is controlled remains controversial.[2]

By content regulation we understand various state-initiated efforts to control the *substance* of the Internet rather than its *technical* aspects. Although the regulation of Internet technologies can and does have an impact on its content, the problem of content control primarily concerns direct regulation of content. Content control may be defined as an effort to ensure that certain types of information on the Internet are not seen, or are seen by certain groups of users only or under certain circumstances only. In broadest terms, this is simply the question of whether a particular content can legally be put on the Internet in a certain jurisdiction, the circumstances under which this can be done, the regime for enforcing it and the consequences of the breach.

The measures through which content is controlled may involve public law, such as criminal or administrative sanctions, or private law, such as the law of defamation or intellectual property law, or hybrid branches, such as media and telecommunications law. In this chapter, content regulation is looked at through a number of issues which are conceptually connected and which are chosen for their practical importance. The first is the control of illegal and harmful content. The second is free speech and defamation. The third is copyright infringement. The final two are sexually explicit speech and hate speech.[3] Before we briefly look

---

[1] On this, see Chapter 1.

[2] For an overview of filtering across the Globe, see R. Deibert *et al.*, *Access Denied: The Practice and Policy of Global Internet Filtering* (MIT Press, Cambridge, MA, 2008).

[3] Criminal law related problems such as hacking and terrorism are addressed in Chapter 10.

at each, we will give a concise overview of the forms of regulation in the European Union and the constitutional principles that govern it.[4]

1 INTRODUCTION: FORMS OF REGULATION AND CONSTITUTIONAL PRINCIPLES

The legal framework for content protection is constitutionally divided between the EU and the Member States. Unlike the Single Market, where EU competence is clear, the majority of areas concerning content regulation fall squarely within national competence with the EU acting from the periphery only. Its main influence comes in the form of general constitutional principles which have an indirect bearing on the subject. In addition to this, the EU regulates content directly in certain narrow areas. This form of regulation is possible where the legal basis arises from other Treaty Articles. For example, the Audiovisual Media Services Directive (AVMS, discussed in section 2.2 below) regulates, in addition to other issues, some forms of audio-visual content. Finally, both the EU and Member States employ a range of soft-law instruments. This form of regulation relies on recommendations, codes of conduct and similar documents. These often concern non-digital issues and only deal with the Internet indirectly[5] but, occasionally, they are devoted mostly to content.[6]

Basic European constitutional principles govern the area of content control and have some influence over it. Among these, general free movement principles and principles governing freedom of expression are of particular relevance. Articles 49, 54 and 114 of the Treaty on the Functioning of the European Union (TFEU), the standard sources for regulating electronic commerce, do not have a direct impact on the *nature* of the regulated content. On the other hand, they do ensure that free movement of goods and services are EU-protected values. The goods

---

[4] For a general overview of issues concerning speech regulation see E. Laidlaw, *Regulating Speech in Cyberspace* (CUP, Cambridge, 2015).

[5] See European Parliament, *Report on Eliminating Gender Stereotypes in the EU*, 2012/2116(INI) (6 December 2012), which calls for a 'policy to eliminate stereotypes in the media' which will 'involve action in the digital field' and 'the launching of initiatives coordinated at EU level with a view to developing a genuine culture of equality on the internet' and the eventual creation of a Charter that would address this.

[6] Decision No. 276/1999/EC of the European Parliament and of the Council of 25 January 1999 adopting a multiannual Community action plan on promoting safer use of the Internet by combating illegal and harmful content on global networks [1999] OJ L033/1, 6 February 1999.

and services, which may be carriers of content, are therefore free to move between Member States. Where a limitation on Internet content is imposed at national level but the situation involves free movement of goods or services across EU borders, the principles can be invoked to protect the content. In that case, a discriminatory limitation can only be defended by invoking a specific exception, such as public policy, and other exceptions in Article 36 TFEU. A non-discriminatory limitation can also rely on a court-created list of mandatory exceptions. A putative national law prohibiting the distribution of obscene material which would include particular kinds of pornography would be scrutinized for its validity in light of free movement provisions but could be justified in principle.

Freedom of speech is constitutionally protected in Article 10 of the 1950 European Convention on Human Rights (ECHR):

1.   Everyone has the right to freedom of expression. This right shall include freedom to hold opinions and to receive and impart information and ideas without interference by public authority and regardless of frontiers. This article shall not prevent States from requiring the licensing of broadcasting, television or cinema enterprises.
2.   The exercise of these freedoms, since it carries with it duties and responsibilities, may be subject to such formalities, conditions, restrictions or penalties as are prescribed by law and are necessary in a democratic society, in the interests of national security, territorial integrity or public safety, for the prevention of disorder or crime, for the protection of health or morals, for the protection of the reputation or rights of others, for preventing the disclosure of information received in confidence, or for maintaining the authority and impartiality of the judiciary.

This constitutional protection is repeated in the constitutions of the Member States, including the formalities and conditions mentioned in paragraph 2. Government actions which limit free speech on the Internet are subject to regular challenges for violation on freedom of expression grounds.[7]

An important line of cases interpreting Article 10 ECHR has been developed by the European Court of Human Rights (ECtHR). In *Pravoye Delo*,[8] the ECtHR expressly acknowledged that Article 10 ECHR imposes an obligation on states to ensure protection of the freedom of

---

[7]   UN General Assembly, *Report of the Special Rapporteur on the Promotion and Protection of the Right to Freedom of Opinion and Expression*, A/HRC/14/23 (20 April 2010).
[8]   *Pravoye Delo and Shtekel v Ukraine*, App. No. 33014/05, 5 May 2011.

speech on the Internet. Further to that, the ECtHR emphasized that political reporting and journalists enjoy a high level of Article 10 protection.[9] On the other hand, the Court is also ready to conduct a balancing of various interests (such as the right of privacy, the right of reputation, etc.) against freedom of expression and to set clear limits to Article 10 in cases where that was demanded by other interests.[10]

Article 11 of the 2000 Charter of Fundamental Rights of the European Union provides similar protection:

1. Everyone has the right to freedom of expression. This right shall include freedom to hold opinions and to receive and impart information and ideas without interference by public authority and regardless of frontiers.
2. The freedom and pluralism of the media shall be respected.

The EU declares itself committed to opening up access, although it does not constitutionally protect it. In the Digital Agenda 2010–2020,[11] for example, it lists a number of required actions which can be interpreted as an effort to reduce national content control and open up access to content. Among them, the first key action is to 'simplify copyright clearance, management and cross-border licensing' while key action 5 introduces a review of EU standardization policy.

An example of the EU soft law approach at constitutional level are the 2014 Guidelines on Freedom of Expression.[12] Their aim is to provide 'political and operational guidance' on how to track and prevent potential violations. The addressees are both the EU and Member States. The document lists certain 'Priority Areas of Action'. It addresses combatting prosecution and harassment of both individuals and journalists for expressing their opinions, promoting laws and practices that protect freedom of opinion and discouragement of authorities' unwarranted interference with media freedoms. A separate heading is dedicated to

---

[9] See *Times Newspapers Ltd v United Kingdom*, App. Nos. 3002/03 and 23676/03, 10 March 2009.

[10] On details of how Art. 10 ECHR is applied in the Internet context see European Court of Human Rights, Research Division, *Internet: Case-law of the European Court of Human Rights* (June 2015), available at www.echr.coe.int/Documents/Research_report_internet_ENG.pdf.

[11] COM(2010)245 (19 May 2010).

[12] Council of the European Union, EU Human Rights Guidelines on Freedom of Expression Online and Offline (12 May 2014), available at https://ec.europa.eu/digital-single-market/en/news/eu-human-rights-guidelines-freedom-expression-online-and-offline.

'Promoting and respecting human rights in cyberspace and other information and communication technologies'. Six action areas are listed
there, the most prominent of them being 'unhindered, uncensored and
non-discriminatory access to ICTs and online services for all' and work
against 'any attempts to block, jam, filter, censor or close down communication networks or any kind of other interference that is in violation
of international law'. The governance model promoted is the 'multi-
stakeholder model' which simply means that the aim is to bring various
stakeholders, including industry representatives and non-governmental
organizations (NGOs), together.

In spite of this, the constitutional framework of the EU, while
protecting content through free movement, freedom of expression and
other constitutional provisions, stops short of proclaiming absolute freedom of speech akin to the First Amendment to the US Constitution.[13] A
number of Member States have express provisions against speech that
incites racial hatred.

The EU has no laws which directly regulate illegal and harmful
content[14] but engages instead in a number of initiatives and self-
regulatory policy initiatives which are meant to have an impact on
Internet content. A prime example of this approach is the Safer Internet
Action Plan 1999–2004.[15] It forms part of a set of policies at EU level
designed to fight illegal and harmful content on the Internet but, in
reality, has rather limited ambitions. It primarily encourages self-
regulation and the use of codes of conduct and promotes filtering tools.

A number of EU initiatives specifically target children and the young.
For example, the European Framework for Safer Mobile Use by Young
Teenagers and Children[16] was created in 2007. It introduces principles
and measures designed to improve the safety of the young on mobile
platforms. In 2012, the Commission created the Strategy for a better

---

[13]   On the First Amendment's importance and history, see B. Neuborne,
Madison's Music: On Reading the First Amendment (New Press, New York,
2015).
[14]   The exception is found in limited efforts to regulate child pornography, see
Child Pornography Directive 2011/92/EU [2011] OJ L26/1, 17 December 2011
and Chapter 10 and, partially, the AVMS Directive (section 2.2 below).
[15]   See note 6 above. A follow up was drafted in 2005, see Decision No.
854/2005/EC of the European Parliament and of the Council of 11 May 2005
establishing a multiannual Community Programme on promoting safer use of the
Internet and new online technologies [2005] OJ C017, 11 June 2005.
[16]   SIPMC 07 26 (February 2007); see also Commission Press Release
IP/10/704 (9 June 2010).

Internet for children.[17] The Strategy aims to stimulate the production of creative and education content, improve digital literacy, stimulate age-appropriate privacy settings and combat child sexual abuse. The document's addressees are Member States, the industry and the EU itself. Another example is found in the Safer Social Networking Principles for the EU,[18] which is a self-regulatory agreement. The agreement contains guidelines for the use of social networking sites by children and has been adopted by a number of players in the industry.

2 ILLEGAL AND HARMFUL CONTENT

2.1 EU Approach to Harmful Content Regulation

Liability for illegal and harmful content posted on the Internet may arise in parts of the world where legal subjects do not expect it. There are potentially numerous instances of such extra-territorial reach. Liability, from the viewpoint of the claimant, is territorially indeterminable or difficult to localize, and therefore costly. A statement published on a French website may have effects in England, where the claimant has an interest which English courts would be prepared to protect. A person accessing and storing photos containing child pornography or illegally sharing movies may be located in the Cayman Islands but will easily be subject to the jurisdiction of the US courts on the ground of business contacts there. What is criminally punishable hate speech in Germany is constitutionally protected in the United States.

Liability in such cases may be criminal, in cases such as child pornography or counterfeiting and piracy, or it may be civil, in cases where the injured party sues for damages or restitution. The problem of liability arises, in case of individuals, out of illegal acts performed on or with the aid of the Internet. Internet service providers (ISPs) as intermediaries may also be subject to legal action where unlawful and illegal content is posted by others but transmitted through or stored on their servers.

---

[17] Communication from the Commission to the European Parliament, the Council, the European Economic and Social Committee and the Committee of the Regions, *European Strategy for a Better Internet for Children*, COM(2012)196 final (2 May 2012).

[18] See V. Donoso, *Assessment of the Implementation of the Safer Social Networking Principles for the EU on 9 Services: Summary Report* (European Commission, Safer Internet Programme, Luxembourg, August 2011).

For purposes of determining liability, the actors on the Internet can be distinguished based on the *capacity* in which they come in touch with the information, that is, whether they create, transmit or receive it. The first category involves posters of illicit content. A pirate who illegally obtains a copy of a movie and posts it on the Internet is primarily liable for copyright infringement and a person who distributes false information about another person is primarily liable for defamation. The second involves those who illegally access them. A user accessing and storing child pornography, for example, may be liable under these provisions. The third category involves intermediaries: this liability concerns ISPs understood in the wide sense of the word (i.e. including universities, Internet cafes or other entities that make the Internet available). Whereas the third category is insulated from liability under conditions which will be discussed in the next chapter most categories of illegality on the Internet apply to the first two. Thus, a copyright infringement action may hit both the original poster of a link to a pirated movie and the end-user. The same is true of other categories of illicit content, for example, content harmful to minors or content inciting racial hatred.

The same phenomenon (e.g. a publication of a defamatory statement) can be looked at either from the perspective of the *publication*, or the *transmission*. The first mentioned form of liability is the direct liability of individuals based on *information content*. This is liability that arises from material posted on the Internet and concerns individual posters and recipients (users). The typical categories here include defamation (libel), intellectual property infringements or the distribution of pornography. This is the liability of somebody who posts or accesses illegal content on the Internet and not of persons who transmit or distribute it through technological means. In the division of the Internet into layers, discussed in Chapter 1,[19] this liability concerns actions on the content layer.

The second is the liability of *intermediaries* such as ISPs, whose accountability arises not because they originated the content itself, but because they transmitted it. The existence of this category is intuitively understandable, as the anonymity that arises from the architecture of the Internet shields the individual users. It is in this context inevitable and financially viable to target the intermediaries.[20] Postings on the Internet are identifiable by their IP numbers but the practical accessibility of Internet users may be limited or, alternatively, it may be economically

---

[19]   See Chapter 1, note 10.
[20]   This has been, until the Recording Industry Association of America (RIAA) started individual lawsuits against file-sharers in 2004, the accepted route in the United States.

more efficient to target the ISPs. The idea behind this is that the ISPs, much like publishers, should bear the responsibility for content that is placed on their servers.

In spite of these attempts at categorization, the actors on the Internet are difficult to classify as they often play multiple (and occasionally conflicting) roles and are therefore difficult to make liable. In the EU, the E-Commerce Directive takes a broad definition of services for remuneration, therefore extending the scope of the protective provisions. It specifies in article 2 that these are 'information society services', thus extending the application of the Directive and its insulation against liability well beyond simple ISPs. Webpages hosted on private computers or those belonging to universities will typically fall within this category. In such cases, the Internet service need not be provided against payment.

Finally, the last category includes liability that cannot be included in either of the first two categories as it is triggered neither by posting material nor by transmitting. Tentatively, this category covers acts against the security of computer systems. These are typically hacking attacks perpetrated by third parties on illegally hijacked computers. The essence of the problem is in the fact that the party in question, either an ISP or an individual, unknowingly acts as a host for the attack that affects a third party. The benefit of such an approach is in the accessibility of hosts, as the actual attacker may be and usually is anonymous. The justification for making hosts liable is in the fact that hosts ought to have effective security measures in place, in the same way a proprietor of a dangerous manufacturing facility ought to secure it against attacks from the outside that may result in injury to passers-by. This may also be economically the most effective solution but no case law has emerged yet. It is to be expected that future attempts may be made in the law of torts.[21]

More widely, the last category can be described as comprising acts that take place on the Web and result in some form of disruption and damage to the affected party. Potentially, a whole range of acts may result in this kind of liability, such as breaking or hacking into computer systems that results in damage to, loss or theft of data; hacking into others' webpages and defacing them or changing their content; denial of service attacks; invasion of privacy; transmission of viruses or other malware; and threats to release confidential information.

In spite of the above provisional categorization, it appears difficult to summarize liability for acts taken on the Internet in the EU. The liability based on information content is not separately regulated in the EU but is

---

[21] For details, see Chapter 10.

affected by national criminal, civil and administrative law and a number of EU instruments, including the Brussels I Regulation (Recast). The most obvious forms of liability arise from defaming others, from infringing copyright, from circulating obscene material and from hate speech. These will be analysed below.

2.2   Audiovisual Media

The Audiovisual Media Services (AVMS) Directive,[22] which amended the Television Without Frontiers Directive (89/552/EC), imposes certain public policy obligations on editorially responsible service providers (including Internet-based ones) and subjects them to the law of their home state. In terms of content control this means that the providers based in one state would, in principle, avoid restrictive rules of another state (except in some special cases) in the coordinated areas, which, at present, include incitement to hatred, advertising and protection of minors.

Two things are of particular importance for content regulation on the Internet. First, Recital 25 underlines the importance of editorial responsibility for the activation of the Directive's functions. As per Recital 26, a person or a legal entity will not be treated as a media service provider if they are merely transmitters and do not bear editorial responsibility. This has the important effect of extending the effects to all who exercise editorial control but also of protecting those who only transmit.

Secondly, the Directive regulates both traditional television (linear services) and video-on-demand (non-linear services, 'TV-like' services), although it subjects the latter to a somewhat less demanding regime.[23] Recital 22 is clear about the Internet falling within the scope of the Directive as it talks of all websites except those 'the principal purpose of which is not the provision of programmes, i.e. where any audio-visual content is merely incidental to the service and not its principal purpose'. Recital 24 emphasizes that 'on-demand' services inclusion is thanks to their ability to compete for the same audience and the users' desire to have the same protection. The word 'programme' must here be interpreted in a dynamic way. Recital 27 specifically names 'analogue and digital television, live streaming, webcasting and near-video-on-demand'. Recital 27 also emphasizes that, where both linear and non-linear services are offered, and they differ, both are covered in their own right.

---

[22]   Audiovisual Media Services Directive 2010/13/EU [2010] OJ L95/1, 15 April 2010.
[23]   Recital 58.

An important grey area is audio-video content distributed through platforms and intermediaries that cannot easily be subsumed under the rather wide definition of article 1(g). That article, namely, defines 'on demand' services as those:

> provided by a media service provider for the viewing of programmes at the moment chosen by the user and at his individual request on the basis of a catalogue of programmes selected by the media service provider.

A website such as YouTube would likely fall within the scope of the Directive but a website containing short clips or animations might not. In a judgment from 2015, the Court of Justice of the European Union (CJEU) ruled that the AVMS Directive covers 'the provision of videos of short duration consisting of local news bulletins, sports and entertainment clips' which is taking place under the subdomain of a newspaper website.[24] In that case, what was important was whether the video clips were 'independent' of the journalistic activity or not. The European Regulators Group for Audiovisual media services, established in 2014 to provide an advisory function, published a Report in 2016,[25] in which it analysed the complex situation concerning, among others, 'TV-like' programmes. It recommended that the definition in article 1(b) be revisited with a view to increasing certainty.

Article 2 of the Directive introduces the country of origin principle and subjects service providers to the law of their own country, defined in paragraph 2 of that article, with the exception for broadcasters from third states using an up-link in an EU country. The latter are to be subject to the law whose up-link they use or, if that is not the case, the law of the state whose satellite capacity they use. The provision applies primarily to providers established in a Member State, irrespective of the place where the editorial control is undertaken.

The relevant content control rules are found in article 3, which provides:

> Member States shall ensure freedom of reception and shall not restrict retransmissions on their territory of audiovisual media services from other Member States for reasons which fall within the fields coordinated by this Directive.

---

[24]   C-347/14 *New Media Online GmbH v Bundeskommunikationssenat,* ECLI:EU:C:2015:709, 21 October 2015.

[25]   ERGA, *Report on Material Jurisdiction in a Converged Environment,* ERGA2015(12) (18 December 2015).

Member States are allowed to derogate from article 3(1) in special cases concerning on-demand services. If they wish to do so, article 3(4) provides that measures: (i) must be necessary; (ii) must be taken against services which 'prejudice' the objectives mentioned in paragraph (i); and (iii) must be proportionate. Article 3(4)(i) clarifies that the objectives for which derogations can be obtained relate to public policy and, in particular:

- the prevention, investigation, detection and prosecution of criminal offences, including the protection of minors and the fight against any incitement to hatred on grounds of race, sex, religion or nationality, and violations of human dignity concerning individual persons;
- the protection of public health;
- public security, including the safeguarding of national security and defence;
- the protection of consumers, including investors.

Article 4 allows Member States to introduce more stringent and detailed rules. Where a broadcaster establishes itself in another Member State to circumvent stricter rules in the second state, the first state has jurisdiction to apply the appropriate measures.

Article 6 prohibits 'incitement to hatred based on race, sex, religion or nationality'. Article 9 addresses audio-visual commercial communications and provides that they must not use 'subliminal' techniques which, in this context, must be understood as those that appeal to the consumer's subconscious. Additionally, commercial communications must not prejudice respect for 'human dignity' or incite discrimination based on 'sex, racial or ethnic origin, nationality, religion or belief, disability, age or sexual orientation', encourage behaviour prejudicial to health and safety or to the protection of the environment. The advertising of tobacco products is banned and that of alcohol products must not be directed at minors, while commercials for medicaments only available on prescription are prohibited. Commercial communications must not cause 'physical or moral detriment' to minors.

Special rules apply to on-demand services. Article 12 protects minors, stating that services which may 'impair the physical, mental or moral development of minors' must be delivered in such a way as to ensure that minors will not 'normally' be able to see them. The article does not give details as to what measures constitute effective filtering. The European Regulators Group for Audiovisual Media Services (ERGA) Report on minors[26] recommended that the regulatory delimitation between linear and non-linear be revised since both the access and content harmfulness differ significantly. They recommended the creation of an EU-wide list of content that is 'likely to impair' or content that 'might seriously impair'.

Article 13 requires that on-demand services promote, 'where practicable', the production of and access to European works.

While the extension of the Directive to on-demand services is to be congratulated, a number of questions remain. One of them relates to the status of services provided mainly and exclusively on the Internet that are subject both to the general electronic commerce regime and the regime created under the AVMS Directive. Video distribution sites such as YouTube or Vimeo are available both as traditional websites (and thus clearly under the scope of the E-Commerce Directive) and as on-demand services through television and video sets that are increasingly connected to the Internet. Such sites should be able to avail themselves of the home country control principle of article 3 of the E-Commerce Directive but may also be subject to the circumvention control regime of article 4 of the AVMS Directive. The question is of importance in all instances where competitive services are under asymmetric treatment but have a similar competitive impact on the market.

Another question is the potential extension of the Directive's scope beyond the current definition of 'non-linear' services, the inclusion of which currently hangs on whether such activities are independent of the main journalistic activity or not. It would seem that an extension of the Directive's sphere of application to all services, which compete with regular TV distribution, would be a possibility. Further to this, the current regime does not apply to services based in non-EU countries but targeting EU customers. The inclusion of those services would potentially make sense, since the demand for American TV streaming services, in particular, is high.

A proposal for revision of the AVMS Directive was tabled in May 2016.[27] The Proposal is meant to strengthen the country of origin principle on which the Directive is based, simplifying the rules on the basis of which the state's jurisdiction over the provider is determined. In addition to that, the Proposal contains new rules on commercial communication and the percentage of European works that on-demand services need to broadcast is set at 20 per cent. The grounds for

---

[26] ERGA, *Report on the Protection of Minors in a Converged Environment*, ERGA(2015)13 (27 November 2015).

[27] Brussels, COM(2016)287 final (25 May 2016).

prohibiting hate speech are to be aligned to those in the Framework Decision on combating certain forms and expressions of racism and xenophobia.[28]

An important change comes for video sharing platform providers, which are put under an obligation to 'protect minors from content which may impair their physical, mental or moral development' and protect everybody from hate speech.[29] The measures include the use of terms and conditions, mechanisms for reporting or flagging the inappropriate content, age verification and rating systems and parental control. While Member States are not allowed to impose stricter measures than those prescribed in respect of ordinary content, they will be able to do so in respect of illegal content.

3 DEFAMATION

3.1 Some Regulatory Models: Australia, United Kingdom and the United States

The law of defamation plays a vital role in attempting to 'reconcile the competing interests of freedom of expression and the protection of individual reputation'.[30] The regulation of defamation on the Internet varies widely across the globe.[31] In the EU, civil lawsuits for defamatory acts are the norm but criminal sanctions have not completely been abandoned. In a 2014 report analysing criminal defamation and insult laws, the International Press Institute concluded that, although the general trend is to abandon criminalization of defamatory acts, a number of EU Member States still have such laws on the book. The majority of states, worryingly, still have criminal laws punishing insult to state symbols.[32]

Most significant disagreements concerning defamation on the Internet today are about the place where the defaming material was 'published'.

---

[28]   Decision 2008/913/JHA.
[29]   Proposal, art. 28(a).
[30]   M. Collins, *The Law of Defamation* (3rd edn, OUP, Oxford, 2010), p. 4.
[31]   See A. Kenyon, *Comparative Defamation and Privacy Law* (CUP, Cambridge, 2016).
[32]   For an overview of EU laws, see International Press Institute, *Out of Balance: Defamation Laws in the European Union and its Effect on Press Freedom* (July 2014), available at https://ec.europa.eu/digital-single-market/en/news/out-balance-defamation-law-european-union.

This question has two sides. The first is: who is considered to be a 'publisher', and the second: in which jurisdiction will the publisher be liable? In principle, in the United Kingdom and in Australia, the publisher is anyone who posts or transmits the material and the liability will arise where the material is accessed. In the United States, however, liability arises only in cases where the material was directed or targeted towards a particular jurisdiction. In response to the first question, most EU Member States provide that publishers who with intention or negligence publish material are as responsible as the original author.

In 2002, the Australian High Court decided *Gutnick v Dow Jones*.[33] The case concerned defamation proceedings brought in Australia by Mr Gutnick against Dow Jones, a US company owner of *Barron's* magazine, where allegedly defamatory statements concerning Mr Gutnick were published. Most of the readership of that magazine was located in the United States, but a minority also existed in Australia. The offending article was published in the print version of the magazine but also in its online version. In the proceedings, Dow Jones claimed that publication occurred where the material was placed on the Internet – in the United States – and that a single publication rule, which provides that publication occurs only when material is placed in circulation for the first time and not on subsequent occasions, should apply to subsequent dissemination. Mr Gutnick claimed that publication occurs every time an item is read and comprehended – in this case in Australia. The Australian High Court took the view that an Internet article is published where it is *accessed and comprehended*, that is, downloaded, therefore potentially opening the gates to litigation in all cases where the material is accessible in another country.

In the United Kingdom, the position is underlined by several cases. In *Godfrey v Demon*,[34] a statement defamatory of the plaintiff was posted on an Internet bulletin board in the United States. It appeared in the United Kingdom through Godfrey's own Internet service provider, Demon. Having unsuccessfully notified Demon and tried to have them remove the offending posting, Godfrey sued in defamation. The ISP defended itself by claiming that it is only a passive distributor and therefore should not be held liable for publication. The court held that transmitting and/or hosting the material *with actual knowledge* amounted to publication. Similar reasoning was seen in *Loutchensky v Times*,[35] where a Russian

---

[33]   [2002] HCA 56.
[34]   [1999] 4 All ER 342.
[35]   [2002] QB 321 and [2002] QB 783.

businessman brought a libel case against *The Times* newspaper. The Court of Appeal accepted the defence of qualified privilege, which provides immunity from damages for material published in the public interest the truth of which cannot be proved in court, but rejected the contention that the same defence should apply to the archived parts of *The Times* newspaper. *Harrods v Dow Jones*[36] rested on similar facts as the Australian *Gutnick* case. Dow Jones sought a stay of English proceedings claiming that England was not the proper forum to hear the case. The High Court refused to stay, saying that publication took place where the material was downloaded and read – in England. Therefore, two separate publications took place: one in the United States, where the magazine was distributed, and one in England, where the website was accessible. In *Don King v Lennox Lewis*,[37] a defamatory statement was made in the United States and both the defendant and the plaintiffs were based there. An application was made to serve out of jurisdiction, which the defendants sought to set aside. This was rejected, with the court emphasizing that Don King enjoyed a substantial reputation in England and that English law regards Internet publication to have occurred where the material was accessed. In *Bunt v Tilley*,[38] various defendants, three of which were ISPs, posted defamatory statements on websites. The judge said that the three ISPs had not 'in any meaningful sense, knowingly participated in the relevant publications'. After the cases cited, it seems clear that while a knowledgeable intermediary is liable, a mere conduit one is not.

The position in the United States is markedly different from that in both Australia and the United Kingdom. The two important early cases are *Cubby, Inc. v CompuServe Inc.*[39] and *Stratton Oakmont, Inc. v Prodigy Services Company.*[40] *Cubby* revolved around an online forum on journalism, owned by CompuServe, but independently managed by another firm, Cameron Communications. The latter had a contract with a third firm, Don Fitzpatrick Associates, for the provision of a gossip newsletter named *Rumorville USA*. Under that contract, Don Fitzpatrick accepted full responsibility for the content. The plaintiffs, publishers of a rival service, claimed that they were defamed in several editions of *Rumorville USA*. The judge equated Compuserve's status to that of a

---

[36]   [2003] EWHC 1162 (QB).
[37]   [2004] EWHC 168 (QB).
[38]   [2007] WLR 1243.
[39]   776 F. Supp. 135 (SD NY, 1991), US District Court, Southern District of New York.
[40]   1995 WL 323710, New York Supreme Court.

public library or a newsstand. The former has as much control over the content of the publication as the latter, and to make it liable as a publisher would be to seriously hamper the freedom of speech protected by the First Amendment of the US Constitution. It would be observed here that the result under the limitation of liability provisions of the E-Commerce Directive would have been the same, provided that the ISP had no actual knowledge of the information or activity.

In *Stratton Oakmont*, Prodigy was hosting a financial bulletin called *Money Talk*. The plaintiffs alleged that they have been defamed by statements posted on the board. It was held that Prodigy was a publisher, not a distributor, under the law of the state of New York. Prodigy, unlike CompuServe in the previous case, had exercised editorial control over the content and also used automatic screening software and content guidelines.

On 19 May 2003, the Supreme Court confirmed a case decided by a Court of Appeal in *Young v New Heaven Advocate*.[41] In that case, it was held that defamation proceedings for material published in Connecticut could not be commenced in Virginia simply because defamatory statements were accessible there. It was held that the alleged defaming newspapers did not target their websites towards a Virginian audience.

Zeran v AOL[42] involved defamatory statements posted on AOL's bulletin board. The poster was unidentified, but Zeran notified AOL, which assured Zeran that postings would be removed, but subsequently failed to act. Zeran filed a lawsuit against AOL, claiming that AOL was liable for defamation. The court rejected this argument, saying that, pursuant to section 230 of the Communication Decency Act (CDA) 1996, the Internet service provider is never liable for defamatory material posted by third parties, even where the ISP has been previously notified.[43] The court, defending the vigour of Internet communication, said that to impose tort liability in cases concerning ISPs would force the latter to constantly monitor the traffic on their networks. This would have a negative impact both on their business and, more importantly, on freedom of speech. But, this case also highlights the problematic implications of encouraging the ISPs to have editorial control, which was also evident in the *Prodigy* case (above). Put in different terms, it seems that the price that the ISPs have paid for this effective insulation from

---

[41]   315 F. 3d 256 (4th Cir. 2002).
[42]   129 F. 3d 327 (4th Cir. 1997), US Court of Appeals, Fourth Circuit.
[43]   For this line of reasoning, see also *Blumenthal v Drudge*, 992 F. Supp. 44 (DDC 1998) and *Doe v America Online*, 718 So. 2d 385 (4th Cir. 1999), US Court of Appeals, Fourth Circuit.

liability is the loss of it in all cases where they have exercised editorial control, placed adequate filtering or have done anything else to insulate themselves.

3.2   Defamation in the EU

The described provisions of the previous three jurisdictions relate to situations where national courts (Australian, English, US) take jurisdiction for material accessible on their territory and apply their defamation law. The EU has not harmonized substantive law on defamation, but it has dealt to a considerable extent with jurisdiction and choice-of-law issues and its general rules on ISP limitation of liability, located in the E-Commerce Directive, apply. There are, therefore, three European sources that have an impact on domestic defamation law in general, and on defamation on the Internet in specific. The first is the Brussels I Regulation (Recast). That Regulation contains jurisdiction rules that determine which courts will hear the case concerning defamation online.[44] Together with this may be considered the Rome II Regulation on the law applicable to tort.[45] The final source is the E-Commerce Directive and its provisions on ISP liability. The last of these, it has to be remarked, concerns only the liability of intermediaries and normally has no impact on national defamation cases involving subjects which are not transmitters but are primary publishers (see below).

When will courts of Member State A take jurisdiction for a defamatory article posted on the Internet in Member State B? Article 7(2) of the EU Regulation on jurisdiction and judgments provides that:

> A Person domiciled in a Member State may, in another Member State, be sued … in matters relating to tort, delict or quasi-delict, in the courts for the place where the harmful event occurred or may occur.

The CJEU in *Shevill v Presse Alliance*[46] ruled that the victim of libel by a newspaper article distributed in several Member States may bring an action in damages against the publisher either in the court of a Member State where the publisher was established or before the courts of each Member State in which the publication was distributed. In the case of the former, the court has jurisdiction to award damages for all the harm

---

44   Notably art. 7(2) on tort. See Chapter 3.
45   See Chapter 3.
46   C-68/93 *Shevill v Presse Alliance* [1995] ECR I-415.

caused by defamation; in respect of the latter, only in respect of the harm caused in the Member State of the court seized.

In light of the *eDate* case discussed in Chapter 3,[47] an action can be brought 'in respect of all the damage caused, either before the courts of the Member State in which the publisher of that content is established or before the courts of the Member State in which the centre of his interests is based'. Additionally, in respect of the damage caused in the territory of the Member State only, an action can be brought before the courts of that state if the content was placed online or has been accessible there. This decision is important as it makes the claimant's position more certain. Instead of suing in a number of Member States, only one will be enough, but where the plaintiff is interested in covering one state only, this will also be possible. The general problem, however, may be to locate the defendant. A statement published on an Internet blog, for instance, may be signed with a pseudonym, making identification difficult and requiring a further action to reveal the identity of the publisher. More importantly, the claimant may not have the financial and legal resources to bring an action in a state other than the home state in which he is located. In that respect, the other option – to sue in the state where the content has been distributed – may not be better.

As for the role of intermediaries, taking articles 12 to 15 of the E-Commerce Directive into account, it can be said that intermediaries who knowingly host defamatory material would not be able to avail themselves of the protection in that article. If intermediaries are 'mere conduits', as per article 12, the protective provision would be effective as long as the conditions of that article are fulfilled. Taking into consideration the present EU case law, which remains fairly consistent,[48] those intermediaries who host or cache material published by others ought to avoid liability as long as they remove it in a manner that articles 13 and 14 prescribe. Article 15, which prohibits monitoring, must be consistently applied here, which means that no legal obligation to actively look for and remove defamatory material exists. The same can be said of search engines, which cannot be held liable for displaying results which contain potentially defamatory material.[49]

The rights and freedoms enshrined in the European Convention on Human Rights form part of the laws of Member States. Of primary

---

[47]   Joined Cases C-509/09 and C-161/10 *eDate Advertising GmbH v X*; *Olivier Martinez and Robert Martinez v MGN Ltd.*, ECLI:EU:C:2011:685, 25 October 2011.

[48]   See Chapter 5 for details.

[49]   For exceptions relating to issues involving privacy, see Chapter 8.

importance here is Article 10[50] ECHR which can potentially come into conflict with defamation verdicts in favour of claimants.[51] The greatest protection in the ECHR is afforded by the court to political speech.[52] Similar levels of protection are afforded to other matters of public concern. On the other hand, commercial and artistic speech, while also deserving protection, are not accorded the same level of protection. There are, as yet, no direct cases that deal with this problem but the general jurisprudence of the Court can be extrapolated onto Internet cases.[53] In *The Times v United Kingdom*,[54] the Court said that the publisher's Article 10 ECHR right could be interfered with in cases where a defamation action was brought against it for material *archived* on the Internet. Article 8 ECHR, which protects private and family life, may be an element in a defamation action where a severe attack on the personal integrity of the applicant exists.[55] In such cases, Articles 8 and 10 may have to be weighed and balanced. The ECtHR has, in recent years, read the 'right to reputation' into Article 8 which did not originally contain it. In order to balance Articles 8 and 10, it suggested a number of criteria.[56]

4   COPYRIGHT INFRINGEMENT AS A TOOL FOR CONTENT CONTROL: DAMAGES, MORAL RIGHTS AND PARODY

Copyright protection is the subject of a separate chapter in this book. In this section we look at copyright rules from the prism of content control only. The idea is that copyright protection can be used as a tool for monitoring which groups of users access the material in a manner

---

[50]   Also of some importance may be other Articles, such as Article 6 (right to a fair and public hearing) or Article 8 (privacy and family rights).

[51]   On how the ECtHR has dealt with the problem of intermediaries in this context, see Chapter 5.

[52]   See M. Collins, *The Law of Defamation and the Internet* (2nd edn, OUP, Oxford, 2005), ch. 30.

[53]   Collins, *The Law of Defamation and the Internet*, note 52 above, pp. 461–3.

[54]   [2009] EMLR 14.

[55]   Collins, *The Law of Defamation and the Internet*, note 52 above, p. 464.

[56]   *Axel Springer v Germany* [2012] ECHR 227; *Von Hannover v Germany (No. 2)* [2012] ECHR 228. See H. Tomlinson, 'Privacy and Defamation, Strasbourg Blurs the Boundaries', Inform's Blog (23 January 2014), available at https://inforrm.wordpress.com/2014/01/23/privacy-and-defamation-strasbourg-blurs-the-boundaries-hugh-tomlinson-qc/.

inconsistent with the regular exercise of IP rights. A copyright holder is granted rights defined by law which are supposed to be exercised under strictly defined circumstances but when these rights are drafted too broadly or enforced in a manner inconsistent with the purpose for which they were given, copyright obtains the capacity to be used as a tool for content control. This is happening when the enforcement tools given to right-holders enables them to assert their copyright not to protect their economic interests (or, at least, not primarily so) but to control the distribution of content unfavourable to them. This can take place in the form of illegitimate notifications of copyright infringements to public platforms such as search engines, forums and video distribution sites but also in the form of real or threatened litigation. Thus, a large corporation who is suffering critical comments on social media may assert its intellectual property rights (e.g. its trademark or copyright) not for economic reasons but to prevent the publication of information unfavourable to its interests. A threat of litigation would often be sufficient for the material to be removed. Two aspects of copyright have the potential to be used to control content: the enforcement mechanisms and the moral rights. These will be briefly looked at in turn.

Liability for violation of intellectual property rights arises from Directive 2001/29/EC ('Copyright Directive') and Directive 2004/48/EC[57] ('Copyright Enforcement Directive').[58] Copyright Directive, article 8(2) obliges Member States, in a general manner, to have an effective system of remedies:

> Each Member State shall take the measures necessary to ensure that right-holders whose interests are affected by an infringing activity carried out on its territory can bring an action for damages and/or apply for an injunction and, where appropriate, for the seizure of infringing material as well as of devices, products or components referred to in Article 6(2).

Injunctive relief is also available against intermediaries whose services are used by third parties.[59] The actual remedies are regulated in more detail in the Copyright Enforcement Directive. The crucial provision there is found in article 13, which provides that damages are due for infringements committed with knowledge or with reasonable grounds for

---

[57] Copyright Enforcement Directive 2001/29/EC [2004] OJ L195/16, 2 July 2004.

[58] For more details on the IP regime, see Chapter 6.

[59] See Chapter 5.

it, on application by the injured party to the appropriate judicial authorities. These damages are to be appropriate to the actual injustice suffered as a result of the infringement. The article also includes the rules for setting the amount of damages. These provide that the courts shall take into account all aspects of the case, including negative economic consequences, lost profits, unfair profits made by the infringer, and other, non-economic, factors. As an alternative to such a way of measuring damages, the courts can, in appropriate cases, set a lump sum which is to be no less than the amount of royalties which would have been due, had the infringer requested authorization. If the infringement was committed without knowledge, a Member State may provide either the recovery of profits or payment of pre-established damages.

The Copyright Enforcement Directive in its draft form caused a positive reaction from the entertainment industry but strong opposition from the telecommunications companies, part of the computer industry, most of the national press and the public, on account of the draconian ways in which infringements were to be treated. In terms of liability, the draft Directive introduced criminal liability for deliberate violations of intellectual property conducted in the course of business. The provision on criminal liability in the draft Directive was replaced with article 16, allowing the Member States to apply 'other appropriate sanctions' where IP rights have been infringed, without prejudice to the civil and administrative measures. This, in effect, turns the Copyright Enforcement Directive into a civil enforcement instrument.

An important aspect of copyright law's capacity to control content comes from moral rights. These rights, which have their origin in European law and are still more prominent there than in the United States, are rights which normally do not relate to the author's ability to control the *economic* side of their works but to their ability to have the works attributed to them and not to have the work treated in such a way as might harm the author's reputation. Article 6*bis* of the Berne Convention provides:

> Independent of the author's economic rights, and even after the transfer of the said rights, the author shall have the right to claim authorship of the work and to object to any distortion, modification of, or other derogatory action in relation to the said work, which would be prejudicial to the author's honor or reputation.

The content control aspect arises either where authors abuse their moral rights to illegitimately influence content or where moral rights are enforced in such a manner which objectively restricts the rights of others to comment on, parody and use the work in other ways consistent with the law. The CJEU has not addressed moral rights extensively[60] but has infrequently touched upon some of their aspects.

Of particular importance here is parody, which is imitation for purposes of creating a comic or critical effect. It is expressly allowed in Copyright Directive, article 5(3)(k) which permits copying for 'use for the purpose of caricature, parody or pastiche'. If the parody exception is allowed to operate in a restrictive manner and only if national laws allow it, significant avenues for content control could be opened. The Court had the opportunity to address this issue in the 2014 *Deckmyn* case.[61] There, a Belgian politician had a page from a well-known comic book modified by superimposing the image of another politician on it and had it distributed in the form of a calendar. The right-holders brought action against Mr Deckmyn alleging infringement of their copyright. Mr Deckmyn's defence was that this was a political cartoon which fell under the category of parody which was accepted under Belgian law. The question referred to the CJEU was, essentially, if the concept 'parody' has an autonomous meaning in EU law and if it must satisfy particular conditions in order to be treated as such. The Court ruled that, where no reference is made to national law in an EU Directive, the concept must be given an autonomous EU meaning. The Court further ruled that 'the essential characteristics of parody, are, first, to evoke an existing work, while being noticeably different from it, and secondly, to constitute an expression of humour or mockery'. It is not necessary that the parody 'should display an original character of its own', 'that it could reasonably be attributed to a person other than the author of the original work itself' nor 'that it should relate to the original work itself or mention the source of the parodied work'. The Court was very clear, however, that the right balance must be struck between the right-holders' interests on one side and the freedom of expression of the user of a protected work on the other. It is for the national courts to determine whether the fair balance has been achieved in any individual case. The case is important not only because parody is given an autonomous meaning but also because the CJEU suggested in paragraph 31 that right-holders have a 'legitimate interest' in not having their work associated with certain problematic messages which, inevitably, opens the complicated balancing question.

---

[60] In the Opinion in the *Deckmyn* case (below), the Advocate General emphasized that moral rights are out of the scope of Copyright Directive harmonization.

[61] C-201/13 *Deckmyn*, ECLI:EU:C:2014:2132, 3 September 2014.

5   SEXUALLY EXPLICIT SPEECH

In terms of its capacity to distribute harmful material, the Internet is possibly more powerful than any media before it. But, what is considered to be obscene in one part of the world would hardly deserve notice in another. Different standards may not easily be reconciled and actors from more liberal legal regimes may find themselves on the receiving end in more stringent jurisdictions. The freedom of speech protection in such cases may be overruled by other interests. The problem of liability for obscene material is twofold. First, criminal liability may arise out of providing illegal material, with individual posters, hosts and transmitters all being affected. Secondly, civil liability may arise out of removing the material deemed to be offensive that turns out not to be, by ISPs acting out of their own accord.

The American history of regulating obscenity is of interest here too. The first attempt to tackle the problem was the Communication Decency Act (CDA) 1996[62] which set out to limit the distribution of indecent speech in cases where it can be accessed by a minor. Effectively, it made all manner of speech illegal. In *Reno v ACLU*,[63] the US Supreme Court struck down the indecency provisions, holding that they were an unconstitutional abridgement of the right to free speech as guaranteed in the First Amendment. In reality, what the Act did was to limit the acceptability of speech on the Internet to that of a minor where this restriction does not exist for other forms of communication. Two later attempts to deal with the same issue were equally unsuccessful: the Federal Government was enjoined from enforcing the Child Online Protection Act (COPA) 1998[64] and the Children's Internet Protection Act (CIPA) 2000 was challenged.

Importantly, however, section 230(c) of the CDA 1996 states that providers and users of computer services shall not be treated as publishers or speakers of information given by another information content provider. Also, they will not be held liable for action to restrict access to or availability of material considered to be obscene. The first part of the section, in other words, insulates ISPs from liability while the second part enables intermediaries to remove offensive material without fear of

---

[62]   47 USC s. 230(c) (1996), Title V of the Telecommunications Acts 1996 (US).

[63]   *Reno v American Civil Liberties Union* 521 US 844 (1997).

[64]   In *Ashcroft v American Civil Liberties Union* 542 US 656 (2004), the Supreme Court affirmed the injunction. The actual law only concerned commercial speech by US providers.

being sued. Although parts of the CDA 1996 were declared unconstitutional in *Reno v ACLU*, this section was not. As for the first part of the section, it will be observed that the said defence is considerably more specific (if not wider) than the defences in articles 12–15 of the E-Commerce Directive (see below). It applies to all providers/users, not just to conduits/intermediaries. Secondly, the section protects the subjects even where they are fully aware of the content.[65]

The European Union did not attempt to regulate obscenity on a general level and it did not pass laws to limit adult pornography. While it is possible that different standards in different Member States may lead to cases alleging violation of the Single Market provisions of the TFEU, such cases would be defendable under Treaty provisions or mandatory requirements. In *Henn and Derby*,[66] the CJEU ruled that:

> a Member State may, in principle, lawfully impose prohibitions on the importation from any other member-State of articles which are of an indecent or obscene character as understood by its domestic laws and that such prohibitions may lawfully be applied to the whole of its national territory even if, in regard to the field in question, variations exist between the laws in force in the different constituent parts of the member-State concerned.

Such a prohibition cannot be arbitrary and presupposes the absence, on the territory of the Member State in question, of trade in the said goods.

More comprehensive attempts have been made to fight *child* pornography. The first documents of some importance are the 1997 Joint Action to combat trafficking in human beings and sexual exploitation of children,[67] the Recommendation on protection of minors and human dignity[68] and the Safer Internet Action Plan (1999–2005).[69] These were

---

[65] For how the article is applied by the courts, see *Zeran v AOL* 958 F. Supp. 1124 (ED Va. 1997), Eastern District Court of Virginia.

[66] C-34/79 *R v Maurice Donald Henn and John Frederick Ernest Darby* [1979] ECR 3795.

[67] Joint Action 97/154/JHA of 24 February 1997 [1997] OJ L63, 4 March 1997, amended by Council Framework Decision 2002/629/JHA of 19 July 2002 concerning trafficking in human beings [2002] OJ L203, 1 August 2002.

[68] 98/560/EC (October 1998), which provides national legislative guidelines regarding illegal and harmful content over electronic media [1998] OJ L270, 7 October 1998.

[69] Decision No. 276/1999/EC of the European Parliament and of the Council of 25 January 1999 adopting a multiannual Community action plan on promoting safer use of the Internet by combating illegal and harmful content on global networks [1999] OJ L108/52, 27 April 1999. Extended by Decision No. 1151/2003/EC of 16 June 2003 [2003] OJ L162, 1 July 2003. See the action

followed by the Council Decision of 29 May 2000 to combat child pornography on the Internet[70] and Council Framework Decision 2004/68/ JHA.[71]

The 1997 Joint Action aimed to establish common rules for action to combat human trafficking and the sexual exploitation of children, to fight against certain forms of unauthorized immigration and to improve judicial cooperation in criminal matters.[72] Member States undertook the obligation to review their national legislation with a view to eliminating human trafficking and the sexual exploitation of children. Although the measure did not specifically address the Internet, it did have some importance for it. One of the three behaviours specifically identified is 'sexual exploitation', in relation to a child, means:

> the inducement or coercion of a child to engage in any unlawful sexual activity; the exploitative use of a child in prostitution or other unlawful sexual practices; the exploitative use of children in pornographic performances and materials, including the production, sale and distribution or other forms of trafficking in such materials, and the possession of such materials.

Most of this can be mediated through the use of emails, chat rooms, portals, real-time text messaging services, and so on. The Action Plan did not introduce specific criminal measures. Its main areas of activity were: establishing a safer environment through a network of hotlines and the encouragement of self-regulation and rules of conduct; filtering technologies; awareness campaigns; and support activities.

Real progress has been achieved with the 2011 Directive specifically aimed at fighting child pornography.[73] This instrument, which replaced

plan, Safer Internet Plus (2005–2008): Decision No. 854/2005/EC of the European Parliament and of the Council of 11 May 2005 establishing a multiannual Community Programme on promoting safer use of the Internet and new online technologies [2005] OJ L149, 11 June 2005.

[70]   Council Decision 2000/375/JHA of 29 May 2000 to combat child pornography on the Internet [2000] OJ L138, 9 June 2000.

[71]   Council Framework Decision of 22 December 2003 on combating the sexual exploitation of children and child pornography [2004] OJ L13/44, 20 January 2004.

[72]   It was replaced by Directive 2011/36/EU of the European Parliament and of the Council of 5 April 2011 on preventing and combating trafficking in human beings and protecting its victims, and replacing Council Framework Decision 2002/629/JHA [2011] OJ L101, 15 April 2011.

[73]   Directive 2011/92/EU of the European Parliament and of the Council of 13 December 2011 on combating the sexual abuse and sexual exploitation of

the above-mentioned ones,[74] obliges Member States to criminalize offences concerning sexual abuse, sexual exploitation and child pornography. Although the main thrust is towards criminal measures, article 25 also addresses content by providing:

1. Member States shall take the necessary measures to ensure the prompt removal of web pages containing or disseminating child pornography hosted in their territory and to endeavour to obtain the removal of such pages hosted outside of their territory.
2. Member States may take measures to block access to web pages containing or disseminating child pornography towards the Internet users within their territory. These measures must be set by transparent procedures and provide adequate safeguards, in particular to ensure that the restriction is limited to what is necessary and proportionate, and that users are informed of the reason for the restriction. Those safeguards shall also include the possibility of judicial redress.

6 HATE SPEECH

Hate speech is a synonym for written or oral communication or public behaviour that invites prejudice based on ethnicity, race, gender or religious, sexual, political, social or other characteristics. Defining it properly is difficult, as it can extend well beyond the most commonly found forms (such as racial hatred) and cover the territory that some label as 'controversial' although legal speech. The most important feature, however, is that it is based on publicly expressed judgement which is not based on evidence and which invites discrimination towards a group of people individualized by one of their common features. The regulation of hate speech has considerable importance for the Internet. Speech legally placed on the Internet in Member State A is accessed in Member State B where it might be illegal. Liability arising out of this action may be both criminal (as, for example, in the case of Holocaust denial) and civil (as in the case of defamation).

A marked difference exists between the United States, where the First Amendment protects freedom of speech, including hate speech, and Europe, where hate speech attracts criminal and/or civil liability. Member States have regulated it differently. Holocaust denial, for example, is illegal in a number of EU Member States, including Germany, Austria

---

children and child pornography, and replacing Council Framework Decision 2004/68/JHA [2011] OJ L26/1, 17 December 2011.

[74] For details on its operation, see Chapter 10, section 5.

and France, but not in others. Incitement of hatred based on racial or ethnic origins is illegal in all EU Member States. From the viewpoint of certainty, the desirable situation is either complete lack of regulation of hate speech, which is the American model, or legal harmonization, which is the European model.[75] Put in simple terms, American society believes that hate speech can best be eliminated by allowing all opinions to be voiced and letting the public choose. Europeans, on the other hand, derive their views from different political traditions and their experience during the two World Wars, and allow speech in general while reserving the right to regulate some forms of hate speech.

Although the EU did not regulate hate speech directly, problems caused by increasing volumes of hate speech on the Internet have caught its attention and led to calls for Member States to criminalize it at national level.[76] This further underlines the difference in the American and EU models. Nevertheless, another European instrument has a clear prohibition on hate speech. The European Convention on Cybercrime, adopted by the Council of Europe,[77] in its amended version,[78] prohibits:

> any written material, any image or any other representation of ideas or theories, which advocates, promotes or incites hatred, discrimination or violence, against any individual or group of individuals, based on race, colour, descent or national or ethnic origin, as well as religion if used as pretext for any of these factors.[79]

The first main provision of the amending Protocol is Article 3, which deals with dissemination of racist and xenophobic material on computer systems. It places an obligation on Member States to criminalize intentional 'distributing, or otherwise making available of racist and xenophobic material to the public through a computer system'. If other effective remedies are available, a party may choose not to attach

---

[75]   The United States has joined in the European Cybercrime Convention effective from 1 January 2007 but not the Additional Protocol. Concerns were voiced by the US government during negotiations that the final Protocol would not be compatible with the US Constitution.
[76]   V. Jourová, Concluding Remarks at the Colloquium on Fundamental Rights, 2 October 2015, available at http://europa.eu/rapid/press-release_SPEECH-15-5765_en.htm.
[77]   And, strictly speaking, falling outside the scope of the EU. For more on these issues, see Chapter 10.
[78]   Additional Protocol to the Convention on Cybercrime Concerning the Criminalisation of Acts of a Racist and Xenophobic Nature Committed Through Computer Systems, Strasbourg, 7 November 2002, PC-RX(2002)24.
[79]   Additional Protocol, art. 2.

criminal liability to the described conduct, provided other effective remedies are available and where the material promotes or incites discrimination that is not associated with violence. Irrespective of this exception, a party may reserve the right not to apply the Article to those cases of discrimination for which there are, due to the national system of freedom of expression, no effective remedy.[80] This latter has been inserted to address the concerns of those Member States that constitutionally protect free speech.

Article 4 criminalizes racial and xenophobic threats. The offence consists of threatening, through a computer system, the commission of a serious criminal offence as defined under domestic law. The threat has to relate to a group, distinguished by race, colour, descent or national or ethnic origin, as well as religion, if used as a pretext for any of these factors, or a group of persons which is distinguished by any of these characteristics.

Furthermore, Article 5 deals with intentional racially motivated insult. This consists of insulting publicly, through a computer system, persons belonging to a group distinguished by race, colour, descent or national or ethnic origin, as well as religion, if used as a pretext for any of these factors, or a group of persons that is distinguished by any of these characteristics. A party may additionally require that the person or group in question is exposed to hatred, contempt or ridicule or reserve the right not to apply the Article whatsoever.

Article 6 covers what is colloquially referred to as 'Holocaust denial' but in fact encompasses denial, gross minimization, approval or justification of genocide or crimes against humanity and is therefore much wider in scope, both in terms of historical periods covered and the geographical extent. The criminal offence consists of:

> distributing or otherwise making available, through a computer system to the public, material which denies, grossly minimises, approves or justifies acts constituting genocide or crimes against humanity, as defined by international law and recognised as such by final and binding decisions of the International Military Tribunal, established by the London Agreement of 8 April 1945, or of any other international court established by relevant international instruments and whose jurisdiction is recognised by that Party.

The party may require that the denial be committed with intent to incite hatred, discrimination or violence or otherwise decide not to apply the Article at all.

---

[80] Additional Protocol, art. 3(3).

Intentional aiding or abetting in any of the acts in Articles 3 to 7 is criminalized in Article 7 of the Protocol.

A number of European countries already have laws that cover racial hatred. The changes, from their perspective, may not look revolutionary. More importantly, though, a proportion of racist sites are also hosted in the United States, which is not bound by the Protocol. This is further complicated by the consequences of the American position in the US *Yahoo!* case,[81] which can be summarized as protecting freedom of speech in the First Amendment through refusing recognition and enforcement of judgments that do not respect it.

* * *

The European Union, unlike most of its Member States, does not have a consistent policy on regulating Internet content. Most of its regulatory efforts are sector specific. This is not surprising, since the EU usually lacks competence to directly regulate non-economic issues. Where such a policy exists, it is limited to specific problems that arise indirectly, such as content control in the AVMS Directive. This is also true of the EU's work on protecting minors, which has resulted in efforts to combat child pornography and harmful advertising.

On the other hand, a number of issues of importance continue to affect the daily lives of EU citizens and may call for more harmonization in the future. This is particularly true of defamation, where national differences both in criminal and civil law are considerable.

---

[81]   See Chapter 3.

5. Liability of intermediaries

1 INTERMEDIARIES AND THE INTERNET

The Internet's unique layered structure[1] creates three separate relevant categories of actors or subjects. The first are those who create or post information. The second are those who this information targets: the recipients. Although the two roles can be blurred in real life (e.g. the same user can both post information on a blog and read other users' posts), legally the roles are distinct in that legal action would normally target a subject in one of its roles only.

The third actor, the intermediaries, plays an essential role which revolves around three points. First, they enable the flow of information between the two other subjects without contributing to the content. Secondly, they act as guardians of the users' identity and anonymity. Thirdly, they are in a unique position to prevent or mitigate the damage that may be inflicted by the other two categories' illegal activity. As such, they may, under certain circumstances, be liable as contributors and are inevitably put under more pressure both by the potential claimants and state law enforcement bodies.

Internet service providers (ISPs) are usually commercial entities guided by commercial logic. Their operation, however, is not solely determined by market forces but is influenced by groups who desire to control the Internet. In the first place, these are the federal and regional governments[2] who exercise pressure on ISPs to control undesirable behaviour on the Internet. The ISP's actions, their cooperation or the lack thereof, can influence a whole range of government policies concerning, among other things, defamation, sexually explicit speech or copyright infringement. For corporations, the intermediaries who possess knowledge of possibly illegal downloading patterns are valuable holders of information concerning potential end-users and their behaviour. This

---

[1]　See Chapter 1.

[2]　In the United States, for instance, some states have enacted child protecting legislation. See *Center for Democracy and Technology v Pappert* 337 F. Supp. 606, US District Court for the Eastern District of Pennsylvania.

information can be extracted with relative ease, depending on the court system.[3] For individual users, the intermediaries are guardians of their privacy, without which it would be difficult to trace them, but also guarantors of their ability to meaningfully exercise free speech.

As will be seen further in this chapter, the prevailing model since the Internet rose in popularity in the 1990s has been to insulate from liability the intermediaries who do not post material themselves. Recently, however, calls have been intensified for enhanced intermediary liability due to real or imagined threats. When we analyse the general push towards more intermediary liability, we can see that more liability is sought from the intermediaries at both international and national levels, that there are increased calls for safe harbour rules reform but also for proactive monitoring and filtering.[4]

The promoters of the idea that more liability is needed claim that the present model is no longer suited to the realities of modern Internet and that more intermediary involvement is needed to fight threats arising from, among other things, intellectual property (IP) infringement and defamation. The Commission is ready (in theory at least) to reopen the discussion on intermediary liability.[5] In the 2015 Digital Single Market Strategy, it commented that it would look into 'whether to require intermediaries to exercise greater responsibility and due diligence in the way they manage their networks and systems – a duty of care'. Worryingly, it did not explain what it meant by the 'duty of care', nor why it thought that the present model needed to be looked into. At the same time, the European Court of Human Rights (ECtHR), contrary to the position normally taken by the Court of Justice of the European Union (CJEU), also signalled that intermediaries ought to play a more active role in monitoring content.[6]

The choice of the regulatory model applied to the intermediaries may have important consequences for the development of the Internet. Economically, there is a direct relationship between regulatory burden and development. The more exposed the intermediaries are to liability,

---

[3]   The CJEU affirmed that right-holders may seek injunctions against ISPs in file-sharing cases. See C-557/07 *LSG-Gesellschaft zur Wahrnehmung von Leistungsschutzrechten* [2009] ECR I-01227.

[4]   G. Frosio, 'Digital Piracy Debunked: A Short Note on Digital Threats and Intermediary Liability' (2016) 5(1) *Internet Policy Review*.

[5]   See public consultation on platforms, opened September 2015, available at https://ec.europa.eu/digital-single-market/en/news/public-consultation-regulatory-environment-platforms-online-intermediaries-data-and-cloud.

[6]   See section 4 below.

the less likely they will invest in the Internet's development. The stricter the regulation, the more restraint it will place on the development of the medium. The link between development and regulation is specifically recognized in the Preamble to the US Communication Decency Act 1996, section 230, the aim of which is, among other things:

(1) to promote the continued development of the Internet and other inter-active computer services and other interactive media;
(2) to preserve the vibrant and competitive free market that presently exists for the Internet and other interactive computer services, unfettered by Federal or State regulation;
(3) to encourage the development of technologies which maximize user control over what information is received by individuals, families, and schools who use the Internet and other interactive computer services.

There is little doubt that strict liability of providers would result in their withdrawal from the market and the limitation of the type and range of the services they provide. But, even a slight change in the liability model may increase the incentive to preventively monitor and delete content and thus change the look and feel of the Internet as it is known today.

The question concerning liability deals with allocating the legal responsibility for actions on the Internet that cause harm to others. By exposing our actions worldwide, the borderless instantly accessible Internet poses a challenge to the traditional notion of civil liability where this allocation is easier to perform. In 'real life', we are liable for harm we cause to others. Mostly, it is easy to localize this kind of liability: it takes place on the territory of a determined or determinable state(s) and results from conscious actions of particular individuals or corporations (such as driving negligently or violating the terms of a contract). The standard is set by the state, in the form of private and public laws, and its violation leads to liability. Sometimes, the liability is strict (as in the case of faulty equipment). In that situation, one is liable regardless of culpability. In most other situations, liability arises because there is fault that can be ascribed to an individual or a corporation. All of this can tentatively be called the standard model of regulation. That model is effective for allocating liability in all cases where the perpetrator is known but begins to fail in those cases where there is either no such knowledge or it is difficult/costly to engage in fact finding.

Liability of intermediaries is widely accepted today: those who store or transmit data can be and are made liable for the damage arising from data even when they are not producers, but the conditions set for such liability are relatively strict. Here we will look at how EU liability regimes reflect this. There are two important points that need to be considered. The first question is: under what circumstances will liability be imposed on intermediaries? This will be discussed in section 2 below. Furthermore, on the Internet, the intermediaries are in the unique position of power, with the ability to introduce private control, in the form of filtering or self-censoring measures. The second question is: under what circumstances can intermediaries be requested to submit information they hold about users so that the claimant can pursue action against the primary infringer? This will be addressed in section 3 below. Finally, the ECtHR has also looked at intermediaries from the viewpoint of whether potential liability violates the freedom of expression enshrined in the European Convention on Human Rights (ECHR). Their views will be analysed in section 4 below.

1.1   Choice of Regulatory Regime

Hosting, transmitting and publishing form the main, revenue-generating part of the ISPs' business. The problem concerning liability, which is contemporary with the popular spread of the Internet in the mid-1990s, is caused by the ISPs' fear of civil liability for the material they host, transmit or publish. Conceptually, the regulators distinguish these activities. Hosting involves keeping and/or managing websites for end-users. All webpages require hosting on a computer from which other users will access them. This can be performed on a local computer (i.e. a university, a corporation or a tech-savvy user will host their own webpages) or it can be hosted on the ISP's equipment, usually for a monthly or yearly fee. In any case, hosting does not involve the intermediary's editorial intervention. Publishing involves making content available on a webpage hosted or controlled by the intermediary with that intermediary's more or less active editorial participation. A typical example is a moderated web forum or a chat group but can also include auction sites, search engines or any situation where an intermediary itself provides content.[7] Transmitting involves providing access to the Internet (normally for a subscription) and sending and receiving signals from other computers without intervening with that content. To this must be added caching, which is the making of temporary local copies the sole purpose of which is to make Internet traffic more efficient. The main distinguishing factor in all these cases must be whether the intermediary only hosts/transmits content made by others or publishes/transforms/moderates the content. Keeping

---

[7]   An example would be an auction site facilitating the sale of items on its pages.

within the boundaries of the former normally maintains its insulation from liability whereas venturing into the latter exposes it to such liability.

As a rule, ISPs prefer not to be involved in disputes between the injured party and the end-user. Allowing them to escape liability satisfies this need but normally comes at a price. Right-holders will seek injunctions asking courts to force intermediaries to deliver names and addresses of file sharers and such injunctions are routinely granted in almost all Member States. The CJEU has confirmed their legality several times, most recently in the 2014 *UPC* case,[8] which will be analysed below.

Clearly, the regime where there is no liability for ISPs satisfies the providers but very few other parties. Alternatively, the regime which puts the entire burden on the ISPs introduces self-censorship, limits their capacity to introduce new services and exposes them to risk from transmitting material by third parties. The appropriate regime, therefore, needs to strike the right balance between the interests of the injured parties and those of the transmitters.

Currently, there exist three theoretically possible regimes for liability of intermediaries on the Internet based on the degree of control imposed on the providers.[9] The first of these involves direct application of criminal sanctions on ISPs for non-compliance with the imposed regime. Under this regime, ISPs are to be liable criminally for material that is hosted on or transmitted through their computers but can also be liable civilly. Even though it might have a limited effect in the case of obscene material, for which it was designed, it has little or no effect on other material. For reasons mainly to do with the ability to implement it, this regime has been abandoned in all but a handful of countries.[10] The second regime insulates ISPs from liability almost completely by granting them immunity and encouraging them to self-regulate. The ISP liability regime in the United States belongs to this model and will be looked at briefly in section 1.2 below. The third regime limits the liability of ISPs, normally on the condition that any infringing material is

---

[8] C-314/12 *UPC Telekabel Wien GmbH v Constantin Film Verleih GmbH and Wega Filmproduktionsgesellschaft mbH*, ECLI:EU:C:2014:192, 27 March 2014.

[9] For a detailed discussion of these regimes, see L. Edwards, 'Articles 12–15 ECD: ISP Liability' in L. Edwards (ed.), *The New Legal Framework for E-Commerce in Europe* (Hart, Oxford/Portland, OR, 2005), p. 106 et seq.

[10] For example, the Australian Broadcasting Services Amendment (Online Services) Act 1999 which was eventually watered down to a point where ISPs in Australia had immunity.

removed upon notification. This regime is similar to the previous one but with a more rigid structure. The EU E-Commerce Directive (2001/31/EC) takes this approach. This regime will be analysed in section 2.

Some states have recently attempted to introduce legislation which invites a more active role from ISPs without introducing the obligation to monitor, otherwise prohibited in article 15 of the Electronic Commerce Directive. The French HADOPI-1 Bill[11] invites copyright owners to report potential infringements to a specially created authority which, in turn, consults other parties involved including the ISPs. While the law does not impose extra liability on ISPs nor does it demand that they 'police' the Internet, it encourages them to cooperate with the authorities, raising questions about collaboration. Similar efforts have been extended in the United Kingdom with the Digital Economy Act (DEA) 2010,[12] which not only requires ISPs' cooperation but imposes heavy fines where that cooperation is not given without good reason.

1.2   US Approach

The US approach to Internet liability has its foundation in the First Amendment which guarantees freedom of speech and freedom of the press, the values which US courts have repeatedly protected. As a result, the model developed in the United States was never based on strict but on limited liability, with the main idea being that a distributor or deliverer that is considered a passive conduit would not be found liable unless there is fault on its part.[13]

The American statutory response to the Internet was robust and involved two separate statutes. The first of these is section 230 of the Communication Decency Act (CDA) 1996 which deals with the problem of intermediaries' liability *in general*. The second is the Digital Millennium Copyright Act (DMCA) 1998 which only deals with providers' liability *for copyright infringement*. CDA 1996, section 230 stipulates:

> No provider or user of an interactive computer service shall be treated as the publisher or speaker of any information provided by another information content provider.

---

[11]   Loi favorisant la diffusion et la protection de la création sur Internet [Creation and Internet Law], Loi no. 2009-669 du 12 June 2009, JO no. 135 du 13 juin 2009.

[12]   2010 c. 24.

[13]   See T. Ludbrook, 'Defamation and the Internet, Part 2' (2004) 15 *Entertainment Law Review* 203.

Here, an 'interactive computer service' specifically includes the Internet, and an 'information content provider' is taken to mean anybody who is responsible for the creation of information provided through the Internet. Although the broad immunity which is evident from this section may sound excessive, in practice it is counterbalanced by a more aggressive role reserved for ISPs, who are supposed to self-regulate the dissemination of material.[14]

Liability for IP violation is regulated in the DMCA 1998.[15] This Act introduces in section 512 limitations of liability in respect of online material and states that a provider shall not be liable for intermediate storage or transmission of material, for system caching or 'for infringement of copyright by reason of the storage at the direction of a user of material that resides on a system or network controlled or operated by or for the service provider'. The provider is not liable for offering information location tools such as search engines. The hosting exception has detailed conditions which need to be fulfilled before protection could be invoked. These include the lack of actual knowledge of an infringement or circumstances from which such an infringement could be inferred and expeditious removal of material upon notification. The removal is subject to a 'notice and take-down' procedure, which involves a notification to the provider with the possibility of the material being put back if it is proven that no violation had taken place. In reality, the vast majority of material is never put back and the number of frivolous take-down requests stands at close to one in three.[16] Unlike Europe, the DMCA 1998 introduces a special standard of liability for non-profit educational institutions.[17]

One of the earliest cases to examine ISP liability in the defamatory context was *Cubby*.[18] CompuServe was an ISP that provided access to the Internet in addition to a variety of special services only available on

---

[14]   See comments on *Zeran*, below.

[15]   DMCA Title II or 'The Online Copyright Infringement Liability Limitation Act' (OCILLA) Bill Number H.R.2281 for the 105th Congress, 112 Stat. 2860 (1998).

[16]   A research project published in 2016 claims that 28 per cent of take-down notices sent to Google were such. See J.M. Urban, J. Karaganis and B.L. Schofield, *Notice and Takedown in Everyday Practice* (29 March 2016), available at SSRN: http://ssrn.com/abstract=2755628.

[17]   Section 512(e). For a wider comparison, see L. Tiberi and M. Zamboni, 'Liability of Service Providers' (2003) 9 *Computer and Telecommunications Law Review* 49.

[18]   *Cubby, Inc. v CompuServe, Inc.* 776 F. Supp. 135, United States District Court for the Southern District of New York.

CompuServe, such as various forums. One of these was the Journalism Forum and part of it was a daily newsletter called *Rumorville USA*. CompuServe was not reviewing the contents of the newsletter nor was it in any way in charge of the publication as it was uploaded. The plaintiffs were Cubby, Inc. and Robert Blanchard, publishers of Skuttlebut, a gossip column intended to compete with *Rumorville*. The plaintiffs claimed that the defendant published defamatory statements on separate occasions. CompuServe's defence was that it was a distributor and not a publisher and it did not know and had no reason to know of them. The court took the view that CompuServe, as a news distributor, would not be held liable if it neither knew nor had reason to know of the allegedly defamatory *Rumorville* statements. In other words, the court took the view that CompuServe is more like a distributor than like a publisher.

In another case, *Stratton Oakmont*,[19] defamatory statements were made against the defendants in a bulletin board in 1994. Prodigy was 'the owner and operator' of the computer network on which these statements appeared. At the time, Prodigy had two million subscribers and the bulletin in question, *Money Talk*, was possibly the most widely read such publication on the Internet. The plaintiffs alleged that Prodigy should be considered a publisher and not a distributor. In claiming this, they relied on Prodigy's stated policy which stated that it was a family oriented network. This policy was widely advertised by its executives who repeated on many occasions that they exercised editorial control over the contents on the network.

Zeran v AOL[20] confirmed that section 230 'creates a federal immunity to any cause of action that would make service providers liable for information originating with a third-party user of the service'. The court emphasized that 'lawsuits seeking to hold a service liable for its exercise of a publisher's traditional editorial functions – such as deciding whether to publish, withdraw, postpone or alter content – are barred'. As will be seen in section 2 below, this is a significantly stronger insulation than the one the EU E-Commerce Directive offers.

In the context of copyright infringement, a number of cases have come through the US courts, but few are as significant as the US Supreme Court case *Grokster*.[21] The case can be seen as a re-examination of the

---

[19]   *Stratton Oakmont, Inc. v Prodigy Services Co.*, New York Supreme Court 1995, 1995 WL 323710.

[20]   *Zeran v America Online, Inc.* 129 F.3d 327, US Court of Appeals, Fourth Circuit.

[21]   *MGM Studios, Inc. v Grokster, Ltd* 545 U.S. 913 (2005). See also D. Sheridan, 'Zeran v. AOL and the Effect of Section 230 of the Communications

Sony Betamax case,[22] which held that producers of a technology were not responsible for copyright violations as long as that technology had substantive non-infringing uses. In *Grokster*, the main question was whether the operators of a point-to-point file-sharing facility were liable or could avail themselves of the Sony defence. The Supreme Court said that Grokster should be liable for inducing copyright infringement. Groskter was, in the view of the Court, manufacturing and distributing not just a neutral device (such as the VHS tape recorder in the *Sony* case) but a device 'with the object of promoting its use to infringe copyright, as shown by clear expression or other affirmative steps taken to foster infringement'. Although the case had never been discussed in light of DMCA 1998, section 512, it is nevertheless important for establishing that a primary infringer or an inducer do not fall within the protective provisions.[23]

A clearer application of DMCA 1998, section 512 happened in the *Viacom*[24] case. There, the main issue was whether YouTube was liable for copyright infringement for allowing its users to post videos on which Viacom claimed to have copyright. The court ruled that Google, as the owner of YouTube, was protected under section 512, absence a finding of intentional copyright infringement. In spite of having general knowledge that some material must be infringing it did not possess information of specific clips (which it would have obtained in a notice and take-down procedure). The judge emphasized that proactive monitoring is precisely what the DMCA 1998 aims to avoid.

2 EUROPEAN APPROACH TO INTERMEDIARY LIABILITY

2.1 Information Society Services

The E-Commerce Directive provisions on ISP liability are relatively wide in scope. The Directive operates with the concept of 'information society

---

Decency Act upon Liability for Defamation on the Internet' (1997–1998) 61 *Albany Law Review* 147.

[22] 464 U.S. 417 (1984), US Supreme Court.

[23] The same logic applies to the Swedish *Pirate Bay* case. See Stockholms tingsrätts avgörande den 17 April 2009 i mål nr B 13301-06.

[24] *Viacom International Inc. v YouTube, Inc. and Google, Inc.*, No. 07 Civ. 2103, US District Court for the Southern District of New York. See also the appeal judgment of the Court of Appeals (Second Circuit), 10 Civ 3270.

services' (ISSs). These are defined as services provided for remuneration and at a distance by means of electronic equipment, for the processing and storage of data, and at the individual request of a service recipient.[25] Remuneration does not normally mean that the services need to be directly paid for by the end-users. It is sufficient that they are economic in nature. A website which is funded through advertising is, therefore, included. The fact that services need to be provided on request excludes services where the recipient plays little or no role in selecting individualized content, such as television or radio.

Information society services defined in this manner encompass a broad range of activities as long as they take place online and as long as one of the sides in the transaction reaps economic benefits. As emphasized in Recital 18 of the E-Commerce Directive, these roughly fall in three categories: transmission of information; access to communication networks; and hosting of information content. Such a definition also includes ISPs, which typically provide access to communication networks but can also provide hosting and other services. Importantly, ISPs are intermediaries but not all intermediaries are ISPs.

Recital 18 of the E-Commerce Directive explains that ISSs include not only economic activities relating to online contracting but any activities which are not remunerated by those who receive them. This distinction is of importance, as it extends the scope of possible insulation from liability to a great number of actors. Television broadcasting is excluded but audio-visual services that are provided on-demand are presumably within the scope. Thus, television signal provided through a regular broadband connection is out of the scope of the Directive but on-demand streaming or extra content provided through the same network is not.

In early US case law, there was some doubt as to the circumstances at which access providers ought to be treated as intermediaries. The doubt arose because access providers typically engage in a number of activities which involve some degree of providing primary content or editing. This is typically the case where they exercise a degree of editorial control. In Europe, the CJEU confirmed in the *LSG* case that access providers 'which merely provide users with Internet access, without offering other services such as email, FTP or file sharing services or exercising any

---

[25]   The definition has been taken from, among others, Directive 98/34/EC of the European Parliament and of the Council of 22 June 1998 laying down a procedure for the provision of information in the field of technical standards and regulations and on rules on information society services [1998] OJ L204/37, 21 July 1998 ('Technical Standards Directive').

control ... must be regarded as "intermediaries"'.[26] In other words, as long as the access provider does not engage in controlling the content, it retains its status as an access provider. That distinction is crucial, taking into consideration the fact that many intermediaries give the users much more than pure access.

Articles 12–15 of the E-Commerce Directive, together with some provisions of the Copyright Directive (2001/29/EC), establish an EU regime for the liability of intermediary service providers. The disparities that existed between Member States in this area were seen as a burden to the smooth functioning of the Internal Market and removing them was identified as one of the priorities. More importantly, however, insulating the providers from liability was seen as an encouragement to the development of services which would otherwise be lacking for fear of legal reprisals. The absence of the limitation would either prevent the providers from entering the market or would severely reduce the content they were offering.

It is important to understand which situations articles 12–15 of the E-Commerce Directive exactly apply to. These articles cover the liability of intermediaries in their role as *intermediaries*, not as primary publishers. The *First Report on the Application of the E-Commerce Directive*[27] throws light on the original intentions of the draftsmen:

> The Directive does not affect the liability of the person who is at the source of the content nor does it affect the liability of intermediaries in cases which are not covered by the limitations defined in the Directive. Furthermore, the Directive does not affect the possibility of a national court or administrative authority to require a service provider to terminate or prevent an infringement. These questions are subject to the national law of the Member States.

Put in other words, the Directive envisages limitations on civil and criminal liability within its sphere of application, but does not influence the liability of the primary infringer nor does it prevent Member States from introducing measures to stop the infringement.

---

[26] C-557/07 *LSG-Gesellschaft zur Wahrnehmung von Leistungsschutzrechten GmbH* [2009] ECR I-1227.

[27] Report from the Commission to the European Parliament, the Council and the European Economic and Social Committee, *First Report on the Application of Directive 2000/31/EC of the European Parliament and of the Council of 8 June 2000 on Certain Legal Aspects of Information Society Services, in particular Electronic Commerce, in the Internal Market*, COM(2003)0702 (8 June 2003).

In the 2014 *Papasavvas* case,[28] the CJEU had an opportunity to discuss the differences between an intermediary and a primary publisher. There, Mr Papasavvas brought an action for damages for defamation against a newspaper publishing company who allegedly defamed him in two articles published online. The question was, among other things, whether provisions on intermediary liability 'cover online information services the remuneration for which is provided not directly by the recipient, but indirectly by means of commercial advertisements' and whether the 'mere conduit' or 'caching' or 'hosting' provisions of articles 12–14 apply to a newspaper website? The Court held that these provisions:

> do not apply to the case of a newspaper publishing company which operates a website on which the online version of a newspaper is posted, that company being, moreover, remunerated by income generated by commercial advertisements posted on that website, since it has knowledge of the information posted and exercises control over that information, whether or not access to that website is free of charge.

Essentially, what the Court is saying is that exercising regular editorial control, which inevitably involves knowledge of the information posted, takes the website out of the scope of the protective provisions irrespective of the business model which the website employs.

2.2 Mere Conduits

E-Commerce Directive, Article 12 covers the liability of passive inter-mediaries. This refers to the situation where the information society service provider (ISSP) has not produced the information or chosen the intended recipient but acts as a mere transmitter of the information. Article 12(1) stipulates that the provider will not be liable where it:

● does not initiate the transmission;
● does not select the receiver; and
● does not select or modify the transmission in transit.

The conditions imposed describe the passive status of the transmitter. The first condition, that the ISP did not initiate the transmission, relates to the fact that it is always the users who requests information in an Internet context. The second condition refers to the fact that the intermediary

---

[28] C-291/13 *Sotiris Papasavvas v O Fileleftheros Dimosia Etairia Ltd, Takis Kounnafi, Giorgos Sertis*, ECLI:EU:C:2014:2209, 11 September 2014.

must not filter the recipients, that is, it must not restrict access to some but not to others. The final condition describes editorial control, which must be absent. Any of the actions mentioned in article 12(1), however, would equate the intermediary with the creator/poster of information and expose it to liability.

Transmissions here include temporary storage for the sole purpose of carrying out the transmission and under the condition that the information is not stored for periods longer than is reasonably necessary. Such storage is normally automatic and takes place in the course of the transmission and not for other, data gathering, purposes. A further condition is the temporary nature of the storage.

The transmission consists of communication of information to a recipient of the service, defined in Recital 20. The recipients are defined in that Recital as anybody who seeks information either for private or professional uses, irrespective of the nature of that information.

The liability in question must be understood to comprise both civil and criminal liability. The possibility exists[29] for courts or administrative authorities to terminate or prevent the infringement, which is normally achieved through an interlocutory measure.

The crucial element of this provision is that the transmitter is passive. It does not create the information, has no knowledge of it and does not control it. This solution is necessary and understandable and the alternative regime would require the intermediary to constantly monitor the traffic on its network for any potential infringements – a prospect that is as difficult as it is ineffective. The experience of other jurisdictions confirms this view.

It is not clear from the wording of article 12 whether ISSPs need to act on information that infringing content is passing through their network. Unlike articles 13 and 14, no such obligation is imposed in the article itself. On the other hand, both article 12(1) and Recital 42 would seem to indicate that knowledge and control removes insulation from liability. Additionally, article 12(3) allows action for prevention and termination of infringement which would indicate that, although a *bona fide* ISSP is not liable, the one who learns of an infringement is exposed to regular legal action and liability after the moment where the infringement had been communicated.

A separate question arises in situations where a mobile operator enters into a contract with a content provider, controlling the applications and/or the content available on its network or in its 'app store'. Thus, an app

---

[29] E-Commerce Directive, art. 12(3).

store operator may choose to approve an app or not or to limit its functionality. Whereas there is no clear answer to this question due to the lack of a definition of 'selecting or modifying information' under article 12(1), it would seem that an intervention of that kind would remove the protection of article 12.[30]

A further interpretation of the 'mere conduit' provision is expected to come in the *McFadden* case.[31] There, an owner of a lighting and sound equipment rental business provided a free Wi-Fi connection as a way of promoting his business. The connection was open (not password-protected) and a file on which the respondent claimed ownership had been downloaded through the connection. The store owner-claimant started a negative declaration case, claiming the article 12 'mere conduit' protection whereas the respondent maintained that the article did not cover free services. The case revolved around a number of questions that the Advocate General grouped in two clusters.

The first concerned the applicability of article 12 to situations involving free Wi-Fi connections. The Advocate General emphasized that 'only services of an economic nature are covered by the provisions of the TFEU Treaty' but also that 'the concepts of economic activity and of the provision of services in the context of the internal market must be given a broad interpretation'. The main idea is that the provision of Internet access 'takes place in an economic context' even when it is ancillary to the provider's principal activity.

The second group of questions concern the delimitation of the liability of a provider of mere conduit services. The question is, first, whether injunctions, damages and court costs can be awarded against intermediaries for violations by third parties; secondly, 'whether a national court is entitled to order an intermediary service provider to refrain from doing something which would enable a third party to commit the infringement in question'; and, thirdly, whether any conditions such as those in article 14 could be imposed on an intermediary. In answer to the first part of the question, the Advocate General emphasized that liability insulation extended in all directions, for 'criminal law, administrative law and civil law, and also to direct liability and secondary liability for acts committed by third parties'. If the conditions from article 12 had been fulfilled, the intermediary should not be held liable for damages or court

---

[30]   See S.S. Jakobsen, 'Mobile Commerce and ISP Liability in the EU' (2010) 18 *International Journal of Law and Information Technology* 1, 12.

[31]   C-484/14 *Tobias Mc Fadden v Sony Music Entertainment Germany GmbH* (not yet decided), Advocate General Opinion delivered on 16 March 2016, ECLI:EU:C:2016:170.

costs. In terms of the third question, the purpose of which is to determine that the intermediary has neither knowledge of nor control over the information, the Advocate General stated that the conditions in article 12 were exhaustive and could not be supplemented with any other. In answer to the second question, and in line with other decisions of the CJEU, an interim measure could be ordered against an otherwise non-liable 'mere conduit' intermediary.[32]

2.3 Caching

A further exemption from liability exists in article 13 which deals with caching. Caching is defined as automatic, intermediate and temporary storage of computer data for later faster and easier access. It can take place not only at ISP level, but at any point between them and the end-user and also at the end-user's computer. It was mentioned that article 12 exempts providers from liability for temporary storage. Article 13 has a similar purpose as article 12, the difference being in the length and nature of the storage. In terms of the length of storage, caching is storage on a temporary basis that is meant to speed up access to content by keeping it stored on a local server, rather than retrieving it constantly for every transaction.

The transmissions covered in this article are automatic, intermediate and temporary. The automatic element refers to the absence of a deliberate and targeted human intervention. For example, the operator may initiate the taking of a 'snapshot' of the system, but this cannot be for the purpose of storing specific information from a specific email or webpage. The intermediate nature of the transmission refers to the fact that the ISSP is neither the initial poster nor the intended recipient. The temporary nature refers to the fact that information cannot be retained indefinitely. In any case, the sole purpose of the storage must be to facilitate the flow of information to the intended recipient.

To insulate itself from liability, the provider would have to refrain from modifying the information (for this prevents it from being treated as an intermediary); would have to comply with any conditions on access to information (the cached page should follow the same conditions that exist for the main page, if the latter is available in different versions depending on access privileges, the former cannot ignore that), with rules regarding the updating of information (for only updated information guarantees that a cached page is the same as the original). The provider is not allowed to

---

[32] See section 3 below.

interfere with the lawful use of technology used to obtain usage statistics. Finally, the information should be as accurate as possible.

It is currently unclear whether caching which mainstream search engines (such as Google) provide as part of their service qualifies as caching under article 13. The said cached copies typically appear as part of search results, in the form of a link or a button. The problem is that the cached copies, although automatic and temporary, do not seem to be intermediate but rather a permanent, albeit updated, feature. It is also possible to envisage a service where the search engine provides several copies, taken at different times. As in article 12, courts or administrative authorities can require the termination or prevent an infringement. Also, as in that article, interlocutory measures can be used as well as regular actions.

No direct ruling on article 13 in the context of intermediaries exists.

2.4 Hosting

Article 14 of the Directive regulates hosting. Hosting, unlike transmitting or caching, is the act of methodical and permanent storage of information, based on a contract between the provider and the user. Under this contract, the information is placed on the host's servers from where it is made available to the general public. In modern times, hosting can take more complex and more ambiguous forms.[33] User-generated content (UGC) sites allow users to store information they created independently (photos, videos, music, text, etc.) and typically use a particular structure to display these files. File hosting sites allow users to store their files in general without structuring the content. A number of websites share links only, often of infringing content (movies, software) which can be obtained from file hosting sites. Other sites manipulate the links, aggregating them and making indexes available to users. The status of some of these will be tested in the courts in the years to come.

Article 14 stipulates that the provider will not be liable for the information if either of two conditions have been met. The first is that the provider must not have actual knowledge of illegal activity or information and 'as regards claims for damages, is not aware of facts or circumstances from which the illegal activity or information is apparent'. This condition will not be fulfilled where the provider is aware that a

---

[33]   For classification of hosting business models, see J.B. Nordeman, 'Liability for Copyright Infringements on the Internet: Host Providers (Content Providers) – The German Approach' (2011) 2 *Journal of Intellectual Property, Information Technology and E-Commerce Law* 37, 38.

significant proportion of the activity on its servers is illegal in nature (such as in the case of popular file-sharing websites).

The second condition is that the provider who has obtained knowledge or awareness of the illegality must act quickly to remove or disable access to information. This is the case where the right-holder informs the ISSP of the alleged infringement. The second condition may lead to considerable difficulties in cases where a provider is notified by a third party that the information put on the Web by the recipient is illegal. The provider may act quickly, fearing exposure to liability. This may lead it to effectively censor content on the Internet at a mere notice from the affected party. At the same time, the provider is concerned that removing the material prematurely may expose it to action by the recipient. In practice, the evidence has shown that providers are prepared to remove content at a mere notice from the affected party, since the risk of a lawsuit from the right-holder is higher than the corresponding risk of a lawsuit from the customer.

Article 14(3) allows Member States to terminate or prevent an infringement. Importantly, it also allows Member States to establish procedures governing the removal or disabling of access to information. This is the possibility to issue an injunction to prevent access to infringing content, which has been confirmed in the CJEU's case law.[34]

The first opportunity for the Court to interpret the operation of article 14 came in the *Google France v Louis Vuitton* case. There, the issue was whether the use of a registered trade mark in an Adword link within the Google search system constituted an infringement of that registered trademark.[35] The Google corporation operates an advertising system whereby customers are allowed to purchase a number of 'Adwords'. The purchase of these allows the paying company's link to appear higher in the list of search results than it otherwise would do, albeit in a section which is clearly marked as advertising. Google does not monitor whether their customers actually own trademarks which they purchase. Louis Vuitton Corp., which engages in the manufacture of luxury goods such as leather bags, began trademark infringement proceedings against Google. One of the questions was whether Google, in its capacity of a referencing service, fell under the protective provisions of article 14.

---

[34] For more on the case law dealing with this see section 3 below.
[35] Joined Cases C-236/08 and C-238/08 *Google France SARL and Google Inc. v Louis Vuitton Malletier SA and others* [2010] ECR I-02417.

The question revolved around the amount of control that the hosting service exercised. The CJEU held that search engines must be treated as hosts:

> in the case where that service provider has not played an active role of such a kind as to give it knowledge of, or control over, the data stored.

Where, on the contrary, it has played an active role, it will still be protected for the data which it has stored at the request of an advertiser. Liability comes only where, having obtained the knowledge of the illegal nature of the advertiser's activity, it 'failed to act expeditiously to remove or to disable access to the data concerned'. Importantly, the Court held that the mere fact that the search engine is subject to payment cannot, in and of itself, have the effect of removing the liability protection. Also, the fact that the entry of a search term matches the keyword does not imply the search engine's knowledge.

This answer is not entirely without interest, for what the CJEU is really suggesting is that a network which is set to profit from the customers' actions, and which cannot be entirely in good faith regarding what is going on on its network, will only be liable if it is expressly told about a specific infringement.

The CJEU had another opportunity to interpret article 14 in light of a more active intermediary. This was in *L'Oréal v eBay*.[36] The cosmetics producer L'Oréal operated a closed selective distribution system in which distributors were prevented from cross-supplying to other distributors. In spite of this, many of its products found their way onto the electronic auction site eBay. Some of those were counterfeit whereas others, presumably genuine, were sold without L'Oréal's authorization. L'Oréal sued for trademark infringement and the question revolved around the interpretation of the words 'actual knowledge' or 'awareness' within the meaning of article 14(1). L'Oréal claimed that eBay had active knowledge of the infringements that were constantly taking place. In the view of the Court, the key question was the level of control that the operator (eBay) exercised. eBay was not just a passive storage medium but an active facilitator. The operator of the website, eBay, played such a role when it optimized the presentation of the offers for sale in question or

---

[36] C-324/09 *L'Oréal SA, Lancôme parfums et beauté & Cie SNC, Laboratoire Garnier & Cie, L'Oréal (UK) Ltd v eBay International AG and others*, ECLI:EU:C:2011:474, 12 July 2011.

promoted them. eBay, the Court ruled, was not a passive host but one that arranged the offers and actively profited from them. In the words of the Court:

> Where, by contrast, the operator has provided assistance which entails, in particular, optimising the presentation of the offers for sale in question or promoting those offers, it must be considered not to have taken a neutral position between the customer-seller concerned and potential buyers but to have played an active role of such a kind as to give it knowledge of, or control over, the data relating to those offers for sale.

The CJEU ruled, on the other hand, that the E-Commerce Directive must be interpreted as applying to the operator of an online marketplace where that operator has not played an active role allowing it to have knowledge or control of the data stored. The level of active knowledge and involvement remained for the national court to determine. In such cases, the Court ruled, the operator nevertheless could not rely on the exemption from liability:

> if it was aware of facts or circumstances on the basis of which a diligent economic operator should have realised that the offers for sale in question were unlawful and, in the event of it being so aware, failed to act expeditiously in accordance with Article 14(1)(b) of Directive 2000/31.

The preceding paragraph seems to suggest that an operator well aware of the illegality of operations should not be able to benefit from the protective regime. In practice, this will be difficult to determine. A very stringent interpretation of article 14 may force the operators to monitor, an obligation which is clearly excluded in article 15. Complete insulation from liability, on the other hand, encourages illegal content, as only operators who have been specifically notified by the right-holders cease to be protected.

2.5 Monitoring

Internet service providers have no general obligation to monitor contents that appear on their servers.[37] This is a very important exemption, as some early case law in Member States seemed to suggest the opposite.[38] An obligation to monitor traffic would have been extremely costly and

---

[37] E-Commerce Directive, art. 15.
[38] For instance, the 1998 *Somm (CompuServe)* case in Germany, File No. 8340 Ds 465 Js 173158/95, Local Court Munich.

difficult to enforce, as the volume of Internet traffic increases yearly, particularly on user-generated sites. Although some Internet sites are edited or moderated, in the sense that an ISP-approved individual or individuals are overseeing the traffic and editing or deleting potentially illegal content, the majority are not. The presence of such editing potentially removes liability protection and turns intermediaries into editors who bear primary or secondary liability.

Article 15(1) stipulates that no general obligation to monitor information that the intermediaries transmit or store exists. Additionally, no obligation exists 'actively to seek facts or circumstances indicating illegal activity'. The difference between the two formulations is in the nature of the activity. While the former excludes the obligation to observe the traffic, the latter excludes the obligation to 'hunt down' suspected law-breakers. In the former case, an ISSP would not be liable for not knowing what was being stored on its servers, in the latter for not taking active action against a suspected infringer. On the contrary, article 15(1) seems to allow ISSPs to remain passive until the moment when they receive relevant information from the right-holders.

On the other hand, article 15(2) suggests that Member States may establish an obligation to inform the authorities of any alleged illegal activities or information provided by recipients or, crucially, the obligation to communicate to the authorities, at their request, information enabling the identification of recipients with whom they have storage agreements. In other words, the ISSPs may be required by Member States to facilitate the governments' spying on users.[39]

The CJEU, however, ruled in the *Promusicae* case[40] that article 15(2) does not require Member States to lay down an *obligation* to communicate personal data of suspected copyright violators to right-holders in civil proceedings. It further ruled that other EU Directives do not do so either. Instead, a fair balance between fundamental rights must be achieved.

* * *

Analysing the provisions of the E-Commerce Directive, it would seem that ISS providers cannot be made liable for violations committed by end-users as long as they remain passive and as long as they promptly

---

[39] More on this in D. Wright and R. Kreissl (eds.) *Surveillance in Europe* (Routledge, London/New York, 2014).

[40] Case C-275/06 *Productores de Música de España (Promusicae) v Telefónica de España SAU* [2008] ECR I-271.

remove infringing material upon receiving notification. The *L'Oréal* case suggests that simple knowledge of the incriminating facts may, in some cases, remove the protection of the E-Commerce Directive. In the United States, the options have been somewhat extended in the *MGM v Grokster* case,[41] where the Supreme Court held that 'one who distributes a device with the object of promoting its use to infringe copyright … is liable for the resulting acts of infringement by third parties'. In a manner practically similar to the *L'Oréal* case, but conceptually different, the Supreme Court confirmed that Grokster and others induced the copyright infringement by marketing the file-sharing software. It would, therefore, seem unlikely that a website mainly used for illegal activity could avail itself of the protection available in articles 12–15.

3 INJUNCTIVE RELIEF AND REQUESTS FOR INFORMATION

The intermediaries are unique among the actors on the Internet in that they hold information about the users' surfing habits. This information includes times of access, websites visited, the duration and the actual content. On its own, this information is of limited relevance. Aggregated, it can have damaging effects and is deserving of separate protection. For that reason, it is very important that access to confidential information is under strict control.

The obvious avenue for a plaintiff alleging an infringement is to seek to obtain the details of the alleged primary infringer or, in the alternative, to prevent the ISSP from facilitating the infringement. Two separate issues arise from this. The first is the right of a third party (the purported right-holder) to request an ISSP to release information about the alleged infringer's identity. This is a situation concerning an ISSP that holds the accounts of the alleged infringers. The second is the right of the right-holders to obtain injunctive relief against an ISSP itself rather than the actual infringer, including the demand that the ISSP install filtering. This will typically be the case because it is easier and less costly to begin action against the ISSP than individual violators.

Injunctive relief is available under the TRIPS Agreement, Article 50, as well as under other international and national instruments, including the Brussels I Regulation (Recast), article 35. In the EU, in copyright cases,

---

[41] See note 17 above.

article 8(3) of the Copyright Directive[42] provides that Member States shall 'ensure that rightholders are in a position to apply for an injunction against intermediaries whose services are used by a third party to infringe a copyright or related right'. A similar right exists in article 9 of the Copyright Enforcement Directive (2004/48/EC) that regulates provisional and precautionary measures. Article 9 of that Directive provides:

> an interlocutory injunction may also be issued, under the same conditions, against an intermediary whose services are being used by a third party to infringe an intellectual property right; injunctions against intermediaries whose services are used by a third party to infringe a copyright or a related right are covered by Directive 2001/29/EC.

The Copyright Enforcement Directive, article 8, also allows a 'justified and proportionate' request for information concerning the 'origin and distribution networks' of the infringing goods and services. The subject of the obligation is not only an infringer but also any other person who was, among other things, 'found to be providing on a commercial scale services used in infringing activities' or was indicated by the main infringer as 'being involved in production, manufacture or distribution' of the said goods and services. Either of these two possibilities may include an ISSP, which actively promotes infringement or, although not behind it, is aware of and profits directly from it. In any case, safeguards inserted in article 8(3) serve to prevent abuse.

The earlier-mentioned *Promusicae* case[43] involved an action by Promusicae, the Spanish association of audio-video musical publishers and producers against Telefónica, an ISP provider. The question was whether Telefónica was *obliged* to divulge private information regarding its customers under various EU Directives, including the E-Commerce Directive and its provisions on ISP liability. This information would enable Promusicae to pursue an action for copyright infringement. The CJEU held that there was no *obligation* to do so, but that each Member States' courts *may* develop their own standards as long as they 'do not rely on an interpretation of them which would be in conflict with those fundamental rights or with the other general principles of Community law, such as the principle of proportionality'.

The *LSG* case[44] had a similar factual basis. It concerned an action by the Austrian collecting society on behalf of its members who alleged

---

[42] For the Copyright and Copyright Enforcement Directives, see Chapter 6.
[43] See note 40 above.
[44] See note 26 above.

infringements of their copyright against Tele2 as an ISP. The main issue was whether Tele2 could be forced to hand over information about its users in light of the E-Commerce Directive and Data Protection Directive. The CJEU held that the E-Privacy Directive and Copyright Enforcement Directive do not:

> preclude Member States from imposing an obligation to disclose to private third parties personal data relating to Internet traffic in order to enable them to bring civil proceedings for copyright infringements.

Nevertheless, the Court stated that, when interpreting and applying the Copyright Enforcement and the E-Privacy Directives, national courts must not rely on an interpretation that would conflict with fundamental rights.

In the *Bonnier Audio* case,[45] which involved a request to a Swedish ISP to release the identities of the alleged infringer, the CJEU ruled that the Data Retention Directive (2006/24/EC)[46] must be interpreted as not precluding the application of national legislation based on article 8 of the Copyright Enforcement Directive (right of information). The ruling simply confirms that Member States may introduce legislation obliging ISPs to release data (under the safeguards mentioned above).

All of this clearly puts a significant responsibility on the national courts. EU law does not oblige Member States to release data. They may or may not allow this in their national law but, if they do, this must not be contrary to EU and international fundamental rights. The question that the Court had avoided in this case, however, is the legal status of data released in cases where this does *not* violate fundamental rights. Clearly, the separate development of national practice in this area may lead to further requests for guidance from the CJEU.

An important dilemma concerning the extent of the ISSP's obligation to install filtering was resolved in the *SABAM* case.[47] SABAM was the Belgian management company, which represents the rights of authors of musical works, and Scarlet was an ISSP. SABAM complained that Scarlet's users regularly engaged in distribution of works to which SABAM managed rights. SABAM requested, among other things, that Scarlet install filtering technology that would prevent files from being

---

[45] C-461/10 *Bonnier Audio AB v Perfect Communication Sweden AB*, ECLI:EU:C:2012:219, 19 April 2012.

[46] See Chapter 8.

[47] C-70/10 *Scarlet Extended SA v SABAM*, ECLI:EU:C:2011:771, 24 November 2011.

distributed. Scarlet had several arguments against the claim but the most significant was that filtering of the kind that SABAM requested would mean de facto monitoring and surveillance, which would be contrary not only to the E-Commerce Directive but also to EU data protection laws.

The CJEU ruled that the E-Commerce Directive, the Copyright Directive, the Copyright Enforcement Directive, the Data Protection Directive and the E-Privacy Directive, read together in light of protection of fundamental rights:

- must be interpreted as precluding an injunction made against an internet service provider which requires it to install a system for filtering:
- all electronic communications passing via its services, in particular those involving the use of peer-to-peer software;
- which applies indiscriminately to all its customers;
- as a preventive measure;
- exclusively at its expense; and
- for an unlimited period.

Citing its *L'Oréal* case, the CJEU re-emphasized that measures that would amount to ISSP monitoring are unlawful under EU rules. The problem, in the Court's view, is not the very fact of introducing an injunction to resolve a copyright infringement. This has been and remains possible. The problem is in the nature of the injunction that SABAM requested. Such an injunction was of a duration and nature so restrictive that it clashed both with the EU Directives and fundamental rights. Therefore, put in simple terms, the *SABAM* court prohibited generic filtering but allowed individualized blocking.

Restraining injunctions against ISPs in the context of the E-Commerce Directive remain possible at the national level in those legal systems that allow them. Thus, the Danish courts allowed a restraining injunction in several cases. One of these[48] was a Supreme Court case and the other[49] was a lower court injunction against the service provider who acted as a gateway for the server where files violating the applicant's copyright had been held.[50]

---

[48]   *TDC v IFPI*, Supreme Court Decision 49/2005, 10 February 2006, Danish Weekly Law Report (U.) 2006.1474 H.

[49]   *IFPI v Tele2*, Sheriff's Court Copenhagen, Order F1-15124/2006, 25 October 2006.

[50]   See K. Frost, 'Denmark: Restraining Injunction against Internet Providers' (2007) 2 *Computer Law Review International* 50 and (2007) 3 *Computer Law Review International* 87.

Both the intellectual property and other types of issues are subject to injunctive relief in civil proceedings. Article 35 of the Brussels I Regulation (Recast) specifically allows provisional measures even in cases where other courts have jurisdiction as to the substance of the matter. The application is for such measures 'as may be available under the law of that Member State' which is a recognition of the fact that this area is not harmonized.

The CJEU had an opportunity to revisit the problem in the 2014 *UPC* case.[51] Constantin Film and Wega were two film production companies. Their films were made available for distribution through downloads and illegal streaming through a website located outside the EU. They applied to an Austrian ISSP, UPC, asking it to block access to the website to users in Austria. When UPC declined, the film producers obtained an injunction asking UPC essentially to do everything in its power to block the access to the infringing website, but without specifying the actual measures. One of the questions referred to the CJEU was whether an injunction of the kind described above (not specifying the measures but allowing the ISSP to demonstrate that it had taken all reasonable measures) was compatible with fundamental rights. The Court held that it was, under the following two conditions:

(i) the measures taken did not unnecessarily deprive Internet users of the possibility of lawfully accessing the information available; and

(ii) that those measures had the effect of preventing unauthorized access to the protected subject matter or, at least, of making it difficult to achieve and of seriously discouraging Internet users who were using the services of the addressee of that injunction from accessing the subject matter that has been made available to them in breach of the intellectual property right, that being a matter for the national authorities and courts to establish.

In its analysis of the case, the Court repeated the balancing arguments already encountered in its *Promusicae* line of cases and concluded that the national court in question performed the said test correctly. In balancing the rights of copyright holders with the rights of the ISSPs and the users, the Court said that the measures need not be completely successful but that they needed to be 'sufficiently effective to ensure genuine protection'. The national courts are supposed to perform the

---

[51] C-314/12 *UPC Telekabel Wien GmbH v Constantin Film Verleih GmbH and Wega Filmproduktionsgesellschaft mbH*, ECLI:EU:C:2014:192, 27 March 2014.

function of deciding both whether the injunctions are effective and whether the users are unnecessarily deprived of their right to information by overly eager ISSPs.

The case has brought some confusion. The Advocate General, in his Opinion, suggested that 'outcome prohibitions' of the type in question were *not* compatible with fundamental rights but that specific measures to make it more difficult for customers to access illegal content should be allowed. The CJEU did not follow this, opting for the solution described above instead – a solution which, in reality, leaves a lot to courts of Member States and increases uncertainty.

The latest views on the limits and legality of interim measures came from the Advocate General's Opinion in *McFadden*.[52] In that case, the Advocate General stated that preliminary measures were allowed under article 8(3) of the Copyright Directive and under article 11 of the Copyright Enforcement Directive. In addition to that, the CJEU's case law in construing the mentioned provisions allowed injunctions 'against an intermediary who provides Internet access and whose services are used by a third party to infringe a copyright or a related right'. The Advocate General, in exploring the limits of such measures, encouraged the balancing of the freedom of expression and information and the freedom to conduct business (EU Charter of Fundamental Rights, Articles 11 and 16, respectively) on one side, against the right to the protection of IP rights (Charter, Article 17(2)) on the other. In particular, it was important:

- that the measures in question comply with Article 3 of [the Copyright Enforcement Directive] and, in particular, are effective, proportionate and dissuasive;
- that, in accordance with Articles 12(3) and 15(1) of [the E-Commerce Directive], they are aimed at bringing a specific infringement to an end or preventing a specific infringement and do not entail a general obligation to monitor;
- that the application of the provisions mentioned, and of other detailed procedures laid down in national law, achieves a fair balance between the relevant fundamental rights, in particular, those protected by Articles 11 and 16 and by Article 17(2) of the Charter.

---

[52]   See note 31 above.

The question of whether proper measures exist and whether they are compatible with the EU requirements listed above remains for the national court.

Finally, the Advocate General discussed hypothetical interim measures proposed by the referring court. These were: (1) termination of the Internet connection; (2) the password-protection of the Internet connection; and (3) the examination of all communications passing through that connection. The Advocate General dismissed the first and the third immediately. In his mind, the first was incompatible with fundamental rights while the third was incompatible with the general prohibition to monitor (E-Commerce Directive, article 15). In regard to the second question (making the network secure), the Advocate General pointed out the negative sides that such a requirement would bring. Not only would it change the business model of some ISSPs significantly, but it would also increase the burden of storing data in compliance with privacy laws.

4 EUROPEAN COURT OF HUMAN RIGHTS

The European Court of Human Rights, while not an EU organ, nevertheless plays a significant role in profiling Member States' courts' interpretations of the European Convention on Human Rights. Since the two legal regimes essentially interpret two different sets of legal sources, incompatibilities are possible and occasionally happen. Two lines of cases have particular significance for intermediary liability. They both stem from Article 10 ECHR. In the first, the ECtHR discussed the scope and legality of access to information in the context of blocking injunctions. In the second, the issue was freedom of expression in light of intermediary liability.

In *Ahmet Yildirim v Turkey*,[53] the ECtHR addressed the issue of wholesale blocking. Mr Yildirim was a Turkish student who used the services of Google Sites to create and host his website. At the time in question, access to all Google services had been suspended as a result of an order by a criminal court. The order itself came about after some content allegedly insulting to Kemal Ataturk, founder of the Turkish republic, had been posted. The blocked site was unrelated to the site that provoked the ban. The question posed was whether this was in line with Article 10 ECHR.

---

[53] *Ahmet Yildirim v Turkey*, App. No. 3111/10, 18 December 2012.

The ECtHR held that it was not, in principle, impossible to envisage a restriction on Internet access which would be compatible with the ECHR but that an effective mechanism preventing abuse of power would be needed:

> the Court considers that such prior restraints are not necessarily incompatible with the Convention as a matter of principle. However, a legal framework is required, ensuring both tight control over the scope of bans and effective judicial review to prevent any abuse of power.

The ECtHR noted that the Turkish court had explored neither whether a less restrictive way of blocking existed (including targeting only the offending site), nor what collateral consequences the ban might have. It further noted that no national safeguards for ensuring that a local ban did not turn into a general ban existed. In those circumstances, a generic ban on all Google sites was a violation of the right to free information. In other cases, however,[54] a more targeted filtering was ruled to be in line with the ECHR.

Delfi v Estonia[55] was a case discussing the role of intermediaries in the context of freedom of expression. An Estonian Internet news portal hosted an article with a comments section. It was this section that contained defamatory comments concerning the defendant. The news portal published many articles on a daily basis and a comments section was made available for the users to post in for each of those. The comments were posted automatically without editorial control or moderation. A take-down system was in existence as was an automatic removal process for messages that contained certain obscene keywords. A disclaimer on the website warned users that the comments did not reflect the operator/intermediary's opinions and that comments which were threatening, insulting, hostile, violent, illegal, advertising in nature, off-topic or vulgar would be deleted. According to the Estonian government, Delfi had a reputation for publishing defamatory statements. Comments relating to a member of a supervisory board of a road company had been posted on Delfi in 2006 and he brought civil action for damages against Delfi. The comments were removed six weeks after their publication.

The lower court made a distinction between the site's articles and comments sections. Posting in the former undoubtedly made the site a publisher but the latter fell within the protection afforded by the

---

54   See e.g., *Akdeniz v Turkey*, App. No. 20877/10, 11 March 2014.
55   *Delfi v Estonia*, App. No. 64569/09, 16 June 2015.

E-Commerce Directive where the site was a host and exercised mechanical and passive control. The Estonian Supreme Court, however, took the position that comment publication was not merely of a 'technical, automatic and passive' nature and that it was not subject to the protection provided in articles 12–15 of the E-Commerce Directive.

The ECtHR found the comments 'extreme in nature' and noted the commercial nature of the company, suggesting that this somehow had an impact on the case but not clarifying what exactly this might have been. Having accepted the Supreme Court's idea that Delfi was a primary poster without giving any further thought to the issue, it found the measures taken to remove the comments to be 'insufficient'. Making the site liable was, in its view, not a disproportionate restriction of the applicant's right to freedom of expression. The Court further said that removing content 'without delay' and 'without notice' was fully appropriate in this situation.

The ECtHR judgment is not only fundamentally perplexing but also incompatible with CJEU's case law on intermediaries. As the dissenting opinions pointed out, the judgment created a liability system that imposed a 'requirement of constructive knowledge on active Internet intermediaries' which, in the view of the dissenting judges, was 'an invitation to self-censorship'. As the dissent pointed out, there were two problems with such an approach. First, there was no explanation in the judgment as to why valid provisions of EU law (E-Commerce Directive, articles 12–15) are not applicable. As a result, there is no adequate explanation as to why Delfi had been taken to be an active intermediary in relation to its comments section. Secondly, there was no explanation as to why such intermediaries, even if one accepted the fact that they were active, should exercise *prior* and not *subsequent* restraint. In other words, why would an active intermediary here be obliged to have a monitoring system which caught potential violations rather than be obliged to remove them upon notification, as E-Commerce Directive, article 14 commands. The liability standard applied here was, in fact, one normally used for publishers. No reasons were given in the judgment why an active intermediary should be made equal to a publisher, nor why an economic interest might possibly change the picture.

MTE v Hungary[56] was a first post-*Delfi* judgment on intermediary liability. It involved a civil action by a real estate company for defamation through dissemination of allegedly defamatory comments by two

---

[56] *Magyar Tartalomszolgáltatók Egyesülete and Index.hu Zrt v Hungary*, App. No. 22947/13, 2 February 2016.

intermediaries, a self-regulatory body and an online news portal, both of which carried the same story. Just as in the *Delfi* case, the comments had been posted not in the article itself but in the comments section. The Hungarian courts refused to insulate the intermediaries from liability as per the E-Commerce Directive, claiming that the Hungarian implementation of these provisions was limited to services of a commercial nature. In the view of the Hungarian court, these were private comments and, therefore, outside the scope of the protective provisions of the Directive.

In its earlier case law, the ECtHR ruled that an interference with Article 10 ECHR freedom of expression must be prescribed by law, have a legitimate aim and be necessary for a democratic society. In order to conduct the balancing between competing rights in question (the right to information vs the right to reputation), the following five factors needed to be taken into consideration: the context and content of the comments; the liability of the authors of the comment; the measures taken by the injured party; the consequences of the comment for the injured party; and the consequences for the applicant. Referring to *Delfi*, the ECtHR held that 'if accompanied by effective procedures allowing for rapid response, the notice-and-take-down-system could function in many cases as an appropriate tool for balancing the rights and interests of all those involved'. Having said that, the Court concluded that there had been a violation of Article 10 ECHR since the comments had not been removed with respect to the criteria above.

The *MTE* case brings further confusion into the arena. While reaffirming *Delfi*, it deals with none of the difficulties which that case brought. It still remains unclear how an intermediary is supposed to know of a violation unless it is told of it. In *Delfi*, the ECtHR demanded a full monitoring and filtering – a blatant violation of E-Commerce Directive, article 15. The *MTE* court, although suggesting in paragraph 82 that filtering might be excessive, impractical and undermining of the freedom of information, went (just like *Delfi*) in the direction of allowing national courts to demand more than just notice-and-take-down. In other words, the *MTE* court too was happy with a system of prior restraint.

5 CONCLUSION

There is no doubt that the European rules on intermediary liability, as they stand in the E-Commerce Directive, have stood the test of time. The rules, which largely mirror the model adopted in the United States, provide robust protection for intermediaries who are not publishers. The rules seem to adequately cover all the typical situations that diverse intermediaries might find themselves in, from transient to more permanent.

The CJEU, through its case law, had the opportunity to clarify the operation of these rules. Its case law is largely consistent in reaffirming both that non-active intermediaries who have not been notified can rely on the protection and that only adequate notification followed by refusal to remove can lead to liability (*eBay*, *L'Oréal* cases). Furthermore, a confirmed ban on monitoring, as well as a restriction on the types of filtering (*SABAM*, *UPC*) keep the level of certainty relatively high.

On the other hand, serious problems have been created through both the national courts' lack of understanding of the interface between the E-Commerce Directive and the ECHR and the confusion that the ECtHR had brought to this field. Not only does the ECtHR demand a totally different standard of liability (effectively demanding pre-emptive action and active monitoring) but it does little to clarify when an intermediary remains an intermediary and when it can expect to be treated as a primary publisher.

It is not clear how the mentioned inconsistencies between the two courts can be resolved. In its Communication on copyright reform,[57] the Commission suggested that 'follow-the-money' approach might be something it would be willing to look into further when revisiting the role of the intermediaries. No explanation was given as to what this approach might be and this leaves some space for concern. Neither is this entirely consistent with the ideas found in the 2015 Digital Single Market Strategy mentioned in section 1 above, where the Commission uses yet another undefined term, 'a duty of care'. It is submitted here that the main principles on which intermediary liability rests should not be revised.

---

[57] European Commission, *Towards a Modern, More European Copyright Framework*, COM(2015)626 final (9 December 2015).

6. Intellectual property

The European Union regulates intellectual property (IP) rights compre-hensively.[1] Most of the areas traditionally included in IP law are addressed in various related policies and documents, covered by one or more Regulations or Directives and are frequently addressed in the Court of Justice of the European Union (CJEU). EU law affects national IP rights in two ways. First, it harmonizes various IP rights or establishes unitary EU-wide IP rights. We examine this aspect in the sections below. Secondly, it subjects national IP regimes to free movement provisions.[2] This is mainly seen through non-discrimination cases, which are mostly irrelevant in the Internet context, and the exhaustion of rights doctrine, which is looked at in section 3.7 below. While these approaches are conceptually different, together they produce a very wide coverage of various IP rights.[3]

The EU's international obligations also significantly influence its regulatory model. This influence is apparent either in concrete obliga-tions that stem from these treaties, or from the inspiration that they give the EU law-maker. The Member States individually and the EU as a whole are party to the 1995 Agreement on Trade-Related Aspects of Intellectual Property Rights (TRIPS). Although the Agreement does not have direct effect, it can be and is interpreted and applied at EU level.[4] Similarly, and of equal importance for the present subject, the EU and the Member States are parties to the World Intellectual Property (WIPO) Copyright Treaty 1996 and the WIPO Performances and Phonograms Treaty 1996.[5]

---

[1] For an overview of the field, see T. Cook, *EU Intellectual Property Law* (OUP, Oxford, 2010). For copyright only see I. Stamatoudi and P. Torremans, *EU Copyright Law: A Commentary* (Edward Elgar Publishing, Cheltenham and Northampton, MA, 2015).

[2] On the different effect of these two influences, see Cook, *EU Intellectual Property Law*, note 1 above, especially chs 1 and 2.

[3] The Single Market aspect of the question, while of considerable interest, is only of limited importance for cases involving the Internet.

[4] C-53/96 *Hérmes* [1998] ECR I-03603.

[5] Council Decision of 16 March 2000 [2000] OJ L89/6, 11 April 2000.

This chapter analyses the application of the EU intellectual property regime to the digital world. Two Directives will be analysed in some detail: the Copyright Directive (section 1) and the Copyright Enforcement Directive (section 2). Both have direct application to the Internet and have been tested in national courts and in the CJEU. We also look at how the Court has interpreted the Directives. Some of the other harmonized IP laws *specifically* address the digital world and most are written in a technology-neutral manner, leaving scope for their application to the Internet. These will also be looked at in section 3. Finally, some words will also be dedicated to the future EU IP policy (section 4).

1 COPYRIGHT IN THE INFORMATION SOCIETY DIRECTIVE[6]

The Copyright Directive (2001/29/EC) implements the provisions of the WIPO Copyright Treaty 1996 and WIPO Performances and Phonograms Treaty 1996 into European law. It lays the foundations for modern copyright law in the digital age by harmonizing disparate laws of Member States.[7] While meant as a copyright instrument for the digital age, the Directive also takes account of the four freedoms in copyright regulation. In other words, it fine-tunes copyright law to the demands of the digital economy while maintaining the Digital Single Market context.[8]

The Directive is not an entirely new instrument, but is based on previous Community legislation, such as the Software Directive (Original Version) for the protection of computer programs,[9] the Rental and Lending Rights Directive (Original Version)[10] and the Database Directive.[11] The first proposal for the Copyright Directive dates back to

---

[6] Directive 2001/29/EC on the harmonization of certain aspects of copyright and related rights in the information society [2001] OJ L167/10, 22 June 2001.

[7] See Recital 15 of the Directive.

[8] See Recitals 5–8.

[9] The original version: Council Directive 91/250/EEC of 14 May 1991 on the legal protection of computer programs [1991] OJ L122/42, 17 May 1991.

[10] Council Directive 92/100/EEC of 19 November 1992 on rental rights and lending right and on certain rights related to copyright in the field of intellectual property [1992] OJ L346/61, 27 November 1992.

[11] Directive 96/9/EC of the European Parliament and of the Council of 11 March 1996 on the legal protection of databases [1996] OJ L77/20, 27 March 1996.

1997.[12] The amendments were approved by the European Parliament in 1999[13] and the final support came in 2000. The Directive was not approved until 2001, with the final implementation date in 2002.

Several important points need to be mentioned at the outset. First, the Directive starts from the premise that disparities in copyright laws and related rights harm competition and the development of the Internal Market.[14] This puts it in line with other EU IP instruments, giving it focus but limiting its scope. The Single Market dimension informs the Directive's objectives as well as its approach. Thirdly, the Directive, which has 'a high level of protection' as a basis (Recital 9), is strongly economically oriented, having as its goal increased growth.[15] Recital 4 claims that the Directive:

> will foster substantial investment in creativity and innovation, including network infrastructure, and lead in turn to growth and increased competitiveness of European industry, both in the area of content provision and information technology and more generally across a wide range of industrial and cultural sectors. This will safeguard employment and encourage new job creation.

Finally, although the Directive implements the WIPO Treaty and largely follows the US regulatory model, it deviates from both in some important aspects.[16] The Directive is a minimal and targeted harmonization of copyright law but not a full harmonization measure that is meant to replace national laws.

1.1   Operation of the Directive

The scope of the Copyright Directive is set out in article 1, which highlights its Internal Market aspect but also puts an emphasis on the information society services (ISS). The Directive covers the whole field of copyright, being in that sense a comprehensive harmonization measure. However, the Directive is not a full harmonization of the whole area, but rather one that puts a 'particular emphasis on the information society'. The exceptions are set out in article 1(2) and they include: legal

---

12   [1998] OJ C108/6, 7 April 1998.
13   [1999] OJ C150/171, 28 May 1999.
14   For example, Recitals 1, 6 and 8.
15   For more on the Directive's objectives, see its Preamble, Recitals 1 to 19.
16   Especially in relation to the protection of technological measures.

protection of computer programs;[17] rental right, lending right and certain rights related to copyright;[18] copyright and related rights applicable to broadcasting;[19] term of protection;[20] and legal protection of databases.[21] The Directive covers 'copyright and related rights'. This is an acknowledgment of the existence of two systems, the continental and the common law one, with related rights (also known as neighbouring rights) being typically protected in both the United States and the United Kingdom but less so elsewhere.

The Internal Market dimension of the Directive is emphasized in a general way in the Preamble,[22] which talks of ensuring that competition, marketing and distribution of new products is not distorted. Of more direct relevance, however, is the idea set out in Recital 6 that national action responding to 'technological challenges', already initiated in a number of Member States at the time of drafting, might lead to uncertainty and hinder free movement of goods and services or economies of scale for new products. In other words, one of the aims was to pre-empt Member States from legislating in this important field. The new information society dimension is also recognized explicitly throughout

---

[17] Covered in Directive 2009/24/EC of the European Parliament and of the Council of 23 April 2009 on the legal protection of computer programs (Codified version) [2009] OJ L111/16, 5 May 2009 ('Software Directive (Codified)'). On abortive attempts to protect software with patents, see J. Park, 'Has Patentable Subject Matter Been Expanded?: A Comparative Study on Software Patent Practices in the European Patent Office, the United States Patent and Trademark Office and the Japanese Patent Office' (2005) 13 *International Journal of Law and Information Technology* 336.

[18] Covered in Directive 2006/115/EC of the European Parliament and of the Council of 12 December 2006 on rental right and lending right and on certain rights related to copyright in the field of intellectual property (Codified version) [2006] OJ L376/28, 27 December 2006 ('Rental and Lending Rights Directive (Codified)').

[19] Covered in Council Directive 93/83/EEC of 27 September 1993 on the coordination of certain rules concerning copyright and rights related to copyright applicable to satellite broadcasting and cable retransmission [1993] OJ L248/15, 6 October 1993 ('Satellite and Cable Broadcasting Directive').

[20] Covered in Directive 2011/77/EU of the European Parliament and of the Council amending Directive 2006/116/EC on the term of protection of copyright and certain related rights [2011] OJ L265/1, 11 October 2011 ('Copyright Term Directive').

[21] Covered in Directive 96/9/EC of the European Parliament and of the Council of 11 March 1996 on the legal protection of databases [1996] OJ L77/20, 27 March 1996 ('Database Directive').

[22] Recitals 1–4.

the document. The current law 'should be adapted and supplemented to respond adequately to economic realities such as new forms of exploitation'.[23]

Article 2 deals with reproduction rights. It obliges Member States to provide for the exclusive right to authorize or prohibit 'direct or indirect, temporary or permanent' reproduction 'by any means or in any form, in whole or in part' to authors, performers, phonogram producers, producers of first fixations of films, and broadcasting organizations. The Directive, in Recital 21, calls for a broad definition, in conformity with the *acquis communautaire*, of acts covered by the reproduction right of article 2.

In terms of content, article 2 provides a broad protection of copyright. The exclusive right to authorize reproduction extends to 'direct or indirect, temporary or permanent reproduction by any means and in any form, in whole or in part'. While temporary reproduction is included, a special exception exists in article 5(1) for reproductions that are only part of a technological process. This would cover most instances where temporary electronic copies are made to enable IT functionality. The subjects are defined according to the scope of exploitation specific for the group in question. Authors are covered in general, performers in relation to their performances, phonogram producers in relation to their phono-grams and film producers and broadcasting organizations in the scope of their respective businesses.

Although the protection is broad, it is surprising how little in terms of explanation the Directive offers for the scope of protection offered. Article 2 entails the right to authorize or prohibit both the direct and indirect reproduction of both a temporary or a permanent nature, which covers total or partial reproduction in any form and by any means. This approach provides very wide protection without proper consideration of the technical aspects of the Internet. It is clear that by its very nature, the Internet involves making indirect, temporary or partial reproductions even when the exception from article 5(1) is applied. For example, providing snippets of information from news websites on a commercial webpage would amount to partial reproduction and fall under article 2. In *Infopaq*,[24] the CJEU ruled that storing an 11-word extract from a news website and allowing it to be printed constituted a violation of copyright

---

[23]   Recital 5.
[24]   C-5/08 *Infopaq International A/S v Danske Daglades Forening* [2009] ECR I-6569.

within the meaning of article 2. In light of the rapid development that the Internet had witnessed in recent years, the article may be in need of a revision.

Article 3 covers the right of communication to the public and making available to the public.[25] The right of communication to the public applies to 'wired or wireless means' and includes on-demand uses, 'from a place and at a time individually chosen'. Article 3(3) specifically provides that the right of communication is not exhausted by communication or other acts of making works available. The distinction made in the article between 'communication' and 'making available' of 'other subject matter' refers to the disparity in Member States' laws between those systems that recognize a general right of communication and those which do not. The authors retain, in article 3(1), an exclusive right to control the communication to the public, by 'wire or wireless means'. Importantly, as article 3(2) provides, this includes the right by 'members of the public' to access the works 'from a place and at a time individually chosen by them'. This latter feature is then specifically regulated in the next paragraph, which obliges Member States to introduce this right in respect of performers, phonogram producers and broadcasting organizations. This article simply extends the right of communication, itself well known and protected throughout the Member States, to the new digital subject matter.

The CJEU case law is also clear on the point of communication to the public in different contexts involving technology. In the *Premier League*[26] case, British pub owners legally acquired Greek decoding cards that they then used for showing Premier League matches in their UK establishments where such cards were markedly more expensive. The Court ruled that 'transmission of the broadcast works, via a television screen and speakers, to the customers present in a public house' constituted communication to the public in terms of article 3(1). The same was confirmed in other cases.[27]

---

[25] On making available in the United States and the EU, see J. Ginsburg, 'Where Does the Act of "Making Available" Occur?' in A. Savin and J. Trzaskowski, *Research Handbook on EU Internet Law* (Edward Elgar Publishing, Cheltenham and Northampton, MA, 2013), p. 191.

[26] C-403/08 *Football Association Premier League Ltd and others v QC Leisure and others* and C-429/08 *Karen Murphy v Media Protection Services Ltd* [2011] ECR I-090834.

[27] C-351/12 *OSA – Ochranný svaz autorský pro práva k dílům hudebním o.s. v Léčebné lázně Mariánské Lázně a.s.*, ECLI:EU:C:2014:110, 27 February 2014.

In *TV Catchup*,[28] the question was discussed in relation to an Internet retransmission of terrestrial signals. There, TV Catchup, the provider of live Internet streams of free-to-air television broadcasts, has been accused of copyright violations by various companies holding rights in TV programmes. TV Catchup had only been made available to those who already had access to the content through their regular UK TV licence and this was enforced through IP address monitoring. For its business model, TV Catchup relied on various forms of advertising. The question asked was, essentially, whether article 3(1) covered situations, such as the one in the main case, where legally available signals were accessed through third party servers. The Court ruled that it did:

- where the retransmission is made by an organization other than the original broadcaster;
- by means of an Internet stream made available to the subscribers of that other organization who may receive that retransmission by logging on to its server;
- even though those subscribers are within the area of reception of that terrestrial television broadcast and may lawfully receive the broadcast on a television receiver.

Interestingly, the Court ruled that neither the fact that the retransmitter relied on advertising nor the fact that TV Catchup was in direct competition with the broadcaster had any influence on this solution. This means that a non-profit organization not in competition would also have been found in violation. The conclusion that must be drawn from the previous cases is clearly that the right-holders have full control over Internet retransmission of their programmes.[29]

Of particular importance here is also the right of 'making available to the public'. Unlike communication to the public, where the person communicating chooses the means and the time, here the works are made *available* to the public so that the public can chose where and when to access them. The works can be on offer via downloads or via streaming and the technological means by which this is done are irrelevant. Therefore, all forms of streaming, on-demand or retrieval services where

---

[28] C-607/11 *ITV Broadcasting Ltd, ITV 2 Ltd, ITV Digital Channels Ltd, Channel 4 Television Corporation, 4 Ventures Ltd, Channel 5 Broadcasting Ltd and ITV Studios Ltd v TVCatchup Ltd*, ECLI:EU:C:2013:147, 7 March 2013.

[29] Compare this case with the US Supreme Court *Aereo* case, where similar results were reached on similar facts, *American Broadcasting Companies v Aereo*, 573 U.S. ___ (2014).

the recipient chooses the times and the mode, are covered. Whether the public had accessed the works or not is of no relevance since the act of making available takes place as soon as the possibility to access the work is there.[30]

An important ruling on making available in the Internet context came about in the *Football Dataco* case.[31] The case concerned the re-utilization right under the Database Directive. A German company was alleged to have copied data about football matches from another company and made it available to its customers. In deciding where the act of re-utilization had taken place, the CJEU rejected server location as a determining factor and said, instead, that making available:

> must be interpreted as meaning that the sending by one person, by means of a web server located in Member State A, of data previously uploaded by that person from a database protected by the sui generis right under that directive to the computer of another person located in Member State B, at that person's request, for the purpose of storage in that computer's memory and display on its screen, constitutes an act of 're-utilisation' of the data by the person sending it. That act takes place, at least, in Member State B, where there is evidence from which it may be concluded that the act discloses an intention on the part of the person performing the act to target members of the public in Member State B, which is for the national court to assess.

It is, therefore, for the targeted state to determine whether making available had taken place.

In a series of cases beginning with *Svensson*,[32] the CJEU addressed whether hyperlinking to other sites amounts to communication to the public as per article 3(1). In *Svensson*, an aggregator website provided links to newspaper articles published on a number of other sites. When a customer accessing the aggregator site clicked on a link, they were referred to articles located on the original sites. In the eyes of the right-holders of the latter this was problematic since the referring company made use of their articles without compensation. The question referred to was whether hyperlinking such as this amounted to communication to the public as per article 3(1). The Court held that, in order for article 3(1) to apply, two conditions need to be fulfilled: there has to be

---

[30] On jurisdiction issues concerning making available see Ginsburg, 'Where Does the Act of "Making Available" Occur?', note 25 above.

[31] C-173/11 *Football Dataco Ltd and others*, ECLI:EU:C:2012:642, 18 October 2012.

[32] C-466/12 *Nils Svensson, Sten Sjögren, Madelaine Sahlman and Pia Gadd v Retriever Sverige AB*, ECLI:EU:C:2014:76, 13 February 2014.

an act of 'communication to the public' and there has to be a 'public' to communicate to. The first requires the same works as those covered by the initial communication and the same technical means. The second requires that the communication be directed at a new public, that is, 'at a public that was not taken into account by the copyright holders when they authorised the initial communication to the public'. The Court ruled that the former condition, communication to the public, had been fulfilled, but that the latter had not, since no 'new public' had been granted access to the work. It also confirmed that Member States could not extend the scope of article 3(1).

Some hyperlinking, however, would be illegal, as is made clear in paragraph 31 of the judgment:

> where a clickable link makes it possible for users of the site on which that link appears to circumvent restrictions put in place by the site on which the protected work appears in order to restrict public access to that work to the latter site's subscribers only, and the link accordingly constitutes an intervention without which those users would not be able to access the works transmitted, all those users must be deemed to be a new public, which was not taken into account by the copyright holders when they authorised the initial communication, and accordingly the holders' authorisation is required for such a communication to the public. This is the case, in particular, where the work is no longer available to the public on the site on which it was initially communicated or where it is henceforth available on that site only to a restricted public, while being accessible on another Internet site without the copyright holders' authorisation.

The feature that made the case stand out, however, is the fact that the material hyperlinks referred to were freely and legally available elsewhere. In *BestWater*,[33] however, the same had been confirmed for freely available material for which the author had *not* given authorization. There, some YouTube videos, which had been posted without authorization, had been hyperlinked through 'framing' on the offending site. Like in *Svensson*, the CJEU concluded that no new public had been granted access to the work and no new technical means had been used. What neither case clarified was whether the hyperlinker's awareness and intent played a role at all and the extent to which illegality of the hyperlinked content changed the situation. Paragraph 31 of the judgment in *Svensson* suggested, at least, that hyperlinking to content hiding

---

[33]   C-348/13 *BestWater International GmbH v Michael Mebes and Stefan Potsch*, ECLI:EU:C:2014:2315, 21 October 2014.

behind article 6-type technical measures of protection would be considered a communication to the public. But, what of content that did not use such protection? And what of content that had never been freely circulated?

In the *GS Media* case,[34] which was about the publication of a hyperlink leading to a file depository site containing unauthorized photographs, the Advocate General, repeating the *Svensson* arguments, suggested that 'posting on a website of a hyperlink to another website on which works protected by copyright are freely accessible to the public without the authorisation of the copyright holder does not constitute an act of communication to the public'. This is because the hyperlink only facilitated accessing something which was already communicated elsewhere. This was very different, the Advocate General contended, from a situation in which a hyperlink was 'vital or indispensable' to the act of communication. Further to that, the Advocate General suggested that the poster's awareness played no role in determining whether an act of communication to the public had taken place. In the final judgment, the Court put an emphasis on the combination of the objective (financial gain) and subjective elements (knowledge of illegal nature). If the links have been posted without the knowledge of illegality *and* without the pursuit of financial gain, the posting is not to be considered a communication to the public. If, on the other hand, a financial purpose exists, the knowledge is presumed but could be rebutted. There are two problems with this approach. First, 'for profit' hyperlinking is not defined. Second, it is not at all clear why financial element ought to play a role in deciding whether a work had been communicated to the public or not (although it very well may play a role in determining the amount of damages in case of violation).

The situation after *GS Media* is as follows. First, hyperlinks to protected material legally available elsewhere (e.g. links to news articles) are, as per *Svensson*, not communication to the public since no new public is gained. Second, hyperlinks to material behind protective walls (e.g. paywalls) do, as per *Svensson*, constitute communication to the public. Third, hyperlinks to any other material not available elsewhere (e.g. movies, photos or music) but not involving the act of cracking a protective measure depend on the linker's good faith combined with the financial nature of the case, as per *GS Media*.

---

[34] C-160/15 *GS Media BV v Sanoma Media Netherlands BV, Playboy Enterprises International Inc. and Britt Geertruida Dekker*, ECLI:EU:C: 2016:644, 8 September 2016.

Article 4 covers distribution right, which is different from communication in article 3 and relates to tangible objects. The right applies only to authors and not to holders of related rights. The former have the exclusive right of distribution that is only exhausted in the EU at the first sale or transfer of ownership in the EU. Article 4 obliges Member States to provide an exclusive right to authorize distribution 'in respect of the originals of their work or copies thereof'. Member States are obliged to grant the authors the exclusive right to authorize or prohibit 'any form of distribution to the public by sale or otherwise'. This is a comprehensive distribution control which is not exhausted except where the first sale is made by the right-holder himself.

This article may cause some confusion. First, it relates only to authors and not to other right-holders. Secondly, it does not relate to the distribution channels mentioned in article 3 but, as Recital 28 explains, only to the distribution of works previously incorporated in a tangible form. This should be taken to mean that authors have the right to control distribution of a physical object that incorporates the creation until the first sale is made which would then exhaust the right. Recital 29, on the other hand, is clear that there is no exhaustion for online services where every online act is subject to authorization.

In *Donner*,[35] the owner of a company based in Italy was advertising on the Internet and importing copies of design furniture from Italy, where there was no protection, into Germany where such furniture was protected, including by criminal law. One of the questions directed to the CJEU was whether such a web-based system amounted to a distribution to the public in light of article 4(1). The Court ruled that it did. It looked for evidence of 'targeted activity' and found it in the direction of advertising, a specific delivery system and payment method.

In *Lebianca*,[36] Dimensione offered design furniture for sale on its website. Knoll believed that the said furniture violated its protected designs and took action against Dimensione and Mr Lebianca as its director. In question was the scope of article 4 and, in particular, whether distribution right can be violated just by advertising the goods for sale on the website. The CJEU concluded that it could, thus greatly widening the scope of the distribution right, 'even if it is not established that that advertisement gave rise to the purchase of the protected work by an EU

---

[35] C-5/11 *Titus Alexander Jochen Donner*, ECLI:EU:C:2012:370, 21 June 2012.

[36] C-516/13 *Dimensione Direct Sales Srl, Michele Labianca v Knoll International SpA*, ECLI:EU:C:2015:315, 13 May 2015.

buyer, in so far as that advertisement invites consumers of the Member State in which that work is protected by copyright to purchase it'.

1.2 Exceptions

Achieving the balance between the rights of various right-holders on one side and users on the other is one of the key tasks that a copyright regime needs to fulfil. A system of exceptions maintains that balance by allowing limited use of copyrighted material in specific situations. This means that exceptions enable the user to circumvent the protection where this is justified for good reasons. To ensure that this is done restrictively, and not as a general way of avoiding copyright protection, the Berne Convention Article 9(2) demands, in a clause known as the 'three-step-test', that such exceptions only be available 'in certain special cases, provided that such reproduction does not conflict with a normal exploit-ation of the work and does not unreasonably prejudice the legitimate interests of the author'. In the United States, the exceptions work through a legal doctrine known as 'fair use', which acts as a defence in copyright infringement proceeding. While conceptually significantly different, it serves the same purpose as the European system.

The Copyright Directive contains a somewhat peculiar regime of copyright exceptions in article 5. This peculiarity arises out of a combination of two factors. First, the Directive opts for an exhaustive list of exceptions, limiting Member States' ability to introduce new ones. Secondly, only one exception is mandatory while the others are left at Member States' discretion. This has the effect both of increasing cer-tainty, since the list is closed, and removing the effects of harmonization, since Member States may pick and choose from the list.

The list of exceptions begins with article 5(1), the only mandatory exception, which concerns temporary acts of reproduction. Those acts must be a 'transient or incidental and integral and essential part of a technological process'. Their sole purpose must either be (a) to enable 'a transmission in a network between third parties and an intermediary', or (b) a 'lawful use of a work without independent economic significance'. The first refers to acts of making copies in the normal functioning of transmission on IT systems. This will be the case when data is moving between different computers/servers on its way from the provider to the recipient. The second refers to acts of making copies for regular and lawful use for both private individuals and corporations. Thus, download-ing a purchased copy or making a local hard copy from an external device would fall into this category. It is to be expected that new technological solutions, as long as they are lawful and without 'independent economic significance', would also fall under this article. It is not clear if an act of maintaining a back-up copy in, for example, the Cloud falls under this definition but there are reasons to believe that it does not since it lacks the required transience.

The exception, although phrased somewhat inelegantly, is necessary, as it refers to the process of saving copies locally that enable faster access to content. The exceptions of article 5(1) are the only mandatory ones in the list. Their aim and spirit is mirrored in articles 12–14 of the E-Commerce Directive (2000/31/EC). In the *Meltwater* case,[37] the CJEU had an opportunity to clarify it further and confirm that normal Internet use falls under this exception. Meltwater provided a media monitoring service to its customers, PRCA, an association of public relations professionals. NLA, the collective licensing body for newspaper publishers, took the view that licensing was necessary both for using the media articles and for receiving them. Whereas Meltwater entered into a licensing agreement covering the usage, PRCA did not. The question posed was whether copies being made on the user's (PRCA) computer screen as a result of viewing the website fell under the exception in article 5(1). The Court ruled that:

> the copies on the user's computer screen and the copies in the internet 'cache' of that computer's hard disk, made by an end-user in the course of viewing a website, satisfy the conditions that those copies must be temporary, that they must be transient or incidental in nature and that they must constitute an integral and essential part of a technological process, as well as the conditions laid down in Article 5(5) of that directive, and that they may therefore be made without the authorisation of the copyright holders.

Other exceptions to the reproduction right in article 2 only are provided in article 5(2). Unlike the previous article, these are optional, which is reflected in the phrasing of the article ('may provide'). The first, article 5(2)(a), relates to reproduction on paper made by photographic equipment, except for sheet music, in cases where the right-holders receive compensation. This is simply a right to be compensated for photocopying. It may have a significance in the digital world in situations where the reproduction originates on the Internet but where the output is a paper copy.

---

[37]   C-360/13 *Public Relations Consultants Association Ltd v Newspaper Licensing Agency Ltd and others*, ECLI:EU:C:2014:1195, 5 June 2014.

The second, article 5(2)(b), includes reproductions made by natural persons for private use. This exception allows reproductions on any medium 'made by a natural person for private use' and for non-commercial means provided that right-holders are compensated and that the technological protection of article 6 is taken into account. This exception relates to personal non-commercial use only. This excludes corporate use including works that a person can use at home but are provided by the corporation. It is not clear from the language of the article and the Preamble whether commercial character should be determined by reference to potential markets in a particular product. Whereas the user may argue that making a digital copy of a CD, for instance, is personal non-commercial use, the right-holder will maintain that this limits the potential of developing an independent product based on digital content. The commercial character can be determined by reference to direct or indirect criteria, which may also limit the scope of the article. If national courts, for instance, decide that downloading a small number of copyright-protected songs from the Internet amounts to indirect commercial use, this would significantly limit the usefulness of the exception, provided that a Member State adopts it in the first place.

In any case, article 5(2)(b) requires fair compensation to be paid to the right-holder. In *Padawan*,[38] the CJEU held that fair compensation is an autonomous concept in EU law. It further said:

> fair compensation must be calculated on the basis of the criterion of the harm caused to authors of protected works by the introduction of the private copying exception. It is consistent with the requirements of that 'fair balance' to provide that persons who have digital reproduction equipment, devices and media and who on that basis, in law or in fact, make that equipment available to private users or provide them with copying services are the persons liable to finance the fair compensation, inasmuch as they are able to pass on to private users the actual burden of financing it.

The article was further interpreted in *ACI Adam*,[39] where the manufacturers of blank data media, such as CDs and DVDs, were required to pay a private copying levy. In their eyes, this levy was too high since it included unlawful reproductions. The question presented was whether the Dutch law, which also applied to copies of works made from unlawful sources, was in line with article 5(2)(b). The CJEU ruled that the article precluded national legislation which did not make a distinction between

---

[38] C-467/08 *Padawan SL v SGAE* [2010] ECR I-10055.
[39] C-435/12 *ACI Adam BV and others v Stichting de Thuiskopie, Stichting Onderhandelingen Thuiskopie vergoeding*, ECLI:EU:C:2014:254, 10 April 2014.

lawful and unlawful copying. This means, in effect, that the exception only applies to copies made from lawful sources. The decision is not surprising and is not likely to have an impact on the amount of illegal copies made.

In the most recent case on the subject, *Copydan*,[40] the Danish organization responsible for managing copyright in audio-visual works maintained that mobile telephone memory cards fell under the fair compensation exception whereas the respondent, Nokia, claimed that memory cards only perform an ancillary function and are not normally used for copying. A number of complex questions relating to the operation of article 5(2)(b) were referred to the CJEU. It ruled that requiring fair compensation is lawful even when just the ancillary function of a medium enables copying. On the other hand, the actual amount of the levy will depend on the function and its practical operation. Therefore, the Member States would be able to determine what constituted minimal harm not requiring compensation.

The third exception, article 5(2)(c), relates to 'specific acts of repro-duction' for public libraries, educational institutions, museums or archives, provided that they do not lead to an 'economic or commercial advantage'. Specific acts of reproduction refer to reproduction of indi-vidual works for specific purposes rather than general copying. Also, the exception is not limited to archiving and preservation purposes only (as was the case with the initial proposal). The latter should be interpreted to mean that a library cannot make a copy of a work which is otherwise commercially available in a digital form, neither can it profit from the copies it made (by selling, for instance, extra subscriptions or charging for access). This means that a library can only copy works which are both commercially exploitable and under copyright with the express permission of the right-holder. Works outside of copyright protection, such as ancient manuscripts, collections of old letters, and so on, can freely be put online, including for commercial exploitation (e.g. subscrip-tions). Article 5(2)(c) has special importance for furthering research, innovation and development. In the absence of a collective licence or a similar arrangement under national law, individual acts of copying would otherwise have been illegal under the provisions of the Directive. Since the Directive's entry into force, the libraries' use of digital media has multiplied. It is arguably necessary to thoroughly reform this exception in light of the present technological and social situation.

---

[40] C-463/12 *Copydan Båndkopi v Nokia Danmark A/S*, ECLI:EU:C: 2015:144, 5 March 2015.

The fourth exception, article 5(2)(d), relates to ephemeral recordings for broadcasting purposes and includes recordings made for preservation in the broadcasters' archives. This means that the broadcaster can make a copy for broadcasting purposes *only* and preserve that copy for reuse, but not commercially exploit it or give it away. Broadcasters who wish to make archives of their own works publicly and commercially available (such as archives of a national television or radio) may do so under various national copyright regimes.

The fifth exception, article 5(2)(e), relates to reproductions made by social institutions (such as hospitals) which pursue non-commercial aims. Reproductions are made under the condition on fair compensation.

In summary, article 5(2) does not bring surprises. The exceptions are familiar and did not generate disproportionate interest in national courts. The case is somewhat different only with article 5(2)(b). The wording of that article, which links these measures to fair compensation, would suggest that any application of the exception without legal intervention would either exclude compensation to the right-holder altogether or reduce the amount received by them.[41] This seems to be an economic approach, balancing the costs to society and the benefits received by the right-holders. Whereas this may be so, the complex ways in which technology is used today arguably call for new models of compensating authors.

Exceptions to *both* the reproduction right of article 2 and the right of communication to the public of article 3 are regulated in article 5(3). Just like the exceptions of article 5(2), the ones in article 5(3) are not mandatory, and implementation varies considerably across Member States, which decreases legal certainty.[42] Article 5(3) allows Member States to make exceptions to articles 2 and 3 based on the special status of the beneficiary (as in article 5(3)(b) or (n)) or on the privileges of the public, as in article 5(3)(a) or (c).

The first exception, article 5(3)(a), involves the right to use for 'illustration purposes' for teaching or scientific research, provided the source and name are quoted. The purpose must remain non-commercial. This should be interpreted to mean that displaying the item for teaching must not substitute legitimate commercial acquisition. Thus, a teacher

---

[41]   See K. Koelman, 'The Levitation of Copyright: An Economic View of Digital Home Copying, Levies and DRM' (2005) 16 *Entertainment Law Review* 75.

[42]   More on this in B. Lindner and T. Shapiro, *Copyright in the Information Society: A Guide to National Implementation of the Directive* (Edward Elgar Publishing, Cheltenham and Northampton, MA, 2011).

displaying material from a commercial repository based on the Internet cannot make a copy and make it available for students irrespective of whether the latter have the opportunity to acquire the work commercially or not.

Furthermore, the exclusion in article 5(3)(b) includes reproductions made for the benefit of disabled person(s), as much as necessary in respect of a specific disability and of a 'non-commercial nature'. This would include the right to make a digital audio copy of a book that can then be read aloud, or implementing a device that can put captions on videos. The exception covers only specific disabilities, which affect individual users. It is not clear what status the copies made by associations of disabled people would have but it should be taken that these too would fall within the exception as long as they satisfy the conditions.

The exception in article 5(3)(c) relates to reproductions in the act of communication to the public of 'current economic, political or religious topics' or the 'reporting of current events' unless reserved. In such a case, the source and the author must be named.

Further exemptions, in articles 5(3)(d)–(m), relate to: (d) quotations for purposes of criticism or review; (e) public security or reporting of administrative or judicial proceedings; (f) political speeches; (g) publicly organized religious or official celebrations; (h) public displays of architecture or sculpture; (i) incidental inclusion; (j) advertising of public exhibitions; (k) caricature or parody; (l) demonstration or repair of equipment; (m) reconstruction of buildings.

In *Deckmyn*,[43] the CJEU had an opportunity to interpret the parody exception of article 5(3)(k). There, a Belgian politician distributed a calendar that contained a photo-edited version of a famous comic. His edition had a head of another politician superimposed on one of the characters and action for copyright infringement had been commenced by the right-holders of the original comic. The Court confirmed that parody had an autonomous meaning in EU law and that 'the essential characteristics of parody, are, first, to evoke an existing work, while being noticeably different from it, and secondly, to constitute an expression of humour or mockery'. It is not essential that parody is original but it should be attributable to a person other than the original creator. The Court called for a balance between copyright protection on one side, and

---

[43]   C-201/13 *Johan Deckmyn, Vrijheidsfonds VZW v Helena Vandersteen, Christiane Vandersteen, Liliana Vandersteen, Isabelle Vandersteen, Rita Dupont, Amoras II CVOH and WPG Uitgevers België*, ECLI:EU:C:2014:2132, 3 September 2014.

freedom of expression on the other, but left it to national courts to draw a line between these rights.

Article 5(3)(h) has recently come into the public view. The optional exception allows Member States to allow 'use of works, such as works of architecture or sculpture, made to be located permanently in public places'. The EU Member States are divided on the exception with some adopting it while the recent reform proposals (see section 4) have called for a mandatory panorama exception.

The exception in article 5(3)(n) allows 'use by communication or making available' of electronic services in libraries or universities on 'dedicated terminals' only and 'on the premises' of works not otherwise subject to purchase or licensing terms. The works are the same as in article 5(2)(c), namely works not otherwise covered by a licensing agreement which enables other kinds of distribution. The article does not apply to online distribution in any form, for which a special licence under national copyright law must be obtained.

The exception was interpreted in the *Darmstadt*[44] case. There, the library of the Technical University of Darmstadt had a number of electronic reading terminals installed throughout its premises. These terminals displayed electronic copies of works, but not in greater number than the library possessed. Books could be printed out or stored on electronic media which the users brought with them. Ulmer was a publishing house whose work, otherwise also available in the commercial eBook format, had been made available on the University's terminals. The question referred to the CJEU was whether the exception in article 5(3)(n) applied to the case where the publisher had their own electronic product on offer and, if it did, whether it also covered the possibility to print and copy. The Court ruled that the library and publisher 'must have concluded a licensing agreement in respect of the work in question that sets out the conditions in which that establishment may use that work' but that digitization was allowed 'if such act of reproduction is necessary for the purpose of making those works available to users, by means of dedicated terminals, within those establishments'. This did not extend to printing or copying the work but the Court allowed Member States to introduce such exceptions under the conditions of article 5(2)(a) or (b) (photocopying and reproductions for private use with fair compensation).

The current exception does not allow massive digitization of material (which is already being undertaken by many commercial and non-profit

---

[44] C-117/13 *Technische Universität Darmstadt v Eugen Ulmer KG*, ECLI: EU:C:2014:2196, 11 September 2014.

organizations). The exceptions as they stand only allow digitization upon prior authorization, which is a cumbersome and expensive process. A new approach, possibly based on collective licensing, may solve some of the problems.[45]

A further exception in article 5(3)(o) exists in cases of minor importance, regulated under national law, that involve analogue uses. Member States that maintain their discretion under article 5(2) and (3) may decide to extend the exceptions to the right of distribution of article 4.

Possible limitations and exceptions are restricted by international obligation expressed in the form of the 'Berne three-step test'. The TRIPS formulation of that test is found in Article 13:

> Members shall confine limitations and exceptions to exclusive rights to certain special cases which do not conflict with a normal exploitation of the work and do not unreasonably prejudice the legitimate interests of the rights holder.

Article 5(5) contains the Copyright Directive version of the three-step test. It was first introduced in Article 9(2) of the Berne Convention for the Protection of Literary and Artistic works of 1967 but found its way into a number of other international instruments and national laws. The test says that limitations and exceptions to exclusive rights: (a) will only be applied in certain special cases; (b) will not conflict with normal exploitation of the work or other subject matter; and (c) will not unreasonably prejudice the legitimate interests of the right-holder. The test is of considerable importance as it determines whether exceptions, enumerated in article 5, can be applied to beneficiaries but its vagueness can mean only that courts will have to determine its exact scope. The CJEU has occasionally had the opportunity to rule on it in connection with the cases discussed in this chapter.

It has often been emphasized that the balance between various interests in society has largely been maintained through the system of broad exceptions to very wide rights.[46] The presence of the exceptions in article 5(3)(c)–(m) is thus both understandable and desirable. The exceptions protect certain freedoms, such as the freedom to conduct scientific research or the freedom of speech, which outweigh the right of copyright

---

[45]   See also Section 3.5.
[46]   On how this works in the United States, see J. Litman, *Digital Copyright* (Prometheus, New York, 2001), ch. 3 'Copyright and Compromise'.

holders. On the other hand, article 5 refers to exceptions 'and limitations'. Although this difference is probably without any practical consequence, it could be taken to mean that there are certain points beyond which copyright protection cannot go.[47] Recital 32 provides, on the other hand, that article 5 contains an *exhaustive* list of exceptions. In other words, Member States are not free to introduce new ones but may adopt some or all of the optional ones listed in article 5(2) and (3).

It is surprising that most exceptions have been placed in the non-mandatory part[48] – a significant weakness of the Directive. The fact that the European Union has chosen to make these important exceptions optional might signal indifference to the interests of the public and a certain regulatory disorder not normally characteristic for electronic commerce instruments. There is little doubt that the character of article 5 will be a further source of legal disparity between Member States. Indeed, the Directive itself recognizes so in Recital 31, where it expressly acknowledges the existence of disparities in 'exceptions and limitations'.

1.3 Protection of Technological Measures

The Infosoc Directive (2001/29/EC) takes as a basis a high level of protection.[49] Recital 10 leaves no doubt that the purpose of the Directive is to further enhance the existing protection in this field. Moreover, and in the view of this author more problematic, is the insistence on the protection given by technical measures.[50] Thus, Recital 47 emphasizes that technological developments allow the right-holders to better control the market for the works in question. It warns, however, that the measures can be circumvented and proposes to harmonize the regulation of technological measures in order to avoid possible discrepancies.

Technological measures are those measures introduced by right-holders, usually companies, to prevent illegal access or copying of works. Article 6(3) of the Copyright Directive defines them as:

> any technology, device or component that, in the normal course of its operation, is designed to prevent or restrict acts, in respect of works or other

---

[47] Cf. M. Vivant, 'Directive 2001/29/EC' in A. Lodder and H. Kaspersen, *eDirectives: Guide to European Union Law on E-Commerce* (Kluwer, The Hague, 2002), p. 95 at p. 106.

[48] See art. 5(2), (3) and (4).

[49] Recital 9.

[50] Recitals 13 and 47.

subject-matter, which are not authorised by the rightholder of any copyright or any right related to copyright.

There are two types of such measures: access-protection measures prevent unauthorized access to protected works while copy-protected measures prevent acts of reproduction. An example of the former are password/activation measures for software protection or authentication measures that depend on fingerprints, dongles or similar access technologies. Examples of the latter are measures on video discs that prevent them from playing in any region but the one they were marketed for or Digital Rights Management (DRM) measures that prevent free copying of MP3 files legally purchased in an online store. In both cases, the measures impose protection that is non-related to the copyright status (i.e. it is possible to impose protection on a public-domain work) although they are, in practice, mostly used for providing an extra layer of protection over and on top of something that already enjoys copyright protection.

Article 11 of WIPO Copyright Treaty 1996 requires contracting parties to:

> provide adequate legal protection and effective legal remedies against the circumvention of effective technological measures that are used by authors in connection with the exercise of their rights under this Treaty or the Berne Convention and that restrict acts, in respect of their works, which are not authorized by the authors concerned or permitted by law.

The United States introduced such protection in the Digital Millennium Copyright Act (DMCA) 1998 'anticircumvention provision'.[51] The Act prohibits circumvention of *access control* measures:

> No person shall circumvent a technological measure that effectively controls access to a work protected under this title.

In addition to this, the Act prohibits distribution of tools that circumvent either *access control* or *copy control*:

> No person shall manufacture, import, offer to the public, provide, or otherwise traffic in any technology, product, service, device, component, or part thereof, that:

---

[51]   Section 103 (17 USC s. 1201(a)(1)).

(A) is primarily designed or produced for the purpose of circumventing a technological measure that effectively controls access to a work protected under this title;

(B) has only limited commercially significant purpose or use other than to circumvent a technological measure that effectively controls access to a work protected under this title; or

(C) is marketed by that person or another acting in concert with that person with that person's knowledge for use in circumventing a technological measure that effectively controls access to a work protected under this title.

Section 1201(b)(1) of the DMCA 1998 prohibits the trafficking in tools that circumvent technologies that effectively protect a right of a copyright owner in a work: this is copy control as opposed to the access control of the previous paragraph. The article also provides that the Librarian of Congress shall have the power to determine what the non-infringing uses are and introduces criteria on which these decisions shall be made. In the past, the Librarian has included exceptions for audio-visual works in university libraries, obsolete video games, computer programs protected with dongles, read-aloud functions of e-books, wireless telephone handsets or audio CD protection measures that can damage the computers they are played on, etc.

The American and global academic community extensively analysed the provision. Among many criticisms, it was said that it stifles innovation and research by subjecting new technologies to legal scrutiny; that it significantly reduces the right to fair use by the public; that it limits free speech; and has a negative effect on competition.[52] The wording was described as awkward and incomprehensible and the administrative procedure as cumbersome. Contrary to these views, Ginsburg has concluded:[53]

---

[52] See J. Litman, 'Electronic Commerce and Free Speech' (1999) 1 *Journal of Ethics and Information Technology* 213. See also Electronic Frontier Foundation, *Unintended Consequences: Seven Years under the DMCA* (March 2010), available at www.eff.org/wp/unintended-consequences-under-dmca. See also P. Samuelson, *Freedom to Tinker*, Theoretical Inquiries in Law, UC Berkeley Public Law Research Paper No. 2605195 (11 May 2015), available at SSRN: http://ssrn.com/abstract=2605195.

[53] J. Ginsburg, *Legal Protection of Technological Measures Protecting Works of Authorship: International Obligations and the US Experience*, Columbia Public Law and Legal Theory Working Papers No. 0593 (1 August 2005), available at http://lsr.nellco.org/columbia/pllt/papers/0593. This paper also contains an overview of the Act's effects vis-à-vis international obligations and a summary of the most relevant literature on the technology vs. law debate.

The US experience to date indicates that legal protection for technological measures has helped foster new business models that make works available to the public at a variety of price points and enjoyment options, without engendering the 'digital lockup' and other copyright owner abuses that many had feared. This is not to say that the US legislation and its judicial interpretation represent the most preferable means to making the internet a hospitable place for authors while continuing to enable lawful user conduct. But brooding forecasts and legitimate continuing concerns notwithstanding, the overall equilibrium so far appears to be a reasonable one.

The very first EU anti-circumvention measures are found in the 1998 Conditional Access Directive[54] which harmonizes Member States' laws on audio-visual and Internet content which is offered under 'technical measure and/or arrangement whereby access to the protected service in an intelligible form is made conditional upon prior individual authorisation'. The Directive protects pay-services offered on TV, radio and the Internet. It lists a number of infringing activities in article 4 and obliges Member States to prohibit them and introduce effective remedies into their laws. Article 4 prohibits three types of activities: (a) the manufacture, import, distribution, sale, rental or possession for commercial purposes of illicit devices; (b) the installation, maintenance or replacement for commercial purposes of an illicit device; and (c) the use of commercial communications to promote illicit devices. Like article 6 of the Copyright Directive, the purpose of this Directive is to protect services, not copyright.[55]

Article 6 of the Copyright Directive establishes and regulates the system of technological protection somewhat similar to the one described above and very similar to the US one. It consists of anti-circumvention and anti-trafficking provisions. Article 6(1) is the anti-circumvention provision. It provides that Member States shall give adequate legal protection against the circumvention of 'effective technological measures', which the person concerned carries out with knowledge, or with knowledge on reasonable grounds. Two questions present themselves. First, what is the significance of the subjective element, and second, when can a measure be considered to be 'effective'? As to the first question, the knowledge required does not relate to actual copyright violation but only to the technological measures. The person must know

---

[54]   Directive 98/84/EC of the European Parliament and of the Council of 20 November 1998 on the legal protection of services based on, or consisting of, conditional access [1998] OJ L320/54, 28 November 1998.

[55]   Similar provision is also found in Computer Programs Directive, art. 7(1)(c); see section 3.2 below.

that he is tampering with a protected device. That is all that is needed to trigger the protection of this article. It is irrelevant whether the person believes that he may be entitled to copy the work or if he really is entitled.

The requirement of effectiveness is of uncertain reach, in spite of the attempt to define it in article 6(3). That definition provides that a technological measure is effective:

> where the use of a protected work or other subject-matter is controlled by the rightholders through application of an access control or protection process, such as encryption, scrambling or other transformation of the work or other subject-matter or a copy control mechanism, which achieves the protection objective.

The examples given are encryption, scrambling or other measures that achieve the protection objective. In reality, an effective measure is usually one that completely prevents circumvention or copying, that is, one that either cannot be removed or can only be so with great difficulty or considerable knowledge. An ineffective measure means one that can be circumvented with relative ease. It would seem that, once the protection has been removed, the measure becomes ineffective and the requirement of article 6(1) becomes superfluous, in spite of the standard which the Directive purports to introduce. For example, an 'extension' made available for an Internet browser may very quickly render a measure of protection ineffective and can be updated with ease. However, that does not make the measure 'ineffective' in the eyes of the law. In addition to that, the definition of effectiveness in article 6(3), in reality, provides that any measure is effective that gives the right-holder the ability to control access. This definition does not take into account the technical effectiveness of the measure.

The CJEU had an opportunity to discuss effectiveness of a measure in *Nintendo*.[56] The subject of that case was the encryption system that the video games manufacturer Nintendo installed on its Wii series of consoles. The system would encrypt physical devices carrying the games and only those that satisfied the system as to their authenticity would be allowed to work. These were typically Nintendo-made, which also meant that only Nintendo products worked on Nintendo consoles. PC Box manufactured a device designed not only to enable copying of Nintendo games but also the use of non-Nintendo content on Nintendo consoles.

---

[56] C-355/12 *Nintendo Co. Ltd, Nintendo of America Inc. and Nintendo of Europe GmbH v PC Box Srl, 9Net Srl*, ECLI:EU:C:2014:25, 23 January 2014.

The questions asked were: whether article 6 applied to the system of protection described above and what criteria should be taken into consideration when determining the product's use. The Court ruled that the effectiveness 'does not have to be absolute' and that 'relative costs' and 'practical aspects' needed to be taken into account. The Court held that, to be able to avail itself of article 6 protection, a measure must be proportionate in that it cannot prohibit devices or activities which have a 'commercially significant purpose' other than to circumvent.

Access control devices prevent access to copyrighted content irrespective of whether the person attempting the access has the rights or not, while *copy control*, by preventing duplication, protects actual rights.[57] The ability to copy exists independently of the ability to access. One usually has the ability to access a video disc such as Blu-ray without the immediate ability to copy it. The DMCA 1998 distinguishes between the two in section 1201(2) and (3). This distinction consists of the ban on circumvention of access control but not copy control, the latter being allowed under fair use.[58] The InfoSoc Directive does not. It follows from article 6(3) specifically and from other parts of the Directive that the same protection is given to technologies controlling access and technologies that protect content, with the only circumvention allowed being the one authorized by the copyright holder. This inclusion of copy control, in addition to access control, is in stark contrast with digital media prior to the advance of the Internet.

It is worth noting here that mandatory exceptions, introduced in article 5(1) for temporary acts of reproduction, and optional exceptions, listed in article 5(2) and (3), also apply to prohibition under article 6.

Article 6(2) is the Directive's anti-trafficking provision. It obliges Member States to provide adequate legal protection against the 'manufacture, import, distribution, sale, rental, advertisement for sale or rental, or possession for commercial purposes' of devices, products or components or the provision of services which:

(a)   are promoted, advertised or marketed for the purpose of circumvention of, or

---

[57]   More on this difference in J. Ginsburg, 'From Having Copies to Experiencing Works: The Development of an Access Right in U.S. Copyright Law' (2003) 50 *Journal of the Copyright Society of the USA* 113.

[58]   The ban on trafficking applies to both. On this and other differences between the US and EU regime, see T. Foged, 'US v EU Anticircumvention Legislation: Preserving the Public's Privileges in the Digital Age' (2002) 24 *European Intellectual Property Review* 525.

(b) have only a limited commercially significant purpose or use other than to circumvent, or

(c) are primarily designed, produced, adapted or performed for the purpose of enabling or facilitating the circumvention of any effective technological measures.

No knowledge requirement exists under this provision and the action becomes illegal without the subjective element. The purpose of the measure is to prevent the trafficking of any technological devices which serve the purpose of violating digital copyright.

Article 6(4) is designed to enable the beneficiaries of exceptions and limitations of article 5 to avail themselves of the benefits *in spite* of the technological protection introduced through article 6. The article provides that if voluntary measures are not taken by the right-holders (including agreements between right-holders and other parties concerned), Member States will step in to ensure, through law, the effective application of exceptions which they have otherwise committed to.[59]

The anti-circumvention provisions are problematic for a number of reasons. First and most important, it is unclear how a radical protection of technical measures can be squared with the drive for innovation. Circumvention cannot be and should not be equated with 'piracy'. Furthermore, there is no economic data on its effectiveness. Secondly, equally important, a number of unresolved issues from article 6 will eventually have to be decided by the national courts. These include the definition of technological measures, the issue of effectiveness and the scope and mode of application of any exceptions. This challenges the idea of harmonization that was the main reason behind harmonization.

Under article 7 of the Directive, Member States are under an obligation to provide adequate legal protection[60] against anyone who knowingly removes or alters any electronic rights-management information, distributes, imports, broadcasts or makes available to the public protected works from which rights-management information has been removed or altered without authorization. Rights-management information is understood to be any information provided by the right-holder which identifies the work.

---

[59] See U. Gasser and M. Girsberger, *Transposing the Copyright Directive: Legal Protection of Technological Measures in EU-Member States*, Berkman Working Paper No. 2004-10 (November 2004), p. 10, available at http://ssrn.com/abstract=628007.

[60] This does not have to be criminal, although it may be. See also section 2 below on copyright enforcement.

Sanctions and remedies are covered in article 8. This article provides that adequate sanctions and remedies shall be provided for the infringements set out in the Directive. The sanctions shall be 'effective, proportionate and dissuasive'. These terms are not properly defined in the Directive, leaving them to national authorities. The right-holders are, furthermore, granted the right to bring an action for damages or seek an injunction. They can apply not only for the seizure of the infringing material but also for the seizure of devices, products or components used for circumvention (referred to in article 6(2)). Finally, right-holders are granted the possibility to apply for an injunction against intermediaries whose services are used to infringe copyright. The last provision, in particular, causes concern. The disparity in the system of interlocutory measures in the Member States may lead to serious difficulties for Internet service providers (ISPs) in some Member States, where these measures are in place, and no action in others where they are not.

2   INTELLECTUAL PROPERTY RIGHTS ENFORCEMENT

2.1   Copyright Enforcement Directive (Civil)

The Copyright Enforcement Directive[61] finds its basis in various international instruments, such as TRIPS, Part III, or WIPO Copyright Treaty 1996, Article 14(2), which deal with important aspects of copyright enforcement. The Commission was motivated by what it perceived as 'major disparities'[62] which existed in spite of the obligations imposed in the mentioned international instruments.

The Directive requires all Member States to apply effective, dissuasive and proportionate remedies and penalties against those engaged in counterfeiting and piracy.[63] Thus, the purpose of the instrument is to

---

[61]   Directive 2004/48/EC of the European Parliament and of the Council on the enforcement of intellectual property rights; Communication on the management of copyright [2004] OJ L195/16, 2 June 2004. Original Proposal for a Directive of the European Parliament and of the Council on measures and procedures to ensure the enforcement of intellectual property rights, COM(2003)46 (30 January) 2003.

[62]   Recital 7.

[63]   Article 3(2).

regulate *enforcement* of intellectual property rights, not the rights themselves. The Directive does not aim to harmonize rules of private international law (Recital 11) nor does it affect competition law (Recital 12).

The subject matter of the Directive is defined in article 1. It applies to enforcement of intellectual property rights that include industrial property rights. The scope of the Directive is defined in article 2: it applies to all infringements of IP rights in Community and national law, without precluding more stringent protection that Community or national law may otherwise grant in other instruments. On the other hand, it excludes specific enforcement provisions of the Computer Programs Directive[64] and of the Information Society Directive. In respect of the latter, specifically excluded are the provisions of articles 6 and 8 on circumvention of technical protection measures. Finally, the Directive leaves unaffected the substantive provisions on intellectual property, international obligations of the Member States and national provisions relating to criminal procedure and criminal enforcement. In short, the Directive adds extra measures on enforcement of digital copyright while leaving national law in other areas largely unaffected.

The general obligation in the Directive, article 3, is to provide for remedies necessary to enforce intellectual property rights. These must be 'fair and equitable' and must not be 'complicated or costly, or entail unreasonable time-limits or unwarranted delays'. They must furthermore be effective, proportionate and dissuasive and must not act as barriers to trade.

The persons who are entitled to apply for the remedies (article 4) are primarily the holder of the intellectual property right, but also any person authorized to use it, such as licensees. Collective rights management bodies and professional defence bodies also have this right, provided that they are 'regularly recognized' as having a right of representation and provided they have the permission. A presumption of authorship is introduced in article 5 for people whose name appears on the work.

Section 2 of the Copyright Enforcement Directive deals with obtaining evidence. Article 6 gives the power to the interested party to apply for evidence regarding an infringement that lies in the hands of the other party. The only requirement is for that party to present 'reasonably

---

[64] Directive 91/250/EEC, now Directive 2009/24/EC on the legal protection of computer programs [2009] OJ L111/16, 5 May 2009 ('Software Directive (Codified)').

available evidence sufficient to support its claim' to the court. Confidentiality will be respected. Optionally, Member States may provide that such evidence will only be presented if the applicant gives a 'substantial number of copies' of the protected work. In case of an infringement on a commercial scale, Member States must also take steps to ensure that 'banking, financial or commercial documents' of the opposing party are presented. In both cases confidential information must be protected.

Measures for preserving evidence are available even before the proceedings commence. Article 7 provides that such measures may be granted under the same conditions as under article 6 and include provisional measures such as physical seizure not only of the infringing goods (for instance, hard drives) but also materials used in the production and distribution. Particularly worrying is the provision in that article that such measures may be taken 'without the other party having been heard, in particular where any delay is likely to cause irreparable harm to the rightholder or where there is a demonstrable risk of evidence being destroyed'. These are interlocutory, *ex parte* and *in personam* orders known in English law as '*Anton Piller* orders'.[65] They give the right to search the premises in order to seize the evidence where there is a risk of its disappearance. Since such orders are made on application, without the knowledge of the other party, the safeguards introduced in the *Anton Piller* case were rather strict. First, there has to be a strong *prima facie* case against the respondent. Secondly, the actual or potential damage must be serious. Thirdly, evidence must exist that the respondents possess the incriminating evidence and that they may dispose of it before proper court proceedings are initiated. There is now, in the place of this order, a statutory search order under the Civil Procedure Rules 1998.[66]

Anton Piller orders were applied with caution by the courts before the Civil Procedure Act 1997 came into force and they are even more so since then. There is little reason to believe that continental courts will intuitively understand a common law instrument. There is even less reason to assume that they will be effective. Although such measures are used in trademark and intellectual property cases, the ability to acquire evidence in disputes on the Internet is dramatically increased with the presence of intermediaries. The evidence may be obtained and secured through the ISP, by means of obtaining an order to produce records of electronic transactions. This is often the chosen path in the United States.

---

[65]   *Anton Piller KG v Manufacturing Processes Ltd* [1976] ch. 55, [1976] 1 All ER 779.

[66]   See sections 7(1), 23 and 25.

Arguably, in spite of the privacy issues and concerns, this is both fairer and more effective, at least when properly supervised by a court. Moreover, article 7 orders have the capacity to be combined with the freezing injunctions of articles 9 and 11.

Article 8 covers the 'right of information'. This is a sensitive procedure by which the courts can order, on application by the claimant, that the 'information on the origin and distribution networks of the goods and services which infringe an intellectual property right' be produced. For the information to be provided, the infringer must have been found in possession of or have been using the goods on a commercial scale, or have been commercially providing services or was otherwise involved in manufacture, production or distribution. The information concerned con-sists of names and addresses of people involved in the production/ distribution chain and information on the goods themselves. This applies irrespective of any other statutory provision which may have the same or similar aim.

Article 9 regulates provisional and precautionary measures. At the request of an applicant, the judicial authorities may issue an interlocutory injunction to prevent an 'imminent infringement' of intellectual property rights or to prevent a continuing infringement. In the latter case, the order may be followed by a recurring penalty payment or lodging of a guarantee intended to compensate the right-holder. The court may also order seizure or delivery of the infringing goods.

More problematic than the ordinary injunctions of the previous para-graph are the so-called *Mareva* injunctions of Article 9(2). Article 9(2) provides that, in the case of an infringement on a commercial scale, judicial authorities may order a precautionary seizure of 'movable and immovable property', which includes freezing the bank accounts and other assets. This may only be done if the applicant demonstrates that it is likely that recovery of damages will be endangered. Further to that, documents relating to banking and other financial transactions may be communicated. In common law, these are *ex parte* and *in personam* orders used to freeze assets to prevent abuses of process.[67] They can be issued as worldwide injunctions, preventing worldwide dispersal. In that case, their effectiveness depends on their *in personam* character, as a party who is found to be guilty of disposing of assets will be in contempt of court.

---

[67] *Mareva Compania Naviera SA v International Bulkcarriers SA* [1975] 2 Lloyd's Rep 509. The current scope: *Group Seven Ltd v Allied Investment Corporation Ltd and others* [2013] EWHC 1509 (Ch), para. 63 (6 June 2013).

The effects of this provision may prove to be uncertain. First, *Mareva* injunctions are specialized instruments used in English courts. As such, they mostly do not have an equivalent in continental Europe, with some exceptions (e.g. *saisie conservatoire* in France). Their introduction is a poorly investigated novelty. Secondly, the use of *Mareva* injunctions in English courts is subject to strict tests. The applicant must demonstrate that there is a good arguable case on the merits and that the refusal of an injunction would involve a risk that assets will be removed or dissipated. The standard of 'good arguable case' is not required in article 9(2). Thirdly, the possibility to disclose financial information introduced in article 9(2) is unreasonable and unjustified. Finally, the potential to combine the injunctions with *Anton Piller* orders may have negative effects on the business of the party against which these are used. The disclosure of trade secrets in poorly documented cases may shift the balance in favour of the claimants.

Also resulting from the merits of the case, 'corrective measures' may be taken on application and pursuant to article 10 to recall temporarily or definitely remove the infringing goods from channels of commerce or to destroy them. This decision is without prejudice to any damages that may follow from the main proceedings. The same measures are available for disposal of materials used in creation of the infringing goods. The article demands that the requirement of proportionality between the infringement and the remedies be kept in mind when determining whether this measure will be used.

Article 11 provides that an injunction preventing further infringements can be issued in cases where a decision has already been taken. The substance of the injunction consists of the prohibition of further infringement, and non-compliance may be subject to punitive damages under national law. An injunction can also be issued, under the same conditions, against an intermediary, although these are also covered in article 8(2) of the Information Society Directive and are, in principle, subject to national law. In *L'Oréal*,[68] the CJEU ruled that an online marketplace such as eBay may be ordered not only to bring infringing measures to an end but to prevent any future infringements. The injunctions used for this purpose must be 'effective, proportionate, and dissuasive' but should not 'create barriers to legitimate trade'.

---

[68] C-324/09 *L'Oréal SA, Lancôme parfums et beauté & Cie SNC, Laboratoire Garnier & Cie and L'Oréal (UK) Ltd v eBay International AG and others* [2011] ECR I-06011.

Injunctive relief of Article 9-type can be used against ISPs in cases where they are 'infringers' in their own right. This would be in situations falling under section 4 of the E-Commerce Directive. For example, an ISP host, which is notified of an infringement and does nothing to remove the infringing content, may then be subject to intermediary relief in the national courts. Indeed, article 18 of that Directive specifically allows interim relief. However, as confirmed in the *SABAM* case,[69] the ISPs have no *obligation* to install filtering mechanisms and an injunction cannot be used to make them do so. The decision specifically confirms that this transpires from, among other instruments, the Copyright Enforcement Directive. In the earlier *Promusicae* case,[70] the Court ruled that no ISP obligation to communicate personal data to right-holders arises from, among others, the Copyright Enforcement Directive and injunctive relief could not be used here.

Instead of the corrective measures of article 10 and injunctions of article 11, the national court may, under article 12, impose pecuniary compensation for the injured party, provided that the persons 'acted unintentionally and without negligence' and if the execution of these measures would cause disproportionate harm.

The result of an infringement is the payment of damages. Article 13 obliges Member States to introduce adequate damages for wilful or negligent infringements. In setting the damages, the judicial authorities, under article 13(1)(a), may take into consideration such effects as negative economic consequences and lost profits and any unfair profits made by the infringer and, 'in appropriate cases' only, elements other than economic factors, such as 'moral prejudice'. In the alternative, that is, at their discretion, under article 13(1)(b), they may set lump sum damages based on 'at least' the royalties or fees, which would have been due had the infringer requested authorization.

CJEU cases throw some light on the application of articles 13 and 14. In *Liffers*,[71] a director and a scriptwriter had parts of his work used without authorization in a documentary that had then been shown on Spanish television. He claimed compensation for material and moral damage that he alleged he had suffered. The question directed to the CJEU was whether article 13(1) allowed the plaintiff to ask for moral as

---

[69] See Chapter 5.

[70] C-275/06 *Productores de Música de España (Promusicae) v Telefónica de España SAU* [2008] ECR I-271.

[71] C-99/15 *Christian Liffers v Producciones Mandarina SL and Mediaset España Comunicación SA, formerly Gestevisión Telecinco SA*, ECLI:EU:C: 2016:173, 17 March 2016.

well as material damages. The Court stated that, although article 13(1)(b) did not mention moral prejudice as an element in determining damages, it did not preclude it either. On the contrary, article 13(1)(a) required that damages cover the *actual* prejudice, provided it is proven, and this included moral damages. On the other hand, article 13(1) prevents the calculation of damages based *only* on hypothetical royalties. The conclusion is, therefore, that the amount of material damages is calculated based on fees which would have been due had the infringer requested authorization whereas the amount of moral damages is calculated on the basis of all elements in article 13(1)(b).

In spite of the Court's suggestion that article 13(1)(a) and (b) should be read together, it may be observed that the Directive introduces alternative application of two potentially incompatible regimes. One regime, embodied in (b), bases damages on the sum that would have been due had the legal path been followed from the start. This regime is rational at least in its ability not to prejudice the actual economic loss; or, in other words, it bases the economic loss on measurable elements and then adds to them the punitive component that results from the wilful or negligent behaviour. On the other hand, there are obvious problems in basing damages on putative royalties. The other regime starts from a different premise. It takes 'all appropriate aspects' into consideration. Such aspects include, primarily, 'negative economic consequences' and 'lost profits'. The first is a vague category that is impossible or at least very difficult to measure. The second is known as 'economic damage' in tort law and is either not awarded or very rarely so and only under special circumstances. The fact that the Directive bases damages on 'lost profits' shows confusion concerning the principles on which tort law operates or, at the very least, a lack of real desire to harmonize this area.

In reality, neither approach necessarily gives an accurate picture of the costs involved. A thought experiment with an example of a CD downloaded from the Internet can be made. If such a CD contains 15 songs, what is the appropriate amount of damages under article 13? If one took the second option first, namely article 13(1)(b), one would add up the cost of each individual song as sold on the nearest legal alternative, such as iTunes store or a similar e-outlet, and add to it a punitive amount. If we accept a different path, that of article 13(1)(a), we could take the full price of a retail CD as a basis, even if only one or two songs were taken from each CD. Therefore, this version seems significantly less fair than the previous one. In reality, however, neither may provide adequate compensation. The person who downloaded the songs in the first example need not have purchased them at their full price even if they had opted for the cheaper and more flexible version involving downloading an electronic copy. In addition, digital songs may be sold at different price levels, with different rights management systems, at different bit-rates, increasing the confusion. Had the infringing party in the case of small-scale copying faced a choice between legal and no purchase at all, the applicant may not have suffered any loss.

Article 14 allows the recovery of legal costs. In *Telenet*,[72] the Court of Appeal in Antwerp dealt with an application for patent infringement that United Video Properties (UVP) brought against Telenet. The question referred concerned the scope of the term 'reasonable and proportionate legal costs and other expenses' in article 14. The court ruled that the article allows Member States to set a maximum limit for the recovery of the successful party's legal fees but precludes Member States from requiring that fault be required for ordering the unsuccessful party to reimburse expert costs.

The Directive suffers from serious problems. In the draft, the infringements targeted were those 'for commercial purposes or causing significant harm'.[73] This requirement was deleted in the final document and the text now refers to 'any infringement of intellectual property rights'. Effectively, the change of direction has potentially included everyday practices and very significantly extended the scope of the Directive, which now does not concentrate purely on commercial acts but leaves scope for individual infringements.[74] In fact, very few parts of the Directive are strictly applicable to commercial matters,[75] with the majority of provisions potentially deployable against individuals.[76] Furthermore, there is no definition of 'intellectual property rights' in the Directive or elsewhere in EU law, which further extends its scope of application. The questions concerning the Directive's legality and legitimacy are also serious.[77] The harmful potential of these 'search and seize' orders, which may be used against universities or other places where file-swapping forms part of the daily routine, is considerable.

---

[72] C-57/15 *United Video Properties, Inc. v Telenet NV*, ECLI:EU:C: 2016:611, 28 July 2016.

[73] See art. 2 of the Draft.

[74] Cf. e.g., art. 13(1)(a).

[75] Such as arts. 6(2), 8(1)(a) and (c) or 9(2).

[76] Issues of compatibility with the Human Rights Act 1998 are also potentially raised. See M. Birnhack, 'Acknowledging the Conflict between Copyright Law and Freedom of Expression under the Human Rights Act' (2003) 14 *Entertainment Law Review* 24.

[77] See W. Cornish, *et al.*, 'Procedures and Remedies for Enforcing IPRS: The European Commission's Proposed Directive' (2003) 25 *European Intellectual Property Review* 447, 448.

Problems do not end there. A number of provisions in the Directive can be used against intermediaries, and ISPs have voiced concern over this. The right to obtain information is introduced in Section 3, although even the United States rejects such an approach as unconstitutional.[78] The original but now changed proposal introduced criminal law provisions in article 20, with 'serious infringements' criminalized as well as 'attempts'. These have been deleted after a public outcry. A subsequent attempt to introduce a Criminal Enforcement Directive has failed but may yet be revived. All of this clearly indicates the amount of lobbying that the media industry directed at the EU law-makers but also the confusion as to the right direction which copyright enforcement in the digital world should take.

2.2 Proposed Enforcement Directive (Criminal)

The EU attempted to address enforcement through criminal liability in the proposal dating to 2006.[79] This was accompanied by the Council Framework Decision to Strengthen the Criminal Law Framework to Combat Intellectual Property Offences.[80] These acts, although abandoned, are of some importance not only because they illustrate the current trends and ideas but also because some of the ideas and solutions they suggest occasionally resurface in bilateral trade agreements the EU concludes.[81]

The key provision is article 3, which provides that 'Member States shall ensure that all intentional infringements of an intellectual property right on a commercial scale, and attempting, aiding or abetting and inciting such infringements, are treated as criminal offences'. The introduction of criminal offences is, in itself, inefficient with large-scale violations and unlikely to deter small-scale file-swappers.[82] Particularly worrying is the incrimination of attempting, aiding, abetting or inciting infringements. This latter has been raised as a concern at the introduction

---

[78] *RIAA v Verizon Internet Services* 351 F.3d 1229, 1233 (D.C. Cir. 2003), US Court of Appeals, District of Columbia Circuit.

[79] Proposal for a European Parliament and Council Directive on criminal measures aimed at ensuring the enforcement of intellectual property rights, amended proposal, COM(2006)168 final (27 April 2006).

[80] SEC(2005)848, COM(2005)276 final (12 July 2005).

[81] See J. Drexl *et al.* (eds.), *EU Bilateral Trade Agreements and Intellectual Property: For Better or Worse?* (Springer-Verlag, Berlin/Heidelberg, 2014).

[82] For an analysis of the American experience, see S. Bhattacharjee *et al.*, 'Impact of Legal Threats on Online Music Sharing Activity: An Analysis of Music Industry Legal Actions' (2006) 49 *Journal of Law and Economics* 91.

of the stalled INDUCE[83] and SOPA Acts[84] in the US Congress. The concern is that producers of new technology devices might discontinue their research and production, fearful of the possible outlawing of the devices they are producing.

The penalties are set out in article 4. Custodial sentences are provided for natural persons. Fine and confiscation are provided for both natural and legal persons. A selection of penalties is made available in article 4(2), to be applied at Member States' discretion. This includes destruction of goods; permanent or temporary closure of establishments or a ban on engaging in commercial activities; placing under judicial supervision; winding-up; a ban on access to public assistance; and publication of judgments. The introduction of criminal penalties for natural persons seems a particularly harsh measure, especially given the lack of proof that their introduction has a significant effect on the level of infringement.

The 'commercial scale' criterion was originally contained in Article 61 of the TRIPS Agreement. That Article obliges WTO members to 'provide for criminal procedures and penalties to be applied at least in cases of wilful trademark counterfeiting or copyright piracy on a commercial scale'. Remedies available are supposed to include imprisonment and/or monetary fines, which are sufficient to provide a deterrent, consistent with the level of penalties applied to corresponding crimes. In appropriate cases, the available remedies must also include the 'seizure, forfeiture and destruction of the infringing goods and of any materials and implements the predominant use of which has been in the commission of the offence'. The Member States have freedom to provide for criminal procedures and penalties to be applied in other cases of infringement of intellectual property rights, especially where they are committed wilfully and on a commercial scale. The TRIPS provision is, on the surface, an unremarkable one. Criminal sanctions for counterfeiting have existed for some time in a number of WTO member states. What makes the transposition of this obligation into EU law questionable is the lack of proper definition of a 'commercial scale'. It should, in principle, include larger scale operations conducted for significant profit but it could, in fact, include rather small one-man operations that attract a negligible profit. In practice, this would depend on the interpretation of the national courts.

---

[83] Introduced as s. 2560 by Senator Orrin Hatch on 22 June 2004.
[84] H.R.3261 Stop Online Piracy Act, House Judiciary Committee, 26 October 2011.

3 OTHER INTELLECTUAL PROPERTY INSTRUMENTS

The relatively comprehensive EU intervention in the sphere of intellectual property rights, although based on the Copyright Directive and Copyright Enforcement Directive, includes a number of other special secondary laws that have a direct bearing on the Internet. They will be analysed here in the order in which they have appeared.

3.1 Databases

Of some interest to Internet regulation is the EU Database Directive.[85] The Directive, which defines databases as collections of 'independent works, data or other materials arranged in a systematic or methodical way and individually accessible by electronic or other means', introduces two systems of protection.

In the first category (article 3) are databases which are protected under copyright law since 'by reason of the selection or arrangement of their contents, constitute the author's own intellectual creation'. In order to qualify for the protection, a database needs to fulfil the protection criteria that copyright law imposes. No protection extends to the actual *contents* of the database, which may or may not be subject to their own IP protection (i.e. a photograph). The protection in question is granted to the database itself, which means that the selection or *arrangement* in itself is worthy of copyright protection. This would be the situation with an arrangement of photographic, musical or artistic works.

Since a large number of databases rely on publically available material, such as names and addresses, but require substantial effort in gathering them, the Directive creates a new right. This *sui generis* right, protected in article 7, exists for databases that do not qualify for copyright protection but where qualitatively and/or quantitatively a 'substantial investment in either the obtaining, verification or presentation of the contents' has been made. The new *sui generis* right is a property right, since it can be transferred, assigned or licensed.

The Database Directive applies also in the Internet context, which has been tested in court, both in the context of copyright and *sui generis* rights. The first case of significance was *British Horseracing Board*.[86] In

---

[85]   Directive 96/9/EC of the European Parliament and of the Council of 11 March 1996 on the legal protection of databases [1996] OJ L77/20, 27 March 1996.

[86]   C-203/02 *British Horseracing Board v William Hill Organisation* [2004] ECR I-10415.

the CJEU's view, where a database provided only a by-product of the creator's main business, it could not be granted *sui generis* protection even when substantial effort had been put in it. In *Football Dataco*,[87] following the copyright line of cases, the Court ruled that selection or arrangement of the data must amount 'to an original expression of the creative freedom of its author, which is a matter for the national court to determine'.

3.2 Computer Programs

The Software Directive (Original Version)[88] allows for the protection of computer programs and accompanying design material under copyright law. The functionality and the programming language of the program is not protectable[89] and neither is the graphic user interface.[90] In *SAS*, the CJEU clarified that performing the same function as another program or using the same programming language and format of data files does not infringe copyright. Likewise, decompiling the program to achieve inter-operability should be permitted. On the other hand, copying the source code should not.

Computer programs are, under article 1, protected 'by copyright, as literary works within the meaning of the Berne Convention'. Ideas that underlie the program or its interfaces are not protected. The beneficiaries are all natural and legal persons, including groups of authors (articles 2 and 3). Article 4 grants exclusive rights of control to the copyright owner subject to the exceptions in article 5, which include the right to make back-up copies or study the program's operation.

There does not seem to be anything in the Directive that prevents it from applying purely to programs used or distributed on the Internet. Pieces of code or applications that are designed to run on the Internet itself (i.e. within a web browser) are also covered. In *UsedSoft*,[91]

---

[87] C-604/10 *Football Dataco Ltd v Yahoo! UK Ltd*, ECLI:EU:C:2012:11 5, 1 March 2012.

[88] Council Directive 91/250/EEC of 14 May 1991 on the legal protection of computer programs [1991] OJ L122/42, 17 May 1991, now Directive 2009/24 on the legal protection of computer programs [2009] OJ L111/16, 5 May 2009 ('Software Directive (Codified)').

[89] See C-406/10 *SAS Institute Inc. v World Programming Ltd*, ECLI:EU: C:2012:259, 2 May 2012.

[90] C-393/09 *Bezpečnostní softwarová asociace – Svaz softwarové ochrany v Ministry of Culture of the Czech Republic* [2010] ECR I-13971.

[91] C-128/11 *UsedSoft GmbH v Oracle International Corp.*, ECLI:EU: C:2012:407, 3 July 2012.

the question was whether a company distributing used software licences for software normally available for downloads via the Internet was infringing the Computer Programs Directive and whether the doctrine of the exhaustion of rights applied (see section 3.7 below). The CJEU ruled that article 4(2) should be interpreted as meaning that the right of distribution of a copy of a computer program is exhausted where the right-holder gave authorization for a remuneration. As explained in paragraph 88:

> It follows from the foregoing that the answer to Questions 1 and 3 is that Articles 4(2) and 5(1) of Directive 2009/24 must be interpreted as meaning that, in the event of the resale of a user licence entailing the resale of a copy of a computer program downloaded from the copyright holder's website, that licence having originally been granted by that rightholder to the first acquirer for an unlimited period in return for payment of a fee intended to enable the rightholder to obtain a remuneration corresponding to the economic value of that copy of his work, the second acquirer of the licence, as well as any subsequent acquirer of it, will be able to rely on the exhaustion of the distribution right under Article 4(2) of that directive, and hence be regarded as lawful acquirers of a copy of a computer program within the meaning of Article 5(1) of that directive and benefit from the right of reproduction provided for in that provision.

A question of considerable importance in computer programming is interoperability, which is the ability of one computer system to operate and exchange information with another. The leading case on interoperability in the digital context, decided in the context of competition law, is the Commission's *Microsoft* decision.[92] Sun Microsystems provided workgroup operating systems. In order to create operating systems that would be compatible with Microsoft Windows OS, Sun required interface information. Microsoft refused to provide this information. At the time of the case, Microsoft had dominance in the operating system market. Without making their operating systems compatible with Microsoft, the applicant could not compete. Microsoft argued that reverse engineering was the correct path for obtaining interoperability information. Sun and the others argued that reverse engineering gave few and uncertain results. This, in turn, meant that supply of the original information was necessary, which is a condition for the application of Article 102 of the Treaty

---

[92] *Microsoft*, Commission Decision COMP/C-3/37.792, 24 March 2004.

on the Functioning of the European Union (TFEU). The Commission concluded that Microsoft's refusal amounted to abuse of its dominant position.[93]

In *SAS*, the CJEU addressed this question directly and concluded that:

> Article 5(3) of [the Computer Programs Directive] must be interpreted as meaning that a person who has obtained a copy of a computer program under a licence is entitled, without the authorisation of the owner of the copyright, to observe, study or test the functioning of that program so as to determine the ideas and principles which underlie any element of the program, in the case where that person carries out acts covered by that licence and acts of loading and running necessary for the use of the computer program, and on condition that that person does not infringe the exclusive rights of the owner of the copyright in that program.

3.3 Trademarks

The EU trademark legislation approximates laws of the Member States that relate to trademarks. The legislation, which is the result of a long period of negotiation, consists of the harmonizing 2015 Trade Mark Directive[94] and the 2015 Regulation concerning the Community Trade Mark,[95] both replacing earlier versions from 2008.[96] The first EU trademark harmonization dates to 1988 and the Community Trade Mark (CTM) had first been created in 1996.

Article 1 provides that the Directive applies to every trademark 'in respect of goods or services which is the subject of registration or of an application in a Member State for registration as an individual trade mark, a collective mark or a guarantee or certification mark'. Article 2 provides that the trademark may consist of 'any signs, in particular words, including personal names, or designs, letters, numerals, colours, the shape of goods or of the packaging of goods, or sounds', as long as they are capable of distinguishing goods and services of one undertaking from the other and being able to be represented in an official register.

---

[93] See also the Court of First Instance judgment T-201/04 *Microsoft v Commission* [2007] ECR II-03601.

[94] Directive (EU) 2015/2436 of the European Parliament and of the Council of 16 December 2015 to approximate the laws of the Member States relating to trademarks [2015] OJ L336/1, 23 December 2015.

[95] Regulation (EU) 2015/2424 of the European Parliament and of the Council of 16 December 2015 [2015] OJ L341/21, 24 December 2015.

[96] The new Trademark Directive came into force in January 2016.

The Directive is not a full harmonization but rather one that covers areas where disparities between Member States have in practice proved to be particularly damaging. Thus the Directive provides detailed rules for grounds for refusal and invalidity (articles 4–9); rights conferred (articles 10–13); limitations of a trademark's effect (article 14); and exhaustion (article 15). Furthermore, use (articles 16–17), and revocation (Section 4) are covered. Transfers are covered in Section 5. Chapters 3 and 4 are dedicated to procedures and administrative provisions.

Two recent cases clarified EU trademark protection in the Internet context.[97] The first relates to trademarks on search engines while the second is about their use on online marketplaces. The *Google v Louis Vuitton* case[98] concentrated on Google's advertising practices. Google runs a search engine and operates a paid advertising service, AdWords. A search term entered into the Google search engine triggers a display of both the regular search results and paid-for adverts. Louis Vuitton and others argued that search queries, which contain words over which they owned trademark rights, display not only the legitimate sites (in the regular search window) but also AdWords-type paid sites of competitors who produced and/or sold counterfeit goods. The CJEU ruled that an Internet search engine that stores a keyword, which is a 'sign identical with a trademark', and displays advertisements based on that keyword, does not use the sign within the meaning of article 5(1). On the other hand, an advertiser (in this case not Google but those buying AdWords from Google) may be prohibited from using keywords identical to the trademark where an average Internet user would be confused by such use.

In *L'Oréal*,[99] the online auctions marketplace eBay offered a variety of goods for sale on its website. Among these were goods that infringed the applicant's trademark. The CJEU ruled that, upon proper construction of the Trade Mark Directive, the trademark proprietor was entitled to prohibit the advertising of goods bearing its trademark where a risk of confusion existed but only if certain conditions had been met. This, first,

---

[97] I. Fhima, 'Trademark Law and Advertising Keywords' in A. Savin and J. Trzaskowski, *Research Handbook on EU Internet Law* (Edward Elgar Publishing, Cheltenham and Northampton, MA, 2013), p. 143.

[98] Joined Cases C-236/08 and C-238/08 *Google France SARL and Google Inc. v Louis Vuitton Malletier SA and others* [2010] ECR I-02417.

[99] C-324/09 *L'Oréal SA, Lancôme parfums et beauté & Cie SNC, Laboratoire Garnier & Cie and L'Oréal (UK) Ltd v eBay International AG and others* [2011] ECR I-06011.

depended on whether the sale was in a commercial context or not (paragraph 55):

> Accordingly, when an individual sells a product bearing a trade mark through an online marketplace and the transaction does not take place in the context of a commercial activity, the proprietor of the trade mark cannot rely on his exclusive right ... If, however, owing to their volume, their frequency or other characteristics, the sales made on such a marketplace go beyond the realms of a private activity, the seller will be acting 'in the course of trade' within the meaning of those provisions.

In relation to whether placing the goods on an online marketplace *also* accessible in the EU is covered by the Directive, the Court held that:

> it is the task of the national courts to assess on a case-by-case basis whether relevant factors exist, on the basis of which it may be concluded that an offer for sale or an advertisement displayed on an online marketplace accessible from the territory covered by the trade mark is targeted at consumers in that territory.

This means, essentially, that the proprietor can prohibit the sale as soon as it is clear that the goods are intended for the EU. Since eBay also used trademarked terms in its keywords, thus attracting traffic and, potentially, extra income through advertising, the Court ruled that the proprietor of a trademark may prohibit such use where:

> the advertising does not enable reasonably well-informed and reasonably observant internet users, or enables them only with difficulty, to ascertain whether the goods concerned originate from the proprietor of the trade mark or from an undertaking economically linked to that proprietor or, on the contrary, originate from a third party.

In the *Interflora* case,[100] which is a continuation of the above line of cases, Marks & Spencer used 'Interflora' and other similar trademarks in Google AdWords to attract custom for its flower delivery service. Interflora is a registered trademark owned by Interflora Inc., a US flower delivery company. The CJEU held that, according to article 5(2) of the Trade Mark Directive:

> proprietor of a trade mark with a reputation is entitled to prevent a competitor from advertising on the basis of a keyword corresponding to that trade mark, which the competitor has, without the proprietor's consent, selected in an

---

[100] C-323/09 *Interflora and others v Marks & Spencer* [2011] ECR I-08625.

internet referencing service, where the competitor thereby takes unfair advantage of the distinctive character or repute of the trade mark (free-riding) or where the advertising is detrimental to that distinctive character (dilution) or to that repute (tarnishment).

In all the mentioned cases, the CJEU left scope for further precision to the national courts, which were left with the task of working out the details.

Traditionally an aspect of trademark rights, domain name regulation, including disputes over domain names, is mostly within Member States' competence.[101] The EU regulates only one of its aspects, namely its own domain name, which is covered in the .eu Domain Name Regulation, introducing the .eu domain name.[102]

3.4 Collective Management of Online Music[103]

The process of rights clearance for online music in the European Union appears complex when compared to that in the United States. In Europe, a commercial entity seeking to clear rights would have to engage in negotiations in the Member States' collecting societies, each of which would have jurisdiction to issue clearances for the global catalogue but valid for their territory only. With increasing move to streaming and downloads, the need for a multi-territorial licensing system is high. With a view to reducing the disparities in licensing models for online music, the European Commission gradually introduced measures culminating in a harmonizing Directive in 2012.

The first attempt at regulating was the Recommendation on the management of online rights in musical works in 2005.[104] In the

---

[101] See T. Bettinger and A. Waddell, *Domain Name Law and Practice: An International Handbook* (OUP, Oxford, 2015).

[102] Regulation (EC) 733/2002 of the European Parliament and of the Council of 22 April 2002 on the implementation of the .eu Top Level Domain [2002] OJ L113/1, 3 April 2002. See also Commission Regulation (EC) 874/2004 laying down public policy rules concerning the implementation and functions of the .eu Top Level Domain and the principles governing registration [2004] OJ L162/40, 30 April 2004.

[103] For a detailed critical overview of the system in the EU see G. Mazziotti, 'New Licensing Models for Online Music Services in the European Union: From Collective to Customized Management' (2011) 34 Columbia Journal of Law and the Arts 757.

[104] Commission Recommendation of 18 October 2005 on collective cross-border management of copyright and related rights for legitimate online music services [2005] OJ L276/54, 21 October 2005.

Commission's detailed impact assessment[105] the present structures for cross-border collective management of online content were analysed and three options considered. The first was to take no action and was rejected by stakeholders. The second, favoured by commercial users, was to eliminate territorial restrictions in the existing agreements, thus bringing true multi-territorial licensing into the EU. The third option, favoured by music publishers, was to give the right-holders the option to appoint an EU-wide manager for online content ('EU-wide direct licensing'). The final proposal was a hybrid of the second and third options, while introducing rules on governance, transparency and dispute settlement, and accountability of collective rights managers. It called for the establishment of a multi-territorial licensing policy by inviting the Member States to introduce systems that are best suited to the collective management of online content services. Right-holders should, under this system, have the right to choose the management society of their choice, irrespective of their residence or nationality. Right-holders should, further, have the right to choose the rights entrusted to management and the territorial scope of the mandate but should also be able to withdraw. The 2005 system was criticized for avoiding true harmonization by opting for a soft-law instrument and for avoiding the introduction of a full pan-European licensing system.[106]

In 2012, the Commission proposed[107] a Directive on collective rights management that was adopted in 2014.[108] Among the aims are the increased transparency and better governance of collecting societies and easier licensing of authors' rights for use on the Internet (multi-territorial and multi-repertoire licensing). Article 1 clarifies that the subject matter is online rights in musical works, with the rights in videos, books, video games or any other content not covered in the Directive and left for general EU law principles and national law.

---

[105] Brussels, SEC(2005)1254, 11 October 2005.

[106] See Mazziotti, 'New Licensing Models for Online Music Services', note 103 above, pp. 800–808.

[107] Proposal for a Directive of the European Parliament and of the Council on collective management of copyright and related rights and multi-territorial licensing of rights in musical works for online uses in the internal market, COM(2012)372 (11 July 2012).

[108] Directive 2014/26/EU of the European Parliament and of the Council of 26 February 2014 on collective management of copyright and related rights and multi-territorial licensing of rights in musical works for online use in the internal market [2014] OJ L84/72, 20 March 2014.

The Directive has two main aims. The first is to create a framework for multi-territorial and multi-directory licensing. The key provision is article 5 which allows right-holders to authorize a collective management organization of their choice irrespective of their or the society's nationality, residence or establishment. As a rule, the collective rights management organization is obliged to manage such rights. This right applies to rights or categories of rights of their choice as well as to territories of their choice. The second aim is to improve transparency and governance of collective rights management organizations. As an example, article 16, which regulates licensing as a relationship with the users, provides that collective rights organizations need to negotiate in good faith and offer licensing terms which are objective and non-discriminatory.

Although it is early to judge its impact, the new system seems to have brought a clearer mechanism for control of rights, decision-making, payment and transparency. On the other hand, licensing of audio-visual works is not subject to harmonization and is continuing to be a source of frustration both for businesses and for users.

3.5   Orphan Works

Orphan works are works that are in copyright but whose right-holders cannot be identified or located. Since these works are still protected, clearing the rights may be difficult or impossible, leading the interested parties to either abandon the project or risk potential lawsuits should the right-holder emerge anyway. Although the estimates vary, there is no doubt that a very large percentage of works that are technically protected are, in fact, orphan works. With the mass digitization projects underway (such as Google Books) the need for clearer rules has become acute.

The Commission recognizes that the present non-binding instruments do not address the problem of mass digitization adequately. In order to address this, it adopted a Proposal[109] for a Directive on certain permitted uses of orphan works in 2011 and this became the Orphan Works Directive in 2012.[110] The overall aim of the Directive is to make it easier for certain public entities to use works, upon fair compensation, in cases where the right-holders are unknown. The Directive applies to 'publicly accessible libraries, educational establishments or museums as well as …

---

[109]   Brussels, COM(2011)289 final (24 May 2011).
[110]   Directive 2012/28/EU of the European Parliament and of the Council of 25 October 2012 on certain permitted uses of orphan works [2012] OJ L299/5, 27 October 2012.

archives, film heritage institutions and public service broadcasting organizations'. The Directive does not cover commercial and private entities, which remain under the general regime, requiring them to clear the rights under national laws. This is justified by the 'public-interests' purpose of the Directive.

The aim is to establish common rules on digitization and online display. The key provision is article 3 that introduces the diligent search criteria which must be fulfilled in order to identify something as an orphan work. The article simply makes sure that the necessary effort to find the right-holder has been made. Article 4 confirms that an orphan work considered as such in one Member State will have the same status in all states. Article 5 ensures that the right-holder can end the orphan work status at any time. Permitted uses are covered in article 6 which allows the organizations mentioned in article 1 either to make the works available or to reproduce them. Article 7 of the original Proposal allowed for other uses, including commercial, under some conditions but was of optional nature in the original Proposal and has since been removed from the final version.

3.6 Geo-Blocking and Content Portability

Geo-blocking is the practice of limiting access to Internet content based on geographical location. Usually, various technical measures at hardware or software level are used to achieve this result. Streaming services (such as, for example, Netflix or YouTube) typically offer different content catalogues based on the licensing arrangements in different countries. There is a whole range of reasons behind geo-blocking, from economic, through cultural to legal. In addition to this, geo-blocking usually comes in two forms. The first relates to copyright and its territorial nature. Since rights to audio-video content need to be cleared for each Member State separately, there are often different 'packages' available in each and geo-blocking measures help enforce this.[111] The second relate to various e-commerce geo-blocking measures, which have to do with the provision of goods and services but typically have nothing to do with copyright. This can, for example, be the case where an e-commerce merchant in one country blocks access to consumers in another or where a news portal offers a more limited set of articles to

---

[111]   For the copyright side of the story see G. Mazziotti, *Is Geo-blocking a Real Cause for Concern in Europe?*, EUI LAW 2015/43, available at http://hdl.handle.net/1814/38084.

audiences accessing it from foreign IP addresses. Conceptually, these two are different.

The consumers are increasingly frustrated by such arrangements and seek access to wider catalogues, often resorting to circumventing geo-blocking through proxy services. This frustration has also been recognized at EU level. The 2015 Digital Single Market Strategy[112] emphasized the removal of geographical blocking as one of its three main aims (section 2.3). Recognizing and reacting mostly to the non-copyright side of the problem, the Commission promised legislative action, including potential change to the e-Commerce framework and article 20 of the Services Directive (2006/123/EC). Recognizing the copyright side of the issue (section 2.4 of the Strategy), the Commission suggested (a) measures on portability of legally acquired content; (b) 'ensuring cross-border access to legally purchased online services while respecting the value of rights in the audiovisual sector'; (c) harmonized exceptions for specific purposes such as research, education, text and data mining; (d) clarifying the rules on intermediaries; and (e) modernizing the enforcement of IP rights, especially for commercial-scale infringements.

In 2015, as parts of the announced measures, the Commission published its proposal on the Regulation for online portability of content.[113] The proposal is not meant as a universal measure to remove geo-blocking but rather as a much narrower instrument enabling the subscribers to access the services while abroad. The providers are obliged to enable the subscriber who is *temporarily* present to access the services they are entitled to at home. In such cases, the provision will be deemed to have taken place in the user's home state. The Proposal does not seem to oblige the providers to give the user the local version of the state where the user is temporarily based but rather to enable the user access to their original, home state, version. There does not seem to be any reason to believe that the words 'temporary' should be interpreted extensively in a manner that would enable the territorial nature of copyright to be circumvented.

In the view of this author, removing copyright-related geo-blocking restrictions will be impossible without fully harmonizing copyright laws of Member States or, at the very least, thoroughly reforming the licensing regimes that apply to multi-territorial licensing of video content. Since

---

[112] Communication from the Commission, *A Digital Single Market Strategy for Europe*, COM(2015)192 final (6 May 2015).

[113] Proposal for a Regulation of the European Parliament and of the Council on ensuring the cross-border portability of online content services in the Internal Market, COM(2015)627 final (9 December 2015).

the Parliament expressed its support for copyright territoriality,[114] the former seems very unlikely. There are signs that the latter may be possible, since EU competition authorities are interested in the licensing arrangements that US companies made with EU pay-tv broadcasters, the suggestion being that the contractual restrictions are creating territorial exclusivity and thus violating EU competition rules.[115]

3.7 Exhaustion of Rights

The principle of the exhaustion of rights refers to the idea that the goods already marketed in one Member State should be freely distributable in others without intellectual property rights, such as patents, copyrights or trademarks, coming in the way. The IP rights remain valid but, once the goods have lawfully been placed on the market in EU Member States A and B, parallel imports from and into these states cannot be prevented. Right-holders can therefore choose not to place their goods on certain markets, but if they do, these will be subject to the exhaustion doctrine.[116]

The CJEU indirectly addressed the application of the doctrine in the *Premier League* case.[117] In that case, some UK pub owners had legally acquired Greek decoder cards with which their customers could access and watch Premier League football matches on digital television. Such cards were marketed at much higher prices in the United Kingdom. The question posed was, essentially, whether parallel imports from another EU Member State constitute a violation of IP rights.

The Advocate General suggested in her Opinion that exhaustion of rights ought to extend to services.[118] In its judgment, the Court sidestepped that particular angle of the question but answered it by analysing the free movement of services, saying that Article 56 TFEU:

---

[114] European Parliament Resolution of 9 July 2015 on the implementation of Directive 2001/29/EC of the European Parliament and of the Council of 22 May 2001 on the harmonization of certain aspects of copyright and related rights in the information society, 2014/2256(INI).

[115] European Commission, 'Antitrust: Commission investigates restrictions affecting cross border provision of pay TV services', Press Release, IP/14/15 (Brussels, 13 January 2014).

[116] First introduced for copyright in C-78/70 *Deutsche Grammophon* [1970] ECR 487.

[117] C-403/08 *Football Association Premier League Ltd and others v QC Leisure and others* and C-429/08 *Karen Murphy v Media Protection Services Ltd* [2011] ECR I-090834.

[118] Advocate General's Opinion, para. 188.

precludes legislation of a Member State which makes it unlawful to import
into and sell and use in that State foreign decoding devices which give access
to an encrypted satellite broadcasting service from another Member State that
includes subject-matter protected by the legislation of that first State.

The grant of a limited licence, therefore, does not seem to exhaust a
copyright. On the other hand, the judgment, in focusing on the services
side of the question, may ultimately have far-reaching consequences for
content distribution on the Internet, which also often relies on different
licensing models. The message is that the ownership of intellectual
property rights does not in and of itself suspend the free movement of
services. This may be a significant development, since the judgment's
main message concerning licensing broadcasting rights on a territorial
basis may also have implications for licensing on the Internet. An
analogous application of the *Premier League* reasoning might suggest
that lawfully accessing an online service from one country in another
cannot be prevented. The situation is more complicated, however. The
dissemination of most online content falls within the 'making available'
right under article 3. Article 3(3) is clear in determining that exhaustion
does *not* apply to the right of communication to the public, which would
mean that exhaustion cannot be applied to online distribution. The
alternative route adopted in the *Premier League* case, on the other hand,
leaves open the path that Article 56 provides and it is for future cases to
find the degree to which this can be extended to other media.

4   CONCLUSION: REVIEWING EU COPYRIGHT LAW

There is no doubt that the Copyright Directive has proved robust and
adequate, in spite of the problems associated with it.[119] Its technology-
neutral framework has proved flexible and able to accommodate new
technologies, while its narrow interpretation of exceptions and protection
of technological measures appeals to industry and acts as an incentive to
bring about new technologies. At the same time, it is true that the
exceptions regime is the bottleneck in the current system, at least in
respect of copyright on the Internet. A common objection to copyright
law at EU level is the inability to properly balance the interests of the

---

[119]   Some general recommendations can be found in M. Van Eechound *et al.*,
Harmonizing European Copyright Law: The Challenges of Better Lawmaking,
Information Law Series (Kluwer, The Hague, 2009).

public against those of the right-holders. The rapid development of content distribution modes, at the same time, challenged a number of the Directive's solutions.

In spite of objections that have been heard about the Directive and the draftsmen's apparent desire to follow the US model, the main copyright instrument for the digital age survives. This shows that its technology-neutral approach has had some success. The cautious calls for reform seen in the Commission's policy documents demonstrate that there is space for reform rather than hasty replacement.

The difficulties outlined in the policy documents and which relate to adjusting the Directive to modern technologies exists in spite of the technology-neutral approach. In fact, they are partially caused by the somewhat inflexible approach of articles 5 and 6. The Information Society Directive potentially makes a number of activities illegal: multi-region DVD and Blu-ray players, copying of music for research purposes or parody and criticism. 'Fencing off' targets authorized as well as unauthorized use. Also, it has previously been possible to challenge the *legality* of copyright protection in the courts. But now that *technology* protects the content, and anti-circumvention per se is made illegal, those who might otherwise have relied on an exception may seek alternative ways.

The question of whether and how the European Union could respond to changes brought about by the advance in the knowledge economy was first raised in the Green Paper published in 2008.[120] In that document, the Commission sought answers from stakeholders on a number of issues relating to the operation of the Directive and its exceptions. The Communication on Copyright in the Knowledge Economy,[121] which followed, is based on the material submitted in response to the Green Paper and summarized the Commission's views on future steps. In that document, the Commission identified five areas which are fundamental for the development of the digital economy and on which work would be needed: libraries and archives; orphan works; teaching and research; disabilities; and user-created content. Similar to the Copyright Communication is the 2011 Green Paper on the online distribution of audio-visual works,[122] which looked into the effect of technological developments on audio-visual works. The Green Paper explored three avenues: it looks at the right clearance mechanism for online distribution, explored the

---

[120] Green Paper, *Copyright in the Knowledge Economy*, COM(2008)466/3 (16 July 2008).
[121] COM(2009)532 final (19 October 2009).
[122] COM(2011)427 final (13 July 2011).

problem of remuneration for online works; and looked into possible legislative measures. The Green Paper sought a better understanding of the reasons behind market fragmentation and the methodologies that could maximize the development of the 'digital internal market'. Significantly, the Green Paper explored the facilitation of collective rights management as one of the possible strategies for addressing the issues, seeing 'cross-border and pan-European licences' as playing a significant role.[123]

The copyright reform began in earnest in 2014 with a public consultation[124] the object of which was to gather opinion from all stakeholders. At the same time, a number of earlier-commissioned studies have been published.[125] Shortly afterwards, in 2015, the Reda Report to the EU Parliament came out, outlining the biggest challenges to EU copyright.[126] While not a comprehensive review of copyright law in the EU, it suggested some important changes, including a reduction of geo-blocking, the introduction of new exceptions and portability of content.

The 2015 Digital Single Market Strategy[127] suggested new legislation on portability and cross-border accessibility of content, 'clarifying the rules on the activities of intermediaries in relation to copyright-protected content' and modernizing enforcement 'focusing on commercial-scale infringements'. The latter, labelled 'follow the money' approach has not been further elaborated on.

The 2015 White Paper on Copyright,[128] serving as the Commission's blueprint for further work on copyright, suggested that what is needed is higher levels of harmonization, in particular in relation to territorial aspects of copyright and adaptation of copyright to new technological

---

[123] This is consistent both with the Digital Agenda for Europe, COM(2010)245 (19 May 2010), and with *Single Market Act: Twelve Levers to Boost Growth and Strengthen Confidence, Working Together to Create New Growth*, COM(2011)0206 final (13 April 2011).

[124] Available at http://ec.europa.eu/internal_market/consultations/2013/copyright-rules/docs/consultation-document_en.pdf.

[125] Available at http://ec.europa.eu/internal_market/copyright/studies/index_en.htm.

[126] J. Reda, *Implementation of Directive 2001/29/EC on the Harmonisation of Certain Aspects of Copyright and Related Rights in the Information Society*, 2014/2256(INI) (9 July 2015).

[127] See page 25 above.

[128] Communication from the Commission to the European Parliament, the Council, the European Economic and Social Committee and the Committee of the Regions, *Towards a Modern, More European Copyright Framework*, COM(2015)626 final (Brussels, 9 December 2015).

realities. The document has four themes: wider access; adapted exceptions; better distribution; and better enforcement.

In terms of wider access, the Commission emphasized that the ultimate goal was full cross-border access for all types of content. In addition to the portability proposal discussed above, the Commission announced proposals in 2016 for better cross-border distribution of television and radio programmes online, improving the framework for licences that allow for cross-border access to content and easier digitization of out-of-commerce works.[129]

In the review of copyright exceptions, the Commission has suggested the adoption of the WIPO Marrakesh Treaty.[130] The announced proposals for 2016 include text and data mining, illustration for teaching, preservation by cultural heritage institutions, remote consultation of works held electronically and the exception for works permanently located in public spaces ('panorama exception'). In addition to this, the Commission will review levies for private copying, ensuring that differences in their application at national level do not increase barriers to free movement of goods and services.

The review of 'communication to the public' and 'making available' is to ensure a better functioning marketplace for copyright, as is a review of the position of news aggregators and the remuneration of authors and performers. In reviewing enforcement mechanisms, the Commission has again suggested the 'follow-the-money' self-regulatory approach where codes of conducts could be backed by regulation. It has also suggested a review of the position of online platforms, discussed in Chapter 5.

Fulfilling some of the promises made in the Digital Single Market Strategy and the White Paper, the Commission published in September 2016 a proposal for a Directive on Copyright in the Digital Single Market.[131] The proposal is not the promised comprehensive revision of the InfoSoc Directive but a very selective targeted measure that seems to have been a result of heavy lobbying from the rightholders sector. Three changes are notable. The first concerns exceptions. Article 3 introduces a text and data mining exception for research organizations only, Article 4 applies to digital and cross-border teaching activities and Article 5 to

---

[129] Brussels, 14.9.2016 COM(2016) 594 final.

[130] WIPO, Marrakesh Treaty to Facilitate Access to Published Works for Persons Who are Blind, Visually Impaired or Otherwise Print Disabled, 27 June 2013, available at http://www.wipo.int/wipolex/en/details.jsp?id=13169.

[131] Proposal for a Directive of the European Parliament and of the Council on Copyright in the Digital Single Market, COM(2016) 593 final (Brussels, 14 September 2016).

preservation of cultural heritage. The second concerns protection of press publications. Article 11 grants publishers of press publications the rights from Articles 2 and 3(2) of the InfoSoc Directive. This is, essentially, a new neighbouring right. Although the preamble 33 does say that the new right 'does not extend to acts of hyperlinking which do not constitute communication to the public' the Proposal does not define when a hyperlink (and the potential accompanying snippet of news) is a communication to the public. There is no explanation in the Proposal as to why news publishers are in need of a separate neighbouring right. The third change affects content filtering of user-generated content. Article 13 applies to 'information society service providers storing and giving access to large amounts of works and other subject-matter uploaded by their users'. Information society service providers are required to enter into licensing agreements with rightholders and introduce adequate content recognition technologies. The idea is that licensing agreements and filtering need to be introduced where information society service providers do *not* benefit from the hosting exception from Article 14 of the E-Commerce Directive (Recital 38 of the Proposal). As in Article 11, the explanation as to why the rightholders need this extra protection is lacking. In addition, no explanation is given as to when ISSs do *not* benefit from Article 14 exception. Finally, the proposed article seems to be in direct conflict with the SABAM judgment which prohibits indiscriminate filtering and, possibly, with Article 15 of the E-Commerce Directive. Overall, the Proposal, which does not address any of the criticisms heard in the past 15 years since the InfoSoc Directive came into power, seems to be unfounded and based on vague premises.

The Commission's vision of future digital copyright seems to hang on a number of narrowly targeted interventions, which it hopes to propose in the course of the next couple of years, and rather vague assertions concerning almost everything else. While the flexibility that this approach brings cannot be completely dismissed, the lack of desire to engage with the deeper issues, including a more profound revision of exceptions, the role of intermediaries, copyright terms or even potential unification, will ultimately have a negative impact on the Digital Single Market project.

7.   Consumer protection and marketing

1 CONSUMERS AND THE INTERNET

Consumers are an important actor on the Internet. So important, in fact, that a great part of Internet activity revolves around them.[1] Hosting a website, sending an email, watching content on the Internet, ordering goods online or just visiting a webpage are all inherently, in whole or in part, consumer activities. But the increase of consumer activities also increases the risk and with it the need for protection. One of the more prominent features of EU law is its consumer protection that is not only a constitutional value but an embedded feature in many of its laws.

Consumer transactions initiated and completed on the Internet need not be significantly more different than the offline transactions except in their speed and the relative ease with which they can be conducted. Hosting a webpage is not conceptually different from renting space in a magazine; sending an email can be equated to sending a letter; watching a television series streamed or downloaded from a web-based provider is an experience similar to watching it on a satellite or cable channel; and purchasing a video disc online is similar to ordering it on the phone from the supplier's catalogue. And yet, uncertainties prevail, as consumers seem reluctant to fully commit to cross-border purchases on the Internet.[2] Although some of the effects can be explained by a variety of psychological and economic factors, there is no doubt that the perceived or real lack of protection and lack of knowledge about the rights conferred and the applicable law play a role. Whereas the Internet seems to have revolutionized consumer shopping habits, it would appear that consumer vulnerability has increased as demand for extra information, insurance

---

[1]   Unless otherwise stated, the EU secondary legislation discussed here applies only to business-to-consumer (B2C) transactions.
[2]   See Communication from the Commission, *A Digital Single Market Strategy for Europe*, COM(2015)192 final (6 May 2015) ('2015 Digital Single Market Strategy').

and protection rises along with the number of fraudulent attacks. In dealing with these vulnerabilities, the law-maker usually makes the assumption that consumers deserve a certain minimum level of protection.[3] Moreover, the Commission's default image when proposing laws seems to be the 'vulnerable consumer'.[4] Although this image may, in fact be a mirage, it is a starting position which informs almost all EU consumer protection documents.

The European Union puts a high value on consumer protection,[5] a fact reflected both in the Treaty Articles[6] and in the secondary legislation.[7] Article 169 of the Treaty on the Functioning of the European Union (TFEU) provides that the Community's aim is to protect 'health, safety and economic interests of consumers' and 'their right to information, education and to organise themselves'. The legal basis for consumer legislation in the EU is the Single Market (Article 114 TFEU) but Article 169 also gives the EU the necessary competence to adopt measures that 'support, supplement and monitor the policy pursued by the Member States'. Such measures, unlike laws enacted by reference to Article 114, do not pre-empt more stringent national measures.

An overview of the comprehensive EU web of consumer protection laws reveals a constant set of objectives, which revolve around transparency and certainty. In reality, consumer interests are more complex and can be tentatively divided into three groups, around which the

---

[3]   On the assumption of consumer vulnerability see D. Leczykiewicz and S. Weatherill, *The Images of the Consumer in EU Law: Legislation, Free Movement and Competition Law* (Hart, Oxford, 2016).

[4]   On how the concept evolved and on indicators of vulnerability see European Commission, *Consumer Vulnerability across Key Markets in the European Union, Final Report* (January 2016), available at http://ec.europa.eu/consumers/consumer_evidence/market_studies/docs/vulnerable_consumers_approved_27_01_2016_en.pdf.

[5]   The Commission uses the term 'consumer empowerment' to designate an environment that enables the consumers not only to have rights but also to enjoy them effectively. See Proposal for a Regulation of the European Parliament and of the Council on a consumer programme 2014–2020, COM(2011)707 final (Brussels, 9 November 2011).

[6]   Cf. Arts 39, 107 or 169 TFEU.

[7]   For an overview of consumer law in the EU, see S. Weatherill, *EU Consumer Law and Policy*, 2nd edn (Edward Elgar Publishing, Cheltenham and Northampton, MA, 2014).

EU legislation has been designed.[8] The first relates to fair-trading interests such as information concerning the seller and the product, payment issues and redress in case the transaction goes wrong. The second category relates to privacy: consent to gather information, access to information already gathered and security of information on hold. This category is covered in the EU Privacy Directive (see Chapter 8). The third category relates to morality: issues such as pornography, hate speech and protection of minors against offensive content (see Chapter 4).

There are two sources of consumer threats in all three categories. In the first case, the threat is a result of an open attempt to defraud the consumer. Recent figures confirm that fraud on the Internet is on the rise.[9] Among numerous schemes, the most popular seem to be online auctions, general merchandise fraud, the so-called Nigerian scam, electronic equipment fraud and Internet access fraud. In the second, the threat arises as a result of problematic business practices. These can be described as substandard practices relating to information provided to the consumer, conclusion and performance of the contract, payment and remedies. Consumer law deals with the second only, leaving the first to criminal and administrative law.

In this chapter we will explore how the EU deals with consumer and marketing problems in the digital world. We will focus on four areas. The first relates to consumer sales transactions. Here, the new Directive on Consumer Rights, as well as its predecessors, will be analysed. The second concerns protection of consumers in banking and financial transactions. The third is about marketing and advertising regulation. Although the EU regulates marketing practices extensively, in this chapter marketing practices will be analysed only in as much as they concern consumers on the Internet. The fourth concerns consumer protection in international litigation.

---

[8] See J. Dickie, *Producers and Consumers in EU E-Commerce Law* (Hart, Oxford, 2005), p. 11 *et seq.*

[9] Internet Crime Complaint Centre (IC3), *2015 Internet Crime Report*, available at www.ic3.gov/media/default.aspx.

2 CONSUMER PROTECTION DIRECTIVES

2.1 Consumer Rights Directive

The 2011 Consumer Rights Directive[10] replaces the Distance Selling Directive[11] and the even older Doorstep Selling Directive on contracts negotiated away from business premises.[12] As such, it is a codification of the basic consumer rights covered in the previously mentioned Directives. At the same time, it provides 'full harmonization of some key regulatory aspects' not previously covered. In respect of digital contracts, the Directive has three key regulatory directions. First, it establishes requirements for information to be provided in distance contracts (article 6). In that respect, the Directive is both a continuation of the Distance Selling Directive (which it replaces) and of the E-Commerce Directive (which contains general rules on information in e-transactions). Secondly, the Directive establishes formal requirements for distance consumer contracts (article 8). Thirdly, it regulates the right of withdrawal (articles 9–16). In addition to that, the Directive also covers the delivery (article 18), fees for use of the means of payment (article 19), passing of the risk (article 20) and additional payments (article 21).[13]

Article 2(1) defines a consumer as 'any natural person who … is acting for purposes which are outside his trade, business, craft or profession'.[14] The Directive applies both to contracts for the sale of goods, which are defined in article 2(5) as contracts to 'transfer the ownership of goods to the consumer' against the payment of a price, and to service contracts, which are defined in article 2(6) as contracts for the provision of services against payment. Article 2(7) defines a distance contract as 'organised distance sales or service-provision scheme without the simultaneous physical presence of the trader and the consumer, with the exclusive use of one or more means of distance communication'.

---

[10]   Directive 2011/83/EC of the European Parliament and of the Council on consumer rights, amending Council Directive 93/13/EEC and Directive 1999/44/EC of the European Parliament and of the Council and repealing Council Directive 85/577/EEC and Directive 97/7/EC of the European Parliament and of the Council [2011] OJ L304/64.

[11]   Directive 97/7/EC of the European Parliament and of the Council of 20 May 1997 on the protection of consumers in respect of distance contracts [1997] OJ L144/19, 4 June 1997. See Consumer Rights Directive, art. 31.

[12]   Council Directive 85/577/EEC of 20 December [1985] OJ L372/31, 31 December 1985.

[13]   On these articles, see Chapter 2, section 6.1.

[14]   This excludes SME businesses, no matter how small they are.

Article 3 excludes a number of areas from the scope of the Directive's application, including, among others, social services, healthcare, gambling, financial services, immovable property, building construction, package travel, timeshare agreements, notarial contracts, food supplies, passenger transport, automatic vending machines and single connection Internet contracts. Article 2(5) emphasizes that the Directive does not affect national contract law. Article 2(6) confirms that *traders* (but not Member States) can go beyond minimum harmonization and offer conditions that are even better than the ones the Directive offers. The expectation here is that traders' associations would apply various kinds of soft law and industry standards.

Article 4 explicitly forbids Member States from introducing legislation, which is more or less stringent, thus emphasizing that the Directive is a full-harmonization measure within its scope. Full harmonization is mostly an exception in EU law and the fact that it features prominently, not only in the Consumer Rights Directive but also in the Unfair Commercial Practices Directive (see below), signifies the importance of consumer protection.

The Directive introduces two sets of core rules: one for distance and off-premises contracts and another for non-distance contracts. Article 6 contains a comprehensive set of information to be provided to the consumer in distance contracts. The provision replicates most of the information provisions already seen in the E-Commerce and the Services Directives[15] without replacing them (article 6(8)) but makes them clearer and more favourable for the consumer. The seller is under an obligation to provide the information 'in a clear and comprehensible manner' prior to the consumer being bound. In a digital contract this means either that the information needs to be presented on the screen during the ordering process or that it is confirmed in an email communication, which, in turn, means that the consumer would not be bound before they received the information. The information forms an integral part of the contract (article 6(5)) but can be altered where both parties agree so. The trader, as per article 8(7), must provide the consumer with the confirmation that the contract had been concluded, on a durable medium and within a reasonable time after conclusion but at the latest at the time of the delivery. This confirmation must contain all the information from article 6(1).

---

[15] Directive 2006/123/EC of the European Parliament and of the Council of 12 December 2006 on services in the internal market [2006] OJ L376/36, 27 December 2006.

The information required concerns goods or services (article 6(1)(a)); trader's identity (6(1)(b)); address of the place of establishment (6(1)(c)) and of business (6(1)(d)); total price including taxes and freight (6(1)(e)); the cost of using means of distance communication for the conclusion (6(1)(f)); payment, delivery, performance and complaints arrangements (6(1)(g)); right of withdrawal conditions (6(1)(h) and (k)); potential costs regarding the right of withdrawal (6(1)(i) and (j)); a reminder of the legal guarantee (6(1)(l)); conditions of after-sales service (6(1)(m)); the existence of relevant codes of conduct (6(1)(n)); contract duration (6(1)(o) and (p)); and deposits and technical guarantees (6(1)(q)). Finally, the existence of an out-of-court complaints and redress mechanism must be communicated to the consumer.

Specific to digital contracts is the obligation to provide information on 'functionality, including applicable technical protection measures, of digital content' (article 6(1)(r)). The trader is also under obligation to provide information on the interoperability of digital content with hardware and software (6(1)(s)). These requirements, in a usual digital content transaction, mean that the consumer must be properly informed not only of any digital rights management measures (DRM) but also of any other conditions that might limit the usability of the service. Thus, streaming services that only operate on certain platforms must clearly state so as must products that are only operational on certain operating systems.

Article 8 covers formal requirements for distance contracts. The information demanded in article 6(1) must be made available in the way appropriate for the distance contract and in 'plain and intelligible' language. This requirement very likely puts in doubt a number of typically used online terms and conditions, which may linguistically be intelligible but are often not written in a 'plain' language. The appropriate ways for displaying information are not listed nor defined. For contracts concluded online, the most appropriate way would include displaying information on the website itself but may also involve emails or sending paper copies.

Where payment is required on the consumer's part in an e-commerce contract, the trader must make this obvious 'in a clear and prominent manner' and before the order is placed (article 8(2)). The consumer must explicitly acknowledge, when placing the order, the existence of the obligation to pay. If the ordering process involves a button, the consequences of pressing the button must be explained clearly. This is, by analogy, extended to situations where the trader preselects the options by ticking a box on the website, or preselects the items from the pull-down menu, and so on, before the consumer has had the option to do so. This is expressly acknowledged in article 22 which, dealing with payments in addition to remuneration, provides that the trader needs an express consent for any extra payments and is not allowed to infer it from the default options.

Article 8(3) confirms that trading websites must clearly and legibly indicate, at the latest at the beginning of the ordering process, whether any delivery restrictions apply and what means of payment are accepted. It has become customary for websites to either block IP addresses from countries they do not want to ship to, or simply decline to ship. From the business perspective, this makes sense, since the Brussels I Regulation (Recast) allows consumers to sue in the place of their domicile in all cases where they have been 'targeted'. This has recently been targeted at EU level through a proposed Directive on geo-blocking.[16]

Article 8(4) ensures that, where there are only limited means for displaying the required information (e.g. mobile phone screens), minimum information (listed in the article) regarding the conditions of the transaction must still be displayed. Other information must then be provided in an appropriate way. This can mean either emailing the information of providing it in an accessible form through a mobile application.

Article 9 allows the consumers to withdraw from distance contracts within 14 days, without giving any reason and without incurring any costs. The 14-day limit runs, for service contracts, from the day of the conclusion, and for sales contracts, from the day the consumer took physical possession. If the trader omits the information on withdrawal, article 10 extends the period from 14 days to 12 months. Annex I(B) introduces a model withdrawal form. In electronic transactions, the trader is allowed to present either the Annex I(B) form or one of its own, as long as appropriate information is presented and acknowledgement of receipt of the consumer's withdrawal is sent.

As per article 11, the desire to withdraw must be communicated to the trader either through the I(B) form or in another unequivocal manner. The exercise of the right to withdraw terminates the contract (article 12) and triggers the seller's obligation to reimburse the consumer (article 13) and the consumer's obligation to send back the goods without delay and not later than 14 days (article 14). For digital goods, article 14(4)(b) expressly releases the consumer for the cost of the supply of digital content where they have not consented to the performance beginning,

---

[16] See section 2.3 below.

where they have not acknowledged that they lose the right of withdrawal or where the seller failed to send the required confirmation.

Article 16 introduces exceptions to the rights of withdrawal consistent with modern contract law (e.g. services already performed, perishable goods, etc.) According to article 16(m), the right of withdrawal does not exist in respect of the supply of digital content where no tangible medium is used and the consumer consented in advance to terms of such delivery. This is typically the case with downloading or streaming content such as books, music or videos. In the case of tangible media (CDs, etc.), article 16(i) excludes withdrawal where the seal has been removed after delivery. Even if the consumer is not entitled to withdrawal, they may still be entitled to other remedies provided for in either EU or their national law.

The Directive introduces a comprehensive mechanism for eliminating hidden charges. Article 22 eliminates hidden transaction charges and costs in general. Consumers have to be told in advance of any such charges that are payable above the agreed remuneration and must specifically agree to them. If such consent is only inferred from default options which need to be rejected (e.g. preselected boxes or pull-down menus), the consumer will be entitled to a refund of such charges. Article 19 prohibits charging fees for using specific payment methods which go beyond the real cost. Traders are allowed to request payments for the use of, for instance, specific credit cards, but these must not exceed the real cost. Article 27 relieves the consumer from any obligation to pay for unsolicited goods, digital content or services (inertia selling).

2.2   Unfair Terms in E-Commerce Contracts

The Unfair Terms in Consumer Contracts Directive[17] is one of the most important consumer-protecting legal instruments in the European Union. Although drafted and enacted before the onset of the Internet age, its application to Internet cases and its importance for online transactions is well established. The aim of the Directive is simple: to minimize or eliminate unfair clauses in consumer contracts. The Directive had its origin in the Commission's policy of providing a comprehensive consumer protection system which would extend to civil contracts. Unfair terms in consumer contracts are frequent and disparities between laws of Member States aggravate the situation. The problem, as applied to the

---

[17]   Directive 93/13 [1993] OJ L095/29, 5 April 1993.

Internet, brings with it all the difficulties of instant transactions (click-wrap or browse-wrap).[18] An average consumer does not read standard terms, is not likely to understand them if he does and would in all likelihood not be able to spot them when he saw them.

The present Directive tackles unfairness in a general manner and serves as a fall-back provision applicable when other special laws do not cover the situation. Some EU proposed laws, present and past, do contain separate rules on unfairness. The proposed Directive on certain aspects concerning contracts for the supply of digital content,[19] for example, deals with such terms in articles 15 and 16 (modification and termination of long-term contracts). The now redundant Common European Sales Law[20] contained a special section (Chapter 8) on unfair terms. That proposal contained a duty of transparency for all contractual terms (article 82), had a separate definition of unfairness (article 82) and a closed black list of terms which are unfair by default (article 84). Article 85, on the other hand, introduced a grey list of terms that are presumed to be unfair unless otherwise proven. The proposal also dealt with unfair terms between traders.

Article 3 defines an unfair term as a contractual term that has not been individually negotiated and which, contrary to the requirement of good faith, causes a significant imbalance in the parties' rights and obligations under the contract, to the detriment of the consumer. A term not individually negotiated is one that has been drafted in advance and the consumer was not able to influence its substance. Most, if not all, contractual terms on the Internet are of this type. The article specifically mentions preformulated standard contracts, which are drafted in advance without the consumer's input. The article also provides that the fact that some aspects of the contract have been individually negotiated will not preclude the rest of the contract from benefiting from the protection.

The unfairness of a particular term is not assessed in general but takes into account the nature of the goods or services, the circumstances and other contractual terms (article 4). The unfairness is not assessed with reference to either the subject matter or the price of the contract as long as these are in plain intelligible terms. The sale of an overpriced item is, therefore, not covered, as long as the consumer had properly been made aware of the price. Likewise, the fact that a consumer purchases an item

---

[18]   On click-wrap contracts in general see N. Kim, *Wrap Contracts: Foundations and Ramifications* (OUP, Oxford, 2013).

[19]   COM(2015)634 final (Brussels, 9 December 2015).

[20]   Proposal for a Regulation, COM(2011)635 final (Brussels, 11 October 2011).

that is substandard is unproblematic unless the consumer had been misled, i.e. led to believe that the item will be better than the one they actually received.

The Annex to the Directive contains a non-exhaustive list of terms frequently used in contracts. This list contains a total of 17 examples, most of which can be considered typical in consumer contracts. This includes (a) limitations of seller's liability for death or injury; (b) limiting consumer's rights in case of seller's non-performance; (c) permitting the seller to retain the sums paid by the consumer in cases of withdrawal; (d) requiring the consumer to pay disproportionately high compensation, and others. Some of the terms listed in the Annex are typically found on the Internet.

Article 5 requires that terms of the contract be drafted in plain language intelligible to an ordinary consumer. In cases of doubt, preference is given to terms favourable to the consumer. This provision creates a certain kind of bias in favour of consumers but the fact that full implications of a term can only properly be understood by a trained professional does not, in itself, make the term unfair.

The consequence of the presence of unfair terms is their nullity with the continuing existence of the remainder of the contract, if this is capable of existing without these terms. Importantly, article 6(2) provides that the consumer will not lose the protection granted by the Directive by virtue of the choice of the law of a non-member country as the law applicable to the contract, if the latter has a close connection with the territory of the Member States. In other words, the provisions of the Directive that protect the consumer will be treated as mandatory rules in the international sense. They are applicable irrespective of the law otherwise applicable to the contract.

It is the obligation of Member States, under article 7, to ensure that sellers are adequately monitored for their use of unfair terms. Member States undertake to make efforts to reduce the prevalence of these terms. As an example, article 7(2) provides that various consumer protection bodies and similar organizations should have the right to take actions before courts or other organs to obtain decisions on whether terms of general use are unfair or not.

Article 8 allows Member States to go above the protection provided in the Directive, as long as this is consistent with the Treaty provisions. Member States who decide to follow this path must accordingly notify the Commission (article 8(a)).

The unfairness of a contractual term does not arise out of its length. Also, in spite of its bias towards protection, it is not the purpose of the Directive to correct situations that arise out of a lack of common sense.

Consumers cannot rely, in legal proceedings, on their own ignorance of terms of the agreement, where they clearly had access to these. Clicking on the button 'I Agree' or 'Buy' or any similar such button normally constitutes a binding agreement as long as a link to 'Terms and Conditions' had been made available before such button is clicked. It is true that such terms, just like those in software agreements, are lengthy and that most consumers do not read them. The important point, however, is that the Unfair Terms Directive will provide protection against *unfair* contractual terms, whether these have been read or not, whether they have been automatically agreed or not. In fact, the very point of the Directive is to combat preformulated terms, those over which the consumer has little or no influence.

At present, there exists uncertainty concerning the status of a number of contractual terms that are introduced into consumer contracts with relative frequency, having been brought to Europe from the United States. One of them, consumer arbitration, while increasingly popular in the United States, shows large disparities in regulation across Member States and may be illegal.[21] Non-disparagement clauses,[22] also increasingly popular in United States, may very well be illegal in terms of the Unfair Contract Terms Directive but also, potentially, constitutional provisions protecting freedom of speech.

2.3 Prohibition of Geo-Blocking

Prompted by reports of widespread discriminatory practices, where traders from one state refuse to deliver to customers in another, the Commission published a proposal for Regulation covering geo-blocking and other forms of discrimination based on customers' place of residence or establishment within the internal market.[23] Although article 20(2) of the Services Directive[24] already prohibits discrimination in its own sphere of application (which is severely limited in article 2), customers in the EU are frequently prevented from accessing sites or being sold goods or services based only on their nationality or place of residence.

---

[21]   See Chapter 3, section 5.
[22]   Where the consumer obliges themselves not to act in any way that may harm the trader's reputation, including leaving negative reviews on online sites.
[23]   Proposal for a Regulation, COM(2016)289 final (Brussels, 25 May 2016).
[24]   Directive 2006/123/EC of the European Parliament and of the Council of 12 December 2006 on services in the internal market [2006] OJ L376/36, 27 December 2006.

Article 3 of the Proposal introduces the obligation for traders not to prevent access to their online interfaces based on customers' residence. The obligation is not to use technological means to block or limit access *solely* on the basis of nationality or place of residence or establishment. Traders are also not allowed to reroute customers to a different version of their site unless customers have explicitly consented to this. This provision only deals with the communications interface (webpage, mobile app) used to access the trader, not with the transaction itself.

Article 4 introduces prohibition of discrimination in three situations. The first involves sales of physical goods where the trader is not involved in delivery to the customer. The logic behind this is that traders often refuse to supply, quoting difficulties in shipping. If the seller is not involved in shipping, though, there should be no reason for that seller to refuse custom from another state. The second is the supply of *electronic* services except those that rely on copyright or other protected matter.[25] Although the original idea was to cover copyright, the complexity of the intervention required had discouraged the Commission. Finally, the third situation covers *all* services not already covered in the second point that are provided in trader's premises in a state different than the customer's state. Here, the trader controls the premises and should have no objective reason for being interested in the consumer's nationality.

Special non-discrimination rules in respect of payments are introduced in article 5. The main rule is that discrimination is prohibited in all cases where payments are made electronically, strong authentication is available and payments are in a currency that the payee accepts.

The wisdom of the Proposal can be questioned both from the traders' and the consumers' perspective. Regarding the former, there can be no objective reason why small and medium-sized companies (and sometimes even large ones) should be forced to trade with consumers in *all* Member States. This is not only expensive but not necessarily in the interest of the consumers. In respect of the latter, a consumer who *demands* a sale from a trader ill-equipped to give adequate support and after-sales services may gain little and lose a lot.

---

[25] This obligation does not apply to VAT-exempt traders.

3 BANKING AND FINANCIAL SERVICES

3.1 Distance Marketing of Consumer Financial Services Directive

Whereas the Consumer Rights Directive regulates the distance selling to consumers of all *non-financial* goods and services, the Directive on distance marketing of consumer financial services[26] aims to consolidate the market for consumer *financial* services and open it up for Member States. The guiding motivation is that distance selling of financial services is a growing area that requires additional consumer protection.[27] The Directive is meant to benefit both the traders, who access markets in other Member States with little or no additional cost, and the consumers who benefit from ease of access and lower prices resulting from increased competition. The Internet in particular is well suited for trading in this field as it offers easy and instantaneous comparison. An interested consumer can look up any offers for a particular financial service online and be sure that she would be able to make an informed decision in the belief that the risk of fraud is minimal.

The object of the Directive, as stated in article 1, is the approximation of laws relating to distance selling of financial services. The Directive distinguishes between contracts that involve an initial service agreement and those that do not. The former are agreements, which consist in a series of successive operations forming one whole, irrespective of whether individual operations can also be considered as contracts. These are, for example, the opening of a bank account or a credit card agreement. The opening of the account can be considered as the initial operation and each withdrawal is a successive one. In such cases, the provisions of the Directive will only apply to the initial agreement and not to the successive ones. Importantly, the Directive does not apply to conflict of laws issues. Recital 8 specifically excludes the application of both the Brussels I Regulation (Recast) and the Rome I Regulation on contracts.[28]

The first obligation, set out in article 3, is the duty to provide information prior to the conclusion of the contract. Before the consumer is bound, he must receive information regarding the supplier of the

---

[26] Directive 2002/65/EC concerning the distance marketing of consumer financial services, amending Directives 97/7/EC and 98/27/EC [2002] OJ L271/16, 9 October 2002.

[27] Consumer Rights Directive, art. 3(3)(d), specifically excludes financial services.

[28] See Chapter 3.

service, the financial service itself, the contract and any redress he may be entitled to. In terms of the supplier, such information includes all the usual details which may be expected in such situations, such as the identity, addresses of representatives and any relevant authorization details. The data regarding the financial service include particularly the price to be paid, costs, taxes, any limitation periods and arrangements for payment and performance. Of particular importance for the consumer will be the right of withdrawal, the duration of the contract and any right to terminate it. The consumer must also be informed of any provision relating to the competent court and the applicable law. The Directive has a favourable view of out-of-court settlement and provides that the consumer shall be informed if any such redress exists.

The Directive does not derogate from information requirements contained in other Community instruments and Member States have the right to introduce more stringent criteria as long as they are properly communicated to the Community.[29] In addition, the communication requirements of article 3 and 4(1) must also be forwarded in paper form before the consumer is bound and also immediately after the conclusion of the contract if this has not been done in a form where they are immediately visible (i.e. telephone of VoIP).[30] The consumer may request the terms and conditions in paper form at any time during the duration of the contract and may also change the means of communication, if appropriate.

Article 6 introduces the right of withdrawal. This right can be exercised within 14 days without any obligation to give reasons and without penalty. Life insurance and pensions contracts covered in the Life Assurance Directive[31] have the deadline extended to 30 days. The right does not exist for financial services normally subject to market fluctuations such as trade in foreign exchange, securities and other financial instruments listed in article 6(2)(a), short-term travel insurance or contracts where performance has already taken place. Importantly, Member States may exclude property credits, credits secured by a mortgage and declarations using the services of an official.[32]

Unsolicited services are covered in article 9 of the Directive. The supply of financial services without prior request is prohibited when this request includes payment, prior or deferred. Specifically, the Directive

---

[29]   See art. 4.
[30]   Voice over Internet Protocol, see art. 5.
[31]   Directive 2002/83/EC of the European Parliament and of the Council of 5 November 2002 concerning life assurance [2002] OJ L345, 19 December 2002.
[32]   See art. 6(3).

provides that not replying will not constitute consent and exonerates the consumers from any liability that arises from it. Likewise, article 10 prohibits unsolicited communications by automated calling systems or fax unless prior consent has been obtained from the consumer. Unfortunately, the same standard has not been used for unsolicited email (spam). Article 10(2) gives the option to Member States to choose between two regimes: (a) opt-in or (b) opt-out. Under the first, spam can only be sent if the consumer has expressed consent in advance. Under the second, the consumer only has the right to object once he starts receiving it.

The final provisions of the Directive give extra protection to consumers. Article 11 obliges Member States to introduce adequate sanctions for violations of the provisions of the Directive. Article 12 provides that the Directive has a mandatory nature, from which consumers cannot derogate. Comprehensive obligations lie on Member States in respect of redress.[33] Member States have to: (a) ensure adequate and effective compliance; (b) allow consumer organizations, public bodies and professional organizations access to courts to ensure that national implementing measures are applied; and (c) force the operators and suppliers to stop practices that are incompatible with the Directive. Out-of-court dispute resolution is promoted in article 14.

The Directive has been subsequently amended and needs to be read in conjunction with the Payment Services Directive (see below and Chapter 9). In its 2009 review of the Directive,[34] the Commission suggested that there was no need for a new instrument or amendments.

3.2 Fraudulent Use of Payment Instruments

In the early days of the World Wide Web, Internet sales were limited and so was fraud. With the growth of electronic commerce, the need for accepted means of payment increased and so did fraudulent use of payment instruments. Since financial transaction on the Internet typically take two forms, there are two categories of fraudulent actions that could affect payment. First, a traditional contract may be followed by the issuing of an invoice, the payment by cash, cheque, money order or bank transfer. These transactions differ little from phone or fax orders and the potential fraud takes place in the physical world. Secondly, an online

---

[33] See art. 13.

[34] Communication from the Commission to the Council and the European Parliament, *Review of the Distance Marketing of Consumer Financial Services Directive (2002/65/EC)*, COM(2009)626 final (Brussels, 23 November 2009).

contract could be followed by payment effected by credit or debit card, the use of one of the proxy services (e.g. PayPal) or the use of virtual currencies such as Bitcoin. This brings the added security of a trusted and reputable intermediary but also adds another step in the transaction chain and therefore increases the risk. Payment card details may then be stolen either while in transit (less frequent occurrence) or directly from the trader's servers. It is the latter that is the primary concern of a number of EU laws dating from 1997 onwards.

The Commission's Recommendation on Electronic Payments from 1997,[35] drafted as a non-binding but nevertheless informative document, was the first instrument to cover some of the payment problems mentioned. The user's obligations include the duty to be as diligent as possible about account information, including the duty not to disclose access information or to notify of any theft, loss or unauthorized access. Article 6 of the Recommendation provides that, up to the time of notification, the holder bears the consequence of the loss or theft of the electronic payment instrument up to a certain limit (then ECU 150), unless he had acted negligently, in contravention of his obligations or fraudulently, in which case the limit does not apply. The holder stops being liable from the moment he has notified the issuer. Importantly, however, article 6(3) provided that:

> the holder is not liable if the payment instrument has been used, without physical presentation or electronic identification (of the instrument itself). The use of a confidential code or any other similar proof of identity is not, by itself, sufficient to entail the holder's liability.

The Recommendation exonerates the holder from any liability in the event of his payment data being presented electronically without the actual card. This is the case where credit card numbers and other associated information (start date, end date, name on card, security code) have been stolen, obtained fraudulently or generated. Moreover, the presentation of any extra security information (such as a password or security code) does not make the holder liable. This high standard of consumer protection effectively prevents the banks from claiming, without proving the contrary, that fraudsters have the data because the holder had been negligent.

---

[35] Recommendation 97/489/EC of 30 July 1997 concerning transactions by electronic payment instruments [1997] OJ L208/52, 2 August 1997, since integrated into the Payment Services Directive (see below).

A study on the implementation of the Recommendation has been carried out, resulting in a report published in 2001.[36] The study, based on the analysis of legislation in the then 15 Member States as well as on anonymous questionnaires, found a general lack of transparency from issuers to holders. There was a significant non-compliance in respect of a number of issues, in particular notification of loss or theft and the subsequent liability. Worryingly, in a number of states the burden of proof was placed on holders, and the means of dispute settlement were inadequate. Finally, Denmark was in 2001 the only country to specifically adopt the Recommendation. Most other states complied differently with various parts of the document, either as part of other laws or through voluntary codes.

Fraudulent use of payment instruments is covered in the Distance Marketing of Consumer Financial Services Directive and the Payment Services Directive (2), among others. Article 8 of the Distance Marketing of Consumer Financial Services Directive contains a provision obliging Member States to introduce legislation allowing the consumer to request cancellation of a payment where fraudulent use has been made of his payment card in connection with distance contracts and allowing the consumer to be recredited with the sums paid or have them returned. The provision is relatively simple but is complimented by the newer regime in the Payment Services Directive (2) Directive.

The Payment Services Directive (2)[37] introduces measures for minimizing the fraudulent use of payment instruments. The user of the payment instrument is obliged to notify the issuer of any unauthorized or incorrectly executed payment transactions on becoming aware of them but at the latest within 13 months of the debit date.[38] If the user denies having made a particular payment, the burden of proof will be on the payment service provider, who will have to provide evidence of 'fraud or gross negligence on part of the payment service user'.[39] In such cases, the fact that there is a record of a particular transaction will not of itself constitute proof that the payment was authorized nor that the user had

---

[36] J. Herveg *et al.*, *Study on the Implementation of Recommendation 97/489/EC concerning Transactions Carried Out by Electronic Payment Instruments and in particular the Relationship between Holder and Issuer, Final Report*, XV/99/01/C (Facultés universitaires Notre-Dame de la Paix and Queen Mary and Westfield College, 17 April 2001).

[37] Directive (EU) 2015/2366 of the European Parliament and of the Council of 25 November 2015 on payment services in the internal market [2015] OJ L337/35, 23 December 2015.

[38] See art. 71.

[39] See art. 72(2).

acted fraudulently or in negligence. Article 73 obliges the payment providers to compensate promptly the users who have notified in accordance with article 71.

Exceptions to the regime are introduced in article 61, which provides that the user will be liable up to the amount of €50 in cases of lost or stolen payment instruments or in cases of 'the misappropriation of a payment instrument'. This provision puts a top limit on the user's liability in cases of negligence. Nevertheless, the user who acted fraudulently or failed to follow the terms of use or to notify of loss, theft or misappropriation with intent or gross negligence will be liable in full. This means that a user who loses a credit card or fails to keep the pin code secret (negligence) can avail itself of the upper limit of €50 whereas the one who, for example, writes it down or gives it to another (gross negligence) cannot. Member States may reduce liability in cases where the user, acting neither fraudulently nor with intent, ignored terms of use or the obligation to inform. This will be done by taking the nature of the personalized security features and the circumstances of loss into consideration. The notification has, in any case, the effect of exonerating a *bona fide* user. The provider has an obligation to enable the user to notify properly at all times. This must be taken to mean a '24/7' hotline available at normal telecoms prices.

This leaves a number of cases in a grey area. Should a user who guards his banking details but fails to update its Internet protection (such as anti-virus and similar measures) be able to avail himself of the law's protective provisions? There is no clear answer to this question, and it seems that some disparity will remain between Member States who attempt to deal with these issues. Under most national laws, fraudulent use of credit cards was subject to compensation from the moment the consumer had notified the card issuer even before the entry of the Payment Services Directive (2) intro force. Similar arrangements usually exist for debit cards as a result of an agreement between the banks. It is not clear what happens with transactions that occur between the moment of loss and the moment of notification.

4 MARKETING REGULATION

The Internet revolves around advertising, it requires new models of getting product information to consumers at the lowest possible cost and the consumers' ability to adequately (in the advertiser's view) respond to the products. Advertising on the Internet is a new field for both consumers and corporations. The advertisers, on one hand, are finding consumers inundated with competitive products, often ready to change products and suppliers, ready to use the Internet to explore the alternatives but also increasingly irritated at the vast amounts of adverts directed at them. Consumers, on the other hand, find a bewildering array of products and services advertised on almost every site accessed. In such a climate, choices become difficult and resorting to reputable websites becomes more common.

From the consumer's perspective, Internet advertising suffers from two problems. The first is: how will a consumer be able to choose between a problematic (although not necessarily fraudulent) advert and a good one? A number of adverts promote fake goods or are operated by scammers who do not intend to fulfil their contractual obligations. They sell products that do not exist or their purpose is to extract money without providing adequate goods or services in exchange. Spam attacks in which consumers are offered the opportunity to buy cheap stocks at unrealistically low prices, or phishing attacks where they are coerced into parting with their personal details, which would then be used for criminal purposes, are examples of these. Such advertising is subject to civil and criminal laws at both national and European level. But, goods or services advertised may also be of lower quality than the ones presented in the adverts, or conditions may be imposed on the transaction that were not originally disclosed.

The second problem is: if the advert is genuine, how can a *bona fide* consumer ensure that the goods or services fit the description and the perceived purpose and that the transaction is described in sufficient detail? This problem relates to both the lack of information about a feature or a transaction (i.e. dimensions not stated clearly, hidden charges not declared) and incorrect information (e.g. pictures do not correspond to the goods delivered, specifications omitted, etc.) While the first problem is mainly criminal in nature, the second is subject to marketing law.

The EU body of law that deals with these problems is made up of two types of instruments. The first are comprehensive laws such as the 2005 Directive on unfair commercial practices (section 4.2 below) and the 2006 Directive on misleading advertising (section 4.1 below). The second are rules located in other Internet-related Directives and Regulations that have an impact on advertising. An example of the latter are rules in the AVMS Directive,[40] or E-Privacy Directive.[41] In this section, we look at the former.

---

[40]   See Chapter 4.
[41]   See Chapter 8.

4.1 Misleading and Comparative Advertising

A considerable achievement in furthering consumer protection in the EU
was the Misleading and Comparative Advertising Directive.[42] The aim of
the original 1984 Directive was to protect consumers from misleading
advertising and its consequences and to lay down the conditions for
comparative advertising. With the entry into force of the Unfair Commercial Practices Directive (see below), the scope of the Directive in respect
of *misleading* advertising has been reduced to advertising addressed to
businesses. Provisions applying to *comparative* advertising still apply
both to business and consumer transactions.

The Directive defines advertising in article 2 widely, as representation
in any form in connection with the trade that aims to promote goods or
services. In such terms, it is not limited only to registered corporations
but applies also to individuals (selling through an online auction site, for
instance, falls within the scope of the Directive). Secondly, misleading
advertising 'deceives or is likely to deceive' and because of its deceptive
nature either affects the subject's economic behaviour or injures a
competitor. This includes not only selling goods or services that do not
exist, that is, false advertising, but also any other deception in relation to
the representation of products. Comparative advertising is simply advertising which 'explicitly or by implication' identifies the competitor or
their goods or services.

In the *Belgian Electronic Sorting Technology* case,[43] the question was
whether the concept of advertising covered domain names and metatags.
In that case, two producers of laser sorting products were competing with
each other. One registered domain names and used metatags the other
claimed trademark on. The question referred was whether this constituted
advertising under article 2(1) of the Directive. The Court of Justice of the
European Union (CJEU) ruled that the 'use' of a domain name and of
metatags in the website's data did but that the 'registration' of a domain
name did not.

Article 3 provides that, in determining whether there is misleading
advertising, account must be taken of all the circumstances of the case,
including characteristics and price of the goods and services and the
attributes of the advertiser. In particular, attention must be paid to

---

[42]   Directive 2006/114 of the European Parliament and of the Council on
misleading and comparative advertising [2006] OJ L376/21, 27 December 2006.
The first Directive, dating from 1984, has been amended several times.

[43]   C-657/11 *Belgian Electronic Sorting Technology NV v Bert Peelaers, Visys
NV*, ECLI:EU:C:2013:516, 11 July 2013.

characteristics of the goods or services (such as, for example, availability, purpose, uses, etc.), the price or the manner in which it is calculated and the nature, attributes and rights of the advertiser.

Comparative advertising, defined as that which identifies the competitor, is allowed if all of the eight conditions set out in article 4 are fulfilled. These conditions essentially prevent the comparative advertiser from creating confusion, discrediting or misleading or, in the case of a trademark with a reputation, from taking unfair advantage from such a trademark. Among the conditions are the requirements that advertising must not be misleading under the terms of the Unfair Commercial Practices Directive; that the goods or services compared must be for the same needs or purposes; that the comparison must be objective; and that it must not discredit the competitor.

Article 5 obliges Member States to provide adequate sanctions against misleading advertising and to combat comparative advertising. This includes the possibility for organizations such as consumer associations to bring legal action. Member States must give courts power to order cessation of misleading or unlawful comparative advertising. Voluntary control by self-regulatory bodies is allowed and encouraged (article 6).

As the Directive is a minimum-harmonization instrument, more stringent laws can be adopted at national level by virtue of article 8. Since the entry into force of the Unfair Commercial Practices Directive (below), the Directive's scope has changed. It now covers business-to-business misleading advertising and comparative advertising which may harm a competitor but where there is no direct consumer detriment.[44]

In 2012, the Commission set out to review the Directive.[45] In the Communication, the Commission pointed out the fact that businesses in different Member States are protected very differently, with a great variety of rules going beyond the minimum EU protection. It was pointed out that rules on unfair commercial practices in Austria, Denmark, Germany, France, Italy and Sweden apply not only to consumer but also to business transactions, while rules in Poland, the Czech Republic and the United Kingdom offer only the minimum protection for business-to-business practices. In addition to that, enforcement rules are different, with some states allowing public enforcement while others opting for a system where only victims can seek redress. Based on the input received from the stakeholders, the Commission intended to revise the Directive

---

[44] See Unfair Commercial Practices Directive, art. 14.
[45] Communication from the Commission, COM(2012)702 final (Brussels, 27 November 2012).

with a view to creating a black list of the most harmful practices and harmonizing the penalties regime. This has not happened yet.

4.2   Unfair Commercial Practices Directive

The Unfair Commercial Practices Directive[46] was drafted in 2005 as major reform legislation aiming to improve consumers' rights before, during and after commercial transactions and to positively influence cross-border trade. The Directive is based on two ambitious tasks. The first is to harmonize unfair trade terms across the EU by preventing Member States from distorting the free movement of goods or services for reasons falling within the scope of the Directive.[47] The second is to introduce a general obligation on traders to treat consumers fairly. The Directive is a full harmonization measure, precluding Member States from acting within its scope.[48] The Directive does not affect contract law nor rules determining the jurisdiction of the courts.[49] The consumer protection provisions deriving from either contract law or private international law are therefore left in place.

The Directive applies to unfair business-to-consumer commercial practices.[50] These are defined very widely as those being contrary to the 'requirement of professional diligence' and 'materially distorting the economic behaviour' of the consumer.[51] The Directive covers misleading and aggressive advertising practices (article 5) with misleading practices being divided into actions and omissions.[52] The Directive operates with

---

[46]   Directive 2005/29/EC of the European Parliament and of the Council of 11 May 2005 concerning unfair business-to-consumer commercial practices in the internal market and amending Council Directive 84/450/EEC, Directives 97/7/EC, 98/27/EC and 2002/65/EC of the European Parliament and of the Council and Regulation (EC) 2006/2004 of the European Parliament and of the Council [2005] OJ L149/22, 11 June 2005. Guidance on implementation, SWD(2016)163 final (Brussels, 25 September 2016).

[47]   See art. 4.

[48]   C-540/08, C-304/08, C-261/07 and C-299/07 *Mediaprint; Zentrale zur Bekämpfung unlauteren Wettbewerbs eV; Galatea BVBA v Sanoma Magazines Belgium NV* [2010] ECR I-10909.

[49]   See art. 3(2) and (7).

[50]   See art. 3.

[51]   See art. 5.

[52]   On scope, the CJEU's tasks in interpreting and the behavioural economics aspects, see J. Trzaskowski, 'Behavioural Economics, Neuroscience, and the Unfair Commercial Practices Directive' (2011) 34 *Journal of Consumer Policy* 377.

the notion of an average consumer, which is to be understood in light of the CJEU's interpretation as an 'average consumer who is reasonably well informed and reasonably observant'.[53]

The Directive introduces objective criteria for determining whether a practice is misleading. In Section 1, the Directive particularly lists misleading acts (article 6) or misleading omissions (article 7) and aggressive commercial practices (article 8) or harassment, coercion or undue influence (article 9) as examples of unfair commercial practices. Article 6(1) says that a practice will be misleading action 'if it contains false information and is therefore untruthful or in any way, including overall presentation, deceives or is likely to deceive the average consumer, even if the information is factually correct'. This has to lead to a transactional decision that would otherwise not have been made. The article then lists the criteria in relation to which misleading information is given. Article 7(1) defines misleading omissions as practices that omit 'material information that the average consumer needs, according to the context, to take an informed transactional decision'. Article 8 defines aggressive practices as those which use 'harassment, coercion, including the use of physical force, or undue influence' thus significantly impairing 'the average consumer's freedom of choice'.

The CJEU's interpretation of the foregoing articles has been largely unremarkable. In *Trento Sviluppo*,[54] for example, local supermarkets were distributing leaflets advertising significant discounts on various products. Where a consumer claimed one of these and was told that it was not available, he complained to the consumer protection authorities in Italy, which, in turn, instituted proceedings against the supermarkets. The question revolved around the interpretation of article 6(1) and what constituted a 'misleading' practice under that article. The Court ruled that a practice is misleading where it 'contains false information, or is likely to deceive the average consumer, and is likely to cause the consumer to take a transactional decision that he would not have taken otherwise'.

Whereas the practices in articles 6–9 are assessed judicially on a case-by-case basis, Annex I contains a list of practices that are regarded as being inherently unfair. No analysis is necessary for these as they are unfair in all circumstances. The list contains 31 items, of which many

---

[53] See C-210/96 *Gut Springenheide GmbH and Rudolf Tusky v Oberkreis-direktor des Kreises Steinfurt – Amt für Lebensmittelüberwachung* [1998] ECR I-04657.

[54] C-281/12 *Trento Sviluppo srl and Centrale Adriatica Soc. Coop. Arl v Autorità Garante della Concorrenza e del Mercato*, ECLI:EU:C:2013:859, 19 December 2013.

will be easily recognized in the digital world. For example, the Annex speaks of codes of conduct abuse (item 1), cases where traders falsely claim that their products have endorsements from public or private bodies (item 4), and paying for editorial content in the media without making this known to consumers (item 11).

The Directive has no special provisions for Internet advertising and such provisions do not seem to be necessary. The Directive's general scope should adequately cover most unfair practices on the Internet. Nevertheless, a number of questions specific to the Internet do arise. For example, traders may pay bloggers or other website operators or send them free samples, so that these could promote their products and services. In principle, as long as this is declared, it will not be problematic and not subject to the Directive. In all other cases where the posters are not independent but operated by, paid for or used by the traders to promote their goods or services, the provisions of the Unfair Commercial Practices Directive might be relevant.[55] Similar reaction should be expected for cases where competitors leave fake negative reviews on rating sites.

The CJEU has in the past clarified some of the provisions of the Directive in light of widely used misleading practices that also appear on the Internet. In *Ving Sverige*,[56] the Court had a chance to interpret the widely-practised offers quoting 'from only' or other similarly marked entry-level prices for products or services that are in reality sold at higher prices. There, a travel agency, which engaged in arranging charter holidays and selling individual airline tickets, advertised New York trips in a daily Swedish newspaper. The trips quoted entry-level prices, only some of which were actually on offer or which were obtainable only under certain circumstances. The Swedish consumer protection agency commenced action against it, alleging that Ving's commercial communication in a newspaper was an invitation to purchase containing misleading information and that fixed prices rather than entry-level prices should be given. The national court referred some important questions to the CJEU, including whether an invitation to purchase exists as soon as information on the product and the price is available or whether there actually has to be an opportunity to purchase the goods or services, and whether it exists where there is a verbal or visual reference but there are no further descriptions of the product. The Court held that:

---

[55]   See *Carrefour v Galaec (la coopérative groupement d'achat des centres Leclerc)*, Tribunal de commerce de Paris, 29 March 2007.

[56]   C-122/10 *Konsumentombudsmannen v Ving Sverige AB*, ECLI:EU:C: 2011:299, 12 May 2011.

it may be sufficient for only certain of a product's main characteristics to be given and for the trader to refer in addition to its website, on the condition that on that site there is essential information on the product's main characteristics, price and other terms in accordance with the requirements in Article 7 of that directive.

It follows that a practice of displaying only some of the product's features is not, in and of itself, unfair, as long as there are means for establishing other relevant facts elsewhere. This seems to be a rather low threshold for an invitation to purchase.

In *Purely Creative*,[57] the CJEU dealt with another widely-used practice on the Internet: claims that a consumer had already won a prize where they, in reality have not or would need to complete a commercial transaction with the trader to claim it, or would need to incur substantial costs in order to claim the prize. The Court ruled that the following are illegal:

> aggressive practices by which traders … give the false impression that the consumer has already won a prize, while the taking of any action in relation to claiming that prize, be it requesting information concerning the nature of that prize or taking possession of it, is subject to an obligation on the consumer to pay money or to incur any cost whatsoever.

4.3 Unsolicited Commercial Communications

Spam is one of the costliest problems on the Internet today. For consumers, it represents a never-ending obligation to monitor unsolicited traffic. It detracts from important messages, which often get mixed with spam, and it requires time to be properly disposed of. For Internet service providers it represents extra cost in server time and the risk of clogging. For corporations, it means spending extra financial resources on filtering unsolicited messages using technologies that, although constantly improving, are not fully reliable. For spammers, on the other hand, the issue may be observed as one concerning freedom of commercial speech.

Spam can be defined as any unsolicited communication by means of electronic mail.[58] Such communication is usually commercial, although it does not exclusively have to be in order to qualify as spam. Political speech, for instance, is covered, meaning that the definition of spam is

---

[57] C-428/11 *Purely Creative Ltd and others v Office of Fair Trading*, ECLI:EU:C:2012:651, 18 October 2012.

[58] It is, at this point, not clear whether this also includes other communication means (e.g. instant messages).

not particularly important for the attempts to fight it. The interesting question, however, is what the legal treatment of similar categories is. Such categories comprise pop-ups and pop-unders and other adverts that appear on the user's browser outside the main browsing context. Also, the status of viruses, Trojans, adware and an increasing arsenal of ever more sophisticated tools for exploiting users' computers is an unknown area.

Attempts to regulate spam worldwide have not been particularly successful. This is probably a result of the Internet's architecture, which allows not only easy transfer of hosts actually responsible for sending messages but also hijacking of hundreds of computers for the same purpose. The businesses advertised through spam are equally difficult to trace, either being classified as online services or operating from jurisdictions with lax legal regimes and poor consumer protection.

In the United States, an attempt to fight spam saw light in the form of the Controlling the Assault of Non-Solicited Pornography and Marketing (CAN SPAM) Act 2003.[59] Its main purpose was the imposition of penalties on the transmission of unsolicited email. The Act defined spam as 'any electronic mail message the primary purpose of which is the commercial advertisement or promotion of a commercial product or service (including content on an Internet website operated for a commercial purpose)'. 'Transaction' and 'relationship' messages are excluded from the scope. In order for an unsolicited commercial email to be sent legally under the Act, it must have an opt-out mechanism, a legitimate subject line and header, a legitimate physical address of the mailer and a label if the content is adult. Religious and national security measures are exempt as are messages regulated in other laws.

The CAN SPAM Act text was widely criticized as being inadequate. Its main weakness was the choice of regime, which failed to actively prohibit unsolicited commercial messages. The Act chose the opt-out approach, which specifically required the recipient to take action once they received the first email. In fact, the Act specifically allowed a first email to be sent, as long as it contained an opt-out clause. Arguably, an opt-in approach, requiring the recipient to sign themselves up for the services, would provide better protection.

A number of EU instruments apply to some extent to unsolicited commercial communications. Before the implementation of the E-Privacy Directive, the first instrument of relevance was the Data Protection Directive.[60] It did not specifically address spam but it could indirectly be

---

[59]   Pub. L No. 108-187, 117 Stat. 2699 (2003).
[60]   See Chapter 8.

applied to the gathering of email addresses falling under personal data. The E-Privacy Directive explicitly recognizes its link with this instrument in Recital 10 and in article 1(2). Another instrument of relevance is the Distance Selling Directive,[61] which limits the use of automated calling systems on the opt-in basis, but in article 10(2) seemingly introduces an opt-out regime for 'other means of distance communication'. The Telecommunications Privacy Directive[62] introduced an opt-in regime for direct marketing by automatic systems in article 12 but left it to Member States to choose between an opt-in and opt-out regime for all other means of communication. Finally, the E-Commerce Directive itself explicitly recognized the problem of spam in Recital 30 but did not go far in fighting it. It limited itself to introducing an obligation to clearly label commercial communication when this communication is permitted (and this was left to Member States) and to introducing an obligation to consult opt-out registers.

The inadequacy of these solutions is apparent. The early instruments (such as the Data Protection or the ISDN Directives) were drafted long before spam became a problem. Some of their solutions (such as those applying to purchasing and processing email lists) were, although useful in themselves, inadequate. Directive 2002/58/EC on privacy and electronic communications was drafted to tackle some of the deficiencies of earlier instruments and to deal specifically with problems from the perspective of electronic communications. Specifically, it regulates 'the right to privacy, with respect to the processing of personal data in the electronic communications sector' and ensures that such data and communications move freely.[63]

The provision that relates to spam is article 13.[64] Article 13(1) provides that the use of electronic mail for the purposes of direct marketing is only allowed in respect of subscribers who have given their prior consent. This is the opt-in regime. However, in article 13(2), natural and legal persons

---

[61] Directive 97/7/EC of the European Parliament and of the Council of 20 May 1997 on the protection of consumers in respect of distance contracts [1997] OJ L144/19, 4 June 1997.

[62] Directive 97/66/EC of the European Parliament and of the Council of 15 December 1997 concerning the processing of personal data and the protection of privacy in the telecommunications sector (including Annex) [1998] OJ L24/1, 30 January 1998.

[63] For more on this Directive, see Chapter 8 on privacy.

[64] For a more detailed treatment of spam, see L. Asscher and S.A. Hoogcarspel, *Regulating Spam: A European Perspective after the Adoption of the E-Privacy Directive* (T.M.C. Asser Press, The Hague, 2006).

who have obtained personal details in the course of previous business may use these details for marketing their own similar products or services as long as the customers are given the opportunity to object without charge. The opportunity to object must be given with each communication, if the customer has not already taken advantage of it. Unsolicited communications other than those previously mentioned are not allowed unless the subscriber gives consent. Especially prohibited[65] are messages that conceal the identity of the sender.

The provisions of article 13, except that relating to concealing, only apply to natural persons. Member States only have an obligation to ensure that the 'legitimate interests' of other subscribers are also protected. They have to ensure this obligation through their national law. This is somewhat disappointing, as corporations are subject to spam as much as natural persons.

An earlier version of article 13 referred not only to electronic mail but also to 'other personally addressed electronic communications'. This would have been a welcome addition, as it would have covered SMS and other instant messages directed at mobile phones of newer generation. It is unclear why this has been left out, as national laws sometimes tackle unsolicited SMS messages in the same way as fax messages. Although it is correct that instant messaging spam has not been as much of a problem as spam emails, this is still a gap in the regulation.

Article 4 of the Directive may also have an impact on the issue. It talks about security, obliging the provider of a publicly available electronic communications service to take appropriate measures to safeguard the security of its services. The duty extends to informing the customers of any breaches.[66] Applied to spam, this introduces an obligation of an Internet service provider (ISP) to apply all technical measures to combat spam or viruses. This should probably be interpreted as meaning 'state of the art' technological measures.

Spammers are in the practice of 'harvesting' email addresses. This simply means obtaining as many valid email addresses as possible within the shortest period of time. This is done either by crawling the Internet for emails scattered on various webpages, or more effectively, by breaching the security measures of companies that keep the emails in their databases. The latter can be also done by purchasing the addresses from those who illegally sell them.

---

[65] See art. 13(4).
[66] See art. 4(2).

Certain provisions of the Data Protection Directive along with the E-Privacy Directive may be used to combat this practice. Articles 6 and 7 of the Data Protection Directive prohibit the unlawful processing of personal data, introducing a number of safeguards that determine when data processing is lawful. Collecting emails on the Internet would be against these articles, as it would not constitute fair and purposeful processing within article 6 or meet the legitimacy test under article 7. In terms of the E-Privacy Directive, article 4 imposes the obligation on the ISP to protect the system against harvesting and article 12 ensures that the customer's consent is obtained before being placed in the email directory.

5 CONSUMER PROTECTION IN PRIVATE INTERNATIONAL LAW

Consumer protection in EU private international law predates the emergence of the Internet by more than 20 years. It dates back to the 1968 Brussels Convention on Jurisdiction and Foreign Judgments, which contained special rules on jurisdiction over consumer contracts. The effort to protect consumers was continued in the 1980 Rome Convention on the Law Applicable to Contractual Obligations, which, in Article 5, addressed the issue of 'certain consumer contracts'. In addition to that, a number of Directives mentioned in this chapter have a private international law dimension. This is usually limited to a declaration that consumers shall not lose, by virtue of the operation of choice-of-law rules, a right granted by a particular Directive[67] or that a Directive does not establish additional rules on private international law.[68] In either case the accent is on protection: a consumer must not be deprived of the security that an instrument gives them by virtue of a conflict with private international law.[69]

Consumers are vulnerable to litigation. They do not normally have the financial and other means to fight legal battles, either as plaintiffs or as defendants. This often leads them either to seeking alternative means of

---

[67] Unfair Terms in Consumer Contracts Directive, art. 6.
[68] As is the case with E-Commerce Directive, art. 1(4).
[69] In reality, however, this relationship is more complex, as was demonstrated in the case of E-Commerce Directive, arts. 1(4) and 3.

dispute resolution[70] or simply deciding to cut their losses.[71] Consumers who nevertheless seek to assert their rights through the courts in cross-border disputes face two problems. The first concerns the courts that have jurisdiction to decide the case, whereas the second is about the law applicable to it.

5.1 Jurisdiction Rules

Brussels I Regulation (Recast)[72] harmonizes rules on jurisdiction in civil and commercial contracts and rules on recognition and enforcement of judgments. Section 4 (articles 17–19) are dedicated exclusively to consumer contracts. Their purpose is to enable consumers, who are defined in article 17 as individuals concluding contracts outside their 'trade or profession', to avail themselves of the potentially more favourable jurisdiction regime in the place of their domicile. The protection works on a relatively simple premise: if the consumer finds himself in one of the three defined situations, he would be able to sue and be sued in the place of the consumer's domicile.

The protective regime applies to instalment credit contracts (article 17(a)), loans repayable by instalments (article 17(b)) and all other contracts where commercial or professional activity has been pursued in the Member State of the consumer's domicile or 'by any means' directed towards that state (article 17(c)). If the conditions of article 17 are not fulfilled regular rules on jurisdiction apply.

Article 17(1)(c), which brings a slight change from the Brussels Convention text,[73] caused some controversy in the drafting stages as it was claimed by e-commerce businesses that the 'introduction' of the 'destination principle' would expose them to litigation in all Member

---

[70] Exclusive arbitration clauses in consumer contracts have, in spite of criticism, been upheld in the US Supreme Court. See e.g., *CompuCredit Corp. v Greenwood*, 565 US (2012).

[71] See J. Hill, *Cross-Border Consumer Contracts* (OUP, Oxford, 2008), ch. 2.

[72] Regulation 2015/2012 of 12 December 2012 on jurisdiction and the recognition and enforcement of judgments in civil and commercial matters [2012] OJ L351/1, 20 December 2012.

[73] See art. 13(1), (3). The original Convention activated consumer protection in all cases where the contract was concluded pursuant to specific invitation or advertising and the consumer took the necessary steps for concluding the contract in that state. No policy change was intended by this rephrasing, see P.A. Nielsen, 'Comment on Article 15' in U. Magnus and P. Mankowski (eds.), *European Commentaries on Private International Law: Brussels I Regulation* (Sellier, European Law Publishers, Munich, 2007), p. 315.

States.[74] To the opponent of this provision, it seemed that a mere availability of content on the Internet allows the consumer to invoke the jurisdiction of article 17(1)(c). The article activates special consumer jurisdiction where:

the contract has been concluded with a person who pursues commercial or professional activities in the Member State of the consumer's domicile or, by any means, directs such activities to that Member State or to several States including that Member State, and the contract falls within the scope of such activities.

In reality, the mere accessibility of a website is not, in itself, enough to trigger protective jurisdiction:

The mere fact that an Internet site is accessible is not sufficient for Article [17] to be applicable, although a factor will be that this Internet site solicits the conclusion of distance contracts and that the contract has actually been concluded at a distance, by whatever means. In this respect, the language or currency which a website uses does not constitute a relevant factor.[75]

Further clarification is provided in the Commission's Proposal:

The concept of activities pursued in or directed towards a Member State is designed to make clear that point (3) applies to consumer contracts concluded via an interactive website accessible in the State of the consumer's domicile. The fact that a consumer simply had knowledge of a service or possibility of buying goods via a passive website accessible in his country of domicile will not trigger the protective jurisdiction. The contract is thereby treated in the same way as a contract concluded by telephone, fax and the like, and activates the grounds of jurisdiction provided for by Article 16.[76]

Two things must be clear from this. First, from the litigation management perspective, a consumer *defendant* would, in any case, have to be sued in that consumer's domicile because that is where his assets are most likely to be found. Secondly, the consumer as *plaintiff* will not be able to sue in the state of his domicile simply because he has been able to access a webpage there. On the contrary, more substantial contacts, akin to American 'active websites' would be required. In that respect, it can be

---

[74] See in more detail, J. Øren, 'International Jurisdiction over Consumer Contracts in e-Europe' (2003) 52 *International and Comparative Law Quarterly* 665.
[75] Statement on Articles 15 and 73, available at http://ec.europa.eu/civiljustice/homepage/homepage_ec_en_declaration.pdf.
[76] European Commission, Proposal, COM(1999)348 (14 July 1999).

expected that European courts will develop their own versions of the *Zippo* test.[77]

In the *Hotel Alpenhoff* case,[78] which involved an Austrian consumer and a German website, the CJEU decided that the application of article 17(1)(c) depended on whether:

> it is apparent from those websites and the trader's overall activity that the trader was envisaging doing business with consumers domiciled in one or more Member States, including the Member State of that consumer's domicile, in the sense that it was minded to conclude a contract with them.

If so, the website was directing activities and will be subject to Section 4 jurisdiction. Importantly, the Court provided a non-exhaustive list of factors that should be taken into consideration when deciding whether directing took place:

> the international nature of the activity, mention of itineraries from other Member States for going to the place where the trader is established, use of a language or a currency other than the language or currency generally used in the Member State in which the trader is established with the possibility of making and confirming the reservation in that other language, mention of telephone numbers with an international code, outlay of expenditure on an internet referencing service in order to facilitate access to the trader's site or that of its intermediary by consumers domiciled in other Member States, use of a top-level domain name other than that of the Member State in which the trader is established, and mention of an international clientele composed of customers domiciled in various Member States.

In any case, it will be for the national courts to develop their own approaches which, ultimately, may lead to divergence.

Article 17(2) allows a non-EU website, which otherwise has a 'branch, agency or other establishment' in the EU, to be subject to Section 4, provided that the dispute arises out of the operations of that branch. An American site with a branch in Ireland will therefore be subject to the consumer jurisdiction regime of Section 4 if a consumer contract arises out of a dealing of that branch with the consumer. It will be less clear whether consumers can sue in the state where they are domiciled if their dealings are exclusively with a generic website (e.g. the Facebook company is based in Palo Alto, California but has offices in various EU countries) if they cannot prove that they were dealing directly with the

---

[77] See Chapter 3.
[78] C-585/08 *Peter Pammer v Reederei Karl Schlüter GmbH & Co. KG* and C-144/09 *Hotel Alpenhof GESMBH v Oliver Heller* [2010] ECR I-2527.

branch, agency or establishment. There are some indications in another case, not otherwise related to jurisdiction, that the place where data is being processed may matter. In *Google Spain*,[79] one of the side questions was whether the Google search engine gathered and processed private data of Spanish citizens on its Spanish servers or not. The CJEU considered that it did. In cases of a social networking site, the presence of a branch may be relevant where the branch plays a significant part in the operations of the network.

Article 18 contains the protective regime that is the centre of Section 4 of the Regulation. Article 18(1) provides that a plaintiff consumer may *bring proceedings* either in the state where the defendant is domiciled or in the state where the consumer is domiciled. The discretion, in this case, is the consumer's. Article 18(2), on the other hand, states that proceedings may be brought *against* a defendant consumer only in the state where the consumer is domiciled.

In *Maletic*,[80] the CJEU had an opportunity to rule on the concept of 'other party to the contract' in article 18. In that case, two Austrian citizens booked a holiday from lastminute.com, which had a registered office in Germany. The website stated that it only acted as a travel agent but that the actual trip was operated by TUI, which had its registered office in Austria. Dissatisfied with the performance of the contract, they sought compensation from TUI in an Austrian court which, in turn, referred the question concerning 'other party to the contract' to the CJEU. The Court ruled that article 18 'covers the contracting partner of the operator with which the consumer concluded that contract and which has its registered office in the Member State in which the consumer is domiciled'.

Jurisdiction clauses in consumer contracts are subject to the special regime of Section 4. A choice-of-forum clause that violates the consumer protection provisions will normally be invalid. Article 19 provides that the mandatory protective provisions of Section 4 of the Regulation may only be departed from after the dispute has arisen, or if they allow plaintiff consumers extra forums, or if both parties are domiciled or habitually resident in the same Member State at the time of conclusion and if the agreement confers jurisdiction on that state. A choice-of-court

[79] C-131/12 *Google Spain SL and Google Inc. v Agencia Española de Protección de Datos (AEPD) and Mario Costeja González*, ECLI:EU:C: 2014:317, 13 May 2014.
[80] C-478/12 *Armin Maletic and Marianne Maletic v lastminute.com GmbH and TUI Österreich GmbH*, ECLI:EU:C:2013:735, 14 November 2013.

agreement that satisfies the general conditions of article 25 remains valid if it does not contradict the provisions of article 19.

The majority of contracts concluded on the Internet that contain a clause to the effect that 'parties submit to the exclusive jurisdiction' of a state other than the state of the consumer's domicile will simply have the effect of allowing the consumer to sue in that state but cannot have the effect of preventing the consumer from taking action in the state provided for in article 18. The reason for this lies in article 19 that explicitly allows clauses derogating from consumer protection only in a very limited number of cases. The article possibly also applies to jurisdiction agreements in favour of courts of third states.[81] Similar logic is valid for arbitration agreements (see Chapter 3, section 5) forcing consumers to arbitrate and depriving them of the protective provisions of Section 4.

The Consumer Injunctions Directive codified EU law concerning injunctions that may be applied for and used in protecting consumers' interests.[82] The Directive harmonized national law relating to injunctions aimed at protecting consumers' collective interests arising out of the Directives specifically listed in the Annex. The obligation lies on Member States to designate bodies (article 2) that can respond to actions brought by qualified applicants (article 3). The overall aim is to improve the efficiency of consumer protection in the Directives listed in the Annex.

5.2   Choice-of-Law Rules

The Rome I Regulation[83] harmonized national rules on law applicable to contracts. Article 6 of that Regulation introduced a special regime for consumers. Article 6(1) provides that the law of the country where the consumer has his habitual residence shall govern consumer contracts. This will be the case only if one of the two conditions is fulfilled: either the professional had pursued his activities in the country where the consumer is habitually resident (the 'seller moves' situation) or the seller had 'by any means' directed his activities to that country 'or to several countries including that country'. The first situation includes a seller who physically operates on the territory of another country. The second involves a seller who advertises his services and actively seeks custom,

---

[81]   See Chapter 3, section 2.4.

[82]   Directive 2009/22/EC [2009] OJ L110/30, 1 May 2009.

[83]   Regulation (EC) 593/2008 of the European Parliament and of the Council of 17 June 2008 on the law applicable to contractual obligations [2008] OJ L177/6, 4 July 2008 ('Rome I Regulation').

including the situation where the Internet is used for that purpose. Recital 24 expressly admits that it applies to Internet contracts, drawing an analogy with the Brussels I Regulation (Recast). Although the choice of language or the currency will not, on their own, constitute relevant factors, they help determine the seller's intentions. Determining factors may include information displayed in different languages, different currencies, local contact numbers or any attempt to target local customers.[84]

The parties may choose the law applicable to the contract in accordance with the regular rules on choice of law (article 3).[85] Their choice may not have the effect of depriving the consumer of the protection of mandatory rules (which are defined as provisions that cannot be derogated from by agreement) of the law that would have been applicable, that is, the law of the consumer's habitual residence. This should be taken to mean that the parties are freely allowed to choose the law of a country other than the consumer's habitual residence, but that the consumer would always be allowed to invoke its mandatory rules.

Special protective measures do not apply to contracts for the supply of services where these services are supplied in a country other than that of the consumer's habitual residence.[86]

Mandatory rules other than those referred to in article 6(2) may be applicable and some of them will derive directly from Community law. Article 25 of the Consumer Rights Directive, for instance, states that provisions of that Directive are mandatory and cannot be waived.

5.3 Alternative Dispute Resolution

In spite of the existence of a consumer-favourable litigation regime, the low value of most disputes coupled with the intimidating nature of an adversarial resolution mechanism raises consumers' discomfort. This can be resolved with more diversification in the alternative dispute resolution field and the creation of industry-driven mechanisms. The EU, aware of the problem, took modest steps towards these ends with recommendations on out-of-court settlement of consumer disputes[87] as well as with

---

[84] Cf. Chapter 3.
[85] See art. 6(2).
[86] See art. 6(4)(a).
[87] Commission Recommendation 98/257/EC of 30 March 1998 on the principles applicable to the bodies responsible for out-of-court settlement of consumer disputes [1998] OJ L115, 17 April 1998; Commission Recommendation of 4 April 2001 on the principles for out-of-court bodies involved in the

later measures generally aimed at alternative dispute resolution (ADR).[88] In 2011, two specific proposals for ADR in consumer disputes were tabled.

A Directive on consumer ADR has been adopted[89] with the aim of improving 'procedures for the out-of-court resolution of contractual disputes arising from the sale of goods or provision of services' in alternative dispute resolution. The Directive is primarily concerned with the issues of access and principles that govern ADR (Chapter 2) and information and cooperation (Chapter 3). Whereas the former improves general accessibility and makes sure ADR is transparent, impartial and fair, the latter improves communication between the parties. While not directly a consumer instrument, it may bring some minor improvements in cases where ADR is used in consumer cases.

In 2013, the Commission also adopted a Regulation on online dispute resolution for consumer disputes (Regulation on Consumer ODR).[90] The Regulation is aimed at the 'out-of-court resolution of contractual disputes arising from the cross-border online sale of goods or provision of services'. Its main purpose is simply to ensure that adequate online ADR mechanisms exist for the resolution of consumer disputes. Article 5 creates the European online dispute resolution platform in the form of a website accessible locally throughout the EU. The platform's main function is to facilitate ADR rather than act as a tribunal itself. In that sense, it brings the parties together, offers a list of competent ADR bodies and acts as a point of information for all sides. The ODR platform has been accessible since February 2016.

---

consensual resolution of consumer disputes not covered by Recommendation 98/257/EC [2001] OJ L109, 19 April 2001.

[88]   See also the Mediation Directive 2008/52/EC of the European Parliament and of the Council of 21 May 2008 on certain aspects of mediation in civil and commercial matters [2008] OJ L136/3, 24 May 2008.

[89]   Directive 2013/11/EU of the European Parliament and of the Council of 21 May 2013 on alternative dispute resolution for consumer disputes and amending Regulation (EC) 2006/2004 and Directive 2009/22/EC [2013] OJ L165/63, 18 June 2013 ('Directive on Consumer ADR').

[90]   Regulation (EU) 524/2013 of the European Parliament and of the Council of 21 May 2013 on online dispute resolution for consumer disputes and amending Regulation (EC) 2006/2004 and Directive 2009/22/EC [2013] OJ L165/1, 18 June 2013 ('Regulation on Consumer ODR').

8. Data protection and privacy

1 INTRODUCTION

1.1 Private Life in the Digital World

Privacy, as a modern European understands it, is the ability to withhold information about oneself or, put differently, the ability to have a secluded sphere of life and to select which parts of one's life will be accessible to the public. Historically, a 'private' person was one who did not participate in public life.[1] The term was often taken as a pejorative, as an indication of the person's unwillingness to participate or lack of capacity to do so. Privacy as a *desire* to keep one's life from public view only became a value and was legally protected relatively recently.[2]

Until late into the twentieth century the ability to guard one's life from the view of others was rudimentary and enjoyed by the few. This was not because the potential to violate it was absent, but rather because it was omnipresent. In addition, one's life took place in public, on streets, squares and markets, and people were expected to participate in it even before most were accorded the right to vote. An average nineteenth-century European or American would be familiar with the need and importance of confidentiality, understood as a right to protect information one guards in secrecy, but would have difficulties with the notion that *non-confidential* information may also be private. Modern privacy law is still locked into this paradigm of privacy as secrecy.[3]

In the modern age, as life retreated from squares into offices, houses and institutions, privacy became a protected value, and with it came the potential and desire to invade it. Once, the governments were the most likely to profit from such invasions. As late as the beginning of the

---

[1] Privatus, in Latin, denoted an individual deprived of public or military office.

[2] Warren and Brandeis are credited with 'inventing' privacy law in S. Warren and L. Brandeis, 'The Right to Privacy' (1890) 4 *Harvard Law Review* 5.

[3] See also, N. Richards and D. Solove, 'Privacy's Other Path: Recovering the Law of Confidentiality' (2007) 96 *Georgetown Law Journal* 124; and D. Solove, *The Digital Person* (New York University Press, New York, 2004), p. 8.

twentieth century, only a handful of states were democracies and most of them did not accord women the right to vote. The interest was, therefore, to control all elements perceived as being a threat to stability of the regime. Keeping records and spying, an activity as old as political life itself, obtained new dimensions as wealth and with it political freedom spread. But, as threats increased, so did legal responses to them and the first statutes and court cases came into being.

A significant portion of modern life no longer takes place in the public eye. Although homes and family lives, telephone conversations and correspondence may be protected, public participation in the digital world has made everybody exposed to new privacy threats. First, technology has enabled public dossiers to be assembled and be accessible more easily than ever, while the law has made information gathering mandatory in many more situations than has previously been the case. Additionally, the information may be easily collated, creating more meaningful links between previously disjointed pieces of information. Secondly, businesses can assemble large quantities of information about their users with relative ease. The information thus gathered can then be used to target marketing or, being itself a commodity, can be traded. Thirdly, the dynamism of modern digital life requires participation on a level which forces us to voluntarily relinquish information about our activities, the places we visit, the books we read or the people we befriend.

In our times, the desire to invade privacy comes no longer from governments only but also, and possibly primarily, from corporations and our fellow citizens. Governments expend the power of collecting data or accessing data that others have collected, often with little regard to the actual power to process the information and render it useful. Corporations, in a constant bid to gain an edge over the competition, strive to learn consumers' habits and use them to improve their marketing techniques. At the same time, other individuals stand to gain from having an insight into our lives. Their reasons range from illegal ones, such as identity theft, to illegitimate ones, such as gaining advantage by learning what our superiors think of us, to relatively harmless ones driven by curiosity about others' television or reading habits.

In the digital age, the potential to gather data is vast, the means to violate accessible and cheap and the potential damage high and un-predictable. The reason for legislative intervention seems, therefore, to be obvious. On the other hand, lack of privacy has other unforeseen and deeper circumstances. It reduces the willingness to engage in activities that 'promote democratic self-rule'.[4] 'A realm of autonomous, un-monitored choice ... promotes a vital diversity of speech and behaviour'[5] and is essential for developing and maintaining a democratic society.

The availability of data, in itself, is not a novelty. Neither is the ability to access it quickly, which has existed for several decades. Automatically processed data has been the subject of regulation for some time now and long before the advance of the Internet in the 1990s. What makes databases in the digital age sensitive, however, is their ability to be quickly and accurately brought into relation with other databases. This ability has been created by the emergence of cheap raw processing power. Searching for a name, a telephone address or an email on the Internet will often result in data being presented which contains other information of which the search term is just a part. Such information may contain property or tax records, political interests or medical history.

Privacy needs to be in balance with other constitutionally protected values, such as the right to free speech, the right of the public to know or the right to security. It is normally assumed by Internet scholars that the advent of the digital age presents particular problems for privacy, but the relationship between technology and privacy is old and complex.[6] While the debate continues, it seems increasingly clear that some features of the Internet do pose a particular threat to privacy. Among those is the decreasing cost of storage capacity, the ease of access to networked systems, as well as the ability to collate information.[7]

In the United States, the right to privacy in common law came to be discussed only towards the end of the nineteenth century.[8] The United States Constitution does not protect privacy directly but infers it from other constitutional provisions or other laws. Initially, the right to privacy was cast as 'the right to be let alone' but, as Solove puts it, has in the twentieth century also been conceptualized as 'limited access to the self',

---

[4] P. Schwartz, 'Privacy and Democracy in Cyberspace' (1999) 52 *Vanderbilt Law Review* 1609.

[5] J. Cohen, 'Examined Lives: Information Privacy and the Subject as Object' (2000) 52 *Stanford Law Review* 1373.

[6] See R. Posner, 'Orwell versus Huxley: Economics, Technology, Privacy and Satire' in A. Gleason *et al.* (eds.), *On Ninety Eighty-Four: Orwell and Our Future* (Harvard University Press, Princeton, NJ, 2005), p. 183.

[7] Cf. P. Bellia, P. Berman, B. Frischmann and D. Post, *Cyberlaw: Problems of Policy and Jurisprudence in the Information Age* (4th edn, West, St Paul, MN, 2011), pp. 625–7.

[8] On 'second generation of information privacy principles', see M. Kirby, 'Privacy in Cyberspace' (1998) 21 *University of New South Wales Law Journal* 323.

secrecy, control over personal information, personhood or intimacy.⁹ An important element of privacy, which protects against government surveillance, came through the Fourth Amendment. In *Katz v United States* the US Supreme Court ruled that privacy can not be invaded where reasonable expectations of privacy exist unless there is prior judicial authorization.¹⁰ *Katz* was extended to electronic communications in the Electronic Communication Privacy Act 1986.¹¹ The Act prohibits or limits the interception of electronic communications, the access to stored data and access to dialling and signalling information. The contribution of the American debate is in emphasizing those concepts and definitions of privacy that can be of particular importance for the Internet.

Any debate on privacy today is complicated by the many aspects it presents itself in. Privacy today, apart from being a philosophical concept, acquires specific flavours. Looking at privacy from the viewpoint of media requires different analytical instruments than looking at privacy in the context of surveillance, national security, health records, financial records, consumers, employment or education. In spite of this multiplicity of contexts, it is possible to argue that the most significant area that needs regulation is privacy protection of natural persons. This chapter, just like the main EU laws in this sphere, deals therefore only with that aspect.

1.2   EU and Privacy

The European Union places a high value on privacy. Member States' Constitutions directly grant protection while several EU constitutional documents do the same at EU level. The European Convention on Human Rights (ECHR)¹² protects privacy through Article 8:

1. Everyone has the right to respect for his private and family life, his home and his correspondence.
2. There shall be no interference by a public authority with the exercise of this right except such as is in accordance with the law and is necessary in a democratic society in the interests of national security, public safety or the economic well-being of the country, for the prevention of disorder or

---

⁹   On the definition, see D. Solove, 'Conceptualizing Privacy' (2002) 90 *California Law Review* 1087.
¹⁰   Supreme Court, 389 US 347 (1967).
¹¹   18 USC ss. 2510–22.
¹²   Which, in turn, was inspired by the United Nations Declaration of Human Rights of 1948.

crime, for the protection of health or morals, or for the protection of the rights and freedoms of others.

The Article is the subject of a number of decisions of the European Court of Human Rights (ECtHR), which reflects its complex nature and which largely mirror the difficulties encountered in US courts in defining privacy.[13] This chapter looks into some of the important EU legal instruments that apply to Internet privacy but does not reflect upon deeper underlying issues not specific to the European Union.[14]

EU constitutional law also regulates privacy. The Charter of Fundamental Rights of the European Union ('Charter') provides in Article 8:

1. Everyone has the right to the protection of personal data concerning him or her.
2. Such data must be processed fairly for specified purposes and on the basis of the consent of the person concerned or some other legitimate basis laid down by law. Everyone has the right of access to data that has been collected concerning him or her, and the right to have it rectified.
3. Compliance with these rules shall be subject to control by an independent authority.

Finally, the Treaties also protect privacy.[15] Article 16 of the Treaty on the Functioning of the European Union (TFEU) specifically provides a legal basis for action:

1. Everyone has the right to the protection of personal data concerning them.
2. The European Parliament and the Council, acting in accordance with the ordinary legislative procedure, shall lay down the rules relating to the protection of individuals with regard to the processing of personal data by Union institutions, bodies, offices and agencies, and by the Member States when carrying out activities which fall within the scope of Union law, and the rules relating to the free movement of such data. Compliance with these rules shall be subject to the control of independent authorities.

The rules adopted on the basis of this Article shall be without prejudice to the specific rules laid down in Article 39 of the Treaty on European Union.

---

[13] For a more detailed overview of the ECtHR's involvement see 'Internet: Case-law of the European Court of Human Rights, Council of Europe, June 2015, Section II', available at www.echr.coe.int/Documents/Research_report_internet_ENG.pdf.

[14] For an overview of data protection laws from the United Kingdom's perspective, see P. Carey, *Data Protection: A Practical Guide to UK and EU Law* (4th edn, OUP, Oxford, 2015).

[15] Article 39 TEU; Art. 16 TFEU.

The fundamentals of EU data protection were built into the 1995 Data Protection Directive.[16] In 2002, the E-Privacy Directive[17] addressed some of the challenges of the digital world while leaving the main Directive in place. Acutely aware of the technological challenges of modern life, the Commission reassessed the regime in the 2010 Communication on Data Protection,[18] proposing a new General Data Protection Regulation[19] and a new Police and Criminal Justice Authorities Directive[20] in 2011. Both texts were adopted, following an intense public debate and after substantial revisions, in early 2016. In the following chapters, we will address the currently applicable Data Protection Directive first, following with the analysis of the new Regulation which is only applicable from 25 May 2018.

---

[16] Directive 95/46 of the European Parliament and the Council of 24 October 1995 on the protection of individuals with regard to the processing of personal data and on the free movement of such data [1995] OJ L281/31, 23 November 1995. For more details, see H. Kaspersen, 'Data Protection and E-Commerce' in A. Lodder and H. Kaspersen, *eDirectives: Guide to European Union Law on E-Commerce* (Kluwer, The Hague, 2002).

[17] Directive 2002/58/EC of 12 July 2002 of the European Parliament and of the Council concerning the processing of personal data and the protection of privacy in the electronic communications sector [2002] OJ L201/37, 31 July 2002. Amended by Directive 2009/136/EC [2009] OJ L337/11, 18 November 2009.

[18] Communication from the Commission to the European Parliament, the Council, the Economic and Social Committee and the Committee of the Regions, *A Comprehensive Approach on Personal Data Protection in the European Union*, COM(2010)609 final (Brussels, 4 November 2010).

[19] Proposal: COM(2012)11 final (25 January 2011). Final text adopted as Regulation (EU) 2016/679 of the European Parliament and of the Council of 27 April 2016 on the protection of natural persons with regard to the processing of personal data and on the free movement of such data, and repealing Directive 95/46/EC ('General Data Protection Regulation') [2016] OJ L119/1, 4 May 2016.

[20] Proposal: COM(2012)10 (25 January 2012). Final text adopted as Directive 2016/680/EU of the European Parliament and of the Council of 27 April 2016 on the protection of natural persons with regard to the processing of personal data by competent authorities for the purposes of the prevention, investigation, detection or prosecution of criminal offences or the execution of criminal penalties, and on the free movement of such data, and repealing Council Framework Decision 2008/977/JHA [2016] OJ L119/89, 4 May 2016.

2 DATA PROTECTION DIRECTIVE

2.1 Introduction

The current Directive on data protection was not the first European instrument to cover the issue of data protection. It was preceded by the Convention on the protection of automatically processed personal data drafted by the Council of Europe in 1981.[21] The Convention, which came into force in 1985, was a source of law in many European states and the Commission's original plan was for all Member States to ratify it. In the EU, however, not all Member States did. Further to that, there was some dissatisfaction with the rules it provided, which were viewed as antiquated and unsuitable for a digital world. Therefore, the Community began work on its own instrument in the early 1990s, culminating in the adoption in 1995 of the final Data Protection Directive.

The European regime is made up of elements of data protection found in Member States, notably French and German, adopting the best solutions, some of which accord a high level of protection to privacy. As recognized in Recital 8, disparities in levels of protection between Member States may obstruct the flow of data. However, the Directive is used as a framework instrument for national legislators, giving them enough flexibility, as evidenced in article 5 which allows Member States to more precisely determine the conditions under which data protection is lawful. At the same time, the Directive institutes a high level of protection that can be complemented by other EU instruments (as is the case with the E-Privacy Directive or the now void Data Retention Directive).

The Directive aims at a high level of protection. This is based on the idea that an internal market requires not only conditions for a free flow of data but also a high level of protection of fundamental rights, including the right to privacy. The information economy brings with it an increasing flow of data between Member States and with it the increased risk of privacy violations. The Directive aims at full harmonization, precluding Member States' action in the area falling within its scope.[22]

The Directive has dual aims, as evidenced in article 1. The first aim is to enable the free flow of personal data, and in this respect the Member States take the obligation of preventing any obstacles that may arise to

---

[21] Convention for the Protection of Individuals with regard to Automatic Processing of Personal Data, ET No. 108.

[22] C-101/01 *Bodil Lindqvist* [2003] ECR I-1297, paras. 96–7.

this. The second obligation is to protect 'fundamental rights and freedoms of *natural* persons' with the particular aim of protecting the right to privacy. Since the accent is on data of natural persons, protection of data belonging to corporations falls either under other branches of EU law (e.g. competition law, trade secrets law[23]) or fully under national law.

The scope of the Directive is defined in article 2(a): it applies to 'any information relating to an identified or identifiable natural person'. The Directive applies to personal data of natural, not legal, persons. Such information is personal if 'it enables the direct or indirect identification of the person concerned'. This definition creates a sufficiently wide scope for the Directive. The exclusion of corporate data means the exclusion of trade secrets law from the scope of the Directive. It follows from article 2(a) that if the person is not identified or identifiable, the Directive does not apply. Anonymized data is, therefore, not subject to the Directive's rules. 'Big data', which could be defined as very large data sets that cannot be analysed using the traditional methods, often involves anonymized data but where it does involve personal data, it must comply with the EU rules.

The processing of personal data is defined as any operation performed on data, but the Directive only applies to personal data processed 'wholly or partially by automatic means'.[24] Also, it applies to processing other than by automatic means where personal data form part of a filing system.[25] It specifically does not apply to police and judicial cooperation,[26] and also specifically not to security or defence. If processing of data is carried out for journalistic, artistic or literary purposes solely, Member States are allowed to introduce various exceptions 'to reconcile the right to privacy with the rules governing freedom of expression'.[27] Finally, activities of natural persons in a private or household context are also excluded.

---

[23] Directive (EU) 2016/943 of the European Parliament and of the Council of 8 June 2016 on the protection of undisclosed know-how and business information (trade secrets) against their unlawful acquisition, use and disclosure [2016] OJ L157/1, 15 June 2016.

[24] See art. 3. Manual processing is covered only in so far as it forms part of a filing system.

[25] This means, under art. 2(c), a structured set of personal data accessible according to specific criteria.

[26] Which used to be the Second and Third Pillar structure of EU law, now eliminated under the Lisbon Treaty.

[27] See art. 9.

In *Bodil Lindqvist*,[28] the Court of Justice of the European Union (CJEU) had an opportunity to clarify some important Directive concepts in light of the Internet. The case concerned a private individual who, in the course of her engagement with the local church, had a webpage set up. The webpage contained private information about some of the parishioners, including medical data. The questions referred all, essentially, boil down to one: is processing of personal data on an Internet page within the scope of article 3? The Court first ruled that the act of naming persons on the Internet or referring to them by other means constitutes processing of personal data in light of article 3(1) without any of the exceptions of article 3(2) applying. The question concerning article 25 was whether posting of data accessible to the public on a webpage means the transfer of data to a third country. The Court answered that it did not.

The main addressees of the obligations in the Directive are 'controllers' – persons, natural or legal, who 'determine[s] the purposes and means of processing of data'. This is a wide definition but, in practice, applies to *any* body, corporate or not, in the position not only to collect and manipulate personal data but to decide the ultimate purpose of that control. The concept is different from 'processor', which is simply a natural or legal person who manipulates the data on behalf of the controller. A national gas company, an airline and a university are, according to this, all controllers of data. In a situation where a corporation A gathers data on behalf of corporation B, but it is the latter that determines the purpose, the former will be the processor and the latter the controller.

Article 4 regulates the territorial application of EU data protection law. If the controller is established in an EU Member State, the controller will be subject to the law of that state. Where the controller is established in several Member States, the laws of each of them have to be complied with. The controller will also be subject to the laws of the Member States in which the controller is not established but in which the equipment for processing personal data (except for transitory purposes) is situated.

The important question of what happens where the controller is only established in one Member State but processes data from the others had been answered in the 2014 *Weltimmo* judgment.[29] There, the CJEU

---

[28]   See note 22 above.
[29]   C-230/14 *Weltimmo sro v Nemzeti Adatvédelmi és Információszabadság Hatóság*, ECLI:EU:C:2015:639, 1 October 2015.

looked at the application of article 4(1)(a) in the context of a Slovakia-based property website which advertised in Hungary and held data of Hungarian clients. The question asked was whether Hungarian data protection law could be applied to a website only established in another state where that website gathers data from clients in Hungary and which supervisory authority was competent in such a situation. The Court held that Hungarian law could be applied provided that the 'controller exercises, through stable arrangements in the territory of that Member State, a real and effective activity – even a minimal one – in the context of which that processing is carried out'. In such a case the fact that a local language was used and that the controller had a local representative worked in favour of such a solution. In that sense, Hungarian data protection authority is competent for data processing of Hungarian subjects on its own territory. The importance of the decision lies in the change of assumption that controllers established in one Member State only have to comply with the law of that state. This is, after *Weltimmo*, manifestly not the case whenever data processing is also taking place in another Member State.

The chosen territorial regime is awkward.[30] It leads to situations where EU law applies to controllers who have no connection with the EU other than the fact that they use or rent the equipment physically located in the EU. It also leads to situations where EU law does *not* apply to controllers outside the EU who deal exclusively or largely with EU customers and have no processing equipment located in the EU. Most large social networking sites are located in the United States and regularly target EU users. If the line of article 4 is followed, they would only be subject to the EU data protection regime if they had equipment used for processing data (which some probably do). The new General Data Protection Regulation (GDPR) changes the sphere of application dramatically (see section 3 below).

2.2 General Rules on Lawfulness of Processing

A number of principles were developed that bind the controllers in their processing of data. Two key provisions are principles relating to data quality (article 6) and principles related to legitimacy of processing (article 7).[31]

---

[30] See L. Moerel, 'The Long Arm of EU Data Protection Law: Does the Data Protection Directive Apply to Processing of Personal Data of EU Citizens by Websites Worldwide?' (2011) 1 *International Data Privacy Law* 28.

[31] The Directive distinguishes between collection and processing.

The principles in article 6, which all relate to *quality of data*, have been developed from ECHR law, where they have autonomous meaning and have been subject to the ECtHR's practice.[32] The first principles contained in article 6 are the principles of *lawful processing* and *fair processing*: data should be processed 'fairly and lawfully'. The second principle is *purpose specification and limitation*: data must be collected for 'specified, explicit and legitimate purposes'. Moreover, legitimately collected data may be subject to illegitimate processing. For instance, information on online purchasing habits collected with the aid of cookies may be used to push advertising. Therefore, article 6(1)(b) leaves it to Member States to provide adequate safeguards for further processing of such data. This may be for historical, statistical or scientific purposes. The third principle is that personal data must be adequate, relevant and not excessive for the purpose for which they are collected. They must be accurate, and if not, must be erased or corrected.

The third principles are *data quality principles:* relevancy and accuracy. Article 6(c) is the *relevancy* principle: data must be 'adequate, relevant and not excessive in relation to the purposes for which they are collected and/or further processed'. Data *accuracy*, on the other hand, requires that data be 'accurate and, where necessary, kept up to date; every reasonable step must be taken to ensure that data which are inaccurate or incomplete, having regard to the purposes for which they were collected or for which they are further processed, are erased or rectified'. Article 6(e) requires *limited retention of data*, which must be kept 'no longer than is necessary for the purposes for which the data were collected or for which they are further processed'. Member States are allowed to lay down criteria for longer storage for 'historical, statistical or scientific' purposes. Finally, article 6(2) introduces the principle of accountability: it is the controller's duty to ensure that the principles in article 6(1) are complied with.

The rules on lawful processing of data are split into rules on processing of *non-sensitive data* (article 7) and rules on *sensitive* data (article 8).

Article 7 sets out the criteria that make the processing of non-sensitive data legitimate. Personal data, according to that article, may only be processed if any of six conditions are fulfilled. Although it is usually correctly assumed that *consent* is a valid basis for processing of personal data, consent is only one of the six bases that make processing legitimate. Consent is defined in article 2(h) as 'any freely given specific and

---

[32] See Council of Europe, *Handbook on European Data Protection Law* (Publications Office of the European Union, Luxembourg, 2014), ch 3.

informed indication of the data subject's wishes'. It is this definition that gives the conditions for a valid consent under EU law. Such consent must be freely given, which means that no pressure, physical or otherwise, must have been applied on the subject. Secondly, the consent must be specific and not general: the data subject must be consenting to a well-defined gathering process with a determined purpose. Finally, the data subject must have been properly informed about what they are consenting to.

Although consent can be given in the simplest of forms and is, in case of the World Wide Web, normally obtained with the aid of a simple click on the button that signifies the acceptance, it is often problematic in terms of each of the three conditions outlined above. Empirical data shows[33] that the average data subject is ill-informed about what they are consenting to and often willing to give authorization for sweeping collections of data which are then used for a variety of purposes not originally envisaged. To address these deficiencies, the GDPR brings some minor improvements in clarity.

The second option for lawful processing (article 7(b)) is if the processing is necessary for the performance of a contract to which the data subject is a party. An e-commerce sale agreement, for instance, will have a shipping and billing address and credit card details and may have a number of other situation-specific items, some of which may be sensitive (such as data on medicines taken). Other options are if the processing is necessary for compliance with a legal obligation to which the controller is subject (article 7(c)) or if the processing is necessary for the protection of vital interests of the data subject (article 7(d)). The former only applies to controllers in the private sector, since those in the public sector are subject to separate exception in article 7(e). By way of example, hospitals, employers, banks, etc. can be quoted. Processing may also be necessary for the performance of a task carried out in the public interest or in the exercise of official authority (article 7(e)). In this case the authority may either be in the hands of the controller or a third party to whom data is disclosed (such as the police or judicial authorities). Finally, processing may be necessary in pursuing legitimate interests, as long as these are not overridden by the fundamental rights and freedoms of the data subject. The last criterion seems to be too vague.

---

[33]   Consent, EU FP7-SSH project, *Final Report Summary* (2014), available at http://cordis.europa.eu/result/rcn/140471_en.html.

Certain categories of data are treated with extra care and their processing is prohibited in principle, save in special circumstances.[34] These categories, labelled *sensitive data*, can still be processed in a limited number of circumstances, all of which are exhaustively listed in article 8(2). Article 8(1) defines sensitive data as data relating to racial and ethnic origin, political, religious, philosophical beliefs, trade union memberships and those concerning health and sex life. The processing of these will exceptionally be allowed where explicit consent has been given,[35] where employment law so requires or where vital interests of the data subject or another person are concerned and the data subject is unable to give consent. Non-profit bodies and foundations with political, philosophical or trade union aims may process data if it relates to its members. Finally, processing may be carried out for data manifestly made public or necessary for processing of a legal claim. Specific derogation is inserted for 'preventive medicine, medical diagnosis and the provision of care or treatment or the management of health-care services' where these are under the obligation of secrecy.[36] Data concerning criminal convictions, other offences and judgments are subject to specific protection.

Article 9 subjects processing of personal data to a specific derogation in relation to journalistic, literary or artistic purposes where freedom of expression comes into conflict with the right to privacy. In such a case, derogations may be made in relation to Chapter I (general provisions), Chapter IV (transfer to third countries) and Chapter VI (Supervisory Authority and Working Party).

2.3 Data Subjects and the Rights of Information, Access and Objection

The data subject has the right[37] to be adequately informed of the gathering and processing of data, including what is being collected, by whom and who has access to it. Furthermore, the subject has the right to access the data, correct it, object to its processing or object to its use for commercial purposes.

Articles 10 and 11 give the data subject the right to be informed of who the controller is and why data is being collected. The subject of this

---

[34] See art. 8(1).
[35] Although national laws may provide that the data subject cannot give consent.
[36] See art. 8(3).
[37] See arts. 10–15.

obligation is the controller. In cases where information is collected directly from the data subject, that subject has the right to know who the controllers and recipients are, the purposes for which data is collected, whether replies to questions are mandatory or voluntary and the consequences of not replying, that a right of access exists, and that data can be rectified.[38]

Where data has not been obtained from the data subject, the information is subject to the conditions set out in article 11, negligibly different from article 10. This relates to any case where the data subject has no control over whether they give information, such as in public places, but also cases where information is simply compiled without their knowledge. In such cases, the controller is under an obligation to disclose the data to the data subject at the moment when they record the information or, at the latest, when this information is being disclosed to third parties. The conditions include: (a) the identity of the controller; (b) the purpose of the processing; (c) other information, such as categories of data, recipients, the existence of right to access and the right to rectify.

An important right of data subjects is the right to access data.[39] This is exercised by the subject against the controller. The latter must, without constraint, at reasonable intervals, without delay or expense: inform the data subject whether data relating to him are held or processed; why they are processed; what categories of data they include; and who they are disclosed to. If this is performed automatically, the information must also include the logic behind the automation, at least in cases covered in article 15(1). The data subject has the right to obtain from the controller the blocking, erasure or rectification of data that does not comply with the provisions of the Directive and the right to inform third parties that this action has been performed.

Article 14 covers the data subject's right to object and introduces two grounds on which this is possible. The first relates to a situation where data has been gathered in the exercise of the public authority or controller's legitimate interests (article 7(e) and (f)). The objection must be based on 'compelling legitimate grounds relating to his particular situation'. A separate right to object exists in cases where the controller 'anticipates' using data for direct marketing purposes or discloses data to third parties for the first time or uses it for direct marketing on their behalf. Member States have a specific obligation to make the data

---

[38]   See art. 10.
[39]   See art. 12.

subjects aware of the possibility to object to data gathering for commercial purposes.

Both articles 11 and 14 are of considerable importance in practice as the incentive to obtain commercially valuable information at low cost has dramatically increased in recent years. Particularly valuable and marketable information includes names and credit records, valid email addresses and shopping habits. These are traded both legally and illegally for large sums of money. Electronic commerce on the Internet depends on the speed and convenience of transactions. Such speed often results in users overlooking the small print, which may include a consent form for the information to be passed on to 'carefully selected' third parties. Such passing of commercial information is a sensitive issue also covered in national legislation. In a number of test cases in the United Kingdom,[40] certain corporations engaged in advertising practices on their own or on behalf of other corporations. They included distribution of leaflets of third parties (*Midlands Electricity, Thames Water*) or passed on their own customers' details to third parties (*British Gas*) or an electoral register being sold for commercial purposes (*Robertson*). The common thread in all cases was the fact that the data subjects whose information was held and subsequently passed on did not give consent. In some cases (*British Gas*), the data subject had the opportunity to remove his name from the register that the tribunal ruled to be unfair.

Article 15 specifically regulates automated individual decisions. Data subjects, according to this article, have the right not to be subject to automated decisions where the decision has legal effects or affects them in other ways. Automated decisions are defined as 'based solely on automated processing of data intended to evaluate certain personal aspects'. The personal aspects quoted by way of example are: performance at work; creditworthiness; reliability or conduct, etc. The exception is when the decision is authorized by another law or is taken in the course of entering into or performance of a contract, in both cases with proper safeguards.

---

[40] *British Gas Trading Ltd v Data Protection Registrar* [1998] TLR 393, Data Protection Tribunal; *Midlands Electricity Plc v Data Protection Registrar* [1999] TLR 217, Data Protection Tribunal; *Decision by the Data Protection Commissioner re Thames Water Utilities Ltd* (unreported); *Brian Reid Robertson v Wakefield Metropolitan Council and Secretary of State for the Home Department* [2001] EWHC Admin 915.

The reality of automated decision-making, however, is more complex than article 15 would let us believe.[41] The first thing to point out is that article 15 applies to *decision-making* but not profile *creation* itself. There are reasons to believe that profile creation in itself ought to be regulated separately. At present, profile creation is under the general regime of the Directive while decision-making based on the profiles is under the special regime. Whereas the purpose-binding from article 6(b) could be used to delegitimize the use of profiles created in a different context, there are reasons to believe that this is not enough. In recognition of these problems, the GDPR has a somewhat updated approach to this problem (see below).

2.4 Other Provisions

In addition to the above, the Directive contains provisions on confidentiality and security of processing (articles 16–17); notification (articles 18–21); remedies, liabilities and sanctions (articles 22–24); transfer of data to third countries (articles 25–26, see also section 4 below); codes of conduct (article 27) and supervisory authorities (articles 28–30).

Article 16 prohibits unauthorized processing of personal data for anyone under the controller's authority. Article 17 demands that Member States introduce measures protecting against 'accidental or unlawful destruction or accidental loss, alteration, unauthorized disclosure or access', in particular in cases of transmission but also measures against any unlawful processing. This article is the basic measure protecting the data while it is in the controller's keeping as opposed to measures controlling how data is gathered, handled or how it might be transferred. The article calls for 'state of art' protection appropriate to the risk presented. Where the controller engages a processor, article 17(2) calls for sufficient levels of technical and organizational security. In addition to that, processing must be based on a contract and/or legal act.

The section on notification demands, in essence, that national supervisory authorities be notified wherever processing takes place[42] but provides for a simplified procedure in certain cases. If processing presents special risks to 'rights and freedoms' of the subjects, the supervisory authority will conduct a prior check (article 20). Article 21

---

[41]   See also A. Savin, 'Profiling in the Present and New EU Data Protection Frameworks' in P.A. Nielsen, P.K. Schmidt and K. Dyppel Weber (eds.), *Erhvervsretlige emne* (Juridisk Institut CBS, Djøf, 2015), pp. 249–70.

[42]   See art. 18(1). The content of the notification is covered in art. 19.

calls for a public register of all processing, maintained by national supervisory authorities.

The sanctions for violation of the provisions of the Directive are left to Member States but an obligation is imposed to ensure that those suffering damage as a result of unlawful processing are entitled to compensation.[43] The remedy is in the form of 'compensation from the controller', but the latter is exempt if they prove that they are not responsible. Other than this, the Member States must introduce 'suitable measures' to ensure compliance.

The primary addressees of the Directive are not the controllers and processors directly but Member States and the supervisory authorities entrusted with data protection issues. These are independent national data protection agencies (sometimes several units in one country) set up under national law. Article 28 provides that they are responsible for monitoring the obligations under this Directive, must be consulted on data protection issues and are endowed with special powers. These powers are investigative, powers of intervention and power to intervene in legal proceedings. As per article 28(4) the authorities also have the obligation to hear claims lodged by private persons, although this does not exclude judicial redress.

Of particular importance for the consistency of application of EU data protection rules is the Working Party on the Protection of Individuals with regard to the Processing of Personal Data, usually referred to as the 'Article 29 Working Party'. This is the body whose setting up was envisaged in article 29, and which consists of representatives of national supervisory authorities. It is independent in its actions (i.e. it does not depend on EU or national bodies) but its function is purely advisory. Article 30 defines the scope of its work, which is to give opinions and expert advice. Its most important contribution comes in the form of opinions and recommendations, which, although not binding, have significant interpretative power at both EU and national level.

2.5 *Google Spain* and the Right to be Forgotten

One of the most significant data protection cases to come out of the CJEU in recent years is the *Google Spain* case.[44] The case concerned a

---

[43] See arts. 23 and 24.

[44] C-131/12 *Google Spain SL and Google Inc. v Agencia Española de Protección de Datos (AEPD) and Mario Costeja González*, ECLI:EU:C: 2014:317, 13 May 2014.

Spanish citizen who was involved in a real-estate auction as a consequence of an attempt to recover some of his social security debt. When
his name was entered in Google Search, two articles from the newspaper
La Vanguardia appeared. Claiming that 15-year-old information was
harming his reputation, he commenced action against both the newspaper
and Google, asking each to remove or conceal the information in
question. The Spanish court referred a number of important questions to
the CJEU that can be grouped into two. The first group of questions was
essentially about whether Google fell under the data protection rules in
terms of articles 2 and 4. The second group of question was, provided
that it did, how are articles 12(b) on erasure and blocking of data and
14(a) on the right to object to be interpreted in light of the facts of the
case.

   The case is significant for several reasons. The individual in question
claimed that their right to privacy had been violated in that out-of-date
(although factually accurate) information had been presented to the
public every time his name was entered into a search engine. This
directly juxtaposed his right of privacy, a fundamental right, to another
fundamental right – the right of information. Equally significantly, his
action did not target only the newspaper that carried the original article
but also the search engines as the public's primary point of entry into the
world of information. The case was, therefore, more than just an odd
query about how the Directive ought to be interpreted but a much more
significant issue about the Internet in its function as public memory.

   Advocate General Costeja González, in his Opinion, emphasized that a
search engine which 'locates information published or included on the
internet by third parties, indexes it automatically, stores it temporarily
and finally makes it available to internet users' does process information
within the terms of article 2 but that it cannot be considered a 'controller'
in the sense of article 2(d), since the search engine does not control the
original data but only its own index. It may be considered a controller
only in the case where it intervenes with the latter, for example, by not
complying with exclusion codes telling it *not* to index a page. In
answering the second group of questions, the Advocate General suggested that articles 12(b) and 14(a) did not confer the right to request the
search engine to prevent indexing of information 'published legally on
third parties' web pages, invoking his wish that such information should
not be known to internet users when he considers that it might be
prejudicial to him or he wishes it to be consigned to oblivion'. The
argument here is that information which has *legally* been posted cannot
be erased on a whim, simply because the subject desires so.

The CJEU did not follow the Advocate General's Opinion. It said that the operator of a search engine is a controller, not only because the concept 'controller' should be interpreted in a wide sense, but also because the search engine's activities in themselves affect fundamental rights to privacy. In interpreting articles 12(b) and 14(a), the Court said that the obligation to erase exists, also in cases where the information had not previously been erased from the primary source. This can be demanded without it being necessary for a prejudice to exist. The right of privacy as protected in Articles 7 and 8 of the Charter, 'override, as a rule, not only the economic interest of the operator of the search engine but also the interest of the general public in having access to that information upon a search relating to the data subject's name'.

In the view of this author, the CJEU made a mistake and decidedly drifted in the direction of creative interpretation, misinterpreting the Directive and violating EU constitutional documents in the process. First, the arguments given in favour of the opinion that search engines are controllers are simply not convincing. The fact that a search engine may have an impact on the private lives of individuals is not the same as claiming that such a search engine determines the purpose of processing, which is a necessary condition for it being called a controller. The only situation where a search engine exercises any kind of control is where it determines not to index something without it being told so through an exclusion code. In all other cases, it is the operators of sites who determine the purpose of collecting and the search engine only index. Secondly, there is no support in any of the EU constitutional documents (Charter of Fundamental Rights, European Convention on Human Rights, TFEU, Treaty on European Union) for a hierarchy of fundamental rights. There is, therefore, no objective reason to claim that the rights from Articles 7 and 8 override other rights without providing significant reasons for why this might be so. Whereas it may be possible to balance privacy and freedom of expression, the Court did not attempt to give any guidance as to how this could be carried out. This will inevitably lead to indiscriminate removal of information from search engines on trivial grounds as it is simply less costly to remove than to engage with expansive and protracted battles with national authorities or courts.

In December 2015, the Article 29 Working Party issued its updated opinion on the territorial aspects of the case.[45] In it, the Working Party

---

[45]   Article 29 Data Protection Working Party, *Update of Opinion 8/2010 on Applicable Law in Light of the CJEU Judgment in Google Spain*, 176/16/EN WP 179 update (16 December 2015).

emphasized the existence of the 'inextricable link' test for all situations where it may not be clear whether the activity of the processor and the data are linked or not. In cases involving multinational establishments, such as search engines or social media sites:

> so long as a company has establishments in several EU Member States which promote and sell advertisement space, raise revenues or carry out other activities, and it can be established that these activities and the data processing are 'inextricably linked', the national laws of each such establishment will apply.

In other words, it is no longer enough to claim a non-EU establishment in order to extricate oneself from the Directive. It was suggested that other business models may also trigger the application of the Directive.

3   GENERAL DATA PROTECTION REGULATION

The desire to reform the EU data protection framework arises from the challenges posed by modern technology. The new laws, updating the now 20-year-old Directive, aim to strengthen the rights of data subjects while enhancing the internal market dimension and improving enforcement. The General Data Protection Regulation (GDPR)[46] and the Police and Criminal Justice Authorities Directive,[47] proposed in 2011, were finally adopted in a much revised form in 2016. Whereas the former is a replacement for the Data Protection Directive, the latter replaces a Framework Decision on privacy protection in criminal matters.[48] The Regulation entered into force on 24 May 2016 and will apply from 25 May 2018.

---

[46]   See note 19 above.

[47]   See note 20 above.

[48]   In general on the Proposal, see P. Hustinx, 'EU Data Protection Law: The Review of Directive 95/46/EC and the Proposed General Data Protection Regulation', available at https://secure.edps.europa.eu/EDPSWEB/webdav/site/mySite/shared/Documents/EDPS/Publications/Speeches/2014/14-09-15_Article_EUI_EN.pdf. On changes in the final version see C. Burton *et al.*, 'From Proposal to Passage: Critical Insights on the EU Data Protection Regulation', *Privacy and Security Law Report*, 15 PVLR 153, 1/25/16.

3.1 Introduction

The GDPR is based on the new Article 16 TFEU and has been issued in the form of a Regulation to minimize the disparities between the Member States. The new instrument relies on the Data Protection Directive, retaining its key ideas and concepts but also introducing new ones and making a number of provisions more precise. It is worth noting that the final text is a result of a compromise reached after heavy lobbying by a number of stakeholders and that some of the ideas from the CJEU's cases did find their way into the final version. In spite of this, the extended scope, the increased precision in a number of areas and the introduction of new concepts all together make this a very significant change both for the entities in and those out of the EU.

The Regulation does not change the definition of personal data but adds 'identification number, location data, an online identifier' as examples of what might be considered as data. Recital 30 further specifies that such information may particularly be interesting when combined with unique identifiers, suggesting that, in all cases where persons could be identified the information would fall under the Regulation. Article 4(13) and (14) introduce two new categories of data: genetic and biometric data.

A new concept of 'pseudonymization' is introduced in article 4(5) and identified as processing where 'data can no longer be attributed to a specific data subject without the use of additional information' and where such additional information is kept separately. The purpose of pseudonymization is to enable the processors to keep the data and use it while minimizing the risks that can potentially arise from misuse but it is clear that pseudonymized data that can be attributed to individuals are still covered. In addition to that, article 11 provides that processing which does not require identification at all means that the controller will not be obliged to identify the subjects just to be able to comply with the Regulation.

The territorial scope of the Regulation differs fundamentally from that of the Directive. Article 3 provides that the Regulation applies to situations involving controllers established in the European Union, regardless of whether the actual processing has also taken place in the EU. The Regulation also applies to processing of personal data of subjects who are in the union by processors who are not in the Union where goods or services are offered to subjects in the Union (irrespective of whether they are for payment or not) or where the monitoring of the subjects' behaviour takes place in the Union. While the first point presents only a clarification of the one found in the Data Protection

Directive, the latter is essentially an extension of the Regulation's application to all situations where the subjects are targeted, either because goods or services are offered to them or because their behaviour is monitored for advertising or other commercial or non-commercial purposes. Thus, a social networking site with an establishment in the United States or a search engine selling advertising who targets European customers would fall under the scope. Recital 23, however, is very clear that mere accessibility of a website or an app is not enough to trigger the application of the Regulation. In terms of offering goods or services the recital states that:

> factors such as the use of a language or a currency generally used in one or more Member States with the possibility of ordering goods and services in that other language, or the mentioning of customers or users who are in the Union, may make it apparent that the controller envisages offering goods or services to data subjects in the Union.

No such determination is needed in cases where the controller monitors EU subjects, as this will be triggered whenever the individuals are tracked or profiled in order to predict their behaviour, without a potential sale or further action being necessary.

The principles relating to processing of personal data have been only slightly changed. One change is to be found in 'fair and lawful processing' of article 6 of the Directive which becomes 'lawfulness, fairness and transparency' under article 5 of the Regulation. The transparency is now also subject to a very detailed article 12 which puts the principle into practice. Article 5(f) adds a new principle – 'integrity and confidentiality' – which demands that data be secure and be protected against accidental loss, destruction or damage.

3.2 Key Innovations

While the new Regulation maintains the basic framework of the Directive, it changes some of the latter's concepts significantly, while introducing new ones.

Consent as one of the most important bases for data processing remains largely unchanged albeit with some adjustments and a separate article clarifying the conditions for a valid consent. The definition of article 4(11) adds *unambiguity* to consent, which already needs to be freely given, specific and informed. The Proposal called for 'explicit' consent but this has subsequently been changed to the present formulation. An explicit consent would, in the view of this author, have been a better option since the vast majority of consent on the Internet is fictitious, with users clicking and agreeing to things they have not read or do not understand. In addition to the new condition, in assessing whether consent had been freely given, regard shall be had to whether performance of a contract is conditional on consent or not. The idea here is that consent is not freely given where the data subject has no choice. Recital 43 specifically emphasizes that this will be the case where the performance of the contract is in no way dependent on the consent or where the public authority is the controller and can, therefore, exercise pressure on the users for services they depend on.

A new article 7 is introduced, outlining the conditions for consent. The article puts the burden of proof squarely on the controller who should be able to demonstrate the subject's consent. If consent is given in the context of a written declaration concerning another matter, it must be presented in a clearly distinguishable manner. This will, for example, be the case where the user agrees to website terms and conditions which also contain consent for the user's data to be stored, processed and/or shared with partners. Article 7(3) now explicitly confirms that data subjects must be allowed to withdraw their consent in as easy a manner as it was given it and must be told of this right.

Another novelty is a special regime on consent obtained from children (article 8). For a person to be treated as adult in terms of consent, they must be at least 16 years old.[49] If they are below that age, consent is only valid if either given or authorized by the holder of parental responsibility. The controller only has to take 'reasonable' steps to ensure that consent had been obtained by the holder of parental responsibility. It is not specified what these might be but it should be assumed that ordinary warning should be enough in most Member States.

Special categories of data found in article 8 of the Directive have been extended in article 9 of the Regulation. In addition to the old ones, genetic data and biometric data, as well as data relating to sexual orientation, have been added. In addition to the five exceptions that make processing of such data legal in the Directive, the Regulation also includes defence of legal claims (9(2)(f)); substantial public interest (9(2)(g)); medical or social care reasons (9(2)(h)); public health (9(2)(i)); and archiving purposes (9(2)(j)).

The purpose-binding principle has been extended in article 6(4), which applies to all situations where data have been collected for one purpose

---

[49] Member States are allowed to set a lower age, although not below 13 years.

but need to be processed for another. In that case, the default position is that the data subject's consent had been obtained or a law allows the processing. If this is not the case the controller, in determining whether the processing for another purpose is compatible, needs to look at the link between the purposes, the relationship between the subject and the controller, the nature of the data, possible consequences and the existence of safeguards. It must be clear that the criteria listed are only to be used if the data gathered are compatible with the new purpose and not to legitimize a random change of purpose.

The rights of individuals already existing under the Directive have been enhanced in the Regulation. Articles 13 and 14 (replacing articles 10 and 11 of the Directive) require that certain information be given to the data subject in cases where data have been collected from the subject (article 13) as well as when they have not (article 14). Both articles demand the communication of a range of information to the subject, including the identity and contact details of the controller; the purpose for which data is gathered; the recipients; and the fact that data may be transferred to third countries. Article 15 provides a more detailed version of the 'right of access' to that found in the Directive.

Article 17 creates the right to erasure (also called 'right to be forgotten' in the article title itself). The subject can demand erasure from the controller if one of the six conditions have been fulfilled. The first ground is if the data are no longer necessary either for the purpose for which they have been collected or for the purpose for which they are being processed. The subject is also allowed to withdraw consent either for regular or special categories of data and provided no other legal ground exists. This means that a simple withdrawal of consent is enough, without other things being necessary to prove to the controller. The next ground refers to the right to object from article 21 which, in turn, applies to processing in the public interest or the controller's legitimate interest, except where there are overriding legitimate grounds or to processing for marketing purposes for which erasure can be demanded without conditions. The subject can also demand erasure where data has been unlawfully processed (17(1)(d)), where an EU or Member State's law demands it (17(1)(e)) or the data have been collected in relation to offer of services to children (17(1)(f)). As per article 17(2), where the controller has already made the data public, they have the obligation to take reasonable steps to inform any other controller processing the data that erasure had been requested and in particular 'any links to, or copy or replication of, those personal data'. In cases where the primary controller is a news portal and the information is copied or linked to, the primary controller needs to inform all those providing links or copied content.[50] This is clearly aimed at search engines in the sense of the *Google Spain* decision. Article 17(3) provides a number of safeguards, including (a) the exercise of the rights of freedom of expression and of information; (b) compliance with legal obligations; (c) public health; (d) archiving; and (e) legal claims.

A separate right to restriction of processing exists in article 18. This is a completely new right which has some similarities to blocking found in the Data Protection Directive. Restriction of processing is a temporary measure, the aim of which is to isolate the data while the contested facts are checked. The first ground is where a data subject contests the accuracy; the second where processing is unlawful but the data subject requests restriction rather than destruction; the third where the subject no longer needs the data but the controller does for legal reasons. The final reason relates to objection under article 21(1).

The GDPR's vision of the 'right to be forgotten' follows the outlines of the *Google Spain* case, in that it establishes a right separate from the right of rectification. On the other hand, it also manages to address some of the issues left open in the judgment, notably the balance between privacy and other fundamental rights. A person wishing to withdraw data which are not inaccurate but which they believe now harm their reputation, would usually opt to do so under article 17(1)(a) and (b). Article 17(2) now specifically covers entities such as search engines, which is in line with the CJEU's view that these are to be considered controllers in their own right. The scope and operation of the right to be forgotten would, in the future, depend on the balancing between article 17(1) and (2) – the grounds for removal and other interests. This will, in the first instance, be exercised by the controllers but will ultimately have to be interpreted in courts.

A new right to data portability has been created in article 20 on the basis of a general drive to increase interoperability in the EU. The data subject has the right to receive data that relates to them presented in a 'structured, commonly used and machine-readable format'. The data subject should, where possible, have the right to have the data transmitted directly from one controller to another. Two conditions need to be fulfilled: the processing must have been based on consent and be carried out by automatic means.

Significant changes have also been introduced to profiling and automated decision-making. Whereas article 15 of the Directive referred to

---

[50] See art. 17(2).

automated processing only, article 22 now distinguishes between automated processing and profiling. The main idea is similar to the one found in article 15: data subjects should have the right to object to decisions solely based on automated processing of data. Profiling is defined in article 4(4) as:

> any form of automated processing of personal data consisting of the use of personal data to evaluate certain personal aspects relating to a natural person, in particular to analyse or predict aspects concerning that natural person's performance at work, economic situation, health, personal preferences, interests, reliability, behaviour, location or movements.

The definition does not cover profile creation but only the use of profiles.

Article 25 introduces data protection 'by design and by default'. Data protection 'by design' means, in essence, the controller's obligation to build data protection into each aspect of its activities with the aim of best upholding the Regulation (e.g. pseudonymization, minimization, etc.) The obligation is not absolute but depends on the state of the art, the cost, risks, etc. Data protection 'by default' means that 'only personal data which are necessary for each specific purpose of the processing are processed'.

In addition to the substantive changes outlined above, the Regulation also brings some formal and procedural innovations. It is no longer necessary to report the processing to authorities in Member States but it is, as per article 30, necessary to keep records of all the activities. The Regulation establishes a 'one stop shop' for companies established in several Member States. Article 56 establishes the competence of a 'lead supervisory authority', which is the authority of the main establishment of the controller or of the processor. According to article 27, where a non-EU controller or processor targets EU data subjects, they must appoint a representative in the Union. The tasks and powers of the supervisory authorities are now outlined in much more detail in articles 57 and 58, as is the cooperation between the authorities (articles 60–62). The Article 29 Working Group established in the Directive has been replaced by the European Data Protection Board (articles 68–76).

As the GDPR applies to non-criminal matters only, a separate Directive was needed to address data protection issues in criminal matters.[51] The currently applicable EU instrument for personal data protection in

---

[51]   Directive (EU) 2016/680 [2016] OJ L119/89, 4 May 2016.

criminal matters is Framework Decision 2008/977/JHA.[52] This measure is a minimum-harmonization measure that applies to the cross-border exchange of personal data. This instrument has limited scope as it applies only to cross-border data processing and not to processing which takes place only at national level, nor to processing by police and judicial authorities. The new Directive protects individuals in situations where 'competent authorities' process their personal data 'for the purposes of the prevention, investigation, detection or prosecution of criminal offences or the execution of criminal penalties', including threats to public security.[53] The purpose of the Directive is to ensure that fundamental rights are respected in such situations and that exchange of data by these authorities is not restricted or prohibited for reasons concerning data protection rules. The Directive does not apply to issues falling outside the scope of EU law. The Directive subjects data to the principles of article 4 and requires Member States to distinguish between personal data of different data subjects (article 6). These persons are suspects, those convicted of criminal offences, victims and third parties. These categories are granted certain rights (Chapter III), whereas duties of controllers and processors are covered in a separate section (Chapter IV). Data can, under Chapter V, be transferred to third countries under the principles and mechanism similar to those in the GDPR.

4 TRANSFER OF DATA TO THIRD STATES

4.1 Data Protection Directive and GDPR

An essential feature of the data protection regime in the EU is a general prohibition of transfer of data outside the EU except when certain conditions are met. The reason for the prohibition is the fear of losing data protection standards in countries with a lower threshold of protection. Since data is regularly transferred on the Internet in a variety of different contexts, this restriction is of growing political and economic importance. The practice of outsourcing – transferring some of the work to corporations based abroad – is dependent on modern infrastructure, including the Internet. In addition to that, the ease with which clouds of data are established and used increase the need to protect. Finally, the

---

[52] Council Framework Decision 2008/977/JHA of 27 November 2008 on the protection of personal data processed in the framework of police and judicial cooperation in criminal matters [2008] OJ L350, 30 December 2008.
[53] See art. 1.

Snowden revelations about mass monitoring of communications by the United States government has increased the political pressure on the EU to control data transfers to third states.

It is worth noting that data flows *between* EU Member States must not be restricted at all and are not subject to the provisions of this section. Transfer of data to *third* countries is regulated in the Data Protection Directive's Chapter IV. Transfers can be undertaken to third countries with adequate level of protection (article 25), third countries in specific cases (article 26(1)), under contractual clauses or binding corporate rules (article 26(2)) or under special international agreements.

The main provision, article 25, is that data transfers can be undertaken only to countries that ensure an adequate level of protection (adequacy criterion). The Commission is competent to make adequacy findings. As of 2016, a relatively small number of countries have been subject of positive findings as per article 25(6): Andorra, Canada, Switzerland, Israel and New Zealand. Article 25(2) lists the criteria to be taken into consideration when determining if adequacy exists or not, which include the nature of the data, the purpose of processing, country of origin and of destination, the rule of law and professional and security measures.

Exemptions may be granted for the export of data to third countries which do not satisfy article 25 adequacy criteria under the conditions set out in article 26. The conditions which need to be satisfied are: (a) the data subject must have given his unambiguous consent, or (b) the transfer must be necessary, either for the performance of the contract or (c) with a view to entering into a contract, or necessary for entering into a contract between the data controller and a third party but at the request of the data subject. Another ground is (d) if the transfer is necessary for reasons of public interest, or (e) for protecting vital interests of the data subjects, or (f) the transfer is made from a public register normally open to the public.

The third possibility for transfers to third states arises in article 26(2), which allows transfers in cases where the controller 'adduces adequate safeguards with respect to the protection of the privacy and fundamental rights and freedoms of individuals and as regards the exercise of the corresponding rights' from, among others, contractual clauses. This, then, needs to be notified to the Commission and other Member States. Based on this article, specific exemption methods have been created for cases where the controller makes special arrangements ensuring adequate levels of protection. This can be made either through contractual clauses, binding corporate rules or special international agreements.

Article 26(2) of the Directive covers contractual rules. The idea is that a transfer may be authorized in the case where a potential non-EU controller issues guarantees in respect of the protection of privacy and fundamental rights. In particular, the article provides, these may result from standard contracts which the EU controller signs with non-EU controllers or processors. The European Commission has issued a set of standard contractual clauses for non-EU controllers in 2001 that it updated with another version in 2004 and a version for non-EU processors in 2010.[54] The clauses are designed in such a way as to guarantee the rights of data subjects and minimize the potential for exposure of information. Transfers of data to processors in third states, as opposed to controllers, are subject to lower standards.

Another way of transferring data to third countries without an adequacy decision as per Article 26(2) is through binding corporate rules (BCR).[55] These are internal rules which multinational corporations adopt for data transfers within the same corporate group. In principle, BCR must contain privacy principles, tools of effectiveness and a proof that they are binding.

Finally, special international agreements also cover data transfers to third countries. Among these, the Passenger Name Record (PNR) agreements and Terrorist Finance Tracking Programme (TFTP) are possibly the most prominent ones. The EU has signed PNR agreements with the United States in 2012,[56] Canada in 2006[57] and Australia in 2012.[58] The TFTP Agreement had been signed with the United States in 2010.[59]

---

[54]   There exist two alternative sets for EU controller to non-EU controller transfers. Set I: 2001/497/EC: Commission Decision of 15 June 2001 on standard contractual clauses for the transfer of personal data to third countries, under Directive 95/46/EC [2001] OJ L181, 4 July 2001. Set II: Commission Decision of 27 December 2004 amending Decision 2001/497/EC as regards the introduction of an alternative set of standard contractual clauses for the transfer of personal data to third countries [2004] OJ L385, 29 December 2004. A set for EU controller to non-EU processor transfers: 2010/87/EC: Commission Decision of 5 February 2010 on standard contractual clauses for the transfer of personal data to processors established in third countries under Directive 95/46/EC of the European Parliament and of the Council.

[55]   The procedure for BCR is outlined in documents adopted by the Article 29 Working Party, Working Papers 74, 107, 108, 133, 153, 154, 155, available at http://ec.europa.eu/justice/data-protection/international-transfers/binding-corporate-rules/tools/index_en.htm.

[56]   [2012] OJ L215, 11 August 2012.

[57]   [2006] OJ L82, 21 March 2006.

[58]   [2012] OJ L186, 14 July 2012.

[59]   [2010] OJ L195, 27 July 2010.

The GDPR maintains all the basic concepts on data transfers already found in the Directive. The main idea – that transfers can only be undertaken if adequacy exists or companies themselves have taken one of the approved approaches – remains. General principles on transfer have been made more stringent. Transfer may be undertaken pursuant to article 45 when a third country meets the adequacy criteria. Article 45(2) has a much more detailed set of assessment criteria on adequacy which can be broken up into three groups. The first group (a) concerns the rules of law, respect of fundamental rights and a number of other criteria relating to law enforcement and security of data. The second group (b) is about the existence and functioning of a supervisory authority. The third (c) is about international commitments of the third country. An adequacy decision is not the final step as it has to be periodically reviewed and the situation needs to be monitored, and if the country no longer fulfils adequacy criteria, the decision must be repealed. Adequacy decisions already entered into force pursuant to the mechanism found in the Directive remain in force.

Transfers to countries that do not fulfil adequacy criteria can still be made pursuant to article 46 (coinciding with article 26 of the Directive). This can be done through (a) legally binding instruments between public authorities; (b) binding corporate rules; (c) and (d) standard contractual clauses; (e) an approved code of conduct (article 40); and (f) an approved certification mechanism (article 42). BCR are regulated in detail in article 47, which provides that they must be legally binding and expressly provide enforceable rights and which sets a number of minimum elements which they must contain. Adherence to an approved code of conduct or an approved certification mechanism are two new bases for transfer as a valid mechanism for data transfers.

4.2   EU/US Safe Harbour Agreement and CJEU *Schrems* Decision

A separate data transfer regime exists for transfers of data to the United States. The mechanism involved an agreement between the United States and Europe on the basis of which the Commission could make an adequacy decision in 2000. The US and EU data protection regimes differ significantly but the transatlantic trade also depends on free flow of data. In order to bridge the differences and minimize damage to trade, the EU and the United States negotiated a set of principles that enable US companies to comply with the requirements of the Data Protection Directive in a streamlined manner. The principles are based on article 25(1) and (2) of the Data Protection Directive. The significance of the exemption must be seen in light of the volume of data crossing the Atlantic in either direction but also in terms of political events.

The Safe Harbour principles were first agreed in 2000.[60] They are designed to permit the transfer of data to carriers in the United States on the condition that certain standards are respected and that guarantees are given by bodies of the US government which serve as overseers. In order to obtain a Safe Harbour status, an organization can either enter a self-regulatory programme or design one itself. The self-certification is renewable at the Department of Commerce annually. In addition, the Federal Trade Commission or the Department of Transportation acts as overseers. The Safe Harbour regime imposes upon controllers the obligation to inform individuals that their data are held and what the purposes of the collection are. Data subjects are allowed to opt out of uses that fall out of the scope for which they were originally gathered, while the opt-in system is accepted for sensitive information. The data subject must have access to information held about him and the right to amend it. Additional requirements relate to such issues as forwarding of information to third parties or enforcement.

The Safe Harbour regime is enforced both by corporations themselves and by the government. There are, on the other hand, both positive and negative sides to using model clauses and the Safe Harbour regime.[61] The former provides a typical contractual regime, with all its benefits and failings, while the latter benefits from government monitoring.

In 2016, the CJEU *Schrems* judgment[62] invalidated the Safe Harbour agreement, which led to a new round of negotiations and a new agreement concluded in 2016. The case involved an Austrian national, Maximillian Schrems, who had been using the social network Facebook since 2008. European users of Facebook services are required to conclude a contract with Facebook Ireland which, in turn, is owned by Facebook United States. Mr Schrems applied to the Irish data protection authority requesting them to prevent Facebook Ireland's data transfers to Facebook United States, claiming that data protection standards in the latter are inadequate pursuant to Edward Snowden's revelations about the

---

[60] Commission Decision of 26 July 2000 pursuant to Directive 95/46/EC of the European Parliament and of the Council on the adequacy of the protection provided by the safe harbour privacy principles and related frequently asked questions issued by the US Department of Commerce, C(2000)2441) [2000] OJ 215, 25 August 2000.

[61] For more, see Carey, *Data Protection,* note 14 above, p. 122.

[62] C-362/14 *Maximillian Schrems v Data Protection Commissioner, Joined Party Digital Rights Ireland Ltd*, ECLI:EU:C:2015:650, 6 October 2015.

US government's surveillance practices. When the Irish authority refused to accept his claim, he raised a case in court, which in turn, made a reference to the CJEU. Two questions were asked. The formal one was about the distribution of competences between the Commission and the national agencies. The issue here was if the Data Protection Directive prevented a supervisory authority of a Member State from being able to examine the claim of a person when that person contended that the law and practices in force in the *third country* did not ensure an adequate level of protection. The substantive question, however, was about the legality of the Safe Harbour regime and whether US law and practice ensured an adequate level of protection within the meaning of article 25.

In answering the formal question, the CJEU said that national authorities retained full investigative powers. As for the substantive question, after reiterating that there is no agreed definition of an adequate level of protection, the Court moved on to analyse the requirements that article 26(6) imposed on adequacy decisions. This approach was completely different to the one suggested by the Advocate General, who concentrated on the legitimacy of the United States' processing. The Court found that the Safe Harbour Agreement principles only bound US companies but not their public authorities. Another reason discussed was derogations from principles for national security that were introduced without any safeguards. The Court, in conclusion, held that the Commission had not proved that the United States gave an adequate level of protection. The decision has since been subject to numerous comments, official[63] and other.

On 2 February 2016, the EU and the United States agreed on a new framework for data transfers: the EU–US Privacy Shield.[64] The new agreement is meant to address the issues pointed out in the *Schrems* judgment. In that sense, US public authorities accessing data will be subject to conditions, limitations and oversight and European data subjects will have the possibility to raise complaints directly with a dedicated new authority. In addressing the latter, companies would have deadlines to reply, European data authorities could refer complaints to the

---

[63]   Statement of the Article 29 Working Party, Brussels, 16 October 2015. See also Communication from the Commission, *Transfer of Personal Data from the EU to the United States of America under Directive 95/46/EC following the Judgment by the Court of Justice in Case C-362/14 (Schrems)*, COM(2015)566 final (Brussels, 6 November 2015).

[64]   Communication, *Transatlantic Data Flows: Restoring Trust through Strong Safeguards*, COM(2016)117 final (Brussels, 29 February 2016).

Department of Commerce and the Federal Trade Commission, and alternative dispute resolution would be free of charge.

The situation for transfer of passenger data had to be negotiated separately. After the 'September 11' attacks, the United States passed legislation requiring that airlines flying into the United States provide specific information concerning passengers at reservation and check-in time. There were a number of items required, among these names, addresses, dates of birth, nationalities and credit card numbers, referred to as passenger name records (PNR). This information may include private and sensitive data. The US authorities typically demand that PNR be transferred prior to flights taking off for the United States. Non-complying airlines face penalties. Since such data transfers would contravene the Data Protection Directive, a separate agreement was concluded in May 2004.[65] The Parliament objected to the Agreement, claiming that adequate levels of protection were not provided. On 30 May 2004, the CJEU concluded that the transfer of passenger records was a matter of public security and, therefore, outside the scope of the Data Protection Directive. The Court also ruled that the Agreement was illegal, having found that it was based on the wrong legal grounds.[66] In July 2007, the EU and the United States concluded a new agreement (the '2007 Agreement').[67] The new agreement set out requirements concerning the purpose, technology, amount, type, retention, level of protection, access, redress and review. The present regime dates to 2011 and was finally adopted in the Council in 2012.[68]

---

[65] The agreement presently in force is the 2011 Agreement between the United States of America and the European Union on the Use and Transfer of Passenger Name Records to the United States Department of Homeland Security, 2011/0382(NLE) (8 December 2011).

[66] Joined Cases C-317/04 and C-318-04 *European Parliament v. Council of the European Union and Commission of the European Communities* [2006] ECR I-4721.

[67] 2007 Passenger Name Records (PNR) Agreement, Council Decision 2007/551/CFSP/JHA of 23 July 2007 [2007] OJ L204/16, 4 August 2007.

[68] See note 56 above.

5 DATA RETENTION AND *DIGITAL RIGHTS IRELAND* DECISION

The Data Retention Directive was adopted in early 2006[69] with the specific aim of aiding the fight against terrorism and related crime.[70] The Directive mandates the retention of data relating to phone calls and emails for a period of between six months and two years. The data thus gathered is then available to national security authorities. The Directive does not allow retention for any other purpose than those designated nor does it make it available to others than the designated authorities. The Directive also does not demand retention of actual data, only meta information about what was accessed, by whom and at what point in time.

The Directive is a special law in relation to the Data Protection Directive and is related to the E-Privacy Directive and the Framework Directive.[71] The Directive specifically derogates from the E-Privacy Directive according to which data is only retained as long as justified. Article 1 provides that the Directive only applies in respect of communication services and data generated or processed by them. As confirmed in Recital 13, the generated data only refers to communication or the communication service and not to actual content of information communicated. Article 1(2) confirms that data gathered does not relate to actual content. What is retained, therefore, are not copies of data itself but information *about* the data. The data relates to identification of the subscriber or registered user. The Directive applies to traffic and location data for both legal persons and individuals.

The categories of data to be retained are defined in article 5. In general, the data relates to several categories of situations: data necessary to identify the source, the destination, date, time and duration, type of communication and equipment used (whether fixed or mobile). For the Internet and email, the data retained to identify the source is the user ID, the telephone number and the name and address of a subscriber to whom

---

[69] Directive 2006/24/EC of the European Parliament and of the Council of 15 March 2006 on the retention of data generated or processed in communication with the provision of publicly available electronic communications services or of public communication networks and amending Directive 2002/58/EC [2006] OJ L105/54, 13 April 2006.

[70] See Recital 10.

[71] Directive 2002/21/EC of the European Parliament and of the Council of 7 March 2002 on a common regulatory framework for electronic communications networks and services [2002] OJ L108/33, 24 April 2002.

these have been allocated. Article 5(2) specifically prohibits retention of data relating to the content of communication. The period of retention is between six months and two years.[72]

The obligation imposed on the Member States by virtue of article 3 is the retention of data specified in article 5, when this data is generated or processed by public networks. This obligation is in specific derogation of the E-Privacy Directive.[73] The gathering of data does not relate to private networks or to private computers not connected to public networks. This includes the so-called Intranets, which are networks within an organization only available to their own members.

The right of access to data retained in accordance with the provisions of articles 3 and 5 will only be granted to national authorities and even then only in accordance with national law. Each Member State has a right to define the conditions under which this data can be accessed. This right is specifically subject to the European Convention on Human Rights as interpreted by the ECtHR, to international and to EU law, a choice which may lead to disparities between Member States.

Member States are under an obligation to provide supervisory authorities, which may be the same as those required under the Data Protection Directive. These authorities have the task to ensure that the data complies with the requirements of article 7 (which relates to, among other things, quality, integrity and access).

Three important points can be made about the Directive in its present form. First, the Directive is more restrictive than necessary. The European Parliament's Civil Liberties, Justice and Home Affairs (LIBE) Committee recommended that data be retained for up to 12 months only, and be obtainable exclusively upon presentation of a judicial warrant and even then only for crimes that would qualify for an European Arrest Warrant. In this proposal, there would also be compensation for the subjects of the obligation.[74]

The second point is that the Directive is a direct derogation of the important principles relating to security and integrity of information found in the E-Privacy Directive and the Data Protection Directive. The three instruments contain three separate lists of situations under which data may be retained. The derogation in article 6 of the E-Privacy

---

[72] See art. 6.

[73] Specifically, arts. 5, 6 and 9 of that Directive.

[74] See European Parliament, *Report on the Proposal for a Directive of the European Parliament and of the Council on the Retention of Data Processed in Connection with the Provision of Public Electronic Communication Services and amending Directive 2002/58/EC*, A6-0365/2005 (28 November 2005).

Directive says that traffic data must be erased or made anonymous if no longer needed and article 9 states that location data must be made anonymous before processing. Data retention is allowed only in exceptional cases (article 15) for safeguarding national security, defence, public security and prevention, investigation, detection and prosecution of criminal offences or unauthorized use of communications systems. The Data Protection Directive, on the other hand, refers to economic or fiscal interest and regulated professions. These divergent approaches create uncertainty.

The final point is that actual surveillance and extraction of meaningful information, even if the Directive's otherwise questionable legitimacy is accepted, is an expensive and difficult exercise that depends on human resources and adequate technology. Automated data monitoring can help the extraction of such information but meaningful decisions depend on human analysis, which is labour-intensive. Finally, the Directive left the rules regarding the access to data or its use by public authorities to national law-makers.

The Directive's legitimacy had been questioned since its inception. In its judgment of 2 March 2010, the German Supreme Court ruled the German implementation of the Directive to be unconstitutional in its present form.[75] But, the dramatic resolution that culminated in the Directive being declared unlawful came about in a CJEU case from 2014. In *Digital Rights Ireland*,[76] the question referred to the Court was: is the Directive compatible with Articles 7, 8, 11 and 41 of the Charter of Fundamental Rights? In addressing the question, the Court pointed out. first, that the Directive covered 'all persons and all means of electronic communication as well as all traffic data without any differentiation, limitation or exception'. Secondly, the Court noted that there was a general 'absence of limits' in the Directive and an absence of objective criteria by which it was possible to limit national authorities' access to data. Particularly damaging was the absence of 'substantive and procedural conditions' for access of national authorities to data. Finally, the Court pointed out that the minimum and maximum period of retention are not based on the objective criteria. In that sense, the Court concluded, the Directive 'does not lay down clear and precise rules governing the

---

[75] *Vorratsdatenspeicherung* [*Data retention*], judgment of 2 March 2010, 1 BvR256/08, 1 BvR 263/08, 1 BvR 586/08.

[76] C-293/12 and C-594/12 *Digital Rights Ireland Ltd v Minister for Communications and others*; *Kärntner Landesregierung, Michael Seitlinger, Christof Tschohl and others*, ECLI:EU:C:2014:238, 8 April 2014.

extent of the interference'. On the basis of these arguments, the Court annulled the Directive.

Interestingly and somewhat worryingly, a number of national data protection authorities had announced, following the decision, that they did not intend to change their national laws[77] and a new reference was made to the CJEU asking if the ruling in *Digital Rights Ireland* intended to create mandatory requirements of EU law.[78] This reference essentially asked if the conclusion reached in *Digital Rights Ireland* had a wider-reaching impact or was confined to the facts of that case alone. If the former, Member States would be precluded from passing laws that contravene the principles outlined in *Digital Rights Ireland.*

6 E-PRIVACY DIRECTIVE

The Electronic Privacy Directive[79] has been drafted specifically to address the requirements of the new digital technologies, ease the advance of electronic communications services and create favourable market conditions for the digital economy. The development of new technologies should, according to Community drafters, coexist with fundamental rights, of which the most notable is privacy. The Directive complements the Data Protection Directive[80] and applies to all matters which are not specifically covered by that Directive. In particular, the subject of the Directive is the 'right to privacy in the electronic communication sector' and free movement of data, communication equipment and services. While questions concerning the existence of two Directives have regularly been raised, there are currently no plans to join them.[81]

Article 1 delimits the Directive's scope of application. The Directive does not apply to areas falling out of the scope of EU law and it does not

---

[77] And some have passed laws which were considerably more invasive than the original Directive. In the UK, see Investigatory Powers Act 2016 c.25.

[78] C-698/15 *Secretary of State for the Home Department v David Davis, Tom Watson, Peter Brice and Geoffrey Lewis* (not yet decided).

[79] Directive 2002/58/EC of 12 July 2002 of the European Parliament and of the Council concerning the processing of personal data and the protection of privacy in the electronic communications sector [2002] OJ 201/37, 31 July 2002, amended by Directive 2009/136/EC [2009] OJ L337/11, 18 November 2009.

[80] See art. 1.

[81] This is also a consequence of the fact that the E-Privacy Directive was part of the Telecommunications package from 2002 and 2009 and applies both to the *carrier* and the *content* layers.

apply to issues concerning public security and defence, state security and criminal law. As a result, interception of communications of individuals or legal persons is allowed in the cases where state security demands it. At present, such interception is partially covered by various national laws. Importantly, the Directive applies to electronic communications service providers and is a part of the telecommunications framework. This means that its main addressees are not content providers in general but only electronic communications providers in the sense of the telecoms framework.

In spite of its declared compatibility with the Data Protection Directive, the two instruments operate with somewhat different scope. Contrary to the Data Protection Directive, which specifically addresses only individuals, article 1(2) makes it clear that the E-Privacy Directive also protects legal persons' interests. The inclusion of legal persons is an interesting addition. There is no doubt that unsolicited communication, spyware, viruses, and so on, affects corporations and individuals alike and that the cost of such communications to businesses is considerable. On the other hand, the declared aim of the Directive is 'processing of personal data and the protection of privacy', a title distinctly targeting individuals. Recital 12 of the Directive does talk of the 'legitimate interests of legal persons'. These are not defined, but the recital clarifies that Member States will not have an *obligation* to apply the Data Protection Directive to those. It would seem that the Directive does not aim here to fight the more general data protection problems affecting legal persons but rather to protect them in their role as clients of various Internet service providers (ISPs). In other words, the E-Privacy Directive protects ISPs' customers irrespective of the nature of their legal personality.

Article 2 of the E-Privacy Directive adopts the definitions of the Data Protection Directive and the Framework Directive[82] and only introduces definitions that do not feature in these two. Thus, a 'user' is any person who accesses an electronic communications service, and not only a subscriber; 'communication' is any information exchanged electronically; and 'electronic mail' is any text, image or audio which can be stored at the destination until requested.[83] 'Location data' is defined as data

---

[82] Directive 2002/21/EC of the European Parliament and of the Council of 7 March 2002 on a common regulatory framework for electronic communications networks and services [2002] OJ L108/33, 24 April 2002 ('Framework Directive'), as amended by Directive 2009/140/EC [2009] OJ L337, 18 December 2009.

[83] Although not, at this stage, an SMS or another instant message.

indentifying the user's geographical location. 'Communication' is defined as any information exchanged or conveyed between a finite number of parties by means of a publicly available electronic communications service.

The services concerned are described in article 3 somewhat awkwardly as 'processing of personal data in connection with the provision of publicly available electronic communication services in public communication networks'. The definition includes 'data collection and identification devices'. In reality, the aim of such a definition is to include as broad a spectrum of information society service providers as possible as long as personal data is being transferred on their networks and as long as those networks are public. Therefore, anyone who is publicly providing services (not necessarily for remuneration and not necessarily as an ISP) is to be included.

The first general obligation in the Directive is a mandatory obligation to provide security of processing (article 4). The Directive recognizes that information society services (ISS) providers are often not related to network service providers and demands that the two cooperate on providing security. Two factors determine the quality and degree of protection. The first is the risk/threat presented, which is to be understood as real or threatened danger. The second is state of the art of technical solutions needed and their cost. The duty imposed is to ensure, at least, that only authorized persons can access data, that data cannot be destroyed by accident and that a security policy exists. Article 4(2) introduces a general obligation to inform subscribers of the risk of breach and any measures which may be taken. Article 4(3)–(5), added in the 2009 revision, deal with notification procedures in cases of breach.

The second general obligation (article 5) is to maintain the confidentiality of communications. The addressees are Member States, who are required to prohibit listening, tapping, storage or other kinds of interception or surveillance of communication and 'related traffic', unless the users have given their consent or the conditions of article 15(1)[84] have been fulfilled. The confidentiality of communication is not violated by simple caching nor for purposes of providing a proof of the transaction. In reality, it is difficult to keep track of the exact purpose for which the information is stored.

The Directive obliges the providers of services to erase or anonymize the *traffic* data processed when no longer needed, unless conditions in

---

[84] Derogations from the E-Privacy Directive under the conditions set out in the Data Protection Directive.

article 15 have been fulfilled.[85] Retention is allowed for billing purposes but only while the statute of limitation allows the payment to be lawfully pursued. Data may be retained for marketing and value-added services upon the user's prior consent (which may later be withdrawn). Article 6(5) expresses concern that data handling might be outsourced to organizations with low standards outside the EU and restricts the categories of actors who can handle data.

Where data relating to *location* of user or other traffic can be processed, article 9 provides that this will only be permitted if such data is anonymized, where users have given consent or for provision of value-added services. As in the previous case, users must be informed beforehand of the character of information collected and have the option to opt out.

6.1 Cookies

A particular problem concerning the lawfulness of gathered information arises in relation to 'cookies'. Cookies are small pieces of computer code, often no longer than a line, left by a website on the visitor's computer. Cookies have three primary uses: session management, personalization and tracking. They help the website memorize the user's identity and 'steer' his browsing; they 'tailor' the webpage to the needs of individual users; and they gather information about the users' viewing habits. From the viewpoint of those who post the code, cookies are a source of information both of immediate commercial value and a valuable and tradable resource. From the consumers' viewpoint, cookies avoid the need for constant authentication by memorizing the users' preferences.

Cookies do not carry viruses or malware but the risk to privacy they pose arises from their data collecting capacity and the potential to pass this data on to unauthorized persons. Whether cookies are a threat to privacy depends on the amount of privacy-sensitive information they hold and on whether the collector shares the information obtained with others on the Internet. The information held will mostly consist of programming code not comprehensible to an average user. This code may contain sensitive information, such as username and/or password, the collection of which is controlled by the web operator.

---

[85]   See art. 6.

Cookies may be left by the issuer himself or they may be left on behalf of third parties (tracking cookies). In this case, third parties are advertisers who track information about users, such as shopping habits and preferences. What information the cookies store depends on the issuer and user preferences. Some record only the identity of the user's computer but others may contain more sensitive information. The users are able to technically set the browser to accept all, none or only some cookies. Cookies are considered an easy and convenient way for obtaining information about users but may be difficult to manage. First, an average Internet user is not very likely to track the individual cookies stored on the computer. Cookies are easily accessible in most browsers' preferences but need to be looked at and analysed on a case-by-case basis. Secondly, cookies, even if analysed, do not easily reveal what information is being sent back to the service provider.

Where identity information is contained in a cookie, the issuer must comply with data protection legislation contained in the E-Privacy Directive. The Data Protection Directive does not contain special provisions applicable to cookies. The early drafts of the Directive on Privacy and Electronic Communications proposed a ban on the use of cookies without consent. This was a result of the Parliament's fear that customer data is being collected without their knowledge and consent. The threat to consumer privacy was perceived as something that would ultimately undermine consumers' confidence in electronic commerce and seriously damage the prospect of it being at the forefront of development in the EU. The proposed measure, however, would have failed, as most sites today depend on cookies without which basic functionality would have been lost. The later drafts and the final version of the Directive introduced a more flexible opt-out regime: they allow the use of cookies but oblige the issuer to give the final user the opportunity to refuse the storage.[86]

In reality, modern browsers allow different privacy settings and permit the consumers to determine which cookies would be stored, for how long and when. Most consumers would, arguably, use these facilities rather than depend on reading certificates on individual websites. But it is also true that a majority of consumers have poor understanding of the basic technicalities of browser operation.

---

[86] Cf. L. Edwards, 'Articles 6–7, ECD: Privacy and Electronics Communications Directive 2002' in L. Edwards (ed.), *The New Legal Framework for E-Commerce in Europe* (Hart, Oxford, 2005), p. 31, at p. 57.

The 2009 revision of the Directive made changes to article 5(3), which affect information collected from users' computers, including cookies:

> Member States shall ensure that the storing of information, or the gaining of access to information already stored, in the terminal equipment of a subscriber or user is only allowed on condition that the subscriber or user concerned has given his or her consent, having been provided with clear and comprehensive information, in accordance with Directive 95/46/EC, inter alia, about the purposes of the processing.

The addition effectively requires the operators to obtain permission in all cases where information is collected in addition to explaining clearly the purposes and operation of the collection. The solution attracted strong criticism for being practically unworkable or very difficult to achieve. In practice, websites resorted to presenting a simple pop-up to the effect that cookies are used. The Preamble (Recital 66) states that 'where it is technically possible and effective … the user's consent to processing may be expressed by using the appropriate settings of a browser or other application'. Although this almost certainly means that browsers *deliberately* set to accept cookies would satisfy the requirements of article 5(3), problems remain with this solution. First, it leaves important questions to the Recital rather than the main text of the Directive. Secondly, technology, which is capable of reacting more quickly and being more flexible to problems than law, is and will remain a better way of protection against privacy invasion than any regulatory effort in the near future. The article is written in a technology-neutral manner, deliberately not naming any specific technological means which may be used to store data. This leaves it open to future technological developments.

Recital 25 of the Directive helps clarify some of the ambiguities of article 5(3). Among other things, it provides that 'information and the right to refuse may be offered once' but may cover 'any future use'. Practically, this means that the option to opt-in should pop up the first time a webpage is visited but need not reappear again. The general policy of Recital 25 is that cookies should be allowed provided that users are given (a) clear information according to the Data Protection Directive; and (b) the opportunity to reject cookies. The Recital emphasizes the importance of this in cases where third parties may have access to cookies, such as computers in public places (libraries, universities, etc.).

Since article 5(3) is technologically neutral, it covers any other files similar in form and function to cookies. Other files left on the client's computer, with or without their knowledge, can, for example, be the 'keys' that certain credit institutions place on hard drives to enable the users to access Internet banking facilities. Viruses, Trojans, spyware and other similar software left without the user's consent also fall within the principle of lawfulness.

6.2 Spam

The instrument that initially dealt with the protection of personal data in the telecommunications sector was Directive 97/66/EC ('Telecommunications Privacy Directive').[87] It covered such issues as itemized billing or unsolicited calls. The proposal to amend Directive 97/66/EC, ultimately resulting in the E-Privacy Directive, was motivated by the desire to bring it in line with the recent developments in the digital world.

Article 13(1) of the E-Privacy Directive introduced the opt-in regime for email for marketing purposes:[88]

> The use of ... electronic mail for the purposes of direct marketing may be allowed only in respect of subscribers or users who have given their prior consent.

Emails for purposes of direct marketing can be sent only with prior agreement of the recipient. A natural or legal person who initially collected the data has the right to use it for their own commercial purposes, provided the customers have the right to reject such communications, where it was collected either initially or subsequently.[89]

Member States have the obligation to ensure that unsolicited communications, other than those mentioned in article 13(1), are prohibited. There are two exceptions in the 2002 version, either of which the Member States could implement into their legislation at their discretion. The first was situations 'where the consent of the subscribers' had been obtained. The consent required was not 'prior consent'. The second was 'in respect of subscribers who do not wish to receive these communications'. It was unclear in what form this lack of desire was to be expressed and at what point in time. The confusing formulations should be interpreted to mean that the Member States were allowed to choose

---

[87] Directive 97/66/EC of the European Parliament and of the Council of 15 December 1997 concerning the processing of personal data and the protection of privacy in the telecommunications sector [1997] OJ L24/1, 15 December 1997.

[88] The 2002 version of article 13 had 6 sub-articles. The 2009 reform reduced this to two with articles 13(3)–(6) being deleted.

[89] See art. 13(2).

between the opt-in and the opt-out regime. Article 13(1) and (3) apply only to natural persons.

Article 13(2), which applies to both natural and legal persons, allows controllers who have obtained data in the context of a sale of a product or service to use them to market their own products as long as the customers can object to this, included in each email they are sent from the controller. The 2002 version of article 13(5) prohibited communications to which the subscriber cannot respond or which conceals the necessary information.

Article 13(6) allowed information society service providers (ISSPs), as persons having a 'legitimate interest in the cessation or prohibition of such infringements', to bring legal proceedings in respect of the infringements. This measure was intended to enable ISSPs, who have the financial and the legal power, to pursue violations which individual users otherwise would not be interested in.

A particularly sensitive problem is the use of location data – data that can help establish the exact location of the user's mobile device and target marketing to that location (e.g. sending book adverts when the consumer is in a bookstore). Article 9 of the Directive covers such eventuality. The article allows the processing of location data only when processing can be done anonymously or where the user has given consent in advance. Users must be informed, prior to giving their consent, of all the details concerning the processing. The user, in such circumstances, must retain the possibility to opt-out.

The 2009 reform introduced an enforcement mechanism which obliges Member States to introduce civil and criminal sanctions.[90] The Member States retain, in addition to this, the power to order the cessation of any violation.

7   CONCLUSION

There is no doubt that the need to improve the Data Protection Directive, notably in relation to new developments in information technology, new threats to privacy and enforcement issues, has existed for a long time

---

[90]   See art. 15a(1).

now.[91] In the short to medium term, the Commission's aim to concentrate on better enforcement seems both necessary and reasonable.[92]

The new regime, consisting of a General Regulation and a special criminal Directive, goes far in the direction of addressing new technologies and providing better enforcement mechanisms while protecting citizens. At the same time, the reformed E-Privacy Directive successfully supplements the Data Protection Directive while bringing the innovation necessary to cover digital technologies.

On the other hand, a number of uncertainties remain. The sheer size of the new Regulation and the number of new concepts it brings will create uncertainties in the business world for a number of years to come. The important new judgments of *Google Spain*, *Schrems* and *Digital Rights Ireland*, which have already been incorporated in the new Directive, show that the CJEU is ready to intervene in the most contentious issues. Finally, the E-Privacy Directive's awkward sphere of application and the rapid development in localization and advertising technologies prompted calls for its revision, which was expected in late 2016.[93]

Possibly the most controversial aspect of the EU data protection regime is transfer to third states. This is particularly so after the Snowden revelations. At present, it seems clear that the EU has gone further in protecting privacy than the United States, but it is less clear if the new transfer mechanism would satisfy both the public and businesses.[94]

---

[91] European Data Protection Supervisor's Opinion on Data Protection Directive Implementation, 25 July 2007 [2007] OJ C255/1, 27 October 2007.

[92] So much was recognized in the Commission, *Communication on Implementation of Data Protection*, COM(2007)87 final (Brussels, 7 March 2007).

[93] See *EPrivacy Directive: Assessment of Transposition, Effectiveness and Compatibility with Proposed Data Protection Regulation, Final Report*, SMART 2013/0071 (2015), available at https://ec.europa.eu/digital-single-market/news/eprivacy-directive-assessment-transposition-effectiveness-and-compatibility-proposed-data.

[94] Specifically, cf. P. Samuelson, 'Privacy as Intellectual Property' (2000) 52 *Stanford Law Review* 1125.

9. Digital identity and electronic payments

1 IDENTITY AND CYBERSECURITY

Defined strictly, identity is 'the quality or condition of being the same in substance'. In other words, it is the 'condition or fact that a person or thing is itself and not something else'.[1] Digital identity is the quality of sameness as mediated by the Internet. It is the ability of an individual (or legal person) to prove that who they claim to be on the Internet matches who they are in real life. The importance of the quality of identity arises from the desire to treat the Internet as a secure domain. Identity, on the other hand, is also an element of cybersecurity,[2] which, in turn, can be defined as the safety of the Internet as a platform for those who use it. But since the anonymity of the Internet is precisely what attracts the users, securing universally accepted identification is a challenge.

In everyday life, identity is proved in numerous different ways. A good, although not always conclusive proof, comes in the form of a formalized document such as a passport or a national identity card, or a more complex one such as a face-to-face interview often conducted by immigration or passport authorities. Sometimes, presenting documents such as birth certificates, driving licence or utility bills can have the same purpose. What is common to all these forms of identification is that the individual presenting them is usually also present and an assumption is made that the person identified in the documents is also the one presenting them. This is never the case on the Internet where the individual is always absent, thus increasing the need for an approved intermediary to certify the user's identity. Increasingly, proof of identity on the Internet is becoming important for activities ranging from electronic government (e-government services) to commercial transactions.

---

[1] Oxford English Dictionary Online (2016), www.oed.com.
[2] M.C. Rundle and B. Laurie, *Identity Management as a Cybersecurity Case Study*, Berkman Center Research Publication No. 2006-01 (September 2005), available at http://ssrn.com/abstract=881107.

The strictness of the proof of identity is proportional to the sensitivity and importance of the transaction. An e-vote in national elections, for instance, requires conclusive evidence that the individual voting is indeed the individual on the electoral register, whereas registration on an e-commerce site usually only requires a functional email. A purchase of alcoholic beverages, pornography or certain kinds of medicines may only require proof that the individual in question is over 18 years old, without also proving the address or any other information, whereas other kinds of purchases (e.g. subscriptions to media services) may also require a social security/national ID number.

Technical limitations of the Internet as a medium prevented a single identification platform from gaining ground. The methods of proving identity are many.[3] They range from different authentication options operated by businesses or governments (such as government-operated identity schemes or log-in screens on banking websites) or mediated by third parties (such as logging in with a social networking account or a payment service account) to those that also require additional hardware (fingerprint or smart-card readers and iris-scanners attached to clients' computers). What is clear today, after almost two decades of Internet use, is that there is no common platform and that one is not likely to emerge soon. The existence of such a platform would require not only that needs are similar where they are not but also that basic international standards can be adopted where they probably cannot.

At present, proving identity would require a database of records that could be universally consulted. Such a database would have to be managed either by an international body, or by a private corporation or by individual states. The first model is impossible to achieve in reality. The second is possible but sensitive for a number of reasons ranging from security to antitrust. The third model is more easily achievable but suffers from problems of international recognition to which non-electronic documents are also subject. In reality, although individual platforms such as national (electronic identity schemes) or corporate (PayPal, Apple Pay) may work, there is no one efficient way of proving electronic identity today.

Authentication on the Internet can have two distinct aspects. The first concerns authentication of a person or a corporation on the Internet. This aspect relates to situations where an individual or a corporation acting on

---

[3] M.C. Rundle and P. Trevithick, *Interoperability in the New Digital Identity Infrastructure*, Berkman Center Research Publication No. 2006-01 (13 February 2007), available at http://ssrn.com/abstract=962701.

the Internet needs to prove to the other side that they are who they claim to be or need to authenticate a document. Some important aspects of the question have been covered in the EU in the 1999 Electronic Signatures Directive,[4] recently replaced by the 2014 E-Identification and Trust Regulation (eIDAS) Regulation.[5] The second aspect is the simpler and more straightforward question concerning the authentication of one's payments in commercial transactions on the Internet. This is partially covered in the 2009 EU Electronic Money Directive.[6] We will look at these issues in turn.

2 ELECTRONIC IDENTIFICATION, TRUST SERVICES, ELECTRONIC SIGNATURES

When the first Electronic Signatures Directive was drafted in 1999, it was hoped that the regime then introduced would simply complement the classic model of signing contracts in the online world. Instead of signing the contract physically, the parties would do it electronically. A scheme was therefore set up that would enable this. The assumption proved to be faulty; instead of exchanging digitally signed contracts, the parties simply clicked on buttons, thus completely side-stepping the issue.

A new Regulation adopted in 2014 and applicable from 1 July 2016 replaces the 1999 Directive.[7] It maintains the basic concepts behind the Electronic Signatures Directive while now also covering electronic identification and trust services. The main purpose of the Regulation is no longer only to harmonize the regime applying to signatures but also to

---

[4] Directive 1999/93/EC of the European Parliament and of the Council of 13 December 1999 on a Community framework for electronic signatures [2000] OJ L13/12, 19 January 2000.

[5] Regulation (EU) 910/2014 of the European Parliament and of the Council of 23 July 2014 on electronic identification and trust services for electronic transactions in the internal market and repealing Directive 1999/93/EC [2014] OJ L257/73, 28 August 2014.

[6] Directive 2009/110/EC of the European Parliament and of the Council of 16 September 2009 on the taking up, pursuit and prudential supervision of the business of electronic money institutions amending Directives 2005/60/EC and 2006/48/EC and repealing Directive 2000/46/EC [2009] OJ L267/7, 10 October 2009.

[7] On the relationship between the two see J. Dumortier, 'Legal Evidence in a Digital Context: Will Signatures Disappear?' in A. Savin and J. Trzaskowski, *Research Handbook on EU Internet Law* (Edward Elgar Publishing, Cheltenham and Northampton, MA, 2013), p. 3.

ensure that individuals and businesses can use their own national identification schemes, and to create a single market for electronic signatures, electronic seals, time stamp, electronic delivery service and website authentication.[8] In that sense, the Regulation takes over where the Directive left off, but improves upon it significantly. The Commission also passed four implementing decisions on electronic signatures[9] and four on electronic trust services[10] that put some of the ideas in the Regulation into effect.

The Regulation has three parts. The first relates to electronic identification, which is a system for securing access to public sector online services through secure identification of a person. The second relates to trust services, which are services guaranteeing particular qualities of an electronic system. The third part covers the subject area of the old Directive, electronic signatures. After the coming into force of the Regulation, an electronic signature can only be used by a natural person (no longer legal persons) to sign a document. Legal entities are instead supposed to use corporate eSeals that are separately regulated in Section 5.

2.1 Electronic Identification Systems

Article 1(a) defines the Regulation's tasks in this area as laying down 'the conditions under which Member States recognise electronic identification means of natural and legal persons falling under a notified electronic identification scheme of another Member State'. Electronic identification is defined in article 3 as the 'process of using person identification data in electronic form uniquely representing either a natural or legal person, or a natural person representing a legal person'. The Regulation, as per article 2(1), only applies to identification schemes that Member States notify to the EU. The main regulatory idea is mutual recognition and interoperability of eligible schemes under mutual cooperation.

---

[8] See Recitals 4, 5 and 9.
[9] Commission Implementing Decision (EU) 2015/296 of 24 February 2015; Commission Implementing Regulation (EU) 2015/1501 of 8 September 2015; Commission Implementing Regulation (EU) 2015/1502 of 8 September 2015; Commission Implementing Decision (EU) 2015/1984 of 3 November 2015.
[10] Commission Implementing Regulation (EU) 2015/806 of 22 May 2015; Commission Implementing Decision (EU) 2015/1505 of 8 September 2015; Commission Implementing Decision (EU) 2015/1506 of 8 September 2015; Commission Implementing Decision (EU) 2016/650 of 25 April 2016.

Article 6 provides that, when it is necessary to access a public sector body service online, an identification scheme from another Member State will be recognized for such purposes provided that three conditions have been fulfilled. The mutual recognition works only for public sector bodies, not private service providers. A 'public sector body' is defined as a state, regional or local authority, a body governed by public law, or an association or a private entity mandated by at least one of those authorities to provide public services. The conditions are that (a) the scheme must be on the Commission's list; (b) the assurance levels of the identification means is the same as or higher than that which the (foreign) public sector body demands; and (c) the public sector body uses 'assurance level substantial or high in relation to accessing that service online'. An electronic identification scheme is only eligible if all of the eight conditions in article 7 have been met. These conditions are a combination of formal ones (concerning who issued the means and under what conditions) and substantive ones (concerning where the scheme can be used and how). Particularly important is the condition that the scheme must meet one of the assurance levels outlined in article 8.

Article 8 introduces three assurance levels: low, substantive and high. Assurance level 'low' provides only a limited degree of confidence, the purpose of which is to 'decrease the risk of misuse or alteration of the identity'. Assurance level 'substantial' provides a higher degree of confidence 'the purpose of which is to decrease substantially the risk of misuse or alteration of the identity'. Assurance level 'high' provides a higher level of confidence, which is defined in the article as 'prevent[ing] misuse or alteration of the identity'.

Member States have a separate obligation to notify (article 9) as well as obligation to take action in case of security breach (article 10). Liability exists for damage caused intentionally or negligently to natural or legal persons and is ascribed to Member States, the issuing party or the party operating the authentication procedure, depending on the circumstances. Article 12 introduces the obligation of interoperability and for that purpose establishes an interoperability framework.

It is important to remember that the identification scheme only addresses identification at a public sector website in another Member State but not other issues that may be relevant, such as the qualifications of the person accessing the site, their authorization levels, etc. At the same time, the Commission's text does not resolve the practical problem of asking numerous pubic bodies throughout the EU to accept identification schemes from other Member States. This does not seem to be practically possible nor is it necessary. In most cases, all that is required is that a user from another Member State who has a genuine need for a website is not unduly restricted from accessing it: in other words, that they can obtain a local identification scheme as easily as the locals can.

2.2 Trust Services

In order for electronic signatures and other similar services to gain a degree of authority over and above simple copies of written signatures, a state-designated authority needs to be put in charge of issuing and/or overseeing the process. The Directive puts 'trust services' in this role. Trust services[11] can best be defined as assurance services based on a common framework. In other words, these are services that guarantee particular qualities of an electronic system (of which e-signatures are only one part). The Regulation establishes a general legal framework for the use of trust services but emphasizes that only trust services provided to the public and having effect on third parties should be covered. Trust services used within closed systems (i.e. within a corporation) are not covered. The Regulation's task is to enable free movement of trust services and, in particular, those for electronic communications (article 1(b)).

Article 3(16) defines trust services as services provided for remuneration the purpose of which is creation, verification and validation of e-signatures, seals or time stamps, or website authentication or preservation of e-signatures, seals or certificates. Trust services are liable for damage (article 13) but the burden of proof is on the person claiming damages. A supervisory body is established (article 17) with the task of overseeing trust service providers established on the territory of that Member State. Additionally, supervisory bodies of different Member States need to cooperate (article 18).

Section 3 regulates qualified trust services that are defined in a somewhat circular manner as those that meet the requirements imposed in the Regulation. These services have special conditions imposed on them in terms of supervision (article 20); initiation (article 21); Member States' list where they need to be registered (article 22); and can be given an EU Trustmark for qualified services (article 23). A set of detailed conditions has been established in article 24. In that sense, the issuer must verify the identity of the person to whom the certificate is issued but must also fulfil a number of conditions relating to their operation.

---

[11]   On the concept of trust in the Regulation see J. Dumortier and N. Vandezande, 'Trust in the Proposed EU Regulation on Trust Services?' (2012) 28 *Computer Law and Security Review* 571.

2.3   Electronic Signatures

The purpose of electronic signatures is the same as written signatures: they indicate the originator of the document, confirming that the person who claims to have created or signed them indeed did so. The terms 'digital signature' and 'electronic signature' are often taken as being synonyms but, in reality, they may designate different systems. A digital or electronic signature is a digital rendering of an ordinary signature (i.e. a photographic copy) or simply data in electronic form (words typed in the document). A special kind of electronic signature is achieved where a public or private authentication body confirms the identity of the individual using the signature, making such a signature qualified.

There are several approaches to the regulation of digital signatures. The first sets down requirements for the use of a particular technology. Electronic signatures are not recognized as such unless they are rendered in that technology.[12] Under the second approach, electronic signatures are valid in principle, with certain exceptions. Here, electronic signatures may have different impacts based on the strength of the technology used but the choice is left to individual authorities. This approach, which places no restriction on future development of the technology, has been adopted in the United States. Finally, the eIDAS Regulation, just like the Directive before it, combines the two approaches in that it recognizes electronic signatures in principle, but posts guidelines as to what constitutes a reliable technology.[13]

The United Nations proposed the UNCITRAL Model Law on Electronic Signatures in 2001.[14] The Model Law met with success and was adopted relatively widely, being seen as a step forward in facilitating electronic commerce between Member States, where divergent rules and lack of accreditation of certification service providers threatened to create barriers to the use of electronic contracts in business. Article 6 of the UNCITRAL Model Law follows a simple approach to electronic signatures:

> Where the law requires a signature of a person, that requirement is met in relation to a data message if an electronic signature is used that is as reliable

---

[12]   See German law: Informations-und Kommunikationsdienste-Gesetz [Information and Communication Services Act], BT-Drs. 13/7934, 11 June 1997.

[13]   See art. 25 and Recitals 50 and 51.

[14]   This is complementary with the 1996 UNCITRAL Model Law on Electronic Commerce.

as was appropriate for the purpose for which the data message was generated or communicated, in the light of all the circumstances, including any relevant agreement.

An electronic signature is defined in the Regulation as 'data in electronic form which is attached to or logically associated with other data in electronic form and which is used by the signatory to sign'.[15] This definition, which is a simplified version of the one found in the 2001 Model Law, is intended to convey the link between data and the signature used to authenticate it. A signatory is defined in the 2001 Model Law as a 'person that holds signature creation data and acts either on its own behalf or on behalf of the person it represents'. In the Regulation this is simply a person who creates the signature. A certificate in the Regulation is 'electronic attestation which links electronic signature validation data to a natural person and confirms at least the name or the pseudonym of that person'.

The eIDS Regulation makes a distinction between ordinary, advanced and qualified electronic signatures.[16] Article 25 does not set out the requirements for an ordinary electronic signature other than that it has to be electronic. Any signature, therefore, can be recognized as such as the article demands that an electronic signature is not denied legal effectiveness and admissibility as evidence in legal proceedings solely on the ground that it is in electronic form or that it is not based on a qualified certificate. Article 25(2) adds, however, that 'a qualified electronic signature shall have the equivalent legal effect of a handwritten signature'. This does not mean that an ordinary signature will not be recognized as being equivalent to a handwritten one but it does mean that its recognition depends on national law and that national laws must recognize at least qualified signatures. The article further says that if a qualified electronic signature is recognized as such in one Member State then it must be so in all.

Advanced signatures have an additional layer of identification that results from a higher level of certainty that the link between the signatory and the signature is genuine. Advanced signatures have to meet more stringent criteria and are admissible as evidence and, for all purposes, must be taken to play the same role that ordinary hand-written signatures play in administrative and legal proceedings. In order for a signature to be treated as 'advanced' it must be:

---

[15] See art. 3(10).
[16] See arts. 26 and 28.

- uniquely linked to the signatory;
- capable of identifying the signatory;
- created using means that the signatory can maintain under his sole control; and
- linked to the data to which it relates in such a manner that any subsequent change of the data is detectable.

Qualified signatures are, essentially, advanced signatures with an extra layer of protection coming in the form of a qualified authority certifying the signature. Article 32 contains detailed conditions for a qualified electronic signature. Most prominent among these are the requirements that (a) a qualified certificate was used; and (b) that a qualified certificate was issued by a qualified trust service provider. Annex I of the Directive gives criteria for determining a qualified certificate. The *qualified electronic signatures creation devices*, on the other hand, must meet the criteria in Annex II of the Directive.

The Regulation does not define the legal effect that either ordinary or advanced digital signatures have in national law. Recital 49 of the Regulation states that 'it is for national law to define the legal effect of electronic signatures'. The old Directive was even more specific, saying that it was 'without prejudice to the power of a national court to make a ruling regarding conformity with the requirements of this Directive and does not affect national rules regarding the unfettered judicial recital of evidence'. In other words, it left national courts with a free hand in deciding whether to admit evidence based on electronic certificates. The Regulation seems to be on slightly different grounds, since these words have been removed in their entirety. This would suggest that national courts must accept e-signatures and electronic identification provided that they are validly issued, that is – qualified signatures.

The crucial question here is the effect that an electronic signature has in national law. The non-discrimination principles, mentioned above, were also found in the 2001 Model Law, which enabled *any* electronic signature technology to satisfy the technological requirements in article 6(1). Article 6 of the 2001 Model Law provides:

1. Where the law requires a signature of a person, that requirement is met in relation to a data message if an electronic signature is used that is as reliable as was appropriate for the purpose for which the data message was generated or communicated, in the light of all the circumstances, including any relevant agreement.
2. Paragraph 1 applies whether the requirement referred to therein is in the form of an obligation or whether the law simply provides consequences for the absence of a signature.

Article 5(1) of the old Electronic Signatures Directive, following the same lines of argument, provided:

> Member States shall ensure that advanced electronic signatures which are based on a qualified certificate and which are created by a secure-signature-creation device ... satisfy the legal requirements of a signature in relation to data in electronic form in the same manner as a hand-written signature satisfies those requirements in relation to paper-based data.

An important principle – non-discrimination – had been part of the old Directive in article 5(2). That article provided that an electronic signature that otherwise does not satisfy the conditions in the first paragraph will not be denied 'legal effectiveness and admissibility as evidence in legal proceedings' just because it is (a) in electronic form; or (b) not based on a qualified certificate whether issued by a qualified issuer or not; or (c) non created by a secure signature creation device. This can also be seen as an interesting derogation from the requirements of article 5(1) and a silent admission of the difficulty of their satisfaction.

The Regulation has a simpler definition in article 25(2): qualified signatures must be recognized as being equal to handwritten ones. The requirement in article 25(1) that electronic signatures be accepted as evidence seems unnecessary as Member States already all recognize them as such. It will be noted that the requirement that an electronic signature has to fulfil in order to get the status similar to that of a written signature is somewhat different in all the texts. Article 6 of the 2001 Model Law has a flexible solution that expands the number of signatures that can potentially be accorded this status. The Regulation, on the other hand, introduces in article 25 some technical requirements for qualified signatures that need to be fulfilled initially. In the 2001 Model Law, article 6(3), an electronic signature will be considered to be reliable where (a) the signature creation data is linked to the signatory only; (b) the signature creation data were, at the time of signing, under the control of the signatory only; and (c) any alteration to the electronic signature is detectable.

All this has created three tiers of signatures that in everyday life may not be relevant at all. In reality, 'advanced electronic signatures' are not widely accepted and their increased use in the future will depend on market forces. After a number of Member States introduced official and semi-official qualified signatures, the matter seems to have settled itself. On the other hand, the infrastructure (which is meant to make digital signatures widely available and used in daily transactions), still suffers from problems relating to the certification authority's liability, operating standards and security. The technology, although largely in place, is simply too risky both in terms of security and in terms of its openness to litigation.

There is no provision in the Regulation that regulates the conduct of *signatories*. This is an omission, as article 8 of the 2001 Model Law has detailed rules for this area. It provides, among other things, that signatories must exercise reasonable care and notify any person who may rely on the signature that data might have been compromised. Particularly significant here might be the issue of the standard of care that the signatory needs to exercise both in keeping the signature secure and in using it. In the absence of EU regulation, national law will apply.

The 2001 Model Law sets out, in article 9(1), a number of requirements that providers have to fulfil including the consequences they will bear for failing to do so. This includes liability for damage caused by inaccuracies and omissions at the time of issuing and failure to register revocation.[17] In the Regulation, Recital 35 states that all trust service providers are subject to provisions on liability. Article 11 introduces a general regime on liability saying that there exists the liability of the notifying Member State, the party issuing the electronic identification means and the party operating the authentication procedure for failure to comply with the relevant obligations under this Regulation. Liability is applied in accordance with national rules on liability. No national cases exist as yet on the liability of providers. Article 10 of the 2001 Model Law sets out a number of requirements that help determine whether the certification service provider's systems, procedures and human resources are trustworthy. No direct equivalent exists in the Regulation, although some of the other provisions located throughout the Regulation perform the same function. Article 19 also provides for a supervisory body that is responsible for all supervisory tasks.

Trust services offered by trust service providers established in a third state will be deemed to be equivalent to those issued in the EU if third country issuers are recognized in an international agreement.[18]

In addition to electronic signatures, the Regulation also covers electronic seals. Electronic seals are in article 3(25) defined as data in electronic form, which is attached to or logically associated with other data in electronic form to ensure the latter's origin and integrity. Similar to electronic signatures, article 35 provides that an electronic seal will not

---

[17] See UNCITRAL Model Law on Electronic Signatures with Guide to Enactment 2001, art. 9 (United Nations, New York, 2002).
[18] See art. 14.

be denied legal effect and admissibility as evidence solely because it is in an electronic form or that it is not a qualified electronic seal. Electronic seals can be ordinary, advanced and qualified, in a manner similar to electronic signatures. A qualified electronic seal enjoys 'the presumption of integrity of the data and of correctness of the origin of that data to which the qualified electronic seal is linked'. An EU-issued qualified electronic seal must be recognized as such in all Member States. An advanced electronic seal, as per article 36, is one which is uniquely linked to the creator and is capable of identifying him, is created using electronic seal creation data under the creator's control, and is linked to the data so that any subsequent change is detectable. Article 37 separately addresses electronic seals in public services whereas article 38 contains provisions on qualified certificates for electronic seals.

In addition to electronic signatures and electronic seals, the Regulation now also covers electronic time stamps. Article 3(33) defines electronic time stamps as data in electronic form that binds other data in electronic form to a particular time establishing evidence that the latter data existed at that time. The pattern from the previous two sections in repeated. Here too, a stamp is not to be denied legal effect and admissibility as evidence solely because it is electronic (article 41). Here too, there exist separate requirements (article 42). Electronic time stamps have not had a very wide use in the European Union.

Article 3(36) defines electronic registered delivery service as a service that 'makes it possible to transmit data between third parties by electronic means' while providing evidence relating to the handling of the data, such as proof of sending and receiving, and that protects transmitted data against the risk of loss, theft, damage or any unauthorized alterations. The Regulation covers the legal effects of the service (article 43) and requirements for qualified electronic registered delivery services.

Article 3(38) defines certificate for website authentication as an attestation that makes it possible to authenticate a website and links the website to the natural or legal person to whom the certificate is issued. The main purpose of the certificate is to authenticate the website, confirming that it originates with the person or entity claiming it. The practical use of such certificates is relatively small or non-existent as commercial solutions in the shape of trust certificates, rankings and review sites almost entirely cover the needs of the market. The Regulation only introduces the requirements for qualified certificates (article 45 and Annex IV).

In the view of this author, the Regulation will be as insignificant in practice as the Directive had been. The reasons for this are not to be found in the legal sphere. On the contrary, the legal text is both clearer than the 1999 Directive and more comprehensive. The reasons are practical: realities of daily life and commercial solutions have largely removed the need for extra legislation in this area. Digital signatures and digital identification solutions exist and operate without problems in a number of states. Digital signatures have not been widely used for a simple reason – there is no need for them. Digital ID schemes, on the other hand, successfully operate in almost all EU Member States. Cross-border movement of these solutions has not been pointed out as a problem by either businesses or natural persons. Put in simple terms, the Regulation is a solution in search of a problem.

3 ELECTRONIC PAYMENT

The traditional means of payment online for the past two decades has been the use of debit, charge and credit cards, with occasional but rising use of intermediary payment services such as PayPal. The use of means of payment is regulated by various financial and consumer laws, all of which apply also to electronic transactions.[19] The use of such means of payment on the Internet differs little from their use on the telephone, where the transaction is recorded as being conducted with an absent cardholder. The problems of electronic payment can be broken into two big questions. The first question is: what can the regulator do to make using the present payment services (cards, proxies, etc.) safer and more efficient. This question is the subject of finance and consumer laws. The second question is: are there any means of payment that are particularly useful for Internet transactions? In the EU, it was believed in the late 1990s that electronic money was the adequate answer to the second question. E-money, defined usually as a balance held on a card or another instrument, was meant to bring the convenience both to the Internet and the physical world. This never happened[20] but new problems emerged in the meantime, including new payment methods such as Bitcoin. The EU regulation of this area consists of the 2009 E-Money Directive and the Payment Services Directive (2).

Electronic money performs a similar function to a credit card or real money, with the difference that monetary value is stored on the card

---

[19] For issues concerning consumer protection in financial transactions, see Chapter 7.
[20] It is probably not an exaggeration to claim that electronic money is as much a failure as digital signatures are.

itself. The information can normally be read either by specific instruments or by ordinary computers fitted with appropriate readers. For these to be useful in an Internet transaction, a computer would have to be fitted with the appropriate reader. At the beginning of this century this was still a rarity. Today, however, there are a number of devices, notably fingerprint readers or smart-card readers, that are typically found on laptops and, sometimes, on desktop machines. In such a climate, it is easy to envisage a situation where electronic money software is used to store the money and one of the readers is used to authenticate the user. In reality, however, this procedure is not used widely, is nowhere nearly as popular as PayPal or the use of payment cards, and is eclipsed in popularity by emerging technologies such as Bitcoin. A typical user today does not hold a card with a stored value on it but uses a smartphone equipped with a variety of payment systems (such as Apple Pay or Google Wallet).

Electronic money is not restricted to Internet use. On the contrary, it is particularly useful in situations where electronic readers may be widely available, such as in supermarkets, at gas stations, hotels, and so on. The role that electronic money plays on the Internet, however, is directly related to the difficulties, real and perceived, of online payment. Recent surveys show that a large proportion of consumers still feel uncomfortable with making payments online. Some of that fear can be attributed to decreasing safety online, but others are a result of inability or inaccessibility of adequate payment means.

3.1 Electronic Money Directive 2009[21]

The first Electronic Money Directive[22] was drafted at a time when it was widely believed that electronic means of payment would catch up faster than they did. In reality, the majority of consumer transactions on the Internet still use credit cards or electronic payment services such as PayPal. It was felt that the Consolidated Banking Directive,[23] which

---

[21] Directive 2009/110/EC of the European Parliament and of the Council of 16 September 2009 on the taking up, pursuit and prudential supervision of the business of electronic money institutions amending Directives 2005/60/EC and 2006/48/EC and repealing Directive 2000/46/EC [2009] OJ L267/7, 10 October 2009. The Directive entered into force in 2011.

[22] Directive 2000/46/EC of the European Parliament and of the Council of 18 September 2000 on the taking up, pursuit of and prudential supervision of the business of electronic money institutions [2000] OJ L275, 27 October 2000.

[23] Directive 2000/12/EC of the European Parliament and of the Council of 20 March relating to the taking up and pursuit of the business of credit

already allowed electronic money, did not provide an adequate basis for this task.[24] Whereas Recital 4 of the old Directive made clear that the approach adopted was minimum harmonization with the mutual recognition and home country control found in banking and other similar directives, the new Directive (article 12) confirms that the approach now taken is full harmonization.

Article 2(2) defines electronic money as:

> electronically, including magnetically, stored monetary value as represented by a claim on the issuer which is issued on receipt of funds for the purpose of making payment transactions [as defined in the Payment Services Directive (2)] and which is accepted by a natural or legal person other than the electronic money issuer.

Recital 7 confirms that this means 'pre-paid stored value in exchange for funds, which can be used for payment purposes because it is accepted by third persons as a payment'. The aim, as evident from that recital, was to establish a technology-neutral framework that could be used for future products as they were developed.

At present, electronic devices can be understood to be software systems, smart cards or account-based programs.[25] In the first situation, proprietary software is used to store electronic money on the user's hard drive. Such information would normally be encrypted or secured in other ways to ensure that only the user can access it. It is worth remembering that, at the time of drafting, there were actually no successful electronic money products of this sort. The second method involves the use of smart cards that are similar in appearance to credit cards. These seem to have been taken up in limited contexts, although some shops have introduced them, and experiments have been conducted using mobile phones as smart cards. The most typical form of card-based e-money are transport cards (such as, for example, London's Oyster card).

The final method relies on user authentication and is not tied to a specific machine. The user has a registered account with some value

---

institutions [2000] OJ L126/1, 26 May 2000, amended by Directive 2000/28/EC [2000] OJ L275/37, 27 October 2000, see especially point 5 in Annex I.

[24] The problem was that electronic money does not normally constitute deposit-taking activity as deposited funds would be immediately exchanged for surrogate money.

[25] See A. Guadamuz and J. Usher, 'The EC Electronic Money Directive 2000; Electronic Money: The European Regulatory Approach' in L. Edwards (ed.), *The New Legal Framework for E-Commerce in Europe* (Hart, Oxford/ Portland, OR, 2005), p. 173, at p. 176.

stored on it, but authenticates by entering a combination of a password, username and other similar information. By far the most successful system so far is PayPal that has attracted millions of users. The system is simple. The buyer opens a PayPal account and registers and authorizes for use a credit or a debit card. The seller does the same. At the time of transaction, the buyer logs into his PayPal account and authorizes the amount of sale. The seller logs into his and collects the money. It is also possible to preload a certain sum of money or use a credit or debit card. The advantage of the system is in its simplicity. It avoids the complexity and cost of accepting credit and debit cards and gives the option to register different cards with only one account/password combination.

The mentioned issue illustrates the difficulties faced by the drafters in the Commission. On one hand, the Directive proclaims to be technology neutral. On the other, it clearly leans towards smart-card systems that are already out of date. The emerging and controversial Bitcoin, launched in 2009 and widely used in the grey zone of illegal or semi-legal transactions, is an example of this. Bitcoin can best be described as a digital asset and a payment system based on a peer-to-peer technology and a constantly changing value. This decentralized cyber currency does not meet the most basic definition of electronic money of article 2(2).[26] At the same time, other hugely successful electronic money systems have emerged in the developing world.[27] These systems, subject to little or no regulation, are often money-transfer and micro-financing systems rather than traditional e-money.

The Directive applies to electronic money institutions, which means, according to article 2, legal entities which have been granted authorization under Title II to issue electronic money. These requirements, which are in line with the Payment Services Directive (2), relate to prudential supervision and have been made substantially easier to fulfil since the earlier version of the Directive. The Directive explicitly does not apply to monetary value stored on devices or cards which can *only* be used on the issuer's premises.[28] In addition, and according to article 1(5), the Directive does not apply to:

> payment transactions executed by means of any telecommunication, digital or IT device, where the goods or services purchased are delivered to and are to

---

[26] On its status under EU VAT rules, see C-264/14 *Skatteverket v David Hedqvist*, ECLI:EU:C:2015:718, 22 October 2015.

[27] Kenyan M-PESA system has a user base of over 90 per cent of the adult population in Kenya of which over 60 per cent are regular users.

[28] See art. 1(4).

be used through a telecommunication, digital or IT device, provided that the telecommunication, digital or IT operator does not act only as an intermediary between the payment service user and the supplier of the goods and services.

In other words, the Directive does not apply to digital purchases of goods or services used digitally but applies to purchases where the IT equipment is only used as an intermediary, that is, payment is effectuated online but goods are physically delivered.

In order for the payment method to be recognized as electronic money, article 2 provides that it has to be (a) stored electronically or magnetically; (b) represented as a claim on the issuers delivered on the receipt of funds; (c) for the purpose of making payments as defined in the Payment Services Directive (2);and (d) accepted by natural and legal persons other than the issuer. This last point disqualifies various store reward cards (such as those used in supermarkets or chemists) or cards used for paying within corporations (e.g. for meals). Importantly, this would also exclude some digital cash systems used for payment on the Internet where they only operate with a closed number of participating institutions and are therefore more like proprietary cash. Such transactions would still be governed by regular credit laws.

There are some reasons to believe that PayPal does not fall under the provisions of the E-Money Directive.[29] Primarily, the company does not store money in an electronic device but rather uses already existing bank accounts to mediate between the seller and the buyer. More importantly, an account-based organization appears to fall under both the provisions of a traditional credit-taking institution and the provisions of the E-Money Directive. In other words, they appear to be taking deposits within the meaning of the Consolidated Banking Directive.[30] On the other hand, such deposits are not used for investments or for operational costs, taking them out of the scope of provisions applicable to credit institutions.[31] Also, PayPal styles itself as an 'e-money payment service' and is recognized as such in the United Kingdom. The issue remains unresolved but the majority of Member States' legal systems are likely inclined towards recognition of PayPal as electronic money.

---

[29]   For a more detailed discussion, see Guadamuz and Usher, 'The EC Electronic Money Directive 2000', note 25 above, pp. 196–200; and A. Guadamuz, 'PayPal: Legal Implications of a C2C Electronic Payment System' (2004) 20 *Computer Law and Security Report* 1.

[30]   See note 23 above.

[31]   In the United States, the service is explicitly not a bank, as it lacks the all-important charter.

Only credit institutions as defined in article 1(1) may issue electronic money. Such institutions wishing to conduct activities other than issuing electronic money must fall under one or more of the provisions of article 6. Otherwise, for areas out of the scope of this Directive, other EU and national banking provisions will apply to the business of credit institutions.[32]

The Directive introduces a number of specific rules designed to facilitate electronic money transactions. Article 11 provides that electronic money must be redeemable at par value during the period of validity. The initial capital, originally set at not less than €1 million and with own funds amounting to 2 per cent or more of the previous six months' proceedings, has now been lowered to €350,000.[33] The safeguarding requirements of the institutions are regulated in article 7 and serve the purpose of minimizing the risk. Article 9 allows the Member States to waive some of the requirements in a number of exceptional situations.

3.2 Payments Services Directive (2) and Payments Security

The Payment Services Directive (2),[34] just like its 2007 predecessor the Payment Services Directive (1),[35] can be described as an attempt to achieve a single European payments market.[36] Judging the European payments to be fragmented, inefficient and non-competitive, the Commission reviewed the then legislative framework[37] and proposed a new one. The Directive sought to increase competition and market transparency while standardizing providers' rights and obligations. The Directive has importance both for electronic money issues, since it covers the institutions wishing to issue electronic money, and for consumers, since it provides consumer protection in cases of unauthorized payments.

Article 1 establishes rules according to which Member States can distinguish between different categories of payment services providers, including credit institutions, electronic money institutions, giro institutions, payments institutions, the European Central Bank (ECB),

---

[32] See art. 2.
[33] See art. 4.
[34] Directive (EU) 2015/2366 of the European Parliament and of the Council of 25 November 2015 on payment services in the internal market [2015] OJ L337/35, 23 December 2015.
[35] Directive 2007/64/EC [2007] OJ L319, 5 December 2007.
[36] See Recitals 1–3.
[37] See Recitals 3–5.

national central banks or Member States when not acting as public authorities.

The Directive applies to 'payment services provided within the Community' (article 2) but does not apply to a number of specifically listed categories (article 3). This includes a number of transactions involving cash, payments through commercial agents, and others. The Directive does not replace the Electronic Money Directive, which regulates who can issue electronic money and under what conditions.[38] Payment institutions are, therefore, not allowed to issue electronic money but can handle payments where electronic money is used.[39]

Title 2 of the Directive sets out the rules for payment service providers, Title 3 information requirements and transparency conditions, and Title 4 rights and obligations in relation to the provision and use of payment services. Titles 5 and 6 contain transitory and final provisions.

Of particular importance are the Directive's provisions on securing Internet payments. The central point in this is the idea of strong customer authentication. Article 97 on authentication demands that Member States ensure that a payment service provider[40] applies strong customer authentication where the payer accesses its payment account online, initiates an electronic transaction or carries any other action through a remote channel which can imply a risk of fraud or other abuses. The article does not differentiate between regular and mobile payments, seemingly encompassing both. Where the payer initiates the transaction, the payment service provider must initiate strong customer authentication. This is defined in article 4(30) as:

> an authentication based on the use of two or more elements categorised as knowledge (something only the user knows), possession (something only the user possesses) and inherence (something the user is) that are independent, in that the breach of one does not compromise the reliability of the others, and is designed in such a way as to protect the confidentiality of the authentication data.

Payment service providers are under obligation to protect the 'confidentiality and integrity of payment service users' personalised security credentials'.

Although no standards on authentication are part of the Directive itself, article 98 provides that the European Banking Authority shall specify the

---

[38]   See Recital 25.
[39]   See Recital 24.
[40]   A payment service provider is an institution mentioned in art. 1(1).

requirements and the exemptions for authentication, the requirements for security measures and the requirements for common and secure open standards.[41]

---

[41] See EBA, *Final Guidelines on the Security of Internet Payments*, EBA/GL/ 2014/12_Rev1 (19 December 2014).

10. Cybercrime

1 CYBERCRIME IN THE EUROPEAN UNION

Criminal activity on the Web takes many different forms.[1] Identities are stolen, computer systems broken into, software illicitly traded, child pornography peddled, money laundered. Share scams, botnets and key-loggers for hire, hacking, phishing, credit card fraud, espionage and political crime have marked the beginning of this century and ever more sophisticated schemes get invented constantly. The perpetrators are numerous and spread widely over the globe. The cost of this activity is measured in hundreds of billions of dollars[2] and the figures are likely to rise as the numbers of Internet users increase, particularly in the developing world.

This chapter is an outline of some of the issues that have provoked reaction at a European level. There have only been sporadic efforts to regulate criminal issues affecting the Internet in the European Union. The reason is simple: competence in criminal matters still lies mostly with the Member States. In the following sections, we will briefly look at the legal basis for law-making in this area. We will then look at the only comprehensive piece of legislation covering the matter – the Cybercrime Treaty (see section 2 below) – which is a Council of Europe coordinated initiative open to signature by other states. We continue with the past and present EU legislation on network security (section 3) and finish with an overview of legislation on harmful content (section 4).

1.1 Legal Basis

The European Union has limited capacity to legislate in the area of criminal law, which has always been regarded as a symbol of state

---

[1] For an overview of recent issues concerning cybercrime in general see A. Gillespie, *Cybercrime* (Routledge, London/New York, 2016).

[2] Symantec, *Internet Security Threat Report Vol. 21* (Symantec Corporation, Mountain View, CA, 2016), available at www.symantec.threatrepor.com.

sovereignty.[3] Although the EU is primarily a trade organization, it has partial competence to regulate criminal law. This is because crime can be looked at as an obstacle to trade between Member States but also because better cooperation in criminal matters is necessary for a more stable economic and social development.

Both the Maastricht (1993) and the Amsterdam (1999) Treaties introduced changes which affected criminal law to some extent, notably in the field of 'justice and home affairs', but the actual competence to create criminal law was lacking. Approximation of rules in criminal matters was allowed under Article 29 of the Treaty on European Union (TEU).

Article 83(1) of the Treaty on the Functioning of the European Union (TFEU) allows the EU to adopt Directives containing minimum rules defining criminal offences and sanctions. This can only be done for particularly serious crimes with a cross-border dimension, which include:

> terrorism, trafficking in human beings and sexual exploitation of women and children, illicit drug trafficking, illicit arms trafficking, money laundering, corruption, counterfeiting of means of payment, computer crime and organised crime.

The Council may decide that other crimes be added to the list. Another possibility exists in Article 83(2) TFEU in respect of crimes that are normally not 'particularly serious':

> If the approximation of criminal laws and regulations of the Member States proves essential to ensure the effective implementation of a Union policy in an area which has been subject to harmonisation measures, directives may establish minimum rules with regard to the definition of criminal offences and sanctions in the area concerned. Such directives shall be adopted by the same ordinary or special legislative procedure as was followed for the adoption of the harmonisation measures in question, without prejudice to Article 76.

Article 84 further allows promotion and support of actions in Member States, without harmonization measures. EUROJUST, the EU agency for cooperation in criminal matters established in 1999, is entrusted with various coordination tasks.

---

[3] C-176/03 *Commission v Council* [2005] ECR I-7879, where the CJEU held that 'neither criminal law nor the rules of criminal procedure fall within the Community's competence'. On the global approach to regulating cybercrime, see M. Gercke, 'The Slow Wake of a Global Approach against Cybercrime' (2006) 7 *Computer Law Review International* 140.

In recent times, however, a number of developments forced a gradual rethinking of this approach. In *Pupino*,[4] the Court of Justice of the European Union (CJEU) ruled that framework decisions made in the area of criminal law have an effect in national legal systems. In *Commission v Council*,[5] it held that the lack of Community competence in this area does not 'prevent the Community legislature … from taking measures which relate to the criminal law of Member States'. This will be true when taking action as is necessary for the effectiveness of Community law. This means that national criminal law may be used to further a Community policy, but a more direct action to harmonize national law under Article 83 may still be allowed.[6]

Compared to its other IT-related interests, the European Union did relatively little in the area of cybercrime until relatively late in 2001 when two Communications were issued.[7] The Communications were primarily intended to raise awareness of computer security issues but three categories of more recent instruments followed. The first is the noted Council of Europe Convention on Cybercrime ('Cybercrime Treaty') signed in Budapest in 2001.[8] The second can be grouped under a general title of 'computer misuse' and covers a variety of issues of interference with computer systems. This category relates to unsolicited email messages or spam. The final category includes measures for the protection of certain vulnerable groups on the Internet, including women and children.

The Commission published its Cybersecurity strategy in 2013.[9] One of the primary aims of the strategy was to promote the Directive for a common high level of Network and Information Security ('NIS Directive', see section 3 below), which was proposed at the same time. In the

---

4   C-105/03 *Criminal Proceedings against Pupino* [2005] ECR I-5285.

5   C-176/03 *Commission v Council*, note 3 above.

6   Cf. S. Crosby, 'European Criminal Law: Some Introductory Reflections' (2006) 1 *Journal of European Criminal Law* 7. A similar provision existed in Art. III-271 of the proposed 2004 Constitutional Treaty (Treaty establishing a Constitution for Europe).

7   Communication, *Creating a Safer Information Society by Improving the Security of Information Infrastructures and Combating Computer-related Crime*, COM(2000)890 (26 January 2001); and Communication from the Commission, *Network and Information Security: A European Policy Approach*, COM(2001)208 (6 June 2001).

8   Convention on Cybercrime, CETS No. 185.

9   Communication, *A Cybersecurity Strategy of the European Union: An Open, Safe and Secure Cyberspace*, JOIN(2013)1 final (Brussels, 7 February 2013).

NIS Directive proposal,[10] the Commission considered several policy options in the area of cybercrime. Two of the options considered were the 'introduction of comprehensive EU legislation against cybercrime' (policy option 4) and an 'update of the Council of Europe Convention on Cybercrime' (option 5). The Commission was aware of the difficulties which either of these would bring and opted for a more targeted approach instead. Interestingly, referring to option 4, it said that comprehensive law, in its view, would encompass attacks against information systems, financial cybercrime, illegal Internet content, transfer of electronic evidence and jurisdiction rules.

A significant part of EU activity in this area consists in coordinating Member States' efforts. The European Network and Information Security Agency (ENISA) was established in 2004[11] with the object of improving network and information security. The European Cybercrime Centre (EC3) is a EUROPOL body that started operation in January 2013. It is meant as a central hub for intelligence and a body coordinating national efforts in fighting cybercrime.

2   CYBERCRIME TREATY

The Convention on Cybercrime was signed under the patronage of the Council of Europe. Although not an EU instrument, the Convention effectively represents the Community's interests in its field of application.[12] The timing of the Convention coincides with the increased importance of electronic commerce, intellectual property and deeper penetration of fast Internet access and mobile telephony. The perceived borderless nature of the covered offences has prompted an effort on a European level.

The Convention effectively creates an obligation for Member States to introduce the provisions of Chapter II into their substantive law and to enable cooperation in the matters within its subject area.

The Convention has a threefold purpose. First, it defines substantive criminal law (Chapter II, Section 1). This is a harmonizing effort aimed at creating a common base of offences. Secondly, it harmonizes measures

---

[10]   Proposal for a Directive on attacks against information systems, see section 3 below.

[11]   Regulation (EU) 526/2013 [2013] OJ L165/41, 18 June 2013.

[12]   See Commission Staff Working Paper, SEC(2001) 315 (Brussels, 19 February 2001), expressing a desire for a disassociation clause to be inserted, to claim precedence of EU law over the Convention in matters covered in both.

of investigation and criminal proceedings (Chapter II, Section 2). Thirdly, it opens up avenues for international cooperation (Chapter III). These will be analysed in turn.

2.1 Offences

The Convention has a relatively wide scope. The offences are grouped into four categories. The first are breaches of confidentiality, integrity and availability of computer data and systems. These are well-known offences of interference with computer systems that predate the Internet age. The second category includes computer-related offences, such as forgery or fraud. The third category includes offences related to content, primarily child pornography. The final category comprises infringements of copyright and related rights. A Protocol to the Convention, signed in Strasbourg in 2003, adds to these the dissemination, threat or insult by racist and xenophobic material through computer systems and the denial, minimization or approval of genocide.

The first category of offences, those against the integrity of computer systems, covers illegal access.[13] The offence consists of breaking into a system, in whole or in part, without proper permission. Parties may require that the offence is committed by infringing security measures or with the intent of obtaining data or with dishonest intent, or in relation to a computer system that is connected to another system. The Article essentially covers hacking into a computer system. The offence is relatively easily committed on the Internet, which allows several types of connections, from a simple unencrypted connection to a connection with several levels of security. The offence consists of unauthorized access, intention being an optional element. Given the possibility of accidental access this may be too harsh, but is in practice of limited importance, as most computer systems holding data of any value would have such security measures that intent would be a necessary part of the offence anyway.[14]

Article 3 of the Convention introduces the offence of illegal interception. The offence consists of intercepting without right, by technical means, non-public transmission of computer data to, from or within a computer system, including electromagnetic emissions. Dishonest intent, once again, may be added by parties, as may be a connection to another computer system. The offence can also be committed with electronic

---

13   Cybercrime Treaty, Art. 2.
14   The presence of a log-in screen, at least, would leave the potential offender in no doubt.

equipment, provided that the perpetrator was sufficiently sophisticated. In the age of the Internet, the most common form would be unauthorized use of wireless or LAN facilities, but more sophisticated methods may involve reading and extracting data from physical wires or a transmitted non-encrypted signal. This provision has a limited impact on financial fraud targeting individual consumers (such as identity theft or phishing), as fraud is typically committed not by intercepting data but by stealing it in physical form (e.g. paper records) or by illegally obtaining digital data (e.g. by purchasing it). As such, these offences are more effectively covered in other provisions of the Convention or EU law.

Article 4 targets a similar offence of data interference. This involves intentional damaging, deletion, deterioration, alteration or suppression of computer data without right. A party may require that the conduct results in serious harm. The offence involves hacking attacks, the purpose of which is not to obtain access to a system (although most of them will inevitably do) or to intercept data but to *alter* it. A typical Internet example involves hacking into websites to alter their content for the perpetrator's purpose. The presence of Article 4(2) that mentions serious harm serves as recognition that most of the attacks of this type are more akin to vandalism than to criminal behaviour.

Article 5 introduces the offence of system interference, which involves intentional hindering, without right, of functioning of a computer system by the inputting, transmitting, damaging, deleting, deteriorating, altering or suppressing of computer data. This Article largely covers the same subject matter as Article 4. It would seem that the legislator's intent was to distinguish the situation where the purpose of data interference is to *hinder* the functioning of a computer system from the situation that involves only *interference* which does not affect the system. If so, this was unnecessary, as the purpose of the legislation must be to prevent any unauthorized interference, whatever the effect on the system. If interference results in subsequent damage to the system itself that may be taken as an aggravating factor.

Article 6 deals with intentional and unauthorized misuse of devices that can help commit offences mentioned in the previous Articles. The offence can consist in the production, sale, procurement for use, import, distribution or other making available of a device (including a computer program) designed or adapted for the purpose of committing offences in Articles 2–5. Also included are computer passwords, access codes or similar data through which computer systems can be accessed. The possession of the item with the purpose of committing the offences is also criminalized, but a party may put a quantitative limit on items before criminal liability arises. No offence is committed where devices are used

for testing of computer systems' protection.[15] Parties may put a reservation on this Article, with the exception of provision (Article 6(1)(a)(ii))
relating to passwords or access codes.

The Article is underlined by a commendable motive of stopping piracy
on a large scale. Devices, software or access codes for breaking into
commercial systems are widely available on the Internet, often free of
charge. The Article is unambiguous about its target, which is explained in
Article6(1)(a)(i) as comprising devices 'designated or adapted primarily
for the purpose of committing any of the offences'. This leaves a
considerable margin of discretion to national law-makers and to national
judges. A strict interpretation may lead to illegality of a number of
devices that have mixed uses.

Articles 7 and 8 introduce the 'computer-related offences'. Article 7
deals with computer-related forgery, criminalizing intentional and unauthorized input, alteration, deletion or suppression of computer data,
resulting in inauthentic data. The essential element of the offence is the
intent that data be considered or acted upon for legal purposes as if they
were authentic. An intent to defraud or similar dishonest intent may be
additionally required by the party.

This Article covers forgery applied to computers. In reality, an
electronic forgery is not more difficult to commit than an ordinary one.
First, electronic documents are usually not images (either in JPG or PDF
or any other such form) of paper documents, but discreet database entries
that can be transmitted electronically or exported or converted to other
formats. The ability to forge an entry in such a database would depend on
the forger's ability to enter into the system, an offence also subject to
Article 2. A skilled forger would simply illegally enter the system and
change the values in the database.

Article 8 criminalizes computer-related fraud. The offence is committed intentionally and without authorization and involves input, alteration,
deletion or suppression of data or interference with the functioning of a
computer system, in both cases with the fraudulent intent of obtaining an
economic benefit for oneself or another. The offence consists, in other
words, of some or all of the elements of the previous offences, with the
addition of economic motivation. There seems to be some repetition in
this, as most of the offences in Articles 2–7 are normally committed for
obtaining economic benefit.

---

[15] See Art. 6(2).

Article 9, the only content-specific offence, criminalizes child pornography offences. The offence consists of the intentional and unauthorized production, offering, making, distributing, transmitting, procuring or possessing of child pornography. The aggravated nature of the offence is reflected in the criminalization of mere possession, on a computer or on another medium. Child pornography is described as material that visually depicts a minor engaged in sexually explicit conduct or a person appearing to be a minor engaged in sexually explicit conduct or realistic images representing a minor engaged in sexually explicit conduct. A minor is defined as a person less than 18 years of age, although the parties may require a lower age, but not less than 16 years. Parties are free to put a reservation on procuring and possessing as offences and on the definition of 'child pornography' so that it only includes visual depictions of minors engaged in sexually explicit conduct, and not pretend or 'artistic' images.

Article 10 criminalizes certain behaviour relating to infringements of copyright and related rights.[16] The first paragraph of the Article invokes the obligations that parties have undertaken under the Bern Convention,[17] the TRIPS Agreement and the WIPO Copyright Treaty 1996, with the exception of any moral rights. The offences must have been committed wilfully, on a commercial scale and by means of a computer system.

The second paragraph invokes the Rome Convention,[18] the TRIPS Agreement and the WIPO Performances and Phonograms Treaty 1996, with the exception of moral rights, where committed wilfully and on a commercial scale and by means of a computer system. If other effective remedies exist, the parties may reserve the right to impose criminal liability and that party's international obligations remain intact.

Aiding and abetting in committing any of the offences under Articles 2–10 as well as attempting is, under Article 11, also an offence when committed intentionally. An attempt to commit is an offence in the case of Articles 3, 4, 5, 7, 8 and 9(1)(a) and (c) of the Convention.

Corporate liability is established under Article 12. Legal persons are liable for offences committed for their own benefit by a natural person, who acted independently or as part of an organ of a legal person. In the latter case, which is included to ensure that corporations can be held

---

[16]   On the problem of criminal sanctions for copyright violation, see Chapter 6.

[17]   Paris Act of 24 July 1971, revising the Bern Convention for the Protection of Literary and Artistic Works.

[18]   1961 WIPO International Convention for the Protection of Performers, Producers of Phonograms and Broadcasting Organizations.

criminally liable for the actions of directors, managers or other employees, such organ must have a power of representation, or an authority to
take decisions on behalf of the legal person or an authority to exercise
control within the legal person. Article 12(2) emphasizes that liability
exists in cases where the lack of control or supervision over the natural
person has led to the offence. The liability of the corporation in all these
cases can be criminal, civil or administrative and is without prejudice to
the liability of the natural person.

The sanctions for offences in Articles 2–11 must be effective, proportionate and dissuasive and include deprivation of liberty. In the case of
Article 12 (corporations) such sanctions may or may not be criminal but
can in any case be monetary.

2.2 Procedural Measures

Procedural provisions of the Convention establish powers and procedures
for criminal investigations relating to the crimes committed under the
provision of the previous section. Significantly, under Article 14, these
powers and procedures apply not only to criminal offences established in
Articles 2–11, but also to other criminal offences committed by means of
a computer system[19] and to the collection of evidence in an electronic
form.[20] In other words, the Convention's procedural provisions aim to
apply not only to the Convention itself, but to harmonize parties'
procedural law applicable to computer misuse in general.

Article 15 introduces important safeguards for the application of
procedures in Section 2. The powers and procedures of that section are to
be used primarily under the safeguards of domestic law of the party.
Such protection includes human rights and liberties as required under the
1950 European Convention on Human Rights (ECHR), the 1966 UN
Convention on Civil and Political Rights, and other international instruments. The safeguards will include judicial and other independent
supervision grounds justifying application and other limitations of scope
and duration.

The provisions on the scope and the safeguards, contained in Articles
14 and 15, apply to most of Section 2. In fact, most of the Articles
specifically so provide. The exceptions are Articles 20 and 21. Parties are
allowed to place a reservation on the application of Article 20 (real-time
collection of traffic data) so that it will apply only to some offences,

---

[19] Cybercrime Treaty, Art. 14(2)(b).
[20] Article 14(2)(c).

provided that such range is not narrower than that of Article 21 (interception of data).[21] The reservation is understandable, considering the political sensitivity of governmentally sponsored monitoring. A party may also reserve the right not to apply the procedural measures in Articles 20 and 21 to communications within a closed computer system (such as that operated by the military).

Article 16 allows parties to retain computer data, including traffic data, stored by a computer system, especially where that data is vulnerable to loss. Parties are required to pass laws in cases where they make orders to persons to preserve data. In such cases, the maximum duration of data maintenance is 90 days, but is renewable if the parties so wish. Custodians of data may be required to keep such gathering of data confidential. The powers under Article 16 do not depend on the number of service providers involved.[22] Such disclosure of data must involve a sufficient amount to enable identification of service providers.

Article 18 establishes a 'production order'. This order empowers the parties' authorities to request a person to submit computer data, either stored in the computer system itself or in a data storage medium. More significantly, the service provider offering its services in the territory of the state *must* submit subscriber information relating to such services. The importance of the latter provision is reflected in the recent case law in the United States, where the Recording Industry Association of America has successfully requested information held by Internet service providers (ISPs) to facilitate actions against individual file-sharers in copyright infringement cases. The obligation applies not only to ISPs established on the territory of a party but also to any ISP that offers its services in that territory, which significantly enlarges the scope of the provision.

The information that may be requested is referred to as 'subscriber information' and includes: the type of service used, the technical provisions and the period (e.g. ADSL connection); the subscriber's identity and address, contact details and billing and payment information; any other information relating to computer equipment. Such powers are extensive and may force the ISPs to provide more information than is in reality necessary. The order is subject to Articles 14 and 15 and can only be applied to the stipulated criminal offences and under the safeguards. Nevertheless, the scope of such offences is as wide as is the order itself.

---

[21] Article 14(3)(a).
[22] Article 17(1)(a).

It remains to be seen whether the sweeping powers so provided would actually have an impact on combating crime on the Web.

Article 19 introduces the measure of search and seizure of computer data. Either a computer system or a data storage medium may be searched, provided that these are located on the party's territory. This last requirement may turn out to be more elusive than the legislator intended. Is the storage medium located in a contracting party where the business headquarters are in the United States and only a back-up server is physically located in the party? The power under Article 19(1) extends to other computer systems accessible through the primary computer system, provided that both are in the same territory.

The computer data accessed under Article 19(1) and (2) may be seized or secured, copied, rendered inaccessible, removed or its integrity maintained in other ways.[23] Orders may be made to competent persons to make information available to protect data, the search or seizure of which is required.[24]

Jurisdiction is regulated in Article 22. It provides that jurisdiction of national courts over offences in Articles 2–11 will exist where these are committed on their territory, on board a ship flying their flag, on board an aircraft registered under their flag or by one of their nationals, provided that the offence is punishable where it was committed or if the offence is committed outside the jurisdiction of any state. The penultimate provision is problematic. For, if the offence committed by a national of state A in state B is punishable in state B, then surely it is for state B to pursue the matter. If it does not want to or cannot, why would state A show an interest in it, only on the basis of the nationality of the perpetrator? This was recognized and a reservation was allowed to all of the mentioned provisions save for the first one (offence committed on the territory).

A confusing provision on extradition is added in Article 22(3). The paragraph requires the party to establish jurisdiction over the offences referred to in Article 24 (namely Articles 2–11) in cases where the perpetrator is present on its territory but cannot be extradited due to nationality. Apart from being a duplication of Article 24(6), the provision does not make much sense. A party is, according to this, either forced to prosecute or to extradite. If it cannot extradite, because, for example, its Constitution prohibits it from doing so, it must prosecute even where it normally would not.

---

[23]   Article 19(3).
[24]   Article 19(4).

2.3 Data Retention

All EU Member States and all members of the Council of Europe have data protection laws in place.[25] The standard of these laws differs, being stricter in some states while more lax in others. EU data protection laws introduce minimum harmonization in this area. But the operation of these laws is not smooth. The problem of data retention arises out of at least three sources. The first can tentatively be called political: Internet users, whether private or corporate, are wary of any attempts to monitor their activity on the Internet. They are protected with constitutional guarantees of privacy and they see the data retention efforts as an infringement on it. Secondly, the political appetite in the Member States for demanding data retention grows, as they face increasing security problems. Finally, even if one agrees with the statement that data retention is necessary and useful in combating crime (which is at this stage still uncertain), one is faced with the problem of the quality of large amounts of data that cannot be analysed without using significant human and financial resources.[26]

Data retention is covered in two separate Articles in Section 2 of the Cybercrime Convention. Article 20 sanctions real-time collection of traffic data. The Article empowers the parties' authorities to collect or technologically record traffic data in real time, on its territory and transmitted by means of a computer system. It also authorizes parties to compel a service provider to do the same or to cooperate and assist the authorities in collecting data. Provision exists in the second paragraph of the Article, where a party cannot, due to its domestic legal system, comply with the first paragraph, to adopt other measures it can to ensure real-time collection through technological means. The service providers are, under Article 20(3), obliged to keep confidential the fact that any collection is taking place.

Article 21 applies to the interception of content data. Structurally, it is the same as Article 20. It applies only to a range of serious offences to be determined by domestic law. It enables national authorities to collect or record through technological means, content data in real time, on its territory and transmitted by means of a computer system. It may also compel the service provider to collect or record data or to cooperate and assist in its collection.

---

[25] On the data protection regime in the EU in connection with the Internet, see Chapter 8.

[26] On problems of surveillance in general, see S. Singh *et al.*, 'Technology Surveillance' in D. Campbell, *Legal Issues in the Global Information Society* (Oceana TM/OUP, New York, 2005), p. 87.

In 2006, the Commission adopted the (now repealed) Data Retention Directive.[27] The Directive harmonized Member States' laws concerning the obligations of public providers of electronic communication services in respect of the retention of data and was inextricably linked with the Data Protection Directive.[28] Article 13 of the Directive deals with remedies, liabilities and penalties. It provides that Member States must take measures to implement Chapter III of the Data Protection Directive and provide sanctions in respect of data processed under that Directive. In particular, the Directive criminalized the intentional access to or transfer of data retained in accordance with the Directive that was not permitted under national law adopted pursuant to the Directive. Such transfer was punishable by penalties, including administrative or criminal, that were 'effective, proportionate and dissuasive'.

2.4 International Cooperation

International cooperation is established in Article 23 of the Cybercrime Treaty, which simply states that the parties should cooperate in criminal matters applicable to the Internet in all possible ways.

Importantly, Article 24 introduces the possibility of extradition of offenders. Such extradition is possible in respect of offences set out in Articles 2–11, provided that they are punishable by the laws of both parties and would result in deprivation of liberty for a maximum period of at least a year or more. Where a different minimum penalty applies, the minimum is to be taken as a basis. The Convention will serve as a legal basis for extradition even where a treaty normally does not exist between the parties.[29]

Article 25 speaks of mutual assistance in matters that the Treaty covers. One form of such assistance is the spontaneous provision of information.[30] Another form is a request for assistance either where agreements exist or where they are absent.[31]

---

[27] Directive 2006/24/EC of the European Parliament and of the Council of 15 March 2006 on the retention of data generated or processed in communication with the provision of publicly available electronic communications services or of public communication networks and amending Directive 2002/58/EC [2006] OJ L105/54, 13 April 2006.

[28] For more details on its operation, see Chapter 8.

[29] Cybercrime Treaty, Art. 24(3).

[30] Article 26.

[31] Article 27.

2.5 Analysis

The Cybercrime Treaty, in spite of the positive elements that it brings by encouraging a global fight against digital crime, can be criticized on several grounds. Some of the activities it criminalized continue to be condemned by civil liberties groups. It places a massive surveillance apparatus in force, criminalizes a host of activities that were hitherto not deemed to be harmful and imposes rigid standards on a still-developing medium.

As an example, the Treaty makes it a crime to create, download or post on a website any computer program that is 'designed or adapted' primarily to gain access to a computer system without permission. Also banned is software designed to interfere with the 'functioning of a computer system' by deleting or altering data.[32] A number of computer programs that fit the latter description also have a harmless use that is limited by criminalizing their creation or adaptation.

Secondly, it allows governments to order the encryption keys to be revealed.[33] In some states, such the United States, the constitutional provisions on self-incrimination may prevent the correct implementation of this provision. It also allows authorities to order the passphrase for an encryption key to be revealed.

Also worrying is the requirement imposed on ISPs in Articles 16, 17, 20 and 21 to collect information about their users, a rule that would potentially limit anonymous use and that may be in conflict with article 15 of the E-Commerce Directive (2000/31/EC) as well as with the CJEU's case law on this matter.

Finally, the requirements imposed in Chapter III would force governments to help enforce the criminal laws of other Member States, even if those were vastly different or, in their view, unjustified. In cases concerning speech that is protected in state A but illegal in state B, this leads to a serious curtailment of acquired Internet rights. Doubts remain about whether this mode of enforcement is a good use of limited financial and human resources.

---

[32] Article 6.
[33] Article 18.

3 ATTACKS AGAINST INFORMATION SYSTEMS

3.1 Directive on Attacks Against Information Systems

The Framework Decision on Attacks Against Information Systems,[34] adopted in 2005, was intended to address certain forms of criminal activity against information systems.[35] It was replaced in 2013 with a more detailed Directive covering the same scope.[36] In an early proposal for revision of the Framework Decision,[37] the Commission revisited some of the unanswered questions. The desire was primarily to address the new forms of attacks against information systems, such as large-scale attacks. The Directive retains the provisions of the Decision but adds new substantive elements.

The specific aim of the Directive is harmonization of the criminal law relating to information systems in the EU. This is part of a more general objective of achieving an area of freedom, security and justice that has been highlighted in the Tampere European Council in 1999 and in the Lisbon European Council of 2000. The lack of harmonized law was perceived as an obstacle to achieving a proper Community cooperation in criminal matters. The Directive is intended to be consistent with the Cybercrime Treaty although its purpose, however, is not to duplicate but to build upon the work done there.

'Information systems' are defined in article 2 as any device which performs automatic processing of computer data, and the computer data stored, processed, recovered or transmitted by them for the purposes of their operation, use, protection and maintenance. The Directive makes four categories of crime against information systems punishable (articles 3–6); covers tools for committing criminal offences (article 7); and criminalizes incitement, aiding and abetting (article 8).

---

[34] Council Framework Decision 2005/222/JHA of 24 February 2005 on attacks against information systems [2005] OJ L69, 16 March 2005. The legal basis was found in Arts. 29, 30(a), 31 and 34(2)(b) TEU.

[35] The Framework Decision was binding on the Member States as to the result to be achieved but left the choice of form and methods to the national authorities.

[36] Directive 2013/40/EU of the European Parliament and of the Council of 12 August 2013 on attacks against information systems [2013] OJ L218/8, 14 August 2013. This is different from NIS Directive, see note 45 below.

[37] Proposal for a Directive of the European Parliament and of the Council on attacks against information systems and repealing Council Framework Decision 2005/222/JHA, COM(2010)517 (30 September 2010).

The first category (article 2) consists of illegal access to information systems. This comprises a variety of attacks colloquially referred to as hacking. The offence consists of accessing intentionally and without right the whole or any part of an information system. The offence must not be minor. The offence exists when a security measure is breached. The convenience of this measure consists in its flexibility. It comprises not only cases where a person has logged into a computer system with real or false credentials and without authorization, but also all attacks having a further aim which necessarily consists of illegally accessing the system. For instance, in order to send thousands of unsolicited email messages, a perpetrator may use its own resources. More likely, however, an unguarded or poorly secured system will be found which will then be used as a base for launching the attacks. An even more efficient effort would consist of planting a bot, a small piece of computer code that would then hijack the victim's computer and, in turn, start sending email messages on behalf of the perpetrator.

The second offence[38] consists of illegal system interference. It consists of the intentional serious hindering or interruption of the functioning of an information system by transmitting, damaging, deleting, deteriorating, altering or suppressing or rendering inaccessible computer data. As in the previous article, minor offences are excluded. This offence is more flexible than the previous one, as it does not require unauthorized access to the system. This is important as persons otherwise authorized to use the system but misusing it on a particular occasion often commit this crime. The most notorious form of system interference is the denial-of-service attack. To put it simply, this is an attempt to make computer resources unavailable to users. It is usually performed by forcing the victim computer to waste all its resources on the attacker, thus making it unable to respond to users' requests. Other forms that fall under this provision are various kinds of virus attacks. A computer virus in a general sense is any piece of computer code that can copy itself without the user's knowledge. This need not be malicious but nearly always dominates valuable computer resources. A virus often installs malicious code, which in turn, may have various purposes, ranging from simply damaging the user's computer to extracting valuable data (bank and credit card accounts, email addresses, etc.).

Article 5 of the Directive criminalizes illegal data interference. The offence consists of intentional deletion, damaging, deterioration, alteration or suppression of computer data on an information system. The

---

[38]   See art. 4.

difference between this offence and the previous one would appear to be in the purpose. Article 4 covers offences intended against computer systems affected through tampering with data. Article 5, on the other hand, targets attacks against data itself. Much that was said for the previous articles can be repeated here. In fact, it would appear that most cyber-related criminal activities fall under several or even all of the articles mentioned in the Directive. This is not surprising, as much of cybercrime today requires access to or interference with the system and access to data. The two are rarely separable.

Article 6 criminalizes illegal interception that is catching 'by technical means, non-public transmissions of computer data to, from or within an information system, including electromagnetic emissions'. It is punishable when done intentionally and without right and at least in cases which are considered not to be minor.

Article 7 covers intentional production, sale, procurement for use, import, distribution or otherwise making available of tools used for committing offences. The list of tools is a closed one and comprises computer programs 'designed or adapted primarily for the purpose of committing any of the offences' and 'password, access code, or similar data by which the whole or any part of an information system is capable of being accessed'.

Instigating, aiding and abetting is punishable as the criminal offence itself as are attempted offences. Member States are obliged, under article 10, to introduce 'effective, proportional and dissuasive penalties'. In particular, the offences in articles 3–7 must be punishable by criminal penalties of a maximum of at least two years' imprisonment. This is a sensible policy intended to send a clear message about the seriousness with which cybercrime is viewed in the EU. A special case is created for the offences referred to in articles 4 and 5. These should be punishable by criminal penalties of a maximum of at least three years' imprisonment when committed intentionally and through the use of a tool designed to attack a significant number of systems. If the offences in articles 4 and 5 have been committed within the framework of a criminal organization, cause serious damage or affect critical infrastructure, the maximum sentence is at least five years' imprisonment.[39]

An important measure is article 10, which allows legal persons to be prosecuted for crimes under articles 3–8, where they are committed for their benefit by any person who acts either individually or as part of an

---

[39] The definition of a criminal organization was provided in Framework Decision 2008/841/JHA [2008] OJ L300/42, 11 November 2008.

organ and having a leading position as defined in the article. This may be based on a power of representation, authority to take decisions on behalf of the legal person or an authority to exercise control. Liability is also ensured in cases of lack of supervision or control that lead to the committing of the offence. Finally, liability of a legal person itself does not exclude liability of a natural person as a perpetrator, instigator or accessory in the commission.

The penalties for legal persons[40] include criminal or non-criminal fines and other penalties, for example, exclusion from entitlement of public benefit or aid, disqualification from practice, judicial supervision or judicial winding-up.

Jurisdiction for offences committed by Internet use is a contentious issue. In the Directive, jurisdiction for prosecuting crimes exists, under article 12(a), where the offence has been committed wholly or partially on the territory of a Member State; or (b) by one of its nationals. In relation to offences committed on the territory of a Member State, it is enough that the perpetrator is physically located there, irrespective of the actual location of the computer system against which the activity is directed. Likewise, this includes cases where the information system is on its territory but the perpetrator is not.[41]

It should also be clear that a single offence can affect several Member States. For instance, interference with a computer system in country A where data is also affected in countries B and C. On the Internet, this is particularly true of websites/services that typically have a presence in more than one Member State. Likewise, there may be several perpetrators independently targeting the same Internet service, in which case there will be several offences for each event.[42]

Article 10(4) of the former Framework Decision had special provision for cases where more than one state was interested in prosecution.[43] It provided that, where an offence fell within the jurisdiction of more than one Member State and when any of the states concerned could validly prosecute on the basis of the same facts, the Member States concerned would cooperate in order to decide which of them would prosecute the offenders with the aim, if possible, of centralizing proceedings in a single Member State. Member States could avail themselves of any mechanism or body in the EU that would facilitate these aims. A sequence was

---

[40] See art. 11.

[41] See art. 12(2).

[42] Typical examples are concerted attacks, such as denial of service, by hacker groups.

[43] These had not been replicated in the Directive.

suggested (not imposed) that the Member States might follow in deciding which of them would prosecute the perpetrator. The first in line, according to the sequence, was the Member State where the offence was committed. The second was the state of which the perpetrator was a national. The final one was the state in which the perpetrator had been found.

The Directive aims in article 13 to kick-start the 'existing network of operational points of contact'. A General Secretariat and the Council are established as the main bodies for exchanging information regarding information systems crime.

There are some obvious problems with the Directive. The first concerns article 4 and illegal system interference. The article does not differentiate between serious crimes, such as persistent denial-of-service attacks arranged by organized crime with the aim of, for example, extorting money, and attacks arranged by individuals for political purposes. The first is normally malign and violent, the second often peaceful and short-lived. Political campaigning on the Internet is as old as the network itself. It is undeniable that a number of attacks by various political groups can be disruptive, even damaging. It is also undeniable that some of them are harmful and expensive to rectify. On the other hand, it is not clear why some of the milder protests in this group would not benefit from constitutional protection of free speech when their 'real-world' counterparts do.

Another apparent problem is the broadness of definition in article 3. Unauthorized access is normally regarded as hacking which, in turn, has a relatively precise definition. It involves unauthorized access to a protected system, which, in turn, is defined by standards of a reasonably skilled hacker. The Directive, however, refers to 'illegal access'. This includes unauthorized access to what is otherwise an open system. The exclusion of minor offences does not help here in the absence of a proper definition. Neither does article 3(2), a measure that is nearer reality.

There are also differences between the Cybercrime Treaty and the Directive. Article 2 of the Cybercrime Treaty, at the parties' option, criminalizes access by infringing security measures only when this is done with the intention of obtaining data or in the case of a networked computer system. No such requirement exists in the Directive. The latter seems a more sensible solution at first, as the intention of obtaining data may indeed not form part of a serious offence or the offence may not be directed towards a network. On the other hand, the difference may be important for situations involving free speech.[44]

3.2 Directive on Security of Network and Information Systems

The EU Directive on Security of Network and Information Systems ('NIS Directive' or 'Cybersecurity Directive')[45] was proposed in 2013 as part of the Cybersecurity strategy with the main purpose of increasing cooperation between Member States on cybersecurity issues. The Directive obliges companies in critical sectors as well as some online businesses to satisfy certain security obligations. The aims of the Directive are set out in article 1(2) as: (a) obliging Member States to adopt a national strategy on network and information systems; (b) creating a Cooperation Group in order to facilitate cooperation between Member States; (c) improving operational cooperation by creating a Computer Security Incident Response Teams (CSIRTs) network; (d) establishing security and notification requirements for operators and providers; and (e) obliging Member States to establish designated authorities and points of contact.

The Directive does not prejudice the application of the Child Pornography Directive (see below),[46] nor the Cybercrime Treaty, which is not surprising since the aim is to increase cooperation, not to harmonize substantive law. The Directive does not prejudice national laws on security (article 1(6)) nor other EU special laws requiring information security (article 1(7)). The Directive also does not prejudice EU data protection rules. Article 3 allows Member States to adopt higher standards since the NIS Directive involves only minimum harmonization.

'Network and information systems' are defined in article 4 as electronic communication networks within the meaning of the Telecoms Framework Directive (2002/21/EC) or simply as 'any device or group of inter-connected or related devices, one or more of which, pursuant to a program, perform automatic processing of digital data' or digital data stored, processed, retrieved or transmitted by such entities. Their security

---

[44] On the differences between the former Framework Decision and the Cybercrime Treaty, see A. Flanagan, 'The Law and Computer Crime: Reading the Script of Reform' (2005) 13 *International Journal of Law and Information Technology* 98.

[45] Directive 2016/1148/EU of the European Parliament and of the Council concerning measures for a high common level of security of Network and Information Systems across the Union [2016] OJ C218/1, 16 June 2016.

[46] See art. 1(4).

means the ability to resist any action that might compromise them. 'Operators of essential services' are defined in Annex II as those belonging to the energy, transport, banking, financial market, health, water supply and digital infrastructure sectors. 'Digital services' include online marketplaces, online search engines and cloud computing services. Member States are obliged to identify the operators to which the Directive applies for each sector in Annex II. The Member States do not have to identify all services but only those that are essential for societal and economic interests and where incidents would have significant disruptive effects. The significance of the disruptive effect is measured according to criteria set out in article 6. These include the number of users affected, the relative importance of the service, the relative impact of societal and economic interests, market share, geographic spread, etc.

Chapter II regulates national frameworks on security. Article 7 obliges each Member State to adopt a national strategy on security. The security must address a number of issues which are specifically listed in the article. Article 8 obliges Member States to designate national authorities and points of contact. Their task is to monitor compliance with the Directive. Additionally, Computer Security Incident Response teams (CSIRTs) are formed (article 9) with the task of risk and incident handling in (at least) the sectors defined in Annex II and services in Annex III. Finally, a duty of cooperation between authorities at national level is also imposed (article 10).

Cooperation between Member States in the subject of Chapter III. To this effect, a Cooperation Group is formed (article 11), consisting of representatives of the Member States, the Commission and ENISA. The Cooperation Group's tasks are clearly outlined in the article and include, among others, providing intelligence for response teams, exchanging information and best practices, etc. Article 12 establishes a national CSIRTs network, the main task of which is to provide coordinated responses to incidents.

Both the operators of essential facilities (article 14) and digital service providers (article 16) have special security obligations concerning security requirements and incident notification under the Directive.

It is difficult to assess at this stage if the Directive will bring significant improvements to fighting cybercrime in the EU. The effectiveness of any strategy designed to fight cybercrime usually depends on the existence of highly skilled and trained teams at all levels, from corporate to national. The coordinating efforts which the NIS Directive brings may have some impact on the work of these but it is not clear at the present moment if they will materially stimulate their formation or operation. It seems clear, at least, that the Directive will force the traditionally secretive organizations such as banks to notify and cooperate on data breaches. While such demands may increase costs for the subjects involved, it will also add to the overall security.

4 HARMFUL CONTENT

The criminal regulation of harmful content in the EU is limited. The Community regularly drafts 'safer Internet' programmes. The latest is the Safer Internet Action Programme 2009–2013.[47] It promotes safer use of the Internet and emphasizes the distinction between illegal and harmful content. It has four aims: to increase public awareness; to fight against illegal and harmful content; to promote a safer online environment; and, finally, to establish a knowledge base. The new programme includes emerging online technologies and specifically addresses certain categories of harmful conduct (grooming and cyber-bullying).

According to the programme, national authorities, such as the police, must deal with the illegal content but the industry should have the ability to introduce self-regulation schemes, such as codes of conduct and hotlines, in particular in the areas of reducing child pornography, racism and anti-Semitism. Harmful content, on the other hand, should be allowed but should have a restricted circulation, such as rated movies or adult magazines, including content that is offensive to certain categories of people but not to others. The latter category is specifically linked to freedom of speech in the document and includes various forms of hate speech.

The financial resources allocated are limited. The budget of the action plan was €25 million, which is adequate for the aim of promoting a safer Internet but not for establishing effective protection. Although activities such as police cooperation are funded under different arrangements, it is significant that a separate funding project does not exist in the EU for combating cybercrime.

4.1 Obscenity

Pornography is not always the subject of regulation. Although trading or even possession is illegal in a number of countries in the world, in others it is allowed and in some it forms a significant contribution to the gross

---

[47] See Decision 1351/2008/EC of 16 December 2008 establishing a multi-annual Community programme on protecting children using the Internet and other communication technologies [2008] OJ L348/118, 24 December 2008.

domestic product. Regular pornography as content traded on the Internet is not regulated in the EU. The subject of this section is only child pornography, which gained the special attention of EU and other legislators.

There are a number of EU measures directed at preventing the sexual exploitation of children. The European Police Office (Europol) was established in 1995[48] and a joint action (as amended) was drafted as an extension to it and to combat trafficking in human beings and the sexual exploitation of children.[49] According to it, the Member States undertook to review their laws in view of eliminating sexual exploitation by use of coercion, violence, deceit or abuse of authority, trafficking, and the sexual exploitation and trafficking of children. Member States have the obligation to classify the offences as criminal and to punish them effectively. Although the joint action does not specifically apply to the Internet, its general scope ensures that providing child pornography on the Internet is criminally punishable.

The Directive on preventing and combating trafficking in human beings ('Human Trafficking Directive') was adopted in 2011.[50] It replaces Framework Decision 2002/629/JHA[51] with a wider instrument achieving better harmonization at EU level. The new Directive introduces criminal provisions, including a common definition of the crime, aggravating circumstances and different, higher, penalties. Article 1 emphasizes the gender perspective, recognizing the nature of the victims. Furthermore, it includes provisions on prosecution of offenders extraterritorially for crimes committed outside the EU. Special sections protect the victims, in particular, the vulnerable, and introduce provisions

---

    [48]   Council Act of 26 July 1995 drawing up the Convention on the establishment of a European Police Office (Europol Convention) [1995] OJ C316, 27 November 1995.

    [49]   Joint Action 97/154/JHA of 24 February 1997 adopted by the Council on the basis of Article K.3 of the Treaty on European Union concerning action to combat trafficking in human beings and sexual exploitation of children [1997] OJ L63, 4 March 1997. Amended by Council Framework Decision 2002/629/JHA of 19 July 2002 concerning trafficking in human beings [2002] OJ L203, 1 August 2002.

    [50]   Directive 2011/36/EU of the European Parliament and of the Council of 5 April 2011 on preventing and combating trafficking in human beings and protecting its victims, and replacing Council Framework Decision 2002/629/JHA [2011] OJ L101/1, 15 April 2011.

    [51]   Council Framework Decision 2002/629/JHA of 19 July 2002 on combating trafficking in human beings [2002] OJ L203, 1 August 2002.

for victim support. Finally, preventive and monitoring mechanisms are introduced.

4.2   Child Pornography

The early regulation took place through a Council Decision to combat child pornography,[52] which addressed Member States and required them to take steps in several areas. First, they were to encourage Internet users to inform law enforcement authorities in cases where they suspected that child pornography material was being distributed on the Internet.[53] Secondly, they were to make sure that offences were investigated and punished.[54] To this end, they were to set up specialized units within the law enforcement authorities. Finally, they were to make sure that the law enforcement authorities reacted rapidly upon receiving information on alleged cases of the production, processing, distribution and possession of child pornography.[55] The Decision then envisaged wide and fast cooperation between Member States, who should set up points of contact, cooperate both between themselves and with Europol and 'engage in constructive dialogue' with the industry. Of special interest is the important article 4, which obliges Member States to:

> verify whether technological developments require, in order to maintain the efficiency of the fight against child pornography on the Internet, changes to criminal procedural law, while respecting the fundamental principles thereof and, where necessary, shall initiate appropriate new legislation to that end.

Effectively, this obliges Member States to review their criminal procedures to make sure that they are keeping up with developments in technology. This refers to new methods of investigation, special police task forces and gathering and presentation of evidence. In fact, a number of Member States are reporting that they are overwhelmed by the effort required and stated that police investigation of this area is still in its infancy. Member States then have to cooperate with the industry to produce filters and to ease the detection and prevent the distribution of child pornography.

---

[52]   Council Decision of 29 May 2000 to combat child pornography on the Internet [2000] OJ L138, 9 June 2000.
[53]   See art. 1(1).
[54]   See art. 1(2).
[55]   See art. 1(3).

A general Framework Decision was adopted to harmonize the laws of the Member States (i.e. set the minimum standards) in matters concerning the sexual exploitation of children and child pornography,[56] which was replaced by the 2011 Child Pornography Directive.[57] The new Directive criminalizes serious forms of child sexual abuse and exploitation and increases penalties. Further, it introduces aggravating circumstances and deals with jurisdiction and extradition. Conduct that is punishable as 'an offence concerning sexual exploitation of children' (whether undertaken by means of a computer system or not) includes the production of child pornography; the distribution, dissemination or transmission of child pornography; offering or otherwise making child pornography available; and the acquisition and possession of child pornography. Importantly, the Directive recognizes criminal and civil liability for legal persons, which supplements that of the liability of natural persons. A legal person is made liable if the infringement is committed on its behalf by another person, acting either individually or as part of an organ of the legal person, or who has authority to take decisions on behalf of the legal person.[58]

Article 5, which regulates child pornography, criminalizes acquisition or possession (article 5(1)); obtaining access (5(2)); distribution, dissemination or transmission (5(3)); and the offering, supplying and making available of child pornography (5(4)). The Directive is specifically targeting offences committed online or with the aid of telecommunications technology (ICT). Article 2(e) specifically mentions online pornographic performances. Article 5(3) provides that obtaining access to child pornography with the aid of ICT will be punishable. Article 6 criminalizes ICT solicitation of children for sexual purposes, with the attempt also being punishable. Grooming, which is defined in line with the Cybercrime Treaty provisions to include recruiting a child, is covered in article 4.

Article 25(1) obliges Member States to promptly remove webpages containing child pornography 'hosted in their territory' and 'to endeavour to obtain the removal of such pages hosted outside'. Article 25(2)

---

[56] Council Framework Decision 2004/68/JHA of 22 December 2003 on combating the sexual exploitation of children and child pornography [2004] OJ L13, 20 January 2004.

[57] Directive of the European Parliament and of the Council on combating the sexual abuse, sexual exploitation of children and child pornography, repealing Framework Decision 2004/68/JHA [2011] OJ L335/1, 17 December 2011. The Directive incorporates the Decision but includes significant new elements.

[58] See arts. 12–13.

authorizes selective blocking of child pornography websites operational only towards the end-users in the Member State in question. This specific form of filtering must be proportionate and transparent.

In terms of jurisdiction, article 17 of the Directive provides that a Member State will have jurisdiction either where the offence is committed within its territory (the principle of territoriality) or where the offender is one of its nationals (the active personality principle). Further to that, it is possible to extend the Directive's field of application to situations where the offence was committed against persons habitually resident on the Member State's territory, or where the offence is committed for the benefit of a legal person established in the territory of the Member State, or where the offender is habitually resident on its territory.

11. Concluding remarks

A comprehensive analysis of EU Internet regulation leaves the reader with five dominant impressions.

First, a commonly repeated assertion concerning the Internet is that it is changing rapidly. This rapidity is all too apparent in the European Union where law-making is a combination of traditional law, soft law and self-regulation in a continuous state of flux. Competing proposals, multiple revisions, changing agendas and policy statements, to use computer jargon, leave the law in a state of permanent beta. Rather than be seen as a sign of weakness, this fluidity must be understood as an inherent feature of Internet regulation. Many framework EU instruments call for periodic reviews, while major policy documents (agendas) are replaced at regular intervals. These reviews will almost certainly remain a permanent feature of EU Internet regulation.

Secondly, the European Union readily experiments with new regulatory models. The introduction of the country of origin principle in the E-Commerce Directive, the increased role of alternative dispute resolution or comprehensive data and consumer protection frameworks are some of the examples. These new regulatory models result from the need to coordinate a large number of national jurisdictions in a dynamic field. The EU's desire to act as an incubator for new governance models may make it adapt more flexibly to the reality of the modern Internet as a platform rather than a product.

Thirdly, the EU has not demonstrated a desire to deviate from the boundaries set for Internet regulation in the United States. The 2005 Tunisia Internet governance negotiations, the copyright laws and Anti-Counterfeiting Trade Agreement (ACTA) negotiations, among others, serve to demonstrate that this is a rule rather than an exception. While European privacy and consumer protection can generally be said to be stronger than American, electronic commerce, intellectual property, Internet Service Provider (ISP) liability and jurisdiction regulation in both countries follow the same patterns. Historically, this can be seen as a missed opportunity to hold a more distinct position.

Fourthly, the relationship of the Commission's complex system of regulation to innovation and growth is as yet poorly understood. The legal language, which contains frequent references to 'more protection' or 'stronger protection', may make consumers/citizens feel safer but may ultimately not be the crucial factor for growth and development of the digital society in Europe and may, in the worst case scenario, hinder it.

Fifthly, the EU's highly fragmented telecommunications market is falling further behind the rest of the developed world. At present, it is not clear how policy creation and law-making at EU level is influencing this fall but there are indications that reform in the carrier field is not going far enough. Because of the convergence between the content and carrier, this will have a significant impact on the Internet world.

The European Union as a system is based on the idea that the EU is *sometimes* better suited to resolve *some* issues than Member States. The EU does not rest on the idea that harmonization is always good nor on the idea that harmonization is always an answer. In that sense, a certain degree of regulatory confusion is inherent and, to some extent, desirable as it provides the needed flexibility. EU Internet regulation will continue to be fluid and occasionally experimental but it also needs to be more independent and assertive and foster innovation as well as (and not at the expense of) consumer and user protection. Ultimately, the EU's ability to tackle the challenge of Internet regulation will probably depend on its ability to strike the right balance between prescriptive and reflexive law-making. Rather than taking over legal responsibility, the EU would do well to show restraint and continue the effort of fostering self-regulation. That way, it will be in a position to respond adequately to the challenges of a modern collaborative decentralized Internet.

Index